# The Promise of the Eternal Covenant

## GOD'S PROFOUND PROVIDENCE AS REVEALED IN THE GENEALOGY OF JESUS CHRIST (THE POSTEXILIC PERIOD)

Rev. Abraham Park D.Min., D.D.

*"Remember the days of old,*
*Consider the years of all generations.*
*Ask your father, and he will inform you,*
*Your elders, and they will tell you."*
—Deuteronomy 32:7

PERIPLUS EDITIONS
Singapore • Hong Kong • Indonesia

Published by Periplus Editions (HK) Ltd.

www.periplus.com

Copyright © 2014 Periplus Editions (HK) Ltd.
First Korean edition published by Huisun in 2010. www.huisun.kr

Scripture quotations taken from the New American Standard Bible®, Copyright © 1960, 1962, 1963, 1968, 1971, 1972, 1973, 1975, 1977, 1995 by The Lockman Foundation.

ISBN 978-0-7946-0769-2

Distributed by:

**North America, Latin America & Europe**
Tuttle Publishing
364 Innovation Drive
North Clarendon
VT 05759-9436 U.S.A.
Tel: 1 (802) 773-8930
Fax: 1 (802) 773-6993
info@tuttlepublishing.com
www.tuttlepublishing.com

**Asia Pacific**
Berkeley Books Pte. Ltd.
61 Tai Seng Avenue #02-12
Singapore 534167
Tel: (65) 6280-1330
Fax: (65) 6280-6290
inquiries@periplus.com.sg
www.periplus.com

**Japan**
Tuttle Publishing
Yaekari Building 3rd Floor
5-4-12 Osaki, Shinagawa-ku
Tokyo 141-0032
Tel: (81) 3 5437 0171
Fax: (81) 3 5437 0755
sales@tuttle.co.jp
www.tuttle.co.jp

**Indonesia**
PT Java Books Indonesia
Jl. Rawa Gelam IV No. 9
Kawasan Industri Pulogadung
Jakarta 13930
Tel: (62) 21 4682-1088
Fax: (62) 21 461-0206
crm@periplus.co.id
www.periplus.co.id

Printed in Singapore

18 17 16 15     10 9 8 7 6 5 4 3 2     1503CP

# Contents

PART FOUR
# The Genealogy of Jesus Christ: Gaps in the Third Period • 151

# List of Abbreviations

| | |
|---|---|
| ESV | English Standard Version |
| KJV | King James Version |
| NASB | New American Standard Bible* |
| NIV | New International Version |
| NKJV | New King James Version |
| NLT | New Living Translation |
| RSV | Revised Standard Version |
| YLT | Young's Literal Translation |

| | |
|---|---|
| *Ant.* | Josephus. *The Antiquities of the Jews* |
| *War.* | Josephus. *The Wars of the Jews* |
| *Apion.* | Josephus. *Against Apion* |
| | Josephus, Flavius, and William Whiston. *The Works of Josephus: Complete and Unabridged.* Peabody: Hendrickson, 1987. |
| WCF | Westminster Confession of Faith |
| WSC | Westminster Shorter Catechism |
| HALOT | Koehler, L., W. Baumgartner, and J. J. Stamm. *The Hebrew and Aramaic Lexicon of the Old Testament.* Translated and edited under the supervision of M. E. J. Richardson. 4 vols. Leiden, 1994-1999. |

---

* All Bible quotations in this book are from the New American Standard Bible unless indicated otherwise.

# Author's Foreword

The Bible is filled with promises of the eternal covenant that God had sovereignly established according to His decree of salvation for fallen mankind (Gen 9:16; 17:7; Exod 31:16; Ezek 37:26; Heb 9:15). The first promise of the eternal covenant that God made after the fall of man was the *promise of the woman's seed* (Gen 3:15). This promise poured forth a holy river of life, which flowed ceaselessly through all of history's ordeals and Satan's interferences. This river of life has now sublimated into the cross on the hill of Golgotha, blossoming as the *new covenant* that brings His chosen people salvation from all sins and the pitch-dark despair of death (Luke 22:20; 1 Chr 11:25). As the mediator of the *new covenant* (Heb 9:15; 12:24), Jesus Christ—the good and great Shepherd of the sheep—shed His precious blood on the cross for His flock (John 10:11; Heb 13:20). This blood is the blood of forgiveness (Eph 1:7), the blood of the eternal covenant (Ref Exod 24:8; Zech 9:11; Heb 10:29), and the blood that breaks down all the barriers of the world and establishes peace among all (Isa 54:10; Eph 2:13-19).

The *genealogy* is a list of names that encapsulates and summarizes the promises of the eternal covenant and their fulfillments in light of the history of redemption. The Bible places great importance on its genealogies because God's administration of redemption to send the Savior as the woman's seed (Gen 3:15) progresses through the succession of progeny within the genealogies. They are recorded as turning points at every watershed moment in the history of redemption. An era in redemptive history concludes with a genealogy; a new era begins with another. In particular, the genealogy in Matthew 1 is an encapsulation of the entire history of redemption. It proclaims that Jesus Christ is the fulfillment of every promise of the eternal covenant. I sincerely hope and pray that the in-depth study of the Matthean genealogy will endow us with the overflowing grace of our Lord and Savior Jesus Christ, the central figure of the genealogy. As we grow in the knowledge of Him (2 Pet 3:18), may only the name of Jesus be magnified (Acts 19:17) and glorified (2 Thess 1:12)!

As history draws near to its close, the shroud of darkness around the world deepens as it spirals ever deeper into inescapable chaos. What is required of the believer who seeks and waits for the second coming of the Lord during such time? It is *holiness*. Hebrews 12:14 states, "Pursue peace with all men and the sanctification without which no one will see the Lord." According to the original Greek, this passage can be rendered, "without holiness no one will see the Lord." The word emphasized here is *holiness*, which is ἁγιασμός (*hagiasmos*) in Greek, meaning "sanctification." *Sanctification* is having the attitude (heart) of Jesus Christ (Phil 2:5). It is the Christian virtue of conforming ourselves to the image of Christ in order to have Christ fully formed in us (Gal 4:19). All saints who await the second coming of the Lord must attain holiness.

The most important way to attain *holiness* is through the Word of God. First Timothy 4:5 states, "for it is sanctified by means of the word of God and prayer." Ephesians 5:26 states, "so that He might sanctify her, having cleansed her by the washing of water with the word" (John 17:17, 19). We can attain holiness by living a life of reading, hearing, and keeping the Word of God in the Bible (Rev 1:3).

The Bible is the inerrant and infallible Word of God, unrivaled by any other writing in the world. Even the most sophisticated literary works cannot be compared to the Bible. I am completely captivated by the fearfully and wonderfully written Word of God. That is why I never drift away from it wherever I may be. Outwardly, this attachment to the Bible became the impetus in overcoming the long-sufferings of life through thanksgiving and grace. Inwardly, it was the wellspring that allowed me to strive step by step toward attaining to the holiness and to the measure of the stature which belongs to the fullness of Christ (Eph 4:13).

This inadequate servant's books in the History of Redemption series, which are currently in publication, are the fruits of my love for the Bible. Since a book is inseparable from the character of the author's faith, the books of the History of Redemption series form the digest of the entirety of my doctrinal beliefs, faith, philosophy, and character. I sincerely hope that the History of Redemption series may serve as a guide to the Bible and as an instrument of righteousness that will help unveil the Holy Scriptures.

I was able to publish *The Unquenchable Lamp of the Covenant: the First Fourteen Generations in the Genealogy of Jesus Christ* in 2010, and *God's Profound and Mysterious Providence: The Genealogy of Jesus Christ from David to the Exile in Babylon* in 2011. Now, I am overwhelmed as *The Promise of the Eternal Covenant: God's Profound Providence as Revealed in the Genealogy of Jesus Christ (the Postexilic Period)* is finally being published to reveal God's redemptive administration in the third period of Jesus Christ's genealogy.

One of the accomplishments in this humble work is a timeline entitled, "The Third Period in the Genealogy of Jesus Christ and Transitions in World History" (Excursus 1). This timeline is a comprehensive compendium that showcases the rise and fall of world powers during the third period in Jesus Christ's genealogy alongside the activities of Israel—God's instrument in the midst of world powers, and the ministries of the prophets sent by God at various epochs of history.

Based on God's revelation of the future of mankind as given to Daniel, I have provided a redemptive-historical treatment of the unfolding of God's profound and mysterious providence within the rapidly changing history of the world. I have invested much time in trying to accurately understand the events in the Bible and their chronological years in accordance to the command, "Consider the years of all generations" (Deut 32:7). This unprecedented work was so vast and so overwhelming that I spent many sleepless nights with my manuscripts, clinging to the Bible in tearful prayers and searching through various reference works. As a precious baby is born after much labor pain, this humble work was completed as a fruition of a long pursuit of research. It is accomplished all by God's grace and solely by His helping hand (Ezra 7:9; 8:18, 22, 31; Neh 2:8, 18).

As the kingdom of God draws nearer, this fallen world will be filled with greater dismay, perplexed at the roaring of the sea and the waves (Luke 21:25). This is the period of time when the earthly Church needs to be reformed day by day. Without reformation, the Church will be drowned by the raging billows of secularization (Heb 10:39).

True reformation of the Church entails returning to the world of the beginning every single day. For in the beginning (ἐν ἀρχῇ, *en archē*) was the Word, true reformation is accomplished when the Church returns to the Word of the beginning (John 1:1). In every generation of redemptive history, God has brought about a reformation in the Church through the movement of the Word. John Calvin carried out his reformation by preaching that we must return to the Word of God, for God reveals Himself in the Scriptures. I dare to hope with all sincerity that the History of Redemption series may contribute in some small way to the reformation of the Church. It is also my earnest prayer that these books may be used as instruments in the ministry of the Word which will start a new wave in the history of Christianity. The History of Redemption series is moving toward its stated goal of twelve books for the series. I earnestly seek your prayers that I may be able to accomplish this enormous and historic task that God has bestowed upon this elderly servant.

As I reflect upon the Words, "If anyone supposes that he knows anything, he has not yet known as he ought to know" (1 Cor 8:2), I always find myself trembling in fear for I am reminded of my insufficiencies. Then, I am encouraged by the message, "However, let us keep living by that same *standard* to which we have attained" (Phil 3:16). Thus, I hope to go forth in sharing with all of God's churches the grace that He has given to me.

Our Lord has led us thus far through His grace and for the defense of the gospel of truth. I sincerely pray that the same Lord will continue to preserve and guard His children and Church—the recipients of the promise of the eternal covenant—until the end. It is my earnest hope that our God of peace, who is at work in us both to will and to work for His good pleasure, may be with all the churches on earth (Rom 15:33; Phil 2:13; Heb 13:20-21).

Lastly, I would like to express my heartfelt thanksgiving to the beloved congregation and elders of the Pyungkang Cheil Church as well as my fellow ministers for their dedicated love in helping me with prayers and supporting me in publishing the books. I also offer my sincere thanks to all the people who have labored hard to typeset, edit, print, and bind the manuscripts of this unworthy servant to transform them into books. Most of all, I give all glory to the living God.

July 17, 2010

朴潤植

Abraham Park

Rev. Abraham Park
An insignificant member in the body of Christ,
On the sojourner's path to heaven

# Praise for the Author

Dr. Abraham Park's life work in the History of Redemption series draws deeply from the wellsprings of his deep Reformed faith. There is no concept that so marks the reformed pastor more than his commitment to covenant theology. This one topic expresses the singular authority of Scripture, the unique sovereignty of God in directing all of history to serve His saving purpose in the covenant, as well as the uniqueness of Jesus Christ, who as the virgin-born Seed of the Woman is the only Savior of mankind. Dr. Park's life and ministry demonstrate his thorough commitment to everything that is central and crucial to Reformed and confessional theology. His life work sets forth the genealogy of the covenant faithfulness of our Lord God.

Dr. Park has poured out his life and considerable talents in the service of the Savior. His commitment to Scripture (he has read the Bible through more than 1,800 times!) and to pastoral ministry (he has founded hundreds of churches not only in Korea, but throughout the world), demonstrate the large scope of his evangelical vision. His ministry is proven, not simply by the love of scores of thousands whom he has taught to know and love the Bible, but it is especially authenticated by the harsh calumny and criticism and deep suffering he has sustained and through which he has persevered with much prayer for those who troubled him.

Dr. Park needs no earthly vindication for his ministry, for he is vindicated by a ministry that has so effectively lifted up Jesus in the hearts and minds of tens of thousands of thousands and thousands. He is a treasure to Pyungkang Cheil church and to the many thousands of us around the world who have been encouraged in our confidence in Scripture and our love for Jesus by the ministry of this faithful servant of Christ.

Henceforth let no man trouble Pastor Park, for he (literally) bears in his body the wounding marks of Jesus (Gal 6:17). Rather, let Pastor Park be counted worthy of double honor, for I know of no one today who has worked harder at preaching and teaching than our good and faithful pastor, Rev. Dr. Abraham Park (1Tim 5:17).

Rev. Warren A. Gage, J.D., Ph.D.,
Professor Emeritus of Old Testament, Knox Theological Seminary

PART ONE

# The History of Redemption
# and the Covenant of God

The Old and New Testaments are God's Words that record the history of redemption which is centered on Jesus Christ. This history spans from the momentous creation of "the heavens and the earth" to the completion of "a new heaven and a new earth." The history of redemption refers to the entire history in which God saves fallen sinners through the death and resurrection of Jesus Christ according to His decree predestined from before the creation.

The history of redemption can be divided into three main parts: "the creation," "the fall," and "salvation." The man, who was created in the image of God (Gen 1:26-27), disobeyed the Word of God the Creator and fell (Gen 3:6). In order to save this fallen mankind, God proceeded with the work of salvation without sleep or slumber (Ps 121:3-4).

It was God's covenants that enabled the history of redemption to continue without ceasing and flow through the events of the creation, the fall, and salvation. In other words, the link that connects the work of salvation from generation to generation is the covenant and its fulfillment. Therefore, it is necessary for us to examine specifically how this covenant was fulfilled in history within the themes of the creation, the fall, and salvation.

# CHAPTER 1

# The Creation of the Honorable Man

The book of Genesis, which begins the Bible, introduces the beginning of this world and all things that exist in it. Furthermore, it reveals the beginnings of sin and salvation, as well as the beginning of the chosen people of Israel. In particular, Genesis chapters 1 through 3 serve as the Bible's prologue that deals with the origins of the universe, life, and salvation; these chapters also help us in understanding the source and essence of redemption. More specifically, these opening chapters contain the following records: God creating the universe and all things in it (Gen 1); God forming Adam from the dust of the ground (Gen 2:7); God planting a garden toward the east, in Eden (Gen 2:8); God establishing the covenant of works with Adam (Gen 2:16-17); God making a suitable helper from Adam's rib (Gen 2:18-23); Adam becoming one with his wife without any shame despite being naked (Gen 2:24-25); and the serpent's temptation and the fall of man by eating the fruit from the tree of the knowledge of good and evil (Gen 3:1-7).

Such accounts recorded in the beginning of the book of Genesis are certainly not legends or myths, but true historical events. The New Testament also testifies that the entire process of the creation and the fall of man were actual historical events (Rom 5:12-19; 2 Cor 11:3; 1 Tim 2:13-14).

## 1. God who created the heavens and the earth in the beginning

**Genesis 1:1** In the beginning God created the heavens and the earth.

This is how the work of creation begins in the Bible.

This verse is the most compressed expression that resonates the deepest among all sixty-six books of the Bible. It contains the beginnings of the entire history of mankind as well as those of each of our individual lives. It is notable that it does not say God simply *existed* but that He *created*. The word *created* in Genesis 1:1 is the *qal* (basic) stem of בָּרָא (*bārā'*), which is used only to express God's works of creation. From the beginning, God is revealed as the Almighty who is active and working (John 5:17); He is the God who creates something out of nothing (Isa 44:24; Rom 4:17).

### (1) Creation through the Word

The heavens and the earth did not accidentally come into existence but were created through the Word of God (Heb 11:3). Genesis 1:3 states, "Then God said, 'Let there be light'; and there was light." Psalm 33:6 states, "By the word of the LORD the heavens were made, and by the breath of His mouth all their host." Psalm 33:9 states, "For He spoke, and it was done; He commanded, and it stood fast." Also, the Scripture says in Psalm 148:5, "Let them praise the name of the LORD, for He commanded and they were created." The Word that proceeds from the mouth of God has the power to form immediately into being the heavens, the earth, and all things in it (Isa 45:12).

After all things were created through God's Word, the Scripture states in Genesis 1:31, "God saw all that He had made, and behold, it was very good." The Hebrew word for *very* in this verse is מְאֹד (*mĕ'ōd*), meaning "much," "greatly," or "exceedingly" and expresses the greatest extent. God was expressing His utmost satisfaction as He saw all that He had created. All of God's creation was complete and without lack. Moreover, the order of His created world was in perfect harmony and balance. Everything God created is absolutely necessary and was perfectly made to fulfill its role and function in its appointed place.[1]

### (2) The Triune God who created the universe and all things in it

The Triune God created the universe and all things in it. The Bible records in several places that the One who performed the work of creation was simply "God," without distinguishing the three persons of the Trinity (Gen 1:1, 21, 27; 2:3; 5:1; Deut 4:32; Isa 40:28). The Hebrew word for *God* used in these verses is אֱלֹהִים (*'ĕlōhîm*). Grammatically, this word is in the plural form, but it is treated as a singular word because it is followed by a singular verb. The characteristic of *elohim*, the Hebrew name of God, demonstrates the Trinity. It implies that God's work of creation was a joint effort of the Trinity.[2]

*FIRST,* all creation comes from God the Father.

God the Father Himself is the *Originator*. It is stated in 1 Corinthians 8:6, "yet for us there is but one God, the Father, from whom are all things and we exist for Him . . . ." The word *from* in this verse is ἐκ (*ek*) in Greek, meaning "from" or "out from." Thus, the source and origin of all things is God the Father (Ps 136:5-9).

*SECOND,* all things were created through God the Son.

God the Son is the *Executor* in the work of creation. First Corinthians 8:6 continues to state, ". . . and one Lord, Jesus Christ, by whom are all things, and we exist through Him." The word *by* in the verse is διά (*dia*) in Greek, meaning "by" or "through." The verse signifies that all things were created through God the Son.

Another name of God the Son is the *Word*. This Word was with God in the beginning, and the Word was God (John 1:1-2). John 1:3 states, "All things came into being through Him, and apart from Him nothing came into being that has come into being." John 1:10 also states, "He was in the world, and the world was made through Him, and the world did not know Him" (Col 1:16; Heb 1:2). This Word "became flesh and dwelt among us, and we saw His glory, glory as of the only begotten from the Father, full of grace and truth" (John 1:14). Truly, God the Son was the executor in the entire creation work. He created the universe and all things in it together with God the Father.

*THIRD,* all things were created by God the Holy Spirit.

God the Holy Spirit is the *Completer* in the work of creation. In Genesis 1:2, the Spirit of God was moving over the surface of the waters. Psalm 33:6 explains, "By the word of the LORD the heavens were made, and by the breath of His mouth all their host." The word *breath* is רוּחַ (*rûaḥ*) in Hebrew and is the same word used to refer to God's Spirit in Genesis 1:2. Thus, it can be understood that the heavens and all their host were made by God the Spirit (Holy Spirit). Psalm 104:30 also states, "You send forth Your Spirit, they are created; and You renew the face of the ground." When God created man, it was the Holy Spirit who breathed into him the breath of God and vivified him (Gen 2:7; Job 27:3; 33:4).

Therefore, the creation of all things was a joint effort of the three persons of the Trinity. The creation of man can also be considered a joint effort of the Trinity (Gen 1:26-27; 2:7; Job 33:4; 1 Cor 8:6).

## 2. The creation of man was the centerpiece of the entire creation work.

Among God's work of creation, the creation of man was truly profound. William Shakespeare said, "What a piece of work is a man! How noble in reason, how infinite in faculties, in form and moving how express and admirable, in action how like an angel, in apprehension how like a god! The beauty of the world, the paragon of animals!"[3] God has created man as the lord of the creation—supreme over all creatures, with numinous and marvelous power, and most excellent and outstanding. Therefore, among all creatures, man is the preeminent being who is given the task to fulfill God's purpose of creation.

The creation of man was certainly not by accident or evolution. Rather, it was decreed by God's profound and mysterious administration. That is why the psalmist praised God, "I will give thanks to You, for I am fearfully and wonderfully made; wonderful are Your works, and my soul knows it very well" (Ps 139:14). The phrase, "for I am fearfully and wonderfully made," is composed of two Hebrew words, נוֹרָאוֹת נִפְלֵיתִי (nôrā'ôt niplêtî). נוֹרָאוֹת (nôrā'ôt) is the passive participle of the word יָרֵא (yārē'), which means "fear" or "revere." נִפְלֵיתִי (niplêtî) is the passive participle of the word פָּלָה (pālâ), which means "distinguished," "admirable," "wondrous," or "marvelous." Therefore, the expression nôrā'ôt niplêtî signifies a "marvel or wonder that is unfathomable." God's skill in creating mankind is an awesome wonder that man just cannot fathom. Indeed, the human being is God's *magnum opus*.

The account of man's creation was recorded twice, once in Genesis chapter 1 and once in chapter 2. Genesis 1:26-28 speaks of the origin and place of man as part of the entire universe and creation. Genesis 2:7-25 expounds on the state of man who is to receive the covenant.

God created man last among all His creation. This hints at the fact that God had the greatest interest and expectations for man, whom He waited to create at the end. It further hints at the fact that the entire work of creation was done solely for man (Isa 45:18; 51:13; Jer 27:5). Mankind is certainly an honorable being who is clearly distinguished from the rest of creation (Ps 49:12, 20).

Man's honor is seen clearly and continually in the process of creation in Genesis chapters 1 and 2. It is notable that the word בָּרָא (bārā')—which describes God's sovereign work of creation—is used three times in Genesis 1:27 alone, which gives the account of the creation of man.

**Genesis 1:27** God created man in His own image, in the image of God He created him; male and female He created them.

וַיִּבְרָא אֱלֹהִים אֶת־הָאָדָם בְּצַלְמוֹ בְּצֶלֶם

(*wayyibrā' 'ĕlōhîm 'et-hā'ādām bĕṣalmô bĕṣelem*)

אֱלֹהִים בָּרָא אֹתוֹ זָכָר וּנְקֵבָה בָּרָא אֹתָם

(*'ĕlōhîm bārā' 'ōtô zākār ûnĕqēbâ bārā' 'ōtām*)

A literal translation of this verse is as follows: "God created the man in His image, in the image of God He created him; He created them male and female." The fact that the word בָּרָא (*bārā'*)—which is used only to signify the work of creation that God Himself performs—is used three times in Genesis 1:27 implies that God's glory had reached its climax on this day through the creation of man. The word בָּרָא (*bārā'*) appears five times in Genesis chapter 1. Three occurrences are in verse 27 and the other two are in verses 1 and 21, respectively. Therefore, God's attention was focused on man, and the creation of man was the creation par excellence, the crown and climax of all creation.

## 3. God created man through His *agape* love

John 3:16 states, "For God so loved the world, that He gave His only begotten Son, that whoever believes in Him shall not perish, but have eternal life." The Greek word for *loved* in this verse is ἠγάπησεν (*ēgapēsen*), which is the verb form of the word ἀγάπη (*agapē*). This signifies God's unconditional, sacrificial, and infinite love. The word *world* includes all races and kinds of people whom God has created. Therefore, all mankind is created upon the foundation of God's *agape* (ἀγάπη) love. This *agape* love is something only God can give; it is absolute and altruistic. It is a self-sacrificing and perfect love that mankind can never emulate.

Mankind is honored, but brute beasts cannot be honored (Ref Ps 49:12, 20; 73:22). God created only mankind in His own image and allowed him to subdue and rule over all creation (Gen 1:26-28). If God did not have *agape* love for mankind, He would have never made man in His own image nor would He have put him in charge over all creation. Moreover, God in His *agape* love created man as an honorable, eternal being (Ref Ps 12:7). Hence, all mankind has a heart that seeks after eternal life (Eccl 3:11).

God entered into a covenant with man whom He created to be honored. God also placed him in the garden of Eden and had him name every beast of the field and every bird of the sky. Then, He fashioned a helper suitable for him. The foundation to all of this work of creation was the overflowing *agape* love of God.

God redeemed humanity with this *agape* love. *Agape* love is the love in which one gives first and gives freely, without holding anything back. It was by God's *agape* love that He sent His only begotten Son Jesus Christ to this earth in order to fulfill the work of redemption through His sacrifice on the cross. First John 4:8-10 states, "The one who does not love does not know God, for God is love. By this the love of God was manifested in us, that God has sent His only begotten Son into the world so that we might live through Him. In this is love, not that we loved God, but that He loved us and sent His Son to be the propitiation for our sins." By letting His only begotten Son Jesus Christ shed the blood of atonement on the cross to forgive our sins, God demonstrated His boundless *agape* love toward us (Rom 5:8; Heb 9:12, 22). Ephesians 1:7 states, "In Him we have redemption through His blood, the forgiveness of our trespasses, according to the riches of His grace." Matthew 26:28 states, "for this is My blood of the covenant, which is poured out for many for forgiveness of sins."

Every time a person sins, God must feel intense heartrending pain. Nevertheless, He was able to pass over the sins in His forbearance because of the blood of atonement that Jesus shed on the cross (Rom 3:25). This is because Jesus Christ's blood that was shed on the cross is the most precious blood in heaven above and on earth below. His blood can completely forgive all the sins of mankind at once (1 Pet 1:18-19).

It was also by His *agape* love that Jesus prayed, ". . . saying, 'Father, forgive them; for they do not know what they are doing'" (Luke 23:34). The word *saying* in this verse is ἔλεγεν (*elegen*), the imperfect tense of λέγω (*legō*), meaning "to say" or "to speak." The imperfect tense emphasizes the continuity of an action from the past. In other words, Jesus did not simply pray for forgiveness just once on the cross, but continually prayed for the forgiveness of the people who crucified and mocked Him. This is in line with what He had been teaching all along (Matt 5:44, 46). Peter asked Jesus, "Lord, how often shall my brother sin against me and I forgive him? Up to seven times?" Jesus answered, "I do not say to you, up to seven times, but up to seventy times seven" (Matt 18:21-22). Jesus, who had taught this to His disciples, would not have simply prayed for their forgiveness only once. He must have continued to pray for the forgiveness of the rebellious mankind every time they spoke and acted sinfully toward Jesus. *Agape* love has no enemy; it has only unconditional forgiveness.

After answering Peter's question, Jesus continued on to tell a parable of the one who had a debt of 10,000 talents. A king forgave the man with 10,000 talents of debt (Matt 18:23-27); but the man could not forgive the one who owed him only a 100 denarii and threw him in prison (Matt 18:28-30). *Ten thousand talents* is an astronomical amount; one talent is 6,000 denarii, so 10,000 talents is equal to 60 million denarii. One denarius is the wages for one day's labor. For example, if one were to calculate the wages for one day's worth of labor as 50 US Dollars, then 10,000 talents would equate to about 3 billion US Dollars. This was an amount that he could not possibly repay even if he were to sell himself, along with his wife, children, and all that he had (Matt 18:25). The forgiveness that Jesus Christ granted us through His atoning work on the cross is so infinitely great and complete that it is incalculable with the human brain. It was a complete forgiveness based on *agape* love.

Besides such divine love, there are other types of humanistic love in this world. Natural affection for family and kin is expressed with the word στοργή (*storgē*); brotherly love between friends is φιλέω (*phileō*); and the attraction of desire and love between the sexes is ἔρος (*eros*). Because these kinds of humanistic love are often based on selfish motives that serve one's own interest, they can easily fall apart if one's needs or conditions are not satisfied, causing hurt and disappointment to the persons involved.

Those who were created and redeemed through God's love continue to breathe, eat, drink, and do all things through God's love while they live in this world. God's love is the source of strength that sustains the life of a man; it is also the everlasting power of life that saves even those who have come upon death. We, who are fed and nourished by such *agape* love in our lives, should cherish this love deep within our hearts with gratitude and live to share it with our neighbors.

Jesus said that we must forgive our brothers and sisters with this *agape* love. In Matthew 18:35, He said, "My heavenly Father will also do the same to you, if each of you does not forgive his brother from your heart." Anyone who does not love his brother is not of God (1 John 3:10). The Bible also admonishes us, "If someone says, 'I love God,' and hates his brother, he is a liar; for the one who does not love his brother whom he has seen, cannot love God whom he has not seen. And this commandment we have from Him, that the one who loves God should love his brother also" (1 John 4:20-21).

"The one who does not love does not know God" (1 John 4:8). The new commandment that Jesus gave us is to love one another (John 13:34; 15:12). In order for us to become partakers of this divine nature, we must supply love to our faith as well as moral excellence, knowledge, self-control, perseverance, godliness, and brotherly kindness (2 Pet 1:4-7). Love is of the greatest value in all of our lives, the most precious treasure, and the supreme good (1 Cor 13:13).

God's *agape* love was immutably present throughout the entire process of the creation, the fall, and salvation. The moment man—who was created to be honored—sinned and fell, God immediately came to find him in that place. Rather than giving up on the sinful man, God came to take responsibility until the end for the man He created. John 13:1 states, "Now before the Feast of the Passover, Jesus knowing that His hour had come that He would depart out of this world to the Father, having loved His own who were in the world, He loved them to the end."

This *agape* love is clearly manifested in the entire process of God's creation of the honorable man, the fall, and salvation.

## 4. God created man in His image and likeness.

> **Genesis 1:26-27** Then God said, "Let Us make man in Our image, according to Our likeness; and let them rule over the fish of the sea and over the birds of the sky and over the cattle and over all the earth, and over every creeping thing that creeps on the earth." God created man in His own image, in the image of God He created him; male and female He created them.

In the expression "in Our image, according to Our likeness" (כִּדְמוּתֵנוּ בְּצַלְמֵנוּ, *běṣalmēnû kidmûtēnû*), there is no conjunction between the words *image* and *likeness*. Thus, the expressions "in Our image" and "according to Our likeness" possess the same significance in different forms of expression. The words *image* and *likeness* are not referring to something that is identical to the original form, but to something that is similar or alike. That is why man, in some important aspects, resembles God and is created to represent God.

## (1) In Our image

Man is created in the image of God (Gen 5:1; 9:6; 1 Cor 11:7; Jas 3:9). The word *image* is צֶלֶם (*ṣelem*) in Hebrew, derived from an unused root that means "to symbolize" or "to define a contour." Thus, the word is used to refer to a "replica" or a "representation."

This word emphasizes the fact that man was created to be honored as God's representative. Since only man is created in the image of God, he is the only one who can be the lord of creation with the privilege and honor to govern and rule over the rest of creation. For that reason, after creating man, God commanded him, "Be fruitful and multiply, and fill the earth, and subdue it; and rule over the fish of the sea and over the birds of the sky and over every living thing that moves on the earth" (Gen 1:28). God also placed man in the garden of Eden to "cultivate it and keep it" (Gen 2:15) and allowed him to name every living creature (Gen 2:19). This demonstrates that Adam was given sovereignty over all living creatures.

Psalm 8 clearly declares that God made man as His representative to rule over all creation.

> **(Psalm 8:5-9; ESV)** Yet you have made him a little lower than the heavenly beings and crowned him with glory and honor. You have given him dominion over the works of your hands; you have put all things under his feet, all sheep and oxen, and also the beasts of the field, the birds of the heavens, and the fish of the sea, whatever passes along the paths of the seas. O LORD, our Lord, how majestic is your name in all the earth!

Man was given dominion to govern and lead every creature to fulfill their proper roles according to their attributes as assigned by God.

## (2) According to Our likeness

The word *likeness* (or *form*) is דְּמוּת (*děmût*), from the root דָּמָה (*dāmâ*), which means "to be like" or "to resemble." This signifies that man resembles God in respect to his moral image, rational and intellectual image, spiritual image, and image reflected in the body.

*FIRST*, man resembles God in his moral image.

Ephesians 4:24 and Colossians 3:10 summarize the moral image of God.

**Ephesians 4:24** And put on the new self, which in the likeness of God has been created in righteousness and holiness of the truth.

**Colossians 3:10** And have put on the new self who is being renewed to a true knowledge according to the image of the One who created him.

The expression *new self* in Ephesians 4:24 (καινὸν ἄνθρωπον, *kainon anthrōpon*: new man) signifies a new creature who is essentially the opposite of the *old self* (Eph 4:22). Second Corinthians 5:17 states, "Therefore if anyone is in Christ, he is a new creature; the old things passed away; behold, new things have come." A new self is one who has put on the Lord Jesus Christ (Rom 13:14; Col 3:12; Rev 19:8) and has been renewed to a true knowledge. This *knowledge* refers to the true knowledge that cannot be attained from the world, but only through the Word of God.

Also, the new self is to be "created in righteousness and holiness of the truth." In Ephesians 4:24, the words *righteousness* and *holiness* are conjoined with the conjunction καί (*kai*: and), and the word *the truth* (τῆς ἀληθείας, *tēs alētheias*) modifies both *righteousness* and *holiness*. Therefore, the phrase "created in righteousness and holiness of the truth" can be rendered as "created in true righteousness and true holiness."

The fact that man is created in the image of God signifies that he is created with true knowledge, true righteousness, and true holiness. The new self we need to put on is the man in the original state as God created him. He is the universally honored man who serves God in fear and submits to His laws.

### SECOND, man resembles God in his rational and intellectual image.

Created in the image of God, man was given a sound mind and an upright heart. Moreover, proper volition along with sound reasoning intellect allows man to recognize God and comprehend matter while feeling and acting properly. Through the rationality and intellect that God has given, man can appropriately control his instinctive impulses that are present in his body and carry on a proper mental activity with discernment and logical reasoning.

Unlike beasts, man who is created in the likeness of God possesses rationality. Second Peter 2:12 says that people who have lost the image and likeness of God are "like unreasoning animals." Those people come to know things instinctively, and it is exactly by their instincts that they are destroyed (Jude 1:10). Although the rational and intellectual image has been corrupted because of the fall of man, it will be recovered through faith in Jesus Christ.

### THIRD, man resembles God in his spiritual image.

Because God is spirit (John 4:24; 2 Cor 3:17), man who is created in the image of God also possesses His spiritual image. Possessing a spiritual image means to have spirituality and immortality. Those who have spirituality experience God's presence from moment to moment, and thus are able to walk with God and live a dynamic life for His glory. *Adam*, who was endowed with spirituality, was not a being that lived with his mind set on earthly things and the thoughts of the flesh. Though his feet were set on earth, he was a heavenly being whose head was lifted toward heaven, aloft in heavenly thoughts (Col 3:1-3).

Immortality denotes the attribute of eternal life which does not yield to the law of death. God had created man as an eternal being who does not die as long as he does not commit sin. After sinning, however, death came in through sin (Rom 5:12; 6:23; 1 Cor 15:21). Death came upon man because of trespasses and sins (Eph 2:1). Nevertheless, whoever believes in and receives God and Jesus Christ, whom God has sent, will become His children and have eternal life (John 1:12; 3:16; 17:3).

### FOURTH, man resembles God in the image reflected in his body.

Psalm 139:13 states, "For You formed my inward parts (כִּלְיָה, *kilyâ*: kidneys); You wove me in my mother's womb." Because the human body was also created by God (Deut 32:6; Job 10:11), His image is reflected in the body as well. Hence, the human body represents God's image in that it is a vessel for the immortal soul and an instrument used to govern over creation.

On the day of the redemption of our body—when the body, along with the spirit and the soul, will fully recover God's image (Rom 8:23)—our natural body will be transformed into a spiritual body that transcends time and space (1 Cor 15:49-52; 2 Cor 3:18). It will be the fulfillment of God's Word in the following verses: "For this perishable must put on the imperishable, and this mortal must put on immortality" (1 Cor 15:53), and ". . . the Lord Jesus Christ, who will transform the body of our humble state into conformity with the body of His glory, by the exertion of the power that He has even to subject all things to Himself" (Phil 3:20b-21).

As discussed above, man became an honored being for he was created in the image and likeness of God (Isa 62:4). In Psalm 16:3, man is addressed as "the majestic ones in whom is all my delight," and in Isaiah 43:4, God says, "you are precious" and "you are honored." Such saints who were created in God's image are the most honorable beings of whom God is mindful and whom God greatly esteems. Indeed, they are God's crown of glory. Having realized this truth, the psalmist sang the following psalm.

> **Psalm 8:4-5** What is man that you are mindful of him, and the son of man that you care for him? Yet you have made him a little lower than the heavenly beings and crowned him with glory and honor (ESV).

## 5. The living being instilled with life

### (1) Formed of dust from the ground

> **Genesis 2:7** Then the Lord God formed man of dust from the ground, and breathed into his nostrils the breath of life; and man became a living being.

Simply by considering the process of forming man of the dust from the ground, we come to the realization that God's interest is focused heavily on man. The Hebrew words for *dust from the ground* in Genesis 2:7 are עָפָר מִן־הָאֲדָמָה (*'āpār min-hā'ădāmâ*). The word for *dust*, עָפָר (*'āpār*), signifies "fine crumbs (dust) of earth." The expression used in the creation of every beast of the field and every bird of the sky, however, is מִן־הָאֲדָמָה (*min-hā'ădāmâ*) without the word *'āpār* (Gen 2:19). God used "fine crumbs of the earth" to create man, but did not specifically use fine dust to create beasts and birds. This does not only demonstrate the superiority of man over beasts, but also man's incomparable honor even in his physical body.

### (2) Breathed into him the breath of life

When God created man, He breathed into his nostrils the breath of life (Gen 2:7). The words *breath of life* are נִשְׁמַת חַיִּים (*nišmat ḥayyîm*) in Hebrew. The basic form of the word נִשְׁמַת (*nišmat*) is נְשָׁמָה (*nĕšāmâ*), meaning "breath" (Deut 20:16) and "blast" (Job 4:9, NKJV). The word חַיִּים (*ḥayyîm*) is the plural form of חַי (*ḥay*), meaning "life." Hence, God formed man of the dust from the ground and breathed into his nostrils the "breath (blast) of lives." Therefore, man breathes and is active as a conscious being while breath is in him, but his life ceases when there is no more breath.

## (3) He became a psychosomatic unity

The Hebrew words for *living being* in Genesis 2:7 are נֶפֶשׁ חַיָּה (*nepeš ḥayāh*), meaning "being with life" or "a being that is alive." When God's breath of life was breathed into man's nostrils, the man became a living being instilled with life. This signifies that man has become a being that is alive and breathing with a spirit, soul, and body (Ref Matt 10:28; 1 Thess 5:23; Heb 4:12).

When a person dies, his soul and body are separated. When he is alive, however, the soul and body are in unity. This unity is called a "psychosomatic unity." The soul and body are distinguished, but not separated; they form the whole person. On the day of resurrection and transfiguration, which will take place as the last trumpet sounds, it will not be the body without the soul or the soul without the body that will resurrect. Those who had died in Christ will be resurrected into spiritual bodies like the body of Jesus Christ after His resurrection—the entire person with both body and soul. Those who are alive will be transfigured into spiritual bodies (1 Cor 15:51-52; Phil 3:21; 1 Thess 4:16-17).

# 6. The garden of Eden

God planted a garden toward the east, in Eden; and there He placed the man whom He had formed (Gen 2:8). The Hebrew word for *plant* is נָטַע (*nāṭaʿ*), meaning "to plant," "to fix," or "to establish." Just like a farmer who plants trees with much devotion to make a beautiful garden, God poured a great amount of attention and devotion in planting the garden of Eden.

The garden of Eden was a place that actually existed in history. In Hebrew, the *garden of Eden* in Genesis 2:15 is גַּן־עֵדֶן (*gan-ʿēden*). The word גַּן (*gan*) is derived from the root גָּנַן (*gānan*), which means "to defend," "to shield," and "to protect"; and the word עֵדֶן (*ʿēden*) is derived from the root עָדַן (*ʿādan*), which means "soft" and "delight." The garden of Eden was a delightful place that was totally distinguished from other regions; it was a place of God's special protection and loving care. Isaiah 51:3 states, "Indeed, the LORD will comfort Zion; He will comfort all her waste places. And her wilderness He will make like Eden, and her desert like the garden of the LORD; joy and gladness will be found in her, thanksgiving and sound of a melody." The garden of Eden was truly paradise on earth.

The Bible refers to the garden of Eden as "the garden of God" (Ezek 28:13; 31:8-9) and "the garden of the LORD" (Gen 13:10; Isa 51:3). It was certainly a garden that God had planted, and a garden with God in its midst. God placed in the garden the man whom He had formed to cultivate it and keep it (Gen 2:8, 15).

In the garden of Eden, there were trees that were pleasing to the sight and good for food (Gen 2:9, 16); and the tree of life and the tree of the knowledge of good and evil were in the midst of the garden (Gen 2:9b). A river flowed out of Eden to water the garden; and from there it divided and became four rivers: Pishon, Gihon, Tigris, and Euphrates (Gen 2:10-14). Adam and Eve were naked in the garden of Eden, but they were not ashamed (Gen 2:25). Within the garden, their entire bodies were probably covered with the glory of God as with garments (Ref Rom 13:14).

Man was created as the special being in the entire universe; and the garden of Eden clearly demonstrates what a blessed life man had enjoyed within its midst.

## 7. Creation of the honorable woman, a helper suitable for the honorable man

The Scripture records the account of the creation of the woman (Eve) at the end of Genesis 2. God created man (Gen 2:7), planted the garden of Eden (Gen 2:8-15), established the covenant of works with the man (Gen 2:16-17), and then made the woman (Gen 2:18-23).

The account of the making of the woman begins as follows.

> **Genesis 2:18** Then the Lord God said, "It is not good for the man to be alone; I will make him a helper suitable for him."

When God created man and put him in the garden of Eden, he was alone without a helper suitable for him. The word *alone* signifies "living solitarily without aid or help." The *helper suitable* in the New Living Translation is rendered as "helper who is just right for him." The word *helper* is עֵזֶר (*'ēzer*) in Hebrew and means "help," "support," and "guard"; and the word *suitable* is נֶגֶד (*neged*), meaning "in the presence of" or "in the sight of." Therefore, a suitable helper is one who is in sight and gives help or support. Every man needs a suitable helper for it is not good for man to be alone. A suitable helper is especially needed in the life of faith (Rom 16:3-4; Phil 2:22; 4:3; Col 4:7-15; Phlm 1:13, 23-24).

God, who said, "I will make him a helper suitable for him," did not make the suitable helper right away, but formed every beast of the field and every bird of the sky, and brought them to the man. It was to see what he would call them (Gen 2:19). Adam observed the overall ecology of each living creature and gave the appropriate name for it, and whatever he called a living creature, that was its name (Gen 2:19). After Adam gave names to every beast of the field and every bird of the sky, the Scripture mentions again in Genesis 2:20, "but for Adam there was not found a helper suitable for him." This statement emphasizes the fact that man was without a helper suitable for him even after all of the beasts of the field and birds of the sky were made.

Why did God not create a helper suitable for Adam right away? Why did He have Adam give names to every living creature first?

**FIRST, God wanted Adam to realize the need for someone to work with him.**

It is lonesome and more difficult to do any work alone. Even if one may have the best of all things and the skills to match, there is no one who exists on earth that can live without the help of others. The Scripture states, "Two are better than one . . ." and ". . . woe to the one who falls when there is not another to lift him up" (Eccl 4:9-12). Every person needs a suitable helper. Even unmarried people need coworker(s) of faith.

**SECOND, God wanted to teach Adam that there is no helper suitable for him among nonhuman creatures.**

Every animal, without exception, was matched in pairs of male and female. Adam was the only one without a suitable partner. There was, however, no animal suitable for Adam. No beast of the field or bird of the sky could become a helper suitable for the man because the honor of the man, who was created in the image of God, was superior over all other creatures combined. God allowed Adam to realize this truth. There is no creature or thing in the entire world that can satisfy the human soul. One who is "suitable" needs to be a coworker in the same level of rationality, conscience, and spirit—one who can share in sincere understanding and fellowship.

Among God's works of creation, the description of the making of the woman is quite dynamic and profoundly impressive (Gen 2:18-23). Adam was formed of dust from the ground (Gen 2:7), but the woman was fashioned from one of the man's ribs (Gen 2:21-22). God caused a deep sleep to fall upon the man and took one of his ribs and closed up the flesh at that place (Gen 2:21). Then, God fashioned into a woman the rib which He had taken from the man (Gen 2:22). The making of the woman from the man's rib is deeply suggestive of the profound and mysterious providence of God.

First, the woman was made from a part of the man so that as she helps her husband, the two can become one flesh (Gen 2:24). Second, it is to demonstrate the fact that the husband and wife are equal although their roles are different. They may have not been equal if she had been made from a bone of a finger, toe, arm, or leg. Third, because the rib's function is to protect the heart, the most important organ in the body, the man is to love and protect his wife as his own body (Eph 5:33a). He who loves his wife loves himself (Eph 5:28).

As soon as Adam saw the woman that God brought to him, he expressed his surging love in an inspirational poem and named her.

> **Genesis 2:23** . . . This is now bone of my bones, and flesh of my flesh; she shall be called Woman, because she was taken out of Man.

The literal translation of Genesis 2:23 according to the original Hebrew text would be, "The man said, 'This, at last, is bone of my bones and flesh of my flesh. I proclaim that this is woman for she has been taken from man.'"

וַיֹּאמֶר הָאָדָם זֹאת הַפַּעַם עֶצֶם מֵעֲצָמַי

(wayyō'mer hā'ādām zō't happa'am 'eṣem mē'ăṣāmay)

וּבָשָׂר מִבְּשָׂרִי לְזֹאת יִקָּרֵא אִשָּׁה

(ûbāśār mibběśārî lězō't yiqqārē' 'iššâ)

כִּי מֵאִישׁ לֻקֳחָה־זֹּאת

(kî mē'îš luqŏḥâ-zō't)

In Genesis 2:23, the demonstrative pronoun זֹאת (zō't), translated as "this" or "she," appears three times in feminine singular form. It is clearly a poem that carries a cheerful rhythm. This short poem lucidly encapsulates the great satisfaction, overflowing delight, and fullness of love that Adam felt as he was captivated by the woman's gracefulness and exceptional beauty. In summary, Genesis 2:23 is a confession of Adam's heart that this woman is his most precious family member, that he finds great satisfaction in her for she is flawless. It is his confession that he would love only this woman and be grateful for none other.

Since the fall, every woman on the earth has a flaw somewhere and at least one aspect that is not fully satisfactory even if she were the most beautiful woman in the world. Nevertheless, this honorable woman, Eve, whom God fashioned from Adam's rib, was a woman of unsurpassed beauty, possessing everything a woman could have—truth, goodness, and beauty.

Adam's helper, Eve, was a woman created by God's profound and mysterious providence. She was indeed the suitable helper that Adam needed. She was the one and only woman for Adam, and the greatest gift that God had bestowed on him. It was out of special consideration that God gave Adam an honorable woman—Eve—as his suitable helper. It was an expression of God's *agape* love that adds to the man's honor.

In conclusion, Adam (man) whom God created was an exceedingly honorable being. Only man was created in God's image and likeness. Only with man did God ratify a covenant. Only man has received the Spirit of God. Man dwelt in the garden of Eden that God had specially planted. God also made the woman with Adam's rib and made her a helper suitable for him. However, all of man's honor was shattered when he sinned and tragically fell.

CHAPTER 2

# The Tragic Fall

As God put the man He created in the garden of Eden, He gave him two tasks to perform and one that was prohibited. The two tasks that man needed to perform were to "cultivate and keep" the garden of Eden (Gen 2:15). The prohibition he had to obey certainly was to keep himself from eating from the tree of the knowledge of good and evil (Gen 2:16-17). As the domain of God's just reign, the garden of Eden was to be kept in perfect order by fully believing and obeying the Word of God.

## 1. The covenant of works and disobedience

In Genesis 2:16-17, God said, "From any tree of the garden you may eat freely; but from the tree of the knowledge of good and evil you shall not eat, for in the day that you eat from it you will surely die." The matter of eternal life or death depended on whether one obeys or disobeys. That is why this covenant is called the *covenant of works*.

After the ratification of the covenant of works, the serpent—the tempter—came to the woman when she was alone (Gen 3:1). The woman could not overcome the temptation of the serpent and ate from the tree of the knowledge of good and evil. The woman then gave the fruit from the tree of the knowledge of good and evil to the man without telling him about the conversation she had with the serpent; and he also fell (Gen 3:6).

The woman fell to the temptation of the serpent because she did not fully believe in the Word of God, and thus did not obey. What is the evidence for this?

**FIRST, the woman could not cultivate and keep the garden of Eden.**

God had commanded Adam to "cultivate and keep" the garden of Eden (Gen 2:15). Although the woman did not hear the command to "cultivate and keep" the garden directly from God, she must have heard it from Adam with whom she had become one flesh (Gen 2:24).

The word *cultivate* is עָבַד ('ābad) in Hebrew, meaning "to work," "to serve," "to cultivate" (Gen 2:5), and "to labor" (Deut 5:13). The word *keep* is שָׁמַר (šāmar) in Hebrew, meaning "to watch," "to guard," "to give heed," "to care for," and "to observe." Therefore, the command to "cultivate and keep" emphasizes a proactive faith that exerts laborious effort and work to guard the garden of Eden. God knew beforehand that the serpent would come to them; therefore, God commanded the man to cultivate and keep the garden of Eden with proactive faith. Nevertheless, the woman did not fully believe this Word but was rather negligent in regard to the command.

Just as God had warned earlier, the serpent, which was more crafty than any beast of the field, came to the woman (Gen 3:1). The word *crafty* is עָרוּם ('ārûm) in Hebrew and has negative meanings like "cunning," "deceptive," "guileful," "ill-natured," and "shrewd." The word also connotes "false wisdom."

The serpent approached the woman and asked, "Indeed, has God said, 'You shall not eat from any tree of the garden'?" (Gen 3:1). The word *indeed* in this question is אַף ('ap) in Hebrew, meaning "surely" or "really." The serpent did not know in regard to which tree the covenant was made between God and man. He was sounding the woman out to find out this secret. The serpent skillfully tempted the woman in such a way that she could not keep herself from opening her mouth and divulging the secret.

The woman should have sternly repelled the serpent by saying something like, "If you are curious, why don't you ask God yourself? This is a covenant between God and me, and you have nothing to do with it. Did you come into the garden of Eden to try to use your guile to make an unfounded conjecture? You are stepping over your boundaries! Get out of here!" The woman, however, could not overcome the serpent's temptation. Rather, she continued to carry on the conversation with the serpent and ended up giving away the secret that it was "the tree which is in the middle of the garden" (Gen 3:3).

Jesus said in John 12:50, "I know that His commandment is eternal life." The woman did not believe in God's command to "cultivate and keep" the garden of Eden, and thus disobeyed it. Consequently, she forfeited her eternal life (Gen 3:22).

Jesus emphatically commanded that the end-time saints who are awaiting the second coming of the Lord should "be on the alert" (Matt 24:42; 25:13) and "be ready" (Matt 24:44). Also in Matthew 24:43, He said, "But be sure of this, that if the head of the house had known at what time of the night the thief was coming, he would have been on the alert and would not have allowed his house to be broken into." There is a thread of connection in this command that reaches all the way back to God's command to Adam and Eve "to cultivate and keep" the garden of Eden. Therefore, it would behoove the saints living in the end times to believe and obey this Word. We must always be awake with the Word, prayer, and praise. If we are not alert and awake with impregnable faith, then we will be tempted by Satan and drift away from God's Word. Consequently, this will lead us to forfeit our place of blessing and ultimately pair up with the world (Eph 4:27; 1 Pet 5:8).

**SECOND**, the woman freely added and took away from God's Word.

God had permitted man to eat freely "from *any* tree of the garden" (Gen 2:16). The woman, however, did not hesitate to say, "From the fruit of the trees of the garden we may eat" (Gen 3:2), omitting the word *any* (כֹּל, *kōl*: all). She took away from God's Word as she pleased.

Furthermore, God simply said, "... you shall not eat" (Gen 2:17). However, the woman added her thoughts to God's Word and said in Genesis 3:3, "God has said, 'You shall not eat from it *or touch it*, or you will die.'"

We must never take away from or add our thoughts to God's Word (Deut 4:2; 12:32). God said in Revelation 22:18-19, "I testify to everyone who hears the words of the prophecy of this book; if anyone adds to them, God will add to him the plagues which are written in this book; and if anyone takes away from the words of the book of this prophecy, God will take away his part from the tree of life and from the holy city, which are written in this book."

**THIRD**, the woman altered God's Word.

God clearly said, "... for in the day that you eat from it [the tree of the knowledge of good and evil] you will surely die" (Gen 2:17). The phrase *surely die* in Hebrew is תָּמוּת מוֹת (*môt tāmût*), in which the word מוּת (*mût*: die) is used twice. The first of the two occurrences is מוֹת (*môt*), in the infinitive absolute form, which intensifies the cognate finite verb that directly follows. Therefore, God's warning, "you will surely die," is a resolute statement that whoever eats from the tree will certainly die without exception. The woman's answer, "... lest you die" (Gen 3:3; ESV), is evidence that she had already altered and debased the Word of God. Those words, "lest you die," betray the woman's doubt by connoting that one may or may not die[4]. The woman doubted God's Word and ended up diluting His absolute and stern warning into a language that suggested a mere possibility. By doing so, she disdained not only the authority of God's Word but also the authority of God Himself.

God's Word is always clear about whether it is a *yes* or a *no*. One with an uncertain attitude that sways back and forth will surely fall into Satan's temptation. Today, there are many, even among theologians and ministers, who do not believe that the Bible is one hundred percent the inspired Word of God. We must bear in mind that if we doubt God's Word, we will also, like the woman, fall into the serpent's temptation.

Having detected doubt in the woman's heart regarding God's Word, the serpent tempted her more aggressively. The serpent caused the woman to directly challenge God's Word by telling her, "you surely will not die!" (Gen 3:4). The crafty serpent continued on to say, "For God knows that in the day you eat from it your eyes will be opened, and you will be like God, knowing good and evil" (Gen 3:5). With such a cunning lie (John 8:44), the serpent shook up the woman's heart. Moreover, he completely shattered her covenantal relationship with God and destroyed the order in the garden of Eden.

The serpent's lies did not stop there. It went on to instill into the woman's heart the arrogant thought that man can become like God. Then, it drove that arrogance to the point where the woman was gripped by the delusion that it was possible for man to be like God. Despite such lies, man the creature can never become God the Creator.

When the woman was tempted by the serpent's lie, her mind was consumed with greed. God's Word was nowhere to be found; instead, she was captivated by the fruit that seemed "good for food," "a delight to the eyes," and "desirable to make one wise" (Gen 3:6). The woman eventually ate the fruit from the tree of the knowledge of good and evil and gave also to her husband to eat (Gen 3:6). Thus, death came upon both of them. When the serpent tempted the woman, her disregard for God's Word led her to disobey. In turn, she completely forgot her duty as the "suitable helper." Consequently, she led herself to destruction and made her husband fall as well. "When lust has conceived, it gives birth to sin; and when sin is accomplished, it brings forth death" (Jas 1:15).

## 2. The result of the fall

God's judgments were pronounced upon Adam and Eve as a consequence of their sin of not believing the Word of God and disobeying by eating the fruit from the tree of the knowledge of good and evil. The judgments were retribution according to God's justice. What were the judgments?

### (1) The judgment pronounced upon the serpent

> **Genesis 3:14** The Lord God said to the serpent, "Because you have done this, cursed are you more than all cattle, and more than every beast of the field; on your belly you will go, and dust you will eat all the days of your life."

God cursed the serpent because it was the tempter that deceived Adam and Eve to disbelieve and disobey God's Word (2 Cor 11:3). The first curse pronounced upon the serpent was "on your belly you will go." The serpent was the craftiest among all of the beasts of the field that God had made (Gen 3:1). Now, it has been degraded to become a being that moves on its belly unlike the other beasts.

The second curse was "dust you will eat all the days of your life." Serpents do not really eat dust for food, but have become beings that cannot avoid swallowing dust while crawling upon their bellies on the ground. An expression that is similar to "eating dust" in the Bible is "licking dust," which signifies extreme shame and humiliation that the defeated has to experience (Ps 72:9; Isa 49:23; Mic 7:17). The curse that the serpent will eat dust alludes to the shame and humiliation that the serpent—which was used as Satan's tool—would experience in the future.

### (2) The judgment pronounced upon Satan

> **Genesis 3:15** And I will put enmity between you and the woman, and between your seed and her seed; He shall bruise you on the head, and you shall bruise him on the heel.

The pronoun *you* in the above passage initially refers to the serpent. Behind the serpent, however, was Satan working through the serpent. Revelation 12:9 states, "And the great dragon was thrown down, the serpent of old who is called the devil and Satan, who deceives the whole world." Revelation 20:2 states, "And he laid hold of the dragon, the serpent of old, who is the devil and Satan" (Ref Matt 3:7; 23:33; John 8:44).

The *seed* of the woman signifies Jesus Christ (Gal 4:4) and the *you* in Genesis 3:15 is the one that confronts the seed of the woman head on. Therefore, it would be appropriate in this context to apply this *you* directly to Satan who used the serpent as an instrument of temptation.

Genesis 3:15 is the proto-Gospel (*protoevangelium*) and a messianic prophecy. Although Satan will bruise the heel of the seed of the woman by causing Jesus Christ to be crucified, Jesus Christ will bruise Satan on the head and destroy him (1 John 3:8). This Word was accomplished through Jesus' crucifixion and will be consummated through the second coming of Christ when Satan will be thrown into the lake of fire and brimstone (Ref Rom 16:20; Heb 2:14; Rev 20:1-3, 10).

### (3) The judgment pronounced upon the woman

> **Genesis 3:16** To the woman He said, "I will greatly multiply your pain in childbirth, in pain you will bring forth children; yet your desire will be for your husband, and he will rule over you."

God gave three punishments to the woman.

**FIRST**, God greatly multiplied the pain of conception and childbirth.

The words *greatly multiply* are הַרְבָּה אַרְבֶּה (*harbâ 'arbe*) in Hebrew. This is an emphatic repetition of the word רָבָה (*rābâ*) which means "to become great or numerous." This implies that the pain of childbirth will be unimaginably great. Jesus, however, stated in John 16:21, "Whenever a woman is in labor she has pain, because her hour has come; but when she gives birth to the child, she no longer remembers the anguish because of the joy that a child has been born into the world." In speaking of a woman's pain in conception and childbirth turning into joy after the birth of the child, Jesus was speaking figuratively about the agony that the disciples would endure at His crucifixion and the greater joy that they would receive at His resurrection (John 16:22; Ref 1 Tim 2:15). This can also be viewed as an implication that the judgment pronounced upon the woman due to her sin would be resolved by Jesus' crucifixion.

**SECOND**, the woman's desire will be for her husband.

The word *desire* in Genesis 3:16 is תְּשׁוּקָה (*tĕšûqâ*) in Hebrew. This word is used in two other places in the Bible. The word is used in Song of Solomon 7:10, which says, "And his desire is for me." It is also used in Genesis 4:7, which says, "and its [sin's] desire is for you." Both times, the word is used to express a strong longing. The word תְּשׁוּקָה (tĕšûqâ), which means "desire" or "longing," is derived from the root word שׁוּק (šûq), which means, "to overflow" or "to run after." Therefore, the expression in Genesis 3:16, "your desire will be for your husband," signifies that the woman will long uncontrollably for her husband. In sinning, the woman manipulated the man to eat the fruit from the tree of the knowledge of good and evil, but now she has become subordinated to the man. Throughout human history women have possessed rather passive dispositions as subordinates who wait upon men, perhaps as a result of the judgment that fell upon them for encouraging sin.

**THIRD, the woman will be ruled over by her husband.**

Originally, Adam was the head of Eve. First Corinthians 11:3 states, "But I want you to understand that Christ is the head of every man, and the man is the head of a woman, and God is the head of Christ." Apostle Paul also said in 1 Timothy 2:12, "But I do not allow a woman to teach or exercise authority over a man, but to remain quiet." Nevertheless, the woman, who was created after the man, became the head over the man in the garden of Eden when she ate the fruit from the tree of the knowledge of good and evil first and gave it to the man to eat also (Gen 3:6, 12, 17; 1 Tim 2:13-14). Therefore, the fall was a result of destroying the order that God had established. Now, God is reestablishing the order by making the husband rule over the wife and having him become the head of the wife (Eph 5:23). Based on this principle, Apostle Paul mentioned several times that the wife must be submissive to her husband (1 Cor 14:34; Eph 5:22, 24; Col 3:18; 1 Tim 2:11-12; Titus 2:5; 1 Pet 3:1, 5-6).

## (4) The judgment pronounced upon the man
*FIRST*, the man will toil all the days of his life.

> **Genesis 3:17** Then to Adam He said, "Because you have listened to the voice of your wife, and have eaten from the tree about which I commanded you, saying, 'You shall not eat from it'; cursed is the ground because of you; in toil you will eat of it all the days of your life.

The word *toil* is עִצָּבוֹן (*'iṣṣābôn*) in Hebrew and is also used in Genesis 3:16 to refer to the woman's pain in childbirth. This demonstrates that man's sweat-filled toil (Gen 3:19a) is as agonizing as a woman's pain in childbirth (Ref Gen 5:29; Eccl 2:22-23). The Scripture states, "if anyone is not willing to work, then he is not to eat, either" (2 Thess 3:10). Likewise, man, after the fall, can only eat the produce of the ground through hard work and toil; he will eat bread through the sweat of his face.

**SECOND, man will return to dust.**

> **Genesis 3:19** By the sweat of your face you will eat bread, till you return to the ground, because from it you were taken; for you are dust, and to dust you shall return.

This judgment speaks of the way of death, which would come to man as the wage of sin. Every sinner dies, is buried in the ground, and becomes dust (Job 10:9; 34:15; Ps 90:3; Ref Eccl 12:7).

### (5) The judgment pronounced upon the ground

The ground was also cursed because of the fall of man. God said to Adam in Genesis 3:17, "Cursed is the ground because of you." Consequently, the ground is cursed to grow "both thorns and thistles" (Gen 3:18). This implies that, after the fall, the only thing man can reap in this world is the fruit of suffering.

Romans 8:22 describes the cursed state of the whole creation on earth because of man: "For we know that the whole creation groans and suffers the pains of childbirth together until now." Thus, the creation longs for "the revealing of the sons of God" (Rom 8:19) and "the creation itself also will be set free from its slavery to corruption into the freedom of the glory of the children of God" (Rom 8:21). Since the ground was cursed as a result of the fall of man, both the cursed ground and all of creation will be restored when man is restored.

### (6) The judgment of being driven out of the garden of Eden

God drove the fallen Adam and Eve out of the garden of Eden to cultivate the ground. Then at the east of the garden of Eden, He stationed the cherubim and the flaming sword which turned every direction to guard the way to the tree of life (Gen 3:23-24). The Hebrew word for *drive out* in Genesis 3:24 is the intensive (*piel*) stem of גָּרַשׁ (*gāraš*). This signifies that God did not simply send Adam and Eve out, but that He resolutely kicked them out. God drove them out of the garden of Eden because He did not want mankind to obtain eternal life in their fallen state (Gen 3:22).

Now, the way to the tree of life is guarded by the cherubim and the flaming sword which turns every direction (Gen 3:24). However, by the grace of God, the saints will be able to stand before the tree of life again (Rev 2:7; 22:14).

## (7) The judgment of death

The sin of Adam and Eve brought death not only upon them, but also to entire humankind. Romans 5:12 states, "Therefore, just as through one man sin entered into the world, and death through sin, and so death spread to all men, because all sinned." Death of human beings is not a natural phenomenon; it is punishment for sin (Rom 6:23). Before sin, man was originally an eternal being; but he lost that eternal life because he sinned.

### ① Spiritual death

Spiritual death refers to Adam's state of separation from God due to sin. As soon as Adam sinned, he became spiritually dead, and his fellowship with God was lost. Adam and Eve's act of hiding themselves from the presence of God after they sinned demonstrated that they were spiritually dead (Gen 3:8). Ephesians 2:1 confirms, "And you were dead in your trespasses and sins." Such spiritually dead people can restore their fellowship with God only when they become a new creation through regeneration (John 3:3-5; 2 Cor 5:17).

### ② Physical death

Physical death is the separation of the soul and the body. When the soul departs from the body, the body immediately begins to decay and eventually decomposes to become dust. Spiritual death came to Adam immediately after his fall; however, physical death came to him when he reached 930 years of age (Gen 5:5).

Thus far, we have discussed the judgments that God had pronounced after Adam and Eve had sinned. The only One who can resolve the issue of all the judgments, sin, and death is Jesus Christ. Romans 8:1-2 declares, "Therefore there is now no condemnation for those who are in Christ Jesus. For the law of the Spirit of life in Christ Jesus has set you free from the law of sin and of death." Ephesians 1:7 also states, "In Him we have redemption through His blood, the forgiveness of our trespasses, according to the riches of His grace" (cf. Col 1:14). Man can be justified and attain eternal life only through Jesus Christ (Rom 3:22-24; 5:17-18).

# CHAPTER 3

# Salvation and Covenant

From the very moment sin entered, the garden of Eden was no longer Paradise. The glory of God that gives spiritual joy departed from the garden of Eden where man used to enjoy fellowship with God. All that remained was sorrow, grief, shame, fear, and terror. Adam and Eve realized that they were naked and sewed fig leaves together to make for themselves loin coverings (Gen 3:7). Then in the cool of the day, they heard the sound of God walking in the garden and hid themselves from the presence of God among the trees of the garden (Gen 3:8). God, however, came to Adam who was hiding among the trees of the garden, and earnestly called out to him.

> **Genesis 3:9** Then the Lord God called to the man, and said to him, "Where are you?"

The phrase *called to the man* is וַיִּקְרָא...אֶל־הָאָדָם (*wayyiqrā'...'el-hā'ādām*) in Hebrew, meaning "called out to the man (Adam) in a loud voice." It was not because the omniscient and omnipotent God did not know that Adam was hiding among the trees that He called out in a loud voice (Ps 139:1-4; Jer 23:23-24). God was actually asking about the current state of Adam's faith, the whereabouts of his heart.

From a covenantal perspective, the question, "Where are you?" (אַיֶּכָּה, *'ayyekkâ*), can also be understood as asking, "What kind of relationship did you and I have?" This short question expresses God's disappointment and sorrow in Adam, who repaid God's immeasurable love with disobedience. It also expresses God's earnest desire for Adam's repentance. This message must have penetrated and echoed deep within Adam's heart. God's voice calling out, "Where are you?" was the voice of reproach for sinners, the plaintive voice of a parent searching for the lost child, the voice of love that comes first to the transgressor (1 John 4:10, 19), and the voice of mercy that urges repentance. God is merciful and draws near to those who are truly contrite and brokenhearted, forgiving and restoring them no matter how greatly they may have sinned (Ps 32:1-6; 34:18; 51:16-17; Isa 57:15).

## 1. The promise of the *seed of the woman*

God first showed the way of salvation for fallen mankind through the promise of the seed of the woman.

> **Genesis 3:15** And I will put enmity between you and the woman, and between your seed and her seed; he shall bruise you on the head, and you shall bruise him on the heel.

The words "her [woman's] seed" in the verse refers to Jesus Christ who would be conceived in Mary through the Holy Spirit (Mat 1:18-20). Galatians 4:4 states, "But when the fullness of the time came, God sent forth His Son, born of a woman, born under the Law." Jesus was conceived by the Holy Spirit and came as the Savior of this world through the Virgin Mary. Jesus came as the seed of a woman, not of a man. The prophecy in Isaiah 7:14, which states, "Therefore the LORD Himself will give you a sign: Behold, a virgin will be with child and bear a son, and she will call His name Immanuel," was precisely fulfilled (Matt 1:21-23).

In Genesis 3:15, the phrase, "You shall bruise him on the heel," prophesies that Jesus Christ would be crucified; "he shall bruise you on the head" means that Jesus Christ would completely destroy Satan (Ref 1 John 3:8; Heb 2:14). Even in the midst of pronouncing curses and judgments upon the fallen man, God also gave him the promise of salvation.[5]

As an assurance of this promise, God Himself made garments of skin for Adam and Eve.

> **Genesis 3:21** The Lord God made garments of skin for Adam and his wife, and clothed them.

**FIRST**, the garments of skin were to cover the shame of the sinners.

When Adam and Eve's eyes were opened by eating from the tree of the knowledge of good and evil, the first thing they saw was their own nakedness (Gen 3:7). In order to cover their shame, they made loin coverings with fig leaves. What is the difference between the loin coverings made of fig leaves and the garments of skin made by God?

First, the covering made by man covered only a part of the body, whereas the garments which God made for them (Gen 3:21) were complete and covered the entire body. The expression *loin coverings* in Genesis 3:7 is חֲגֹר (*ḥăgōr*) in Hebrew and refers to a piece of clothing that barely covers around the loins. On the contrary, the expression *garments of skin* (כְּתֹנֶת, *kĕtōnet*) in Genesis 3:21 refers to a long garment that covers the body from the top down to the knees like a robe.

Furthermore, the coverings that Adam put together was made of leaves, thus they withered quickly. However, the garments that God made lasted a long time because they were made of leather.

Fundamentally, the garments of skin with which God clothed them foreshadow Jesus Christ, who will come and be offered as the eternal atoning sacrifice on the cross in order to cover the sin and shame of fallen mankind (Isa 53:4-6; Matt 20:28; Mark 10:45).

**SECOND, the garments of skin signified God's absolute protection for sinners.**

God Himself came to Adam and Eve and clothed them with the garments of skin that He specifically made for them. This act demonstrates God's infinite mercy, forgiveness, protection, and love. The fallen Adam and Eve had to go out to the cursed world outside the garden of Eden. The land upon which they were to live was a desolate land that produced thorns and thistles—a place where man must eat of the produce of the ground through the toil and sweat of his face (Gen 3:17-19). For every person living on the earth, there are thorns that can prick and afflict him both mentally and physically. Even people with great faith like Apostle Paul were not exempt (2 Cor 12:7). The garments of skin that God had made for Adam and Eve were signs of protection from being pricked or harmed by any thorn that comes from the accursed ground.

In other words, the garment of skin was the sign that demonstrated the mercy and forgiveness of God, who did not completely forsake mankind even though they had fallen. It was not at Adam and Eve's request, but entirely because God first loved mankind that He showed such mercy (1 John 4:10, 19).

In order to attain garments of skin, the owner of that skin needs to die and shed blood. The sacrifice of an animal was necessary to clothe Adam and Eve with garments of skin. The animal that was sacrificed for Adam and Eve foreshadowed Jesus Christ who would come as the Passover Lamb and become an atoning sacrifice on the cross for us (1 Cor 5:7; 1 Pet 1:19; Rev 5:6). John the Baptist, in reference to Jesus, confessed in John 1:29,

"Behold, the Lamb of God who takes away the sin of the world!"

The love of God, who made garments of skin and clothed Adam and Eve, was accomplished and demonstrated through the atoning work of Jesus Christ on the cross (Rom 5:8). By obtaining "eternal redemption" on the cross (Heb 9:12), Jesus had fulfilled the new covenant (Jer 31:33-34; Luke 22:20; 1 Cor 11:25). Apostle Paul indicated that the moment we experience the grace of eternal redemption is the very moment that we are clothed with Jesus Christ (Rom 13:14; Gal 3:27).

## 2. Jesus Christ, the fulfiller of the new covenant

The promise of the woman's seed was expanded to the covenant with Noah (Gen 6:18; 9:8-17) and the covenant with Abraham (Gen 12:1-3, 6-7; 13:14-18; 15:12-21; 17:9-14; 18:10; 22:15-18). Then it further developed into the Sinaitic covenant (Exod 24:1-8; Ref Deut 29:1) and the Davidic covenant (2 Sam 7:11-16; 1 Chr 17:10-14). Furthermore, God proclaimed the new covenant through Prophet Jeremiah (Jer 31:31-34), and spoke of the covenant of peace through Prophet Ezekiel (Ezek 34:25-31; 37:26-28).

In order to save the fallen mankind, God chose Noah ten generations after Adam, and then Abraham another ten generations later. When Israel, Abraham's descendants, became a great nation, God gave them the Law through Moses and established the first covenant by sprinkling the blood on the book of the Law and all the people (Exod 24:1-8; Heb 9:18-20).

What is the relationship between the Law (the first covenant, also known as the old covenant) and the new covenant?

### (1) Characteristics of being "under the law" of the Old Testament

Until the coming of Jesus, human beings were under the law. Galatians 3:23 states, "But before faith came, we were kept in custody under the law, being shut up to the faith which was later to be revealed."

The word *law* is תּוֹרָה (*tôrâ*) in Hebrew and νόμος (*nomos*) in Greek. This is the law that needs to be kept in our relationship with God and with each other. The law is holy, righteous, and good (Rom 7:12). Nevertheless, man sinned and fell to a state where he could not completely keep the law of God. Thus, he was bound in custody under the law.

Apostle Paul described the wretchedness of life that is under the law in several ways.

**FIRST**, it is the state of being "under sin."

The expressions, "under the law" and "shut up" in Galatians 3:23 are used in parallel with the expression "shut up ... under sin" in Galatians 3:22. Here, Apostle Paul is describing the state before attaining faith in Jesus Christ as being shut up "under the law" and "under sin." In both passages, the Greek word used for the English phrase *shut up* is συγκλείω (*synkleiō*), signifying a state of complete confinement.

Until the coming of Jesus Christ, all human beings were in a wretched state, completely confined by sin and unable to break away with their own strength. Regarding this, Romans 6:14 states, "For sin shall not be master over you, for you are not under law but under grace." Being "under law" is the state in which one is mastered over by sin. The Greek word for *master* is κυριεύω (*kyrieuō*), meaning "to rule over" or "to subjugate."

Therefore, those who were under the law were confined and ruled over by sin, living a tragic life without being able to escape from it. However, Jesus Christ is the One who liberated them from such desperate circumstances (Gal 4:4-5). The blood that Jesus Christ shed on the cross forgave all of our sins and liberated us from them (Matt 26:28; Eph 1:7; Heb 9:12).

**SECOND**, it is the state of being "under guardians and managers."

The state of being "under the law," as mentioned in Galatians 4:4, is described as being "under guardians and managers" in Galatians 4:2. The word *guardian* is ἐπίτροπος (*epitropos*) in Greek, referring to a steward who was put in charge of nurturing, educating, and protecting a young heir until he grows to become an adult. In Galatians 3:24, this guardian is labeled as "tutor." The Greek word for *tutor* is παιδαγωγός (*paidagōgos*), meaning "tutor," "guardian," or "custodian." The Greek word for *manager* is οἰκονόμος (*oikonomos*), referring to a house steward who manages the assets until the young heir of the family grows up. The young heir will live under the care of guardians and managers without any decision-making rights, much like a slave.

Likewise, Christians who are babes in faith are also enslaved under the law, which is like the guardian and manager. Jesus, however, liberated those who were under the bondage of the law and unable to practice their rights even though they are heirs.

**THIRD**, it is the state of being "under the elemental things of the world."

The expression "under the law" in Galatians 4:4 is expressed in Galatians 4:3 as "under the elemental things of the world." The words *elemental things* are στοιχεῖον (*stoicheion*) in Greek, meaning "fundamental principles," "basic components," or "elements." In ancient Greek natural philosophy, the word was used to signify the "proto-elements of the cosmos." Later, it was used to signify the "elementary and rudimentary teachings" or "principles of science or scholarship."

Therefore, the concept of the "elemental things," which symbolically refers to the law, implies the existence of a higher and more complete level; and this is referring to Jesus Christ. This is why Jesus said in Matthew 5:17, "Do not think that I came to abolish the Law or the Prophets; I did not come to abolish but to fulfill." Jesus completes all elementary things.

Galatians 4:3 states, "So also we, while we were children, were held in bondage under the elemental things of the world." The Greek verb for the expression "held in bondage" is δεδουλωμένοι (*dedoulōmenoi*), the perfect passive participle of the word δουλόω (*douloō*). It connotes that we had become enslaved by sin apart from our own volition but that our bondage has finally come to an end after a long time. God sent Jesus Christ at the fullness of the time and freed mankind from the long and abominable slavery. Thus, Galatians 4:4-5 states, "But when the fullness of the time came, God sent forth His Son, born of a woman, born under the Law, so that He might redeem those who were under the Law, that we might receive the adoption as sons."

### (2) Characteristics of the new covenant

The new covenant is the covenant of grace that Jesus executes and fulfills; it is the covenant that Jesus Christ established through His blood (Luke 22:20; 1 Cor 11:25). Thus, Jesus Christ is the "mediator of a new covenant" (Heb 9:15; 12:24). Then, what unique characteristics does the new covenant have in comparison to the law (the old covenant)?

**FIRST**, the new covenant is a covenant written on the heart.

God said in Hebrews 8:8, "I will effect a new covenant." In verse 10, God continues to explain about the covenant that He will make with the house of Israel, "And I will write them on their hearts." This passage is quoting the words written in Jeremiah 31. In Jeremiah 31:31 God said, "I will make a new covenant," then He explicates further and says, "I will put My law within them and on their heart I will write it" (Jer 31:33).

The old covenant was engraved on tablets of stone (2 Cor 3:7). In the new covenant, however, the Word of God is written on tablets of human hearts (2 Cor 3:3). Then, they will become God's people and God will be their God (Jer 31:33). Jesus taught the Word of God (Matt 4:23; 9:35; 22:16; Mark 4:33; Luke 20:21) and engraved the Word on His people's hearts, fulfilling the new covenant of Jeremiah.

**SECOND**, the new covenant is a covenant previously ratified by God.

Galatians 3:17 states, "What I am saying is this: the Law, which came four hundred and thirty years later, does not invalidate a covenant previously ratified by God, so as to nullify the promise." People had been keeping the Law ever since its ratification at Mount Sinai circa 1446 BC. God's covenant, however, was given 430 years before the law. When we trace back 430 years from the time when the law was given on Mount Sinai, we come to the year 1876 BC, which is the year when the seventy members of Jacob's family moved into Egypt. Of course, the year when God gave Abraham the promise of salvation through Jesus Christ as part of the covenant of the torch in Genesis 15 was 2082 BC.

Then, why does the Bible say that the covenant was previously ratified, alluding to 1876 BC as the starting point? This difficulty can only be resolved from God's redemptive-historical perspective. In order to aid us in understanding this issue, let us briefly examine the seemingly contradictory records about the land of Shechem in the Old and New Testaments (from *The Covenant of the Torch*, Book 2 of the History of Redemption series, pp. 270-276). Even though Jacob was buried in the cave of the field of Machpelah (Gen 50:12-13), the martyred Deacon Stephen preached his sermon as if Jacob were buried in Shechem as Joseph had been (Acts 7:15-16). Although Jacob died in Egypt, he was assured in his belief that his children would inherit the land of Canaan just as God had promised. That is why he had given the land of Shechem to Joseph earlier (Gen 48:22). It was Jacob's faith and assurance in the covenant that laid the groundwork for Joseph to be buried at Shechem (Josh 24:32). Hence, in high appraisal of Jacob's faith, the Bible records as if Jacob were buried at Shechem. Moreover, Deacon Stephen also preached that Abraham had purchased the land of Shechem from the sons of Hamor (Acts 7:14-16) when in fact it was Jacob who had purchased, for one hundred pieces of money, the piece of land before the city of Shechem where he had pitched his tent (Gen 33:18-20). Jacob and Abraham dwelt in tents together for fifteen years (Heb 11:9). Thus, Abraham was able to transmit the entirety of the covenant faith to Jacob. Therefore, Jacob purchased that piece of land in full assurance of the covenant that God had bestowed upon Abraham (Gen 12:5-7). Though it is true that Jacob was the one who actually purchased the land of Shechem, from a covenantal perspective, the purchase process had begun with Abraham who had first received the covenant concerning Shechem from God. Since it was Abraham who was decisively influential in the purchase of this land, Deacon Stephen preached that it was Abraham who had purchased the land.

Likewise, the starting point for reckoning the "430 years" in Galatians 3:17 can also be easily understood from a covenantal perspective. When Jacob's seventy family members were about to enter Egypt in 1876 BC, God appeared to Jacob at Beersheba and said to him, "I will make you a great nation there. I will go down with you to Egypt, and I will also surely bring you up again." Thus, God reaffirmed the covenant that He gave to Abraham (Gen 46:1-7). Jacob, who had been fearful for a while, was reassured through the covenant. He firmly believed that the ultimate reason that they were going down to Egypt was not to become strangers in a land that is not theirs, but rather to judge the nation that they were about to serve, to come out with many possessions, and to become a great nation as they return to the Promised Land in the fourth generation (Gen 15:14-16). Therefore, the "430 years" (Gal 3:17) spans from the time that the Abrahamic covenant was reaffirmed with Jacob—and hence the time when its actual fulfillment began—until the Israelites received the law at Mount Sinai. Thus, it was a time reckoned from a covenantal perspective.

Therefore, the covenant was given earlier than the law. The Greek word for *previously ratified* in Galatians 3:17 is προκυρόω (*prokyroō*). It is a compound word comprised of πρό (*pro*: in front of, before) and κυρόω (*kyroō*: ratify, confirm, validate), meaning "ratify beforehand" and "validate in advance." This covenant which was ratified before the law points to the new covenant that will be fulfilled through Jesus Christ.

**THIRD**, the new covenant is an eternal and perfect covenant.

The old covenant grows old, becomes obsolete, and disappears. Hebrews 8:13 calls the old covenant "the first," stating that the first is made obsolete, and "whatever is becoming obsolete and growing old is ready to disappear." The old covenant is replaced by the new covenant, and the old covenant is fulfilled in the new covenant (Matt 5:17). The new covenant is eternal. Therefore, "the promise of the eternal inheritance" is given through Jesus, who is the mediator of a new covenant (Heb 9:15).

Furthermore, the old covenant was not faultless. Hebrews 8:7 states, "For if that first covenant had been faultless, there would have been no occasion sought for a second." The word *faultless* in this verse is ἄμεμπτος (*amemptos*), meaning "blameless" or "faultless." This explains that the old covenant was not perfect and declares the need for a new covenant that is perfect.

**FOURTH**, the new covenant is a covenant of complete forgiveness of sins.

The law of the Old Testament brought condemnation to mankind. Romans 3:20 states, "Because by the works of the Law no flesh will be justified in His sight; for through the Law comes the knowledge of sin." Through condemnation, the law allows people to realize that they are sinners, but it cannot actually forgive sins. Thus, the ministry attained through the law is called the "ministry of death" (2 Cor 3:7) and the "ministry of condemnation" (2 Cor 3:9).*

Under the new covenant, however, iniquities are forgiven and sins are remembered no more (Jer 31:34). Hebrews 8:12 states, "For I will be merciful to their iniquities, and I will remember their sins no more." This is a complete forgiveness, an eternal forgiveness, and an assured forgiveness.

Jesus has fulfilled the new covenant with His blood on the cross (Luke 22:20; 1 Cor 11:25). Therefore, only the blood of Jesus can completely forgive all our sins and liberate us from every curse. This forgiveness is an eternal and perfect atonement. Galatians 3:13 states, "Christ redeemed us from the curse of the Law, having become a curse for us—for it is written, 'Cursed is everyone who hangs on a tree.'" The word *redeem* in this verse is ἐξαγοράζω (*exagorazō*), signifying release and liberation from slavery. Only the new covenant of Jesus' blood on the cross can rescue and liberate us from our sins, curse, and death. Galatians 4:4-5 explains that Jesus was conceived by the Holy Spirit and came as the seed of the woman in order to redeem those who were under the law.

Jesus Himself declared that He is the fulfiller of the new covenant.

---

\* *Ministry of condemnation* signifies the function of the law that brings awareness of sin and confirms the guilt of the sin in the sinner (Rom 7:7-9). The New Century Version of the Bible brings out this meaning by translating the expression as "the law that judged people guilty of sin" while the NIV translates as "the ministry that condemns men."

After He broke the bread at the Last Supper, He took the cup and said, "This cup which is poured out for you is the new covenant in My blood" (Luke 22:20). He also said, "for this is My blood of the covenant, which is poured out for many for forgiveness of sins" (Matt 26:28).

Jesus Himself was hung on the cross and bore all our sins, thus fulfilling the work of saving fallen mankind through His precious blood that He shed on the cross (Eph 1:7; Heb 9:12; 1 Pet 1:18-19; 2:24). Therefore, all covenants are completely fulfilled in Jesus Christ.

## 3. The promise of the eternal covenant

### (1) God's promise

A *promise* is a declaration to someone that something will be done in the future. In the Bible, a promise refers to God's unilateral covenant with mankind (Ref 1 Chr 16:15-17; Ps 105:8-10). The *Merriam-Webster Dictionary* defines *promise* as follows.

① a declaration that one will do or refrain from doing something specified

② hope, reason to expect something, ground for expectation of success, improvement, or excellence

③ something that is promised, that is, to perform, to give, to make, or to obtain

The prophecies concerning Jesus Christ in the Old and New Testaments are encapsulated into the word *promise*. All promises in the Bible are ultimately fulfilled through perfect salvation in Jesus Christ. Jesus Christ came to this world according to God's promise, and His entire ministry on earth was the fulfillment of His promise. God's promise has been enacted by Jesus the Mediator (Heb 8:6; 9:15; 12:24), and this indestructible promise which God made to us is eternal life (Heb 6:18; 1 Jn 2:25).

Therefore, God's promise fills us with great anticipation for Jesus Christ alone, the blessed hope of glory (Acts 26:6-7; Col 1:27; Titus 2:13). This promise was given to Abraham (Heb 6:13-15), and Isaac and Jacob became "fellow heirs of the same promise" (Heb 11:9). In this promise, the Gentiles also became "fellow heirs and fellow members of the body, and fellow partakers" (Eph 3:6).

All of God's promises are invaluable because of their immutability.

**Numbers 23:19** God is not a man, that He should lie, Nor a son of man, that He should repent; has He said, and will He not do it? Or has He spoken, and will He not make it good?

**Psalm 89:34** My covenant I will not violate, nor will I alter the utterance of My lips.

**1 Samuel 15:29** Also the Glory of Israel will not lie or change His mind; for He is not a man that He should change His mind.

God is faithful because He never forgets; He keeps every promise He makes (1 Cor 1:9; 10:13; 1 Thess 5:24; Heb 10:23; 11:11). Our faithful God wears "faithfulness" as a belt about His waist (Isa 11:5; Lam 3:23). He keeps His covenant and His lovingkindness to a thousandth generation with those who love Him and keep His commandments (Deut 7:9). As we have seen, God's promises are certain and absolute. Therefore those who receive His promise will never get lost, feel anxious, or become disappointed. What He says today will not change tomorrow, or His "yes" will never become "no" (2 Cor 1:18-20). Therefore, the value of the promises of God's covenant is intrinsically infinite. Just as Apostle Peter confessed, they are "His precious and magnificent promises" (2 Pet 1:4).

We are the children of promise who have received this precious covenant through Jesus Christ. Therefore, let us not doubt but press on, firmly believing in Apostle Paul's encouragement: ". . . be steadfast, immovable, always abounding in the work of the Lord, knowing that your toil is not in vain in the Lord" (1 Cor 15:58). This magnificent promise will be perfectly fulfilled in those who possess the great faith to believe in and cling to the promise of the eternal covenant.

## (2) God's eternal promise

God's covenant is valid not only in the generation of its ratification, but eternally. The promise contained in this eternal covenant will neither change nor be annulled in midcourse, but it will certainly be fulfilled. That is why it is called the "promise of the eternal covenant." The promise that God gives to His saints is eternal. How is this possible?

*FIRST*, it is a promise made through the eternal Word (Gen 9:16; 17:7, 13, 19; Exod 31:16; Lev 24:8; Judg 2:1; 2 Sam 23:5; 1 Chr 16:17; Ps 105:8-10; 111:5; Isa 24:5; 55:3, Ezek 16:60; 37:26).

God's covenant is always made through the Word. Psalm 105:8 states, "He has remembered His covenant forever, the word which He commanded to a thousand generations." Psalm 105:10 states, "Then He confirmed it to Jacob for a statute, to Israel as an everlasting covenant." God's Word is eternal (Luke 21:33; 1 Pet 1:23-25). Therefore, the covenant made through the Word is eternal and the promise of the covenant is also eternal.

### SECOND, it is a promise made by the eternal God (Deut 33:27; Ps 90:1-2; 93:2; 102:12; Isa 40:28; Lam 5:19).

Since God is eternal, His promises are also eternal. Man's promises, however, are not eternal because man is not an eternal being. Hence, promises made between men cannot be carried out if one dies. The promise given by the eternal God continues to be carried out until its complete fulfillment.

### THIRD, it is a promise that God remembers.

God remembers His holy Word (Ps 105:42) and His holy covenant (Luke 1:72). God remembers His covenant with mankind forever and does not forget them (Ps 106:45; 111:5). Hence, the promises contained in the covenant are also eternal.

### FOURTH, it is a promise made by the faithful God.

God is "faithful" (Rom 3:3; 1 Cor 1:9; 10:13; 2 Cor 1:18; 2 Thess 3:3; 1 Pet 4:19; 1 John 1:9; Ref Titus 1:9; 3:8). Hebrews 10:23 specifically states, "He who promised is faithful," and Hebrews 11:11 states, ". . . she considered Him faithful who had promised." The word *faithful* is πιστός (*pistos*) in Greek, meaning "trustworthy" and "reliable." Our faithful God does not change His mind once He makes a promise. This is why His promise is eternal (Heb 6:17). Psalm 89:33-35 also states, "But I will not break off My lovingkindness from him, nor deal falsely in my faithfulness. My covenant I will not violate, nor will I alter the utterance of My lips. Once I have sworn by My holiness; I will not lie to David."

For the sake of momentary gain, people of the world make promises very easily. Consequently, these promises are also easily broken when they undergo hardships or when there is no more gain to be had. Nevertheless, we can be comforted and find hope in our God, because He is faithful and never breaks the promises He makes.

## (3) Promises of the eternal covenant

All covenants that God has made with His people are eternal covenants which can be classified into a number of promises. The promises found in God's covenants are classified as follows.

### FIRST, the promise of the seed

God has promised "a seed," and that seed is Jesus Christ (Gal 3:16). This promise has been established in the "covenant previously ratified by God" (Gal 3:17). Galatians 3:19 alludes to Jesus as "the seed" that was promised. Romans 1:2-3 states, ". . . which He promised beforehand through His prophets in the holy Scriptures, concerning His Son . . ." and Hebrews 8:6 also states, "He is also the mediator of a better covenant, which has been enacted on better promises." Jesus Christ is the One who came as the son of Abraham and the son of David according to all these promises (Matt 1:1; Acts 13:23). Saints, who are spiritual children of Abraham, are the ones who believe in this promise of the one "seed" and are granted that promise.

### SECOND, the promise of eternal life

Eternal life is having a life of blessings and happiness within unending time. Although we are already tasting eternal life on earth through faith, we will have an everlasting life of complete and eternal blessings from the day our bodies are redeemed (Rom 8:23; Phil 3:21; 1 Thess 4:16-17).

First John 2:25 states, "This is the promise which he Himself made to us: eternal life." Titus 1:2 explains that eternal life was "promised long ages ago." Likewise, God has promised eternal life to us long ages ago.

Who can receive this promise of eternal life? This promise is given to the spiritual children of Abraham who believe in the only begotten Son, Jesus Christ (Gal 3:22, 29). John 3:16 states, "For God so loved the world, that He gave His only begotten Son, that whoever believes in Him shall not perish, but have eternal life."

John 17:3 states, "This is eternal life, that they may know You, the only true God, and Jesus Christ whom You have sent." The word *know* in this verse is γινώσκω (*ginōskō*), referring to a fellowship of union like the relationship of husband and wife. Apostle John states in 1 John 1:3, "What we have seen and heard we proclaim to you also, so that you too may have fellowship with us; and indeed our fellowship is with the Father, and with His Son Jesus Christ." We must share the fellowship we have "with the Father, and with His Son Jesus Christ."

### THIRD, the promise of the Holy Spirit

God gave the "promise of the Holy Spirit" to the spiritual children of Abraham. Acts 2:33 describes it as "the promise of the Holy Spirit"; Ephesians 1:13 describes it as "the Holy Spirit of promise"; Luke 24:49 describes it as "the promise of My Father." The Holy Spirit that was promised is the Spirit of truth (John 14:17; 15:26; 16:13) and the Helper (παράκλητος, *paraklētos*) both of whom Jesus had promised (John 14:16, 26; 15:26; 16:7).

Galatians 3:14 states, "in order that in Christ Jesus the blessing of Abraham might come to the Gentiles, so that we would receive the promise of the Spirit through faith." Those who have received the promise of eternal life by believing in Jesus—the promised seed—will receive "the promise of the Holy Spirit." That is why Jesus said in John 7:37-38, "If anyone is thirsty, let him come to Me and drink. He who believes in Me, as the Scripture said, 'From his innermost being will flow rivers of living water.'" It continues on to explain in verse 39, "But this He spoke of the Spirit, whom those who believed in Him were to receive; for the Spirit was not yet given, because Jesus was not yet glorified."

The Holy Spirit fell upon all those who were listening to the Word of God when Peter was sharing the Word at the house of Cornelius, the Roman centurion. Acts 10:44 states, "While Peter was still speaking these words, the Holy Spirit fell upon all those who were listening to the message." The Holy Spirit comes when the Word is proclaimed. The Holy Spirit also works through the Word. Therefore, those who have received the Holy Spirit, whom Jesus Christ had promised, are able to live in the fullness of the Holy Spirit by living their life centered on the Word (Eph 5:18).

### FOURTH, the promise of the second coming

Having destroyed the power of death and Hades, Jesus Christ was raised back to life in a spiritual body and ascended into heaven after forty days (1 Cor 15:4-6). When Jesus ascended to heaven, angels appeared to the people who were gazing into the sky and said, "This Jesus who has been taken up from you into heaven, will come in just the same way as you have watched Him go into heaven" (Acts 1:9-11; Ref Matt 24:30; Mark 13:26; Luke 21:27).

After the first coming, in which the Word became flesh and came to the earth, the Scripture promises a second coming (Matt 16:27-28; 24:44; 25:31; 26:64; 1 Thess 3:13; 4:16-17; 2 Thess 1:7; Jude 1:14; Rev 1:7; 22:20). Hebrews 9:28 states, "so Christ also, having been offered once to bear the sins of many, will appear a second time for salvation without reference to sin, to those who eagerly await Him."

Many people cannot believe in the promise of the second coming. Second Peter 3:4 says that there will be people who will say, "Where is the promise of His coming? For ever since the fathers fell asleep, all continues just as it was from the beginning of creation." Nevertheless, the Lord is not slow about His promise, but is patient toward us, not wishing for any to perish but for all to come to repentance (2 Pet 3:9).

We must always seek and cherish the promise of the eternal covenant in regard to the second coming. We must be diligent to be found by Him in peace, spotless and blameless, through holy conduct and godliness (2 Pet 3:11, 14). Then we can become "partakers of the divine nature, having escaped the corruption that is in the world" (2 Pet 1:4b).

**FIFTH, the promise of the eternal inheritance**

God has promised through the covenant He made with Abraham that He would eternally grant the land of Canaan (Gen 13:15; Ref Gen 48:4; Jer 7:7; 25:5). Genesis 17:8 states, "I will give to you and to your descendants after you, the land of your sojourning, all the land of Canaan, for an everlasting possession; and I will be their God." This is a promise that God would give the kingdom of heaven as an eternal inheritance to the spiritual children of Abraham. This is a promise of "entering His rest" (Heb 4:1); it is "His precious and magnificent" promise (2 Pet 1:4).

This promise of the eternal inheritance is fulfilled by Jesus Christ, the mediator of the new covenant. Hebrews 9:15 explains, "For this reason He is the mediator of a new covenant, so that, since a death has taken place for the redemption of the transgressions that were committed under the first covenant, those who have been called may receive the promise of the eternal inheritance."

The Greek word used in the New Testament for *inheritance* is κληρονομία (*klēronomia*). This eternal inheritance is imperishable, undefiled, and unfading (1 Pet 1:4). This inheritance is the kingdom which God has promised, the kingdom of heaven (Jas 2:5). It is also the promise of the new heavens and a new earth (2 Pet 3:13). This inheritance is not given through the law but granted by grace through God's promise (Gal 3:18).

As we have discussed in this chapter, the promise regarding Jesus Christ—who was to come as the seed of the woman (Gen 3:15)—became the foundation for the promise of the eternal covenant; and the promise is completely fulfilled through the first and second coming of Jesus Christ.

Therefore, the promise of the eternal covenant is intimately related to the genealogies that describe the path through which Jesus Christ comes. An accurate study of the biblical genealogies opens up the possibility of an in-depth understanding and a more comprehensive view of the promise of the eternal covenant in the profound providence of God.

The next section will discuss the biblical genealogies in detail.

לכל בר דעת דרך המסעות ארבעים שנה במדבר והרוחב והאורך של ארץ הקדושה מנהר

עמלק

מדבר ציז הוא קדש

ים המלח

לוח המסעות במדבר
אשר על פי ה' יסעו ועל פי ה' יחנו

| | | | |
|---|---|---|---|
| טו' רתמה | רט' חרהגדגד | א' רעמסס |
| טז' רמן פרץ | ל' ימבתה | ב' סכת |
| יז' לבנה | לא' עברונה | ג' אתם |
| יח' רסה | לב' עציןגבר | ד' פיהחירת |
| יט' קהלתה | לג' מדברצין | ה' מרה |
| כ' הרספר | לד' הרההר | ו' אילם |
| כא' חרדה | לה' צלמנה | ז' ים סוף |
| כב' מקהלת | לו' פונן | ח' מדברסין |
| כג' תחת | לז' אבת | ט' דפקה |
| כד' תרח | לח' דיבןגד | יו' אלוש |
| כה' מתקה | לט' עלמן דבל' | יא' רפידם |
| כו' חשמנה | מ' הרי עברים | יב' מרברסיני |
| כז' מסרות | מא' ערבת מואב | יג' קברתהתאוה |
| כח' בני יעקן | | יד' חצרות |

PART TWO

# A Study of Biblical Genealogies

The history of redemption proceeds according to God's decrees. Its central themes are the creation, the fall, and salvation. God's boundless love and profound providence can be found in each of these themes. Covenants were ratified between God and men based on His decrees, and redemptive history continued on the basis of those covenants.

The genealogies that appear in the Bible are summarized records of the eternal covenants that God has established with man. Thus, studying the genealogies will lead to profound insights that penetrate through the entire history of redemption.

The biblical genealogies have purpose and content that are distinct from secular genealogies in that they are intimately related to God's history of redemption. The most important element in a genealogy is the *names*. Thus, a study of the redemptive-historical meanings of the names in the biblical genealogies is imperative.

The study of biblical genealogies will become the foundational basis for the study of Jesus Christ's genealogy. Furthermore, the study can serve as a foundation upon which the promise of the eternal covenant in God's profound providence can be abundantly displayed. In this section, we will examine the significance of biblical genealogies, their distinctive features, and their relationships with the history of redemption.

CHAPTER 4

# The Significance of Genealogies

Before we embark upon the study of the third period of Jesus Christ's genealogy in the Gospel of Matthew, we will first review the significance of genealogies. The first topic of discussion will be the general and biblical significances of genealogies and an overview of various genealogies in the Bible.

## 1. General significance of genealogies

A genealogy is a record that charts out the patrilineal descent of a clan that originates from a single ancestor. Moreover, a genealogy explains the path of the generations in a way that is easy to understand. Furthermore, it is a family's historical account that reveals the origins of the clan while honoring its blood descent and lineal succession.[6] In the same way that a nation has the annals or records of its national history, a family or a clan has a family genealogy. The nation of Korea was even considered by some to be the originator of genealogies because of their high regard for genealogies since ancient times. Especially during the Joseon era, bearing a son to continue the patrilineal succession of the family was an important task for a wedded couple. A son was regarded as the pillar that upholds the family. For a woman, not being able to give birth to a son after getting married into a family was deemed to be one of the "seven valid causes for divorce." Some families adopted sons to become their heirs or even used surrogate mothers to beget sons.[7]

As one can see from past generations, the people of Korea respected their ancestry and treasured the genealogy that recorded their lineage. It was through the genealogy that descendants learned to respect their ancestors. Moreover, proper hierarchical order was established through the genealogy, fostering peace and unity in the family. They considered the genealogy a sacred reference book that contains the spirits of their forefathers. Consequently, some families showed respect to their forefathers by placing the genealogy book on a table with a bowl of pure water next to it and bowing down to it as though they were bowing down to their forefathers. Koreans treasured genealogies to such an extent that the genealogy book was the first thing people secured when a fire broke out in the house. Those who brought shame to the family name were removed from the genealogy. Hence, the threat to blot out one's name from the genealogy was the most humiliating statement that could be uttered to a person. Also, in choosing marriage partners, families scrutinized the genealogy of the potential spouse in order to prevent a promiscuous marriage or intermarriage.

The Bible testifies that the Jewish people also had high regard for genealogies for thousands of years. A genealogy is a summarized record of ancestral history; frequent occurrences of expressions such as "my fathers"* (Gen 47:9; Deut 26:7; 1 Chr 29:10; Luke 1:72-73; 3:8; Heb 1:1) and "your fathers" (Gen 48:21; Exod 3:13-16; Josh 24:2-3; Isa 51:2; Jer 7:7) indicate that genealogies were an important aspect of the culture.

Each of the tribes of Israel possessed genealogies in which kinships were recorded (1 Chr 4:33; Ref 1 Chr 5:1, 7, 17; 7:5, 7, 9, 40; 9:1, 22; 2 Chr 31:16, 19; Ezra 2:59, 62; 8:1, 3; Neh 7:5, 64). In the census taken of the Israelites after the exodus, the verses that record the number of people in each tribe repeatedly use the phrase, "their genealogical registration by their families, by their fathers' households" (Num 1:20, 22, 24, 26, 28, 30, 32, 34, 36, 38, 40, 42). In Hebrew, this phrase is תּוֹלְדֹתָם לְמִשְׁפְּחֹתָם לְבֵית אֲבֹתָם (tôlĕdōtām lĕmišpĕḥōtām lĕbêt 'ăbōtām); translated literally, it means, "a genealogy recorded according to their kinsfolk and fathers' household (or generations)." In this manner, the Israelites had their own ancestry by tribe and familial lineage (Num 1:18), and the distribution of the inheritance among the twelve tribes was also carried out "according to their families" (Josh 13:15, 23-24, 28-29, 31).

The Israelites, even until the first century, were able to accurately preserve an amazingly complete genealogy.[8] The Jewish historian Josephus writes that in the case of the priests, the genealogies were strictly managed so that it contained lists of high priests over a period of 2,000 years (*Apion.* 1.35). Jesus Christ's genealogy recorded in Luke chapter 3 is clear evidence that the Jewish people had meticulously preserved their

---

* Fathers: any male ancestor, especially the founder of a race, family, or line; progenitor (Gen 4:20-21)

genealogies. Even after they had returned from captivity in Babylon, Ezra and Nehemiah thoroughly reviewed, supplemented, and organized their genealogies (Ezra 9-10; Neh 13).

In this manner, the Bible assigns great importance to the genealogies. This is because, since Adam's fall, God's plan of redemption—to send the Savior into this world and save the sinners—unfolded and was fulfilled through the line of descent in the genealogies.

## 2. Biblical significance of genealogies

In general, genealogies in the Bible reveal lineages that are passed down from the ancestors. They are sequential records of individual descent or relationships among groups such as families, clans, tribes, or race.[9]

### (1) The meaning of the word *genealogy* in the original language
The following are a few examples of words that mean genealogy in the original language.

① יַחַשׂ (*yaḥaś*)
*Yaḥaś* means "to be enrolled by genealogy." Thus, the word is used for general genealogies which list only names, especially for genealogies kept by individual tribes when a census was taken (1 Chr 4:33; 5:1, 7, 17; 7:5, 7, 9, 40; 9:1, 22; 2 Chr 31:16, 19; Ezra 2:62; 8:1, 3; Neh 7:5, 64).

When we examine the usage of the word *yaḥaś* in 1 Chronicles 9:1, the New American Standard Bible translates as "all Israel was enrolled by genealogies," whereas the New International Version translates, "All Israel was listed in the genealogies." Finally, the English Standard Version translates, "all Israel was recorded in genealogies." Thus, *yaḥaś* or "to be enrolled by genealogy" not only means that the descent and the number of the members of the twelve tribes have been confirmed, but that they have been acknowledged as God's chosen people. Furthermore, it means that they have been enrolled in the genealogy of the covenant people.

Unlike *yaḥaś*, which was mainly used when listing the enrolled names, a *tôlĕdōt* also recorded brief accounts of events associated with the names.

② תּוֹלְדֹת (*tôlĕdōt*)
*Tôlĕdōt*, which is variously translated as "account," "generations," "deeds," "according to their birth," "records of the generations," or "throughout

all generations," originates from the word יָלַד (*yālad*), which means, "to beget." Thus, *tôlĕdōt* is used to mean "birth" or "order of birth" (Exod 6:16, according to their generations), and in many cases, it is also used to mean "generations." The word תּוֹלְדֹתָם (*tôlĕdōtām*), which is translated as "their genealogical registration" in Numbers 1:22, is the masculine third person plural form of the word תּוֹלְדֹת (*tôlĕdōt*), and when translated accurately means "their generations." In this case, there is the premise of one ancestor and the emphasis that the descendants came from him (Num 1:20, 22, 24, 26, 28, 30, 32, 34, 36, 38, 40, 42; 3:1; 1 Chr 1:29; 5:7; 7:2, 4, 9; 8:28; 9:9, 34; 26:31). In other words, the *tôlĕdōt* reveals the genealogy of the person at the starting point, clearly showing how God will work through the descendants and how He will lead His work of redemption through certain descendants.

Furthermore, *tôlĕdōt* is not only used in the narrow sense to refer to "birth" or "generations," but also in a broader sense as a summarized record of the lives and deeds of the people who were born (Gen 2:4; 5:1; 6:9; 10:1, 32; 11:10, 27; 25:12, 19; 36:1; 37:2; Exod 6:16, 19; Ruth 4:18). Thus, a *tôlĕdōt* is not a genealogy that merely lists names, but a genealogy that selectively includes accounts with redemptive-historical significance. Ultimately, the *tôlĕdōt* shows how God's history of redemption unfolded—from the beginning of mankind to the coming of Jesus Christ—and which descendants carried it forward.

③ γένεσις (*genesis*)
The Greek word *genesis* meaning "genealogy," also means "birth," "origin," and "beginning."

> **Matthew 1:1** The record of the genealogy of Jesus the Messiah, the son of David, the son of Abraham
>
> Βίβλος γενέσεως Ἰησοῦ Χριστοῦ υἱοῦ Δαυὶδ υἱοῦ Ἀβραάμ.
>
> **Matthew 1:18** Now the birth of Jesus Christ was as follows . . .
>
> Τοῦ δὲ Ἰησοῦ Χριστοῦ ἡ γένεσις οὕτως ἦν.

The Hebrew counterpart for the Greek word *genesis* is תּוֹלְדֹת (*tôlĕdōt*). It originates from the word γεννάω (*gennaō*) meaning "beget" and shows that the genealogy records the birth of the ancestors from a redemptive-historical perspective.

④ γενεαλογία (*genealogia*)

*Genealogia* is a combination of the word γενεά (*genea*) meaning "genera-tions" or "family" and the word λόγος (*logos*) meaning "the Word." Thus, *genealogia* means "family record." This word appears twice in the Bible, in 1 Timothy 1:4 and Titus 3:9, and refers to a worldly genealogy created by rabbis who liked to embellish things.

> **1 Timothy 1:4** Nor to pay attention to myths and endless genealogies (γενεαλογίαις), which give rise to mere speculation rather than *furthering* the administration of God which is by faith.

> **Titus 3:9** But avoid foolish controversies and genealogies (γενεαλογίας) and strife and disputes about the Law, for they are unprofitable and worthless.

## (2) The genealogies in the Bible

The Bible is the history of a holy genealogy, which—in eager anticipa-tion of the "seed of the woman"—begins with the family of Adam and Eve and continues on by preserving the godly lineage (Mal 2:15). The Bible contains many genealogies in various forms and the following is a summary of a few important ones.

### ① The Genesis genealogies

The book of Genesis contains ten genealogies which summarize God's extensive history of redemption. For this reason, the book of Genesis earns the nickname "book of genealogies." The ten genealogies alternate between genealogies which enumerate names (Gen 5:1; 10:1; 11:10, 27; 25:12, 19; 36:1) and genealogies which record history in a narrative for-mat (Gen 2:4; 6:9; 37:2). These ten genealogies appear to be separated, but are actually connected as one; as one genealogy ends, the next one begins immediately after it. Each of the themes of the genealogies come together to form the overall theme of the book of Genesis. Genesis 5:1 begins with, "This is the book of the generations of Adam," and the words "book of the generations" is סֵפֶר תּוֹלְדֹת (*sēper tôlĕdōt*) and means "book of genealogies." This shows that the genealogy which appears in Genesis 5 is not merely a list of names, but a book that encapsulates God's administration in the vast history of redemption.

The following is a summary of the ten תּוֹלְדֹת (*tôlĕdōt*) which appear in Genesis.

1 – The genealogy of the heavens and the earth (1:1–2:4; 2:4–4:26)

**Genesis 2:4** This is the account (תּוֹלְדֹת) of the heavens and the earth when they were created

2 – The genealogy of Adam's generations (5:1–6:8)

**Genesis 5:1** This is the book of the generations (תּוֹלְדֹת) of Adam.

3 – The genealogy of Noah's family (6:9–9:29)

**Genesis 6:9** These are the records of the generations (תּוֹלְדֹת) of Noah.

4 – The genealogy of Noah's sons (10:1–11:9)

**Genesis 10:1** Now these are the records of the generations (תּוֹלְדֹת) of Shem, Ham, and Japheth, the sons of Noah.

5 – The genealogy of Shem (11:10–26)

**Genesis 11:10** These are the records of the generations (תּוֹלְדֹת) of Shem.

6 – The genealogy of Terah (Abraham) (11:27–25:11)

**Genesis 11:27** Now these are the records of the generations (תּוֹלְדֹת) of Terah.

7 – The genealogy of Ishmael (25:12–18)

**Genesis 25:12** Now these are the records of the generations (תּוֹלְדֹת) of Ishmael, Abraham's son.

8 – The genealogy of Isaac (25:19–35:29)

**Genesis 25:19** Now these are the records of the generations (תּוֹלְדֹת) of Isaac, Abraham's son.

9 – The genealogy of Esau (36:1 – 37:1)

**Genesis 36:1** Now these are the records of the generations (תּוֹלְדֹת) of Esau (that is, Edom).

10 – The genealogy of Jacob (37:2 – 50:26)

**Genesis 37:2** These are the records of the generations (תּוֹלְדֹת) of Jacob.

## ②  The Chronicler's genealogies

It is evident to any reader that the first chapter of 1 Chronicles begins with a genealogy. This genealogy, which continues until chapter 9, replaces the vast Old Testament history with an extensive list of names. The Chronicler's genealogies cover a period of over 3,600 years, starting from Adam until the second return from Babylonian captivity. The genealogy is recorded with a focus on people such as Adam, Noah, Abraham, Jacob, David, and others who were involved in the ratification of important covenants (1 Chr 1:1-4, 5, 8, 17, 24-27, 28, 34; 2:1; 3:1).

The book of Chronicles, which opens with a genealogy, is located at the end of the Hebrew Bible; the Gospel of Matthew, which also opens with a genealogy, is located at the beginning of the New Testament. Hence, genealogies connect the book of Chronicles of the Old Testament and the Gospel of Matthew in the New Testament. The genealogy in 1 Chronicles reveals God's work of salvation within the history of the Israelites, while the genealogy of Jesus Christ in the Gospel of Matthew reveals how God's work of redemption was fulfilled through Jesus Christ.

The Chronicler's genealogies are a distillation of the entire history of the Israelites starting from Adam. If the Genesis genealogies are centered on Abraham and Jacob's twelve sons, then the Chronicler's genealogies is centered on David and the remnant returning to Jerusalem from Babylon.

The long and extensive genealogies in the book of Chronicles act as a bridge that connects the past to the future of the Israelites who have returned from captivity. They also show that God's work of redemption had not once ceased from Adam to Abraham, the father of faith, and until King David. Furthermore, by revealing that the remnants returning from captivity are now standing upon this continuous foundation, the genealogies proclaim God's administration of redemption toward their own generation as well as the generations to come.

In other words, for the Israelites returning from the seventy-year captivity in Babylon, the Chronicler's genealogies reaffirmed the historical root of their lineage and their identity as the people of God's covenant, thereby awakening them to their new task to *rebuild Israel*. This purpose of recording the Chronicler's genealogies is evident in the chiastic structure of the genealogy itself.[10]

## The Chiastic Structure of the Chronicler's Genealogies

A     1 Chr 1:1–54       The world before Israel (root of Israel)
  B      1 Chr 2:1–2         All the sons of Israel
    C      1 Chr 2:3–4:23       Judah – tribe of King David
      D      1 Chr 4:24–5:26     Tribes of Israel
        E      1 Chr 6:1–47         Sons of the high priest and Levi
          F      1 Chr 6:48–49        Duties of the priests
          F¹     1 Chr 6:50–53        The high priests
        E¹     1 Chr 6:54–81        The sons of Levi at the settlement location
      D¹     1 Chr 7:1–40         Tribes of Israel
    C¹     1 Chr 8:1–40         Benjamin – tribe of King Saul
  B¹     1 Chr 9:1ᵃ           All of Israel enrolled
A¹    1 Chr 9:1ᵇ–34    Reconstruction of Israel

The Chronicler's genealogies in 1 Chronicles chapters 1 to 9 is laid out in a chiastic parallel structure. There is a chiastic parallel between 1 Chronicles 1:1-54, which declares the root of Israel, and 1 Chronicles 9:1b – 34, which declares the restoration of Israel with their return from Babylonian exile.

Broadly, the Chronicler's genealogies are divided into three sections. The first section ranges from 1 Chronicles 1:1 to 1 Chronicles 3:24, which lists the genealogy of the family of David. The second section ranges from 1 Chronicles 4:1 to 1 Chronicles 8:40, which lists the genealogy of the twelve sons of Jacob down to the twelve tribes of Israel, just before their deportation to Babylon. The third section is 1 Chronicles 9, which lists the genealogy of each of the tribes that have returned from captivity.

The following is a summary by chapter.

## Summary of Each Chapter in the Chronicler's Genealogies

**First Chronicles 1** – recorded according to the genealogies of Genesis
- Direct line of descendants from Adam to Noah (vv 1-4, Ref Gen 5:1-32)
- Sons of Noah (vv 5-23, Ref Gen 10:1-32)
- Sons of Shem (vv 24-27, Ref Gen 11:10-26)
- Abraham and his descendants (vv 28-33, Ref Gen 25:1-16)
- Sons of Isaac (v 34, Ref Gen 25:19-26)
- Sons of Esau (vv 35-37, Ref Gen 36:1-19)
- Sons of Seir (vv 38-42, Ref Gen 36:20-30)

- Eight kings of Edom (vv 43-50, Ref Gen 36:31-39)
- Eleven chiefs of Edom (vv 51-54, Ref Gen 36:40-43)

**First Chronicles 2** – The descendants of the tribe of Judah until King David

**First Chronicles 3** – The kings of Judah who succeeded David and Solomon, the Babylonian captivity, and the people after the return

**First Chronicles 4** – The other sons of Judah (vv 1 – 23) and the descendants of the tribe of Simeon (vv 24 – 43)

**First Chronicles 5** – The descendants of the tribes of Reuben, Gad, and the half tribe of Manasseh

**First Chronicles 6** – The high priests and the Levites

**First Chronicles 7** – The descendants belonging to the six tribes of Issachar, Benjamin, Napthali, Manasseh, Ephraim, and Asher

**First Chronicles 8** – The descendants of the tribe of Benjamin

**First Chronicles 9** – Those who settled in Jerusalem after their return from Babylonian captivity
- The genealogy of the people who have returned (vv 1-9)
- The genealogy of the priests who have returned (vv 10-13)
- The genealogy of the Levites who have returned (vv 14-34)
- The genealogy of King Saul (vv 35-44)

---

The main characteristics of the Chronicler's genealogies are as follows.

**FIRST, many generations have been omitted.**

Within God's administration of redemption, the Chronicler's genealogies have boldly omitted certain sections while emphasizing certain others.

For example, 1 Chronicles 2:6 states, "The sons of Zerah were Zimri, Ethan, Heman, Calcol and Dara; five of them in all." Zerah's name appears on the list of Jacob's seventy-member family that entered Egypt in 1876 BC (Gen 46:12). On the other hand, Zimri, Ethan, Heman,

Calcol, and Dara, who are listed as Zerah's sons, are presumed to have lived during Solomon's time (970–930 BC; 1 Kgs 4:31). Therefore, there is a gap of about 900 years between Zerah and these five men.

Thus, the Hebrew word בֵּן (bēn) meaning "son" as used in 1 Chronicles 2:6 does not only refer to sons, but also to descendants.

**SECOND, of the many descendants, only those who were involved in the work of redemption were recorded.**

For example, Zerah had a countless number of descendants, but God only listed five of them. Among them, Ethan, Heman, Calcol, and Dara are the same Ethan, Heman, Calcol, and Darda that are mentioned in 1 Kings 4:31. All of them had wisdom to rival that of Solomon. We know that they are the same people because their names, as well as the order in which they are recorded, are the same.

The name *Dara* (דָּרַע) in 1 Chronicles 2:6 is the shortened version of the name *Darda* (דַּרְדַּע) which appears in 1 Kings 4:31. The name *Zerah* in 1 Chronicles 2:6 is זֶרַח (zeraḥ); and the word "Ezrahite" in 1 Kings 4:31 is also derived from the same word זֶרַח (zeraḥ; Ref Ps 89:title).

Notably, 1 Kings 4:31 records Heman, Calcol, and Darda as *the sons of Mahol. The sons of Mahol* in Hebrew is בְּנֵי מָחוֹל (bĕnê māḥôl), meaning "sons of dance." Here, the word for *son*, בֵּן (bēn), does not refer to a son of the same blood line, but rather alludes to members of a certain guild or association. So the phrase, *sons of Mahol*, does not indicate direct descendants, but those who were charged with the godly duty of dancing in God's temple.

Another name mentioned besides Ethan, Heman, Calcol, and Dara, is Zimri, which is זִמְרִי (zimrî) in Hebrew, meaning "to praise or celebrate with singing." If the sons of Mahol served God through dance, then Zimri served God through singing praises.

As one can see, the Chronicler's genealogies omitted all the generations that have no connection with God's work of redemption, only focusing on the people pertinent to God's redemptive work. God promised that the Messiah would come as the "seed of the woman" in Genesis 3:15. Even through dark times in history, such as the period of the Babylonian captivity, God continued His history of redemption without interruption in order to fulfill that promise; and His fulfillments of the promises are clearly manifested in the Chronicler's genealogies.

③ **The genealogy in the book of Ruth**

The book of Ruth records the fall and the salvation of a family (Elimelech, Naomi, Mahlon, Chilion, Orpah, and Ruth) that lived during the spiritually dark period of the judges. Ruth 4 records the genealogy that lists ten people from Perez to David.

> **Ruth 4:18-22** [18] Now these are the generations of Perez: to Perez was born Hezron, [19] and to Hezron was born Ram, and to Ram, Amminadab, [20] and to Amminadab was born Nahshon, and to Nahshon, Salmon, [21] and to Salmon was born Boaz, and to Boaz, Obed, [22] and to Obed was born Jesse, and to Jesse, David.

This short genealogy in the book of Ruth is significant because the Messiah will come as a descendant of David. The book of Ruth concludes with the genealogy of Perez in chapter 4, which reveals the *channel* of the covenant, namely, David. Hence, this genealogy serves as a link between the period of the judges and the period of the kings. Although the period of the judges was a spiritually dark age, the genealogy in Ruth 4 proclaims the hope that God has continued to prepare David and the Messiah who would come as his descendant.

There are many omitted generations in the genealogy in the book of Ruth.* First, most of the 430 years of life in Egypt have been omitted between Ram and Amminadab, who are both listed in Ruth 4:19 (Ref Matt 1:3-4; 1 Chr 2:9-10). Perez's son, Hezron, is mentioned in the list of Jacob's seventy-member family who entered Egypt (Gen 46:12). Hezron's son Ram is the second son born to him by his first wife (1 Chr 2:9), so there are no omissions between Hezron and Ram. However, Amminadab, who is listed as Ram's son, lived at the end of the 430-year period in Egypt. His daughter (Nahshon's sister) Elisheba became the wife of Aaron, a leader during the wilderness journey (Exod 6:23); Amminadab was thus Aaron's father-in-law. Moreover, Amminadab's son Nahshon is listed as a leader of the tribe of Judah during the wilderness era (Num 1:7; 2:3; 10:14; 1 Chr 2:10). All of these facts reveal that most of the 430-year sojourn in Egypt has been omitted between Ram and Amminadab.

---

* **Systematically organized for the first time in history** [see pp. 156-58; also, Abraham Park's History of Redemption series book 3, *The Unquenchable Lamp of the Covenant*, pp. 78-81; History of Redemption series book 4, *God's Profound and Mysterious Providence*, pp. 209-11.]

Second, approximately 300 years in the period of the judges (Ref Judg 11:26) have been omitted between Salmon and Boaz, who are listed in Ruth 4:21 (Ref Matt 1:5-6; 1 Chr 2:11-12). Salmon (Matt 1:5), who married Rahab the harlot of Jericho, lived during the early stage of the conquest of Canaan. However, Boaz, who is recorded as Salmon's son, lived at the end of the period of the judges, and the Bible testifies that there are no time gaps between Boaz, Obed, Jesse, and David (Ruth 4:13-17, 21-22). Thus, about 300 years of the spiritually dark period of the judges (Judg 2:7-10; 17:6; 21:25) have been omitted entirely.

④ **The genealogies recorded in the books of Ezra and Nehemiah**
An interesting characteristic of the Old Testament books of Ezra and Nehemiah is that they repeat series of genealogies with tedious lists of names. These genealogies are: a list of people who took part in the first return from Babylon (Ezra 2:1-63; Neh 7:5-65); the genealogy of Ezra the priest (Ezra 7:1-6); a list of people who took part in the second return from Babylon (Ezra 8:1-20); a list of those who were in charge of building the city walls (Neh 3:1-32); a list of people who vowed to keep the laws (Neh 10:1-27; Ref Neh 9:38); a list of people who settled in Jerusalem (Neh 11:1-36); and a list of priests and Levites (Neh 12:1-26).

Why were so many seemingly meaningless lists recorded?

Most importantly, these genealogies are evidence of the historicity of Israel's return from captivity. They also act as a bridge between the ancestors who were taken captive and the descendants who returned, thereby showing that God's work of redemption had continued without ceasing.

The situation at the time was dismal; the nation was in shambles and its sovereignty had completely collapsed. During such a time, the books of Ezra and Nehemiah enabled the people to prepare for the coming Messiah. Hence, these books are like a *bridge* in the history of redemption, serving as a link that connects the Old Testament to the New Testament.

Ezra and Nehemiah were leaders who encouraged and comforted the people's hearts during the most somber time. They made great efforts to restore the nation's faith so that it may stand before God. They struggled to restore a nation that had been shattered into pieces so that it may be reestablished upon God's administration within redemptive history. As a result, from the moment the Israelites returned from Babylon, the help of the "good hand of God" was upon them until they established their nation again (Ezra 7:6, 9; 8:18, 22, 31; Neh 2:8, 18).

Nehemiah wanted Jerusalem, with its temple and city walls restored, to become the center of the nation of Israel. Thus, he felt the strong need to build a population large enough to resist any enemy attack. In order to relocate people from other regions to Jerusalem, he checked the past record of people who had taken part in the first return: this is "the book of the genealogy of those who came up first" (Neh 7:5). This was after the city walls were rebuilt following the third return in 444 BC, about ninety-three years since the first return.

After the Israelites returned from Babylon and restored the city walls, "the city was large and spacious, but the people in it were few and the houses were not built" (Neh 7:4). It was at this time that Nehemiah first began to review the genealogies. Nehemiah did not arbitrarily begin the work to check and record the names and number of people in the genealogy; he did this according to God's inspiration and guidance. This is evident in his own words at the beginning of the genealogy where he confesses, "Then my God put it into my heart to assemble the nobles, the officials and the people to be enrolled by genealogies" (Neh 7:5). Thus, the recording of the genealogies was done through God's inspiration within His administration of the history of redemption. The genealogies were important for the Israelites because they proved their ancestral legitimacy to qualify as nationals of Israel.

Ezekiel, who was active among the captives in Babylon, proclaimed God's Word that the prophets who see false visions and utter lying divinations will have no place in the "council of My people." Furthermore, these prophets will not be recorded in "the register of the house of Israel." They will not even be able to "enter the land of Israel."

> **Ezekiel 13:9** So My hand will be against the prophets who see false visions and utter lying divinations. They will have no place in the council of My people, nor will they be written down in the register of the house of Israel, nor will they enter the land of Israel, that you may know that I am the Lord GOD.

Anyone who did not have the proper genealogy to prove that they belonged to Israel was excluded from the community of Israel from that moment on.

In fact, Nehemiah 7:61-62 shows that during the first return, 642 people (652 in Ezra 2:59-60) among those who came up from Tel-melah, Tel-harsha, Cherub, Addon (Addan), and Immer could not show whether their fathers' houses or their descendants were of Israel (the sons of Delaiah, the sons of Tobiah, the sons of Nekoda). In particular, Ezra and Nehemiah specifically wrote about the sons of Habaiah (sons of Hobaiah), the sons of Hakkoz, and the sons of Barzillai, who had searched (בָּקַשׁ; *bāqaš*: to seek diligently) for their names among their ancestral registrations, but were unable to locate them. As a result, they were considered unclean and excluded from the priesthood (Ezra 2:61-63; Neh 7:63-65). Priests whose descent was questionable earnestly sought to find their priestly genealogies, but were ultimately stripped of their priesthood when they were unable to find them. This may seem harsh, but service as a priest was a great calling specially granted to the descendants of the tribe of Levi (Num 8:14-16; 16:9-10; 18:2-6; Deut 10:8). Also, a priest's family was especially consecrated according to the law (Ref Lev 21:7-8, 13-15; Ezek 44:22). Therefore, those who could not show their priestly genealogies were precluded from performing their priestly duties.

After the return from captivity, Ezra and Nehemiah also rectified marriage practices among the returnees in order to prevent further intermingling between the Jews and the Gentiles (Ezra 9-10; Neh 13:23-31). Upon his return to Jerusalem, Ezra initiated grand-scale reforms to address the issue of intermarriages with Gentiles. They had worshipped the idols of the Gentiles, performed abominable acts (Ezra 9:1), and took the daughters of the Gentiles as wives and daughters-in-law, compromising the purity of the race. The princes and the rulers were foremost in this unfaithfulness (Ezra 9:2), so Ezra and Nehemiah thoroughly examined the genealogies and reorganized them. Indeed, this was a thorough reformation of faith that stemmed from a wholehearted desire to observe God's strict command not to intermarry with the Gentiles (Deut 7:2-4; Ezra 9:12). Ezra, the scribe and priest, forcefully commanded the people to separate from their foreign wives (Ezra 10:10-11). Then for three months (the first day of the tenth month until the first day of the first month) he again thoroughly investigated (Ezra 10:16b-17) the genealogies and reorganized them. Then came a sweeping command to divorce, which forced married couples to break their bonds from one another and separate from their beloved children.

Ezra's genealogical reforms were so immediate and resolute that the number of people who divorced was as high as 114. Among them, eighteen were from the priestly lineage (five sons of the high priest Jeshua and his brothers), and ten were Levites. All of the foreign wives and their children who were affected by these reformatory divorces were immediately banished from Israel (Ezra 10:18-44).

This extreme measure led to instant breakups of happy families and caused great pain and suffering. Some people opposed these measures perceiving them as being too harsh. A total of four people rose up to oppose this measure. Jonathan and Jahzeiah led the opposition and Meshullam and Shabbethai the Levite supported them (Ezra 10:15).

Ezra's reform was nonetheless a part of God's sovereign work within His administration of redemption. His volition in the reform was very resolute and all those who had returned from captivity followed accordingly (Ezra 10:16-44). Later, when Nehemiah was confronted with the same issue, he excluded from Israel all (כֹּל, kōl: "all, every single one") the mixed multitude who were of foreign descent (Neh 13:3).

As we have seen, the genealogies were truly well preserved although Israel's land had been trampled upon and her people were taken captive to a foreign land for seventy years. They were not preserved merely to confirm one's descent or lineage. It was part of God's providence of redemption to ensure a continuous transmission of the blessed covenant made with Abraham and David, thereby preserving the pure lineage through which the Messiah would come.

## ⑤ The genealogy of Jesus Christ

The genealogy in Matthew chapter 1 lists forty-one persons from Abraham to Jesus Christ in a linear descending order, while the genealogy in Luke chapter 3 lists seventy-seven persons from Jesus Christ until God in a linear ascending order. The genealogy in Matthew 1 shows that Jesus came after forty-two generations (14+14+14), as a fulfillment of God's covenant with Abraham and David (Matt 1:17). Meanwhile, the genealogy in Luke 3 provides a sweeping view of the history of redemption that links Christ to Adam, then ultimately to God.

Summarizing about 2,162 years of Old Testament history from Abraham to the birth of Christ, the Matthean genealogy encapsulates the entire history of redemption. In fact, Matthew uses this short, sixteen-verse genealogy to introduce the enormously vast history of redemption until the coming of Jesus Christ. The reason our Lord was introduced through this encapsulation called *genealogy* was to reveal—in a single sweeping view—that Christ is the essence of the Old Testament and the basis of the New, as well as the turning point of the entire history of mankind. Such a panoramic perspective enables the reader to view the entire Bible through the lens of the overarching narrative of redemptive history. Hence, the genealogy fully captures therein God's administration of the mystery, which He had planned before the ages and has accomplished without fail (Ref Eph 3:9).

### (3) Jesus Christ recorded in the genealogy

For Jesus Christ, the years will never come to an end, and He is self-existing from everlasting to everlasting (Heb 1:12; 7:24; 13:8). He is the eternal life itself (1 John 1:2; 5:11-12). He is, in very nature, God (Phil 2:6), and the One who created the universe and all things in it through His Word. He is the God who was from the beginning (John 1:1-3). It is truly a mystery that the name of such a being is recorded in a genealogy according to the flesh in which life and death repeat. Thus, the knowledge of Jesus Christ's true nature will lead to a deeper understanding of God's great and marvelous administration of redemption hidden in the genealogies.

The Letter to the Hebrews uses Melchizedek, who appears in Genesis 14:18-20, to provide the most exceptional explanation of Jesus Christ's great work as the high priest.

Melchizedek is the king of Salem, which means "king of peace." His name, which originates from the combination of the words מֶלֶךְ (*melek*: *king*) and צֶדֶק (*ṣedeq*: *righteousness*; Heb 7:1-2), also means "king of righteousness." Melchizedek was king and at the same time "the priest of the Most High God" (Gen 14:18; Heb 7:1). When Abraham returned victorious from war, Melchizedek gave him bread and wine and blessed him (Gen 14:18-19), and Abraham gave him a tenth of all the spoils of war (Gen 14:20).

The unique characteristic of the historical Melchizedek is that he is "without father, without mother, and without genealogy" (Heb 7:3). He has "neither beginning of days nor end of life" (Heb 7:3), and is "made like the Son of God" (Heb 7:3). He is not enrolled in the genealogy of the Levites (Heb 7:6), yet "remains a priest perpetually" (Heb 7:3b).

The Letter to the Hebrews proclaims that Jesus Christ is "another priest" (Heb 7:11) who came "according to the order of Melchizedek." In this manner, it firmly testifies that the priesthood of Jesus Christ excels above all others. It also affirms that only Jesus Christ is the perfect mediator for sinners, and that only He is the true Savior who can resolve the problem of sin once and for all (1 Tim 2:5; Heb 7:25).

Unlike the Levitical priests who were replaced continuously because they were not eternal due to death (Heb 7:23), Jesus Christ, like Melchizedek, is the priest who continues forever (Heb 7:24; Ref Ps 110:4; Heb 5:6, 10; 6:20; 7:17). Jesus Christ came according to the order of Melchizedek whose genealogy is not traced from the Levites (Heb 7:6). Indeed, He is the Eternal God who is without genealogy from the beginning, and the high priest according to the power of an indestructible life (Heb 7:16).

Jesus asked the Pharisees, "Then how does David in the Spirit call Him 'Lord'?" (Matt 22:41-45; Mark 12:35-37). This question indicates that even though Jesus came as a descendant of David, He is actually David's Lord (Root of David; Matt 22:45; Mark 12:37; Rev 5:5; 22:16) and God the Son who possesses divinity transcending genealogies. Yet, this God put on human form and dwelt among us (the Incarnation), and He had His name recorded in the genealogy as "the son of David" of the tribe of Judah. This was truly the ultimate work of grace that was accomplished within God's *agape* love and His profound and mysterious providence for the salvation of sinful mankind (Ref Rom 1:3-4; Phil 2:6-8; Heb 2:14-17).

# CHAPTER 5

# Distinctive Features and Roles of Biblical Genealogies

In most biblical genealogies, much like general genealogies, an introduction precedes the enumeration of names. This introduction summarizes the origin and essence of the genealogy and defines relationships that are crucial to understand the names that follow it.

Examples of introductions in biblical genealogies are as follows.

"This is the book of the generations of Adam" (Gen 5:1)

"Now these are the records of the generations of Shem, Ham, and Japheth, the sons of Noah" (Gen 10:1)

"Now these are the records of the generations of Isaac, Abraham's son" (Gen 25:19)

"Now these are the records of the generations of Esau (that is, Edom)" (Gen 36:1)

"These are the records of the generations of Jacob" (Gen 37:2)

"Now these are the names of the sons of Israel, Jacob and his sons, who went to Egypt" (Gen 46:8)

"These are the heads of their fathers' households" (Exod 6:14)

"Now these are the records of the generations of Aaron and Moses" (Num 3:1)

"The record of the genealogy of Jesus the Messiah, the son of David, the son of Abraham" (Matt 1:1)

Biblical genealogies can be classified based on format. *Linear* genealogies trace a single line of descent (Gen 5:1-32; 11:10-26; 1 Chr 1:1-4, 24-27; Matt 1:1-16; Luke 3:23-38), whereas *segmented* genealogies enumerate all or several of the children of one specified ancestor (Gen 10:1-32; 1 Chr 1:5-23, 28-42). Linear genealogies can be further classified into two structures. *Linear ascending* genealogies list up from descendant to ancestor, placing the emphasis on the individual of the starting generation (1 Chr 6:33-48; Luke 3:23-38; Ref Ezra 7:1-5). On the contrary, *linear descending* genealogies list down from ancestor to descendant, emphasizing the legitimacy of the lineage. A majority of the biblical genealogies are in the linear descending format.

Biblical genealogies contain introductions and various structures, which play a variety of important roles. They also contain distinctive features that differentiate them from general genealogies.

## 1. Distinctive features of biblical genealogies

### (1) Biblical genealogies do not contain any forgeries.

Worldly genealogies were used for the purpose of garnering and enjoying the special privileges that are attached to one's honored status or name. They were also used as a means to showcase one's authority and achievements. There were many cases where the ranks of one's official posts were exaggerated or fabricated and parts of the genealogy forged in the process. A person of lowly birth could either forge the genealogy or purchase an elevated status so that a commoner could become a noble; some even changed clans altogether.[11] They made sure that the data from before they became nobles were expunged, and only the new data was preserved for their descendants. However, there were no instances where genealogies in the Bible were forged, nor was one's status or honored name ever exaggerated. They are pure historical records based on facts, without any falsification. This is because all Scripture is inspired by the living God (2 Tim 3:16). The biblical writers, armed with the facts of history, wrote down what they have received from God as they were moved by the Holy Spirit (2 Pet 1:21). Thus, all biblical genealogies are recorded by the Holy Spirit; they contain God's amazing administration of redemptive history and His mysterious and profound providence.

### (2) Biblical genealogies do not contain any interruptions.

From ancient times, there were many instances where even the families of the noblest stock could not preserve their lineage because they did not have progeny.[12] In Korea, the noblest clans are usually the families of the primogenitary line. The primogenitary line consists of the families of the eldest sons who were born through the legal wife (as opposed to a concubine or mistress) of the progenitor. One of the requirements of such a noble clan of the primogenitary line is that they must possess a history of at least fifteen generations in the lineage.[13]

Although some families claim to be of the primogenitary line, such physical lineages rarely exist. Even when such genealogies are found, it is not easy to trace the whereabouts of their progeny.[14] The Goryeo dynasty, one of the longest dynasties in the history of Korea, lasted for thirty-four generations over a period of 475 years (AD 918–1392) from Wang Geon until King Gongyang. The Joseon dynasty founded by Taejo Yi Seong-gye lasted for twenty-seven generations over a period of 519 years (AD 1392–1910) until King Soon-jong.

In the biblical genealogies, however, there was not even a single break in the lineage from Adam until the coming of the promised "seed of the woman" (Gen 3:15). Although one may discover intentional omissions in some of the genealogies in the Bible, when all of the biblical genealogies are examined together, it will be found that there were no interruptions until the coming of Jesus Christ.

The genealogies of the gentile nations surrounding Israel lack continuity and are disconnected with the past. Hence, although they appear temporarily, they are eventually cut off as time passes, never to be mentioned again. The case is altogether different for the genealogies of the holy chosen people—the ones who carry on God's covenants. Their genealogies not only continue on from the firmly established framework of the past genealogies, but they also expand upon the foundations of those past genealogies. For example, the genealogy found in Genesis 29:31-30:24 reveals the names and the meanings of the names of Jacob's eleven sons from his four wives. This genealogy, while maintaining its frame, expands down to the descendants of the fourth generation in Genesis 46:8-27 and Numbers 26:1-62.

## 2. Roles of genealogies

### (1) They reveal the succession of the direct line of descent.

First Chronicles 1:1-4 records the direct line of descent from Adam as it lists "Adam, Seth, Enosh, Kenan, Mahalalel, Jared, Enoch, Methuselah, Lamech, Noah, Shem, Ham and Japheth." Through this kind of lineage, we can determine each person's ancestor.

Each time the Bible introduces a person, it includes a record of the ancestors, or at least a record of the father. Up to five, six, or even seven generations of ancestors (Num 27:1; Josh 17:3; 1 Sam 1:1; 9:1; 1 Chr 4:37; Neh 11:4- 5; Zeph 1:1) are recorded for important figures such as kings, priests, and prophets.

### (2) They record important historical facts.

Biblical genealogies not only show lineal blood relations but also record important historical facts that take place between the generations. For example, 1 Chronicles 1:19 states, "Two sons were born to Eber, the name of the one was Peleg, for in his days the earth was divided, and his brother's name was Joktan." Not only does this explain the familial relationship that Peleg and Joktan were Eber's sons, but it also adds the historical fact that it was during Peleg's time that the earth was divided. One must remember, however, that the purpose of the biblical genealogies is not merely to provide historical information; its greater purpose is to reveal God's administration of redemption through such historical information. In a similar line of thought, Apostle Paul rebuked those who were mindful of Jewish genealogies with no regard for God's administration. Paul asserted that such genealogies only give rise to mere speculation and that they are unprofitable and useless (1 Tim 1:4; Titus 3:9).

### (3) They reveal affiliations and status.

Genealogies reveal a person's tribe and status. Each tribe of Israel possessed a genealogy (1 Chr 4:33; 5:1, 7, 17; 7:5, 7, 9, 40; 9:1, 22 etc.); therefore, the genealogies revealed the tribe to which a person belonged.

An individual's social status and rights were also determined by the genealogies. After the return from the Babylonian exile, those who asserted priestly rights had to prove their descent from a priestly lineage and were forbidden from performing priestly duties if their genealogies were uncertain (Ezra 2:61-63; Neh 7:63-65). People performed their duties based on their affiliations as stated in the genealogies (Ezra 2:36-58; Neh 7:39-60). Taking the genealogies lightly was like taking one's affiliations and status lightly.

# CHAPTER 6

# The Relationship Between
# Biblical Genealogies and
# the History of Redemption

In general, the functions of biblical genealogies include revealing familial relationships and explaining important historical truths. However, from the redemptive-historical perspective, biblical genealogies are much more significant for many reasons.

## 1. Biblical genealogies are summaries and progressive signposts of redemptive history.

Biblical history, which begins with the book of Genesis and ends with the Revelation to John, is the history of redemption. The genealogies are summaries of the essence of the mysterious administration in the history of redemption. In the Bible, at each important moment in the history of redemption, a genealogy is recorded to mark that watershed moment. Genealogies can conclude an era in the history of redemption as well as begin a new one.

The book of Genesis is made up of ten genealogies (Gen 2:4; 5:1; 6:9; 10:1; 11:10, 27; 25:12, 19; 36:1; 37:2). The book of Ruth, at its conclusion, introduces a genealogy that starts with Perez and ends with David (Ruth 4:18-22). First Chronicles, which begins with a genealogy, records within nine chapters an extensive genealogy spanning from Adam to those who returned from Babylonian captivity (1 Chr 1:1-9:44). The Old Testament books of Ezra and Nehemiah also consist of many genealogies, which include lists of those who took part in the first and second return from exile, newly organized genealogies, and many others (Ezra 2:1-70; 7:1-5; 8:1-20; Neh 7:5-73; 11:3-36; 12:1-26).

The Gospel of Matthew, which opens the New Testament, also begins with a genealogy (Matt 1:1-17). In particular, the genealogy of Jesus

Christ summarizes the history from Abraham to Jesus Christ; it is the encapsulation of the entire history of redemption. Because of this, an in-depth study of the genealogy of Jesus Christ will enable us to have a clear grasp of the Christ-centered history of redemption. Moreover, such a study will provide a panoramic view of the overarching thread that runs through the entire history of redemption—a history that God has planned before the foundation of the world and has been fulfilling to this day.

The various genealogies recorded in the different parts of the Bible— from the genealogies in Genesis to the genealogy of Jesus Christ—are not only encapsulations of the history of redemption, but also function as progressive signposts in redemptive history. In other words, within the overarching theme called God's history of redemption, the Scripture— through its genealogies—provides a progressive revelation of the promise of the Messiah's advent as the "seed of the woman." In doing so, the Scripture reveals to us that God's revelation of salvation has never ceased throughout the ages, and confirms repeatedly that this promise regarding the Messiah will surely be fulfilled. Thus, biblical genealogies are signposts of redemptive history that instill hope in all mankind. Moreover, they serve as scriptural landmarks that reaffirm the unwavering nature of God's covenant of salvation.

## 2. Biblical genealogies display the succession of covenant progeny.

In general, genealogies are patrilineal rather than matrilineal, meaning that they record the lineage of the father and his son. For this reason, except for special instances, biblical genealogies rarely contain names of women. Even in the genealogy of Jesus Christ in the Gospel of Matthew, the names of forty-one men make up the majority, while only the names of five women—Tamar, Rahab, Ruth, Uriah's wife, and Mary—appear interspersed among the male names. Not a single woman is mentioned in the genealogy in 1 Chronicles 1:1-31. This signifies that biblical genealogies primarily display the succession of covenant progeny through the male line.

Moreover, biblical genealogies contain omissions[15] and do not necessarily continue the line of descent through the firstborn of the family. This is because biblical genealogies do not merely display the succession of lineal descendants. Rather, biblical genealogies display the succession of progeny that continues the history of redemption through God's covenants.[16] Professor Jong-jin Choi refers to this succession of the covenant progeny as the "redemptive-historical succession of the seed."[17]

Throughout history, Satan had materialized his terrifying plan to interrupt the succession of covenant progeny and thwart God's administration of redemption. Such plans surfaced endlessly within the plethora of events, great and small, interspersed throughout the procession of redemptive history. Three of the most notable incidents are as follows. First, the Egyptian pharaoh sought to kill all the male Hebrew babies and enslave the Israelites forever (Exod 1:18-22). Second, Athaliah, the wife of Judah's King Jehoram and daughter of Israel's King Ahab, sought to annihilate the seed of David (2 Kgs 11:1; 2 Chr 22:10). Lastly, Haman—the son of Hammedatha the Agagite and the prime minister of Persia during the reign of King Ahasuerus—had planned and attempted a complete massacre of the Jews throughout the Persian empire (Esth 3:6-15).

**FIRST, the pharaoh of Egypt, who came to the throne about 1539 BC, sought to permanently enslave the Israelites.**

The Israelites became fruitful, increased greatly, multiplied, and became exceedingly mighty, so that the land was filled with them (Exod 1:7). The Egyptian pharaoh (the king who did not know Joseph; Exod 1:8) became worried because of the numerous sons of Israel. In order to suppress their procreation, the Egyptians afflicted them and made their lives bitter (Exod 1:8-14). The more they afflicted them, however, the more they multiplied and the more they spread out (Exod 1:12).

It was apparent that the policy to suppress their procreation through rigorous labor had failed. Therefore, the Egyptian pharaoh instructed the Hebrew midwives, Shiphrah and Puah, saying, "When you are helping the Hebrew women to give birth and see them upon the birthstool, if it is a son, then you shall put him to death; but if it is a daughter, then she shall live" (Exod 1:15-16). Nevertheless, the midwives feared God and did not do as the king commanded them. They let the boys live, and the people multiplied and became very mighty (Exod 1:17-20).

When his plan to secretly kill the baby boys through the midwives failed, Pharaoh commanded, saying, "Every son who is born you are to cast into the Nile, and every daughter you are to keep alive" (Exod 1:22). He thus called for a ruthless infant massacre on a public, nationwide level.

God, however, raised up Moses in accordance with His profound and mysterious providence of salvation for Israel. He then raised Moses in Pharaoh's palace to be educated in all the learning of the Egyptians (Exod 2:1-10; Acts 7:22). After Moses struck down and killed an Egyptian, God sent the forty-year-old Moses out to the wilderness of Midian. Then, when he was eighty years old, God raised him up as the leader of the exodus (Exod 2:11-3:12; Acts 7:22-34).

God punished Egypt with the ten plagues for attempting to annihilate the Hebrew baby boys and enslave the Israelites permanently (Ref Exod 12:12; Num 33:4). In 1446 BC, on the fifteenth day of the first month, while the Egyptians were wailing in extreme sorrow from the death of their firstborns, the Israelites boldly started out in the sight of all the Egyptians (Num 33:3). Then, God drowned Pharaoh and his army in the Red Sea (Exod 14:27-28, 30; 15:4-5, 10, 19, 21; Ps 78:53; 106:11; 136:15). All of this happened because God remembered the covenant which He swore to Abraham, Isaac, and Jacob; He heard the cries and groaning of the people and took notice of them (Exod 2:23-25).

**SECOND, in 840 BC, Athaliah sought to destroy all of David's royal offspring.**

When Athaliah saw that her son Ahaziah had died, she sought to destroy all of David's royal offspring so that she could become king (2 Kgs 11:1; 2 Chr 22:10). It was truly a critical moment where the succession of the covenant progeny was at the brink of being cut off. Meanwhile, Jehoshabeath (Jehosheba), the sister of Ahaziah, took Joash the son of Ahaziah and stole him, and placed him and his nurse in the bedroom so that he was not put to death (2 Kgs 11:2-3; 2 Chr 22:11-12). After six years of suffering under Athaliah's evil reign, the priest Jehoiada finally made up his mind and sent for the captains of hundreds of the Carites and of the guard, and brought them to him in the house of the Lord. He then made a covenant with them and put them under oath in the house of the Lord, and in absolute secrecy he showed them the seven-year-old prince Joash (2 Kgs 11:4; 2 Chr 23:1). Imagine their surprise and joy when they saw Joash. They had believed that all of David's seed had been destroyed by Athaliah six years ago. Although Joash was just a seven-year-old child, the fact that this Davidic descendant was still alive probably provided immeasurably great hope, comfort, and joy to all who cherished and clung to God's covenant. Joash, who spent six years in hiding in the

Lord's temple, became king at the age of seven and ruled for forty years (2 Kgs 11:3, 21; 12:1; 2 Chr 22:12; 24:1).

Athaliah acted as Satan's pawn for thirteen years (847–835b BC) since her marriage to Jehoram the king of Judah. Then, she died a miserable death when the people struck her with the sword as she arrived at the horses' entrance of the king's house (2 Kgs 11:16, 20b; 2 Chr 23:15, 21b). All the people of the land rejoiced and the city was quiet when she was killed (2 Kgs 11:20a; 2 Chr 23:21b).

As part of His providence, God hid Joash so that David's royal offspring was preserved, and the dying flame of the lamp of Judah the southern kingdom burned brightly once again. With wicked ambition, Athaliah sought to destroy David's royal seed, but she could not thwart God's providence of redemption.

**THIRD, in about 474 BC, Haman, the son of Hammedatha the Agagite (descendant of Amalek; 1 Sam 15:8), planned to annihilate the Jews.**

Haman sought to annihilate in a single day—the thirteenth of the month of Adar (the twelfth month)—all the Jews who lived throughout the 127 provinces of Persia [from India to Cush (Ethiopia; Esth 1:1)]. He commanded "to kill and to annihilate all the Jews, both young and old, women and children" and to seize their possessions as plunder (Esth 3:13). As it turns out, however, Haman was the one to be hanged on the gallows which he had prepared for Mordecai (Esth 7:9-10). His ten sons were also killed together (Esth 9:7-10). Moreover, on the thirteenth day of the twelfth month, 500 men who hated the Jews were also killed at the citadel in Susa (Esth 9:5-6). On the fourteenth day of the twelfth month, 200 additional men were killed (Esth 9:15), and from each of the provinces 75,000 men were killed altogether (Esth 9:16). In this manner, even as the descendants of the covenant faced the threat of annihilation, God miraculously saved them so that His administration of redemption would not be halted. To commemorate this, the Jews observe the Feast of Purim throughout their generations (Esth 9:17-32).

Thus, the threat of the annihilation of the Jews serves as the backdrop of the book of Esther. Professor Jong-jin Choi posits that the book of Esther contains a form of genealogy that uses a narrative style to explain how the Jewish people, whose succession of progeny was threatened, continued on so that the redemptive-historical seed (progeny) was not cut off.[18]

## 3. Biblical genealogies reveal the path of Jesus Christ's coming.

Jesus Christ is the final destination for the godly descendants of the covenant. Through the proto-Gospel (*protoevangelium*) in Genesis 3:15, God had already promised the coming of the *seed of the woman* who would bruise the serpent's head. Biblical genealogies show in a compressed form the lineage through which the *seed of the woman* would come. In Galatians 3:16, Apostle Paul states, "Now the promises were spoken to Abraham and to his seed. He does not say, 'And to seeds,' as referring to many, but rather to one, 'And to your seed,' that is, Christ." According to this, although there were many promises regarding the seed (Gen 15:5; 16:10; 22:17-18; 26:3; 28:14; 32:12), the true seed that those promises ultimately refer to is the One, Jesus Christ. In other words, biblical genealogies reveal the succession of the covenant progeny in order to ultimately show the path of the coming of Jesus Christ.

The various genealogies in the Bible are evidence of a very long wait for the seed of promise. Finally, as the fulfillment of this promise, the genealogy of Jesus Christ in the Gospel of Matthew proclaimed the coming of Jesus Christ, the anticipated true seed. We can most accurately understand the administration of redemption by using the genealogies to examine the process through which Jesus Christ came to this earth in order to save fallen mankind. If Jesus Christ, the core and the fulfiller of the genealogies, is lost in the study of the genealogies, then that study becomes meaningless.

At times, there are people who ask if there is a need to study such complicated genealogies in great detail. The one thing that we need to bear in mind is that the genealogies are summaries of the history of redemption and that they are the most accurate compasses that lead us to the path of the coming of Jesus Christ, the one and only Savior. If we do not properly understand the genealogies recorded at every watershed moment in the history of redemption, then we will inevitably be ignorant of God's administration of redemption. Furthermore, we will also be unable to have proper understanding of Jesus Christ who stands at the center of the history of redemption.

## CHAPTER 7

# Biblical Genealogies and Names

Genealogies are long enumeration of names, and names are the most basic and significant elements of genealogies. The Chronicler's genealogies are lists comprised almost exclusively of names. It spans from chapter 1 to chapter 9 without even a single verse of prefatory material. In the case of 1 Chronicles chapter 1, there are a total of 190 names[19] in a total of 54 verses.

> **1 Chronicles 1:1-4, 24-27** Adam, Seth, Enosh, [2] Kenan, Mahalalel, Jared, [3] Enoch, Methuselah, Lamech, [4] Noah, Shem, Ham and Japheth, . . .
>
> [24] Shem, Arpachshad, Shelah, [25] Eber, Peleg, Reu, [26] Serug, Nahor, Terah, [27] Abram, that is Abraham.

The name listed in the genealogy is the shortest possible summary of a person's life. No matter how vast history may be, when you put together a chronologically ordered list of names of people who have lived and breathed in their respective generations, then you get a genealogy; and the genealogy is the encapsulation of history.

For this reason, if we open up the genealogy and explicate the names listed in them, then the history of those generations will unfold as a panorama. At the most compressed level, the genealogy consists of names and the time that flows between them. It can then be expanded to include the people that lived and breathed within the same period. If we expand further, then we may also include the plethora of events and important achievements that those people have left behind. Finally, when we also include the space in which those people lived and moved, then we have fully attained to the level of history. Conversely, if we compress this vast history into the most condensed form, then we get an enumeration of names, which is called a *genealogy*. Therefore, upon a cursory glance, genealogies may seem like nothing more than long lists of numerous names. Upon closer examination, however, we will find that living and breathing within them are God's mysterious administration of redemption and His profound providence in each and every generation for the salvation of His elect.

Let us now examine the significance of the most basic element of the genealogy: names.

## 1. A name verifies one's existence.

All creation has a name that verifies its existence. After God formed every beast of the field and every bird of the sky, He brought them to Adam and allowed him to name each living creature (Gen 2:19). The moment a name was given to each creature, its existence was verified. God calls each and every creature in this created world by name (Isa 40:26). Eliminating a person's name is tantamount to eliminating the person's existence (1 Sam 24:21; 2 Kgs 14:27; Job 18:17). During the Japanese occupation, the ultimate reason the Japanese coerced Koreans to take on Japanese names was for the total elimination of the existence of the Korean nation.

Ancient conquerors also forced the people of the conquered nation to change their names to conform to that of the conquering culture. The Babylonian commander of the officials changed Daniel's name to *Belteshazzar* (Dan 1:7). The name *Daniel* means, "God is my judge," but the name *Belteshazzar* means, "Bel (the main Babylonian God), protect my life!" Even the names of Daniel's three friends were changed: Hananiah (חֲנַנְיָה: "God is gracious") to Shadrach ("thy command"), Mishael (מִישָׁאֵל: "Who is like God?") to Meshach ("the guest of the king"), and Azariah (עֲזַרְיָה: "God has helped") to Abed-nego ("servant of Nego"). By changing the names of Daniel and his three friends, they sought to erase their Jewish identity so that they can be assimilated as captives of Babylon.

By remembering a person's name, we verify the person's existence. In Hebrew, the word שֵׁם (šēm) is the general term meaning "name," while the word זֵכֶר (zeker) means "remembrance" (Job 18:17; Ps 97:12; 102:12; 112:6; Pro 10:7). זֵכֶר (zeker) connotes that through the name, a person's existence is made known and imprinted into the memory of others.

The life of a righteous person is regarded as precious, and his name is blessed and remembered throughout the generations. The life of an evil person, however, rots and perishes as something eaten away by insects, and his name is neither spoken of nor remembered again (Job 18:17; Ps 112:6; Pro 10:7). Truly, a good name is more fragrant and travels farther than costly perfume (Ecc 7:1a).

## 2. A name demonstrates one's character.

A person's character refers to one's traits, nature, and personality. The name *Jacob* (יַעֲקֹב) means "one who takes by the heel" or "supplanter." The name *Jacob* reveals well his tendency to deceive others. In Genesis 27:36, the Scripture states, "Is he not rightly named Jacob, for he has supplanted me these two times? He took away my birthright, and behold, now he has taken away my blessing."

After spending twenty difficult years in Laban's house, Jacob was completely broken as a human being at the ford of the Jabbok. It was exactly then that God changed his name from *Jacob* to *Israel* (Gen 32:28). His receipt of the name *Israel*, which means "striven with God and prevailed," signified that he was changed into someone who was acknowledged by God. Accordingly, depending on which names are used in the genealogies, one can perceive the changes in a person's character and nature. Hence, the Chronicler's genealogies use the new name *Israel* in place of the name *Jacob* (1 Chr 1:34; 2:1).

## 3. A name displays one's reputation.

When a person becomes famous, his name also becomes famous. At times, the Hebrew word שֵׁם (*šēm*) also refers to "fame" or "reputation" (1 Chr 14:17). Usually, when we recall a person's name, it reminds us of the aura that the person exudes as well as everything else that may be associated with that person, such as hometown, education, parents, occupation, friends, memories, achievements, and/or reputation.

Ruth married Boaz and gave birth to Obed and the women sang praises, saying, "May his name become famous in Israel" (Ruth 4:14). At the time that Jesus was about to be crucified on the cross, Barabbas, the person whom the crowd wanted to be freed in Jesus' place, was so well-known that he was called a "notorious prisoner" (Matt 27:16). Therefore, a person's reputation can change depending on whether his name is included at all in the genealogy and—if it is—by which name he is included. Moreover, the reputation of the family as well as the individual can change depending on the fame of the people listed in the family's genealogy.

## 4. A name reveals the history of redemption.

A name not only contains the parents' hopes for their child, but also God's administration of redemption for that era. Lamech gave birth to a son at the age of 182 and named him *Noah* (נֹחַ, *nōaḥ*: "rest," "comfort"; Gen 5:28-29). Lamech named his son Noah hoping that the extreme suffering that humans experience due to the curse on the land may be resolved through his son. This name also contains God's administration of redemption to save the world—which has been cursed (Gen 3:17) since the fall—through Noah's ark. Furthermore, it also contains the eschatological administration of redemption through Jesus Christ, whom Noah foreshadows, to completely restore the cursed world and give eternal rest.

Although the names that appear in the Bible were given by men, they cannot be totally unrelated to the will of God who allowed them to be recorded in the Bible. Accordingly, a close study of the names in the genealogies will reveal both the person's whole life as well as the history of redemption during that era.

Genealogies substitute names for countless historical events that cannot be explained through spoken or written words; therefore, genealogies contain nothing that is without meaning (1 Cor 14:10). In fact, they contain God's administration of redemption that is as weighty as a massive boulder. Thus, we should not approach the genealogies with the desire to quickly skim through them. Rather, we should examine them closely with earnest hearts so that we may discover the vast current of the history of redemption that is flowing through each and every name in the genealogy. This is the very current that is vigorously rushing towards the One, Jesus Christ. Therefore, we must take a hold of this current so that we may obtain deep insight into God's mysterious administration of redemption. In addition, we must be able to discern and understand the tenacious spiritual vitality, which the descendants of the covenant possessed within God's profound providence for salvation.

Each time we examine the names in the genealogies, we must think about the day when our own names will be recorded in the genealogies. With that in mind, we must inspect our faith to see how we are fulfilling the stewardship that God has given to us (Col 1:25). Furthermore, we must reflect upon how our names would be remembered in the genealogies. The accumulation of each day that passes makes up a year, and eventually, a lifetime. So, today is an encapsulation of our lifetime. At this moment, we must deeply examine ourselves and ask how much we have struggled and labored in order to fulfill God's stewardship. We must check to see if we are living faithful lives worthy of the name that would be passed down to our posterity until the day when our Lord returns. Second Corinthians 13:5 states, "Test yourselves to see if you are in the faith; examine yourselves! Or do you not recognize this about yourselves, that Jesus Christ is in you—unless indeed you fail the test?"

A believer possesses the name *Christian* (Acts 11:26). In Greek, "Christian" is Χριστιανός (*Christianos*), meaning "follower of Jesus Christ" or "belonging to Jesus Christ." Hence, believers must belong to Jesus Christ, follow only Him, and live for Him alone. Then, they can bear fruit worthy of the name.

The third book of the History of Redemption series entitled *The Unquenchable Lamp of the Covenant* focuses on the history of the first period of the genealogy of Jesus Christ in Matthew chapter 1. It covers the period in history from Abraham to King David. The fourth book of the series is entitled *God's Profound and Mysterious Providence* and focuses on the second period of the genealogy of Jesus Christ. It covers the period of history from David until the deportation to Babylon. Now, this fifth book in the series will examine the history of the third period of the genealogy of Jesus Christ.*

We will study God's promise of the eternal covenant within His profound providence that is found in the genealogies. We will do this by examining, in order, the history from the deportation to Babylon until Jesus Christ. We will also explore God's administration of redemption that is contained in the names and lives of the people who appear in the third period of the genealogy of Jesus Christ.

---

* In the third, fourth, and fifth books of the History of Redemption series, all the calculations of years for Judah and its neighboring nations from the time of Solomon until the Israelites' return from Babylon are based on the Tishri (7th month) reckoning method. In the Bible, there are two ways to reckon the regnal years of the kings. The Nisan method counts the regnal year from the month of Nisan (1st month) to the next month of Nisan. The Tishri method, on the other hand, counts one year from the month of Tishri (7th month) to the next month of Tishri. Because the Nisan method is always six months ahead of the Tishri method, it is imperative that one knows which method was used when calculating the years in the Bible (Ref Abraham Park, *God's Profound and Mysterious Providence*, 71-73.).

לכל בר דעת דרך המסעות ארבעים שנה במדבר 'והרוחב והאורך של ארץ הקדושה מנהר ב

עמלק

מדבר צין הוא קדש

ים המלח

עתר
מקדה
עיר כרמל
שבט
ענב
אלהול
שרוחן
באר שבע
שמעון
בית המרכבות
גת
אשקלון
ארץ פלשתים

יהו

מדבר סיני

מדבר פארן

מדבר שור

ארקב נשן
פתם
שרה
צען
אלכסנדרי

לוח המסעות במדבר
אשר על פי ה'יסעו ועל פי ה'יחנו

| | | | |
|---|---|---|---|
| א' רעמסס | טו' רתמה | רעו' חרהגדגד |
| ב' סכת | טז' רמן פרץ | ל' ילבתה |
| ג' אתם | יז' לבנה | לא' עברנה |
| ד' פיהחירת | יח' רסה | לב' עציון גבר |
| ה' מרה | יט' קהלתה | לג' מדבר צין |
| ו' אילם | כ' הרספר | לד' הרההר |
| ז' ים סוף | כא' חרדה | לה' צלמנה |
| ח' מדבר סין | כב' מקהלה | לו' פונן |
| ט' רפקה | כג' תחת | לז' אבת |
| יוד' אלוש | כד' תרח | לח' דיבן גר |
| יא' רפידם | כה' מתקה | לט' עלמן דבל' |
| יב' מדבר סיני | כו' חשמנה | מ' הרי עברים |
| יג' קברתהתאוה | כז' מסרות | מא' ערבה מואב |
| יד' חצרות | | רח' בני יעקן |

# PART THREE

# The Genealogy of Jesus Christ: Individuals in the Third Period

## Fourteen Generations from the Babylonian Exile to Jesus Christ

# The Genealogy of Jesus Christ: Individuals in the Third Period

The genealogy of Jesus Christ in Matthew chapter 1 consists of the first period of fourteen generations from Abraham to David, the second period of fourteen generations from David to the deportation to Babylon, and the third period of fourteen generations from the deportation to Babylon until the coming of Jesus Christ—a total of forty-two generations (Matt 1:17). The fourteen generations in the third period of the genealogy begins with a record of the shameful destruction of Judah, the southern kingdom.

Judah's national power waned drastically after Josiah, the sixteenth king. Jehoahaz succeeded Josiah, but he did evil in the sight of the Lord according to all that his fathers had done and was taken to Egypt by Pharaoh Neco. Jehoiakim was made king in his place (2 Kgs 23:32-34). Nevertheless, Jehoiakim's anti-Babylonian policies resulted in him being bound in chains and taken to Babylon (2 Kgs 24:1-4; 2 Chr 36:5-7).

Jehoiakim's son, Jehoiachin, became king, and he also did what was evil and was taken to Babylon during the second Babylonian invasion (2 Kgs 24:8-17). Zedekiah, Josiah's son, became Judah's last king. Judah was completely destroyed at the hands of Babylon in 586 BC. However, God called the people of Judah back after seventy years of Babylonian exile and continued His work of redemption by rebuilding the temple through Zerubbabel so that the path of the coming of Jesus Christ would not be obstructed by any means.

# An Overview of the 42 Generations in the Matthean Genealogy (The 3rd Period)

## – Fourteen Generations from the Deportation to Babylon until Jesus Christ

| People | History |
|---|---|
| **1st Generation**<br><br>**Jeconiah**<br><br>Ἰεχονίας<br><br>יְכָנְיָה<br><br>or **Jehoiachin**<br><br>Ἰωακιν<br><br>יְהוֹיָכִין<br><br>The Lord establishes | ① "Josiah became the father of Jeconiah and his brothers . . ." (Matt 1:11)<br><br>② He is the first person listed in the third period of Jesus Christ's genealogy (1 Chr 3:16-17). Jeconiah was the 19th king of Judah and was called *Jehoiachin* (2 Kgs 24:6-17; 2 Chr 36:9-10), *Jeconiah* (1 Chr 3:16-17; Esth 2:6; Jer 24:1; 27:20; 28:4; Matt 1:11-12), and *Coniah* (Jer 22:24, 28; 37:1). Although he was Josiah's grandson, he is listed in the genealogy as his son (Matt 1:11), while Josiah's actual sons (all kings of Judah)—Jehoahaz (17th), Jehoiakim (18th), and Zedekiah (20th)—were not recorded in the genealogy.<br><br>③ He was an evil king. He did what was evil in God's eyes according to the deeds of his father (2 Kgs 24:9; 2 Chr 36:9; Jer 22:24-30) during his short reign of 3 months and 10 days (or 3 months).<br><br>④ In 597 BC, King Jehoiachin was taken to Babylon in the second deportation along with his mother, his servants, his captains, and his officials (2 Kgs 24:12-16; 2 Chr 36:10); and Nebuchadnezzar made Zedekiah (real name: Mattaniah) king of Judah in his place (2 Kgs 24:17; 2 Chr 36:10).<br><br>⑤ In the 37th year of the Babylonian exile (561 BC; on the 27th day of the 12th month in the first year that Evil-merodach became king), Jehoiachin's crown was restored on a personal level (2 Kgs 25:27-30; Ref 25th day of 12th month in Jer 52:31-34). This was because Jehoiachin was the only king who surrendered to the king of Babylon (2 Kgs 24:12) in accordance with Jeremiah's prophecy, "If you will indeed go out to the officers of the king of Babylon, then you will live" (Ref Jer 21:9; 27:8, 11-12, 17; 38:2, 17-21). |
| **2nd Generation**<br><br>**Shealtiel**<br><br>Σαλαθιήλ<br><br>שְׁאַלְתִּיאֵל<br><br>I have asked of God | ① ". . . Jeconiah became the father of Shealtiel . . ." (Matt 1:12)<br><br>② He is the second person listed in the third period of Jesus Christ's genealogy (1 Chr 3:17).<br><br>③ He was Jeconiah's first son, and his brothers were Malchiram, Pedaiah, Shenazzar, Jekamiah, Hoshama, and Nedabiah (1 Chr 3:17-18). The meanings of these names each contain Jeconiah's prayer, thanksgiving, and praise to God, reflecting his godly life.<br><br>④ In God's redemptive administration to establish a new covenant (Jer 31:31-34), He said that He would "raise up for David a righteous Branch" (Jer 23:5, 33:15); and thus, in accordance with God's redemptive administration, Jeconiah had seven children including Shealtiel. |

| People | History |
|---|---|
| **3rd Generation** <br> **Zerubbabel** <br> Ζοροβαβὲλ <br> זְרֻבָּבֶל <br> <br> Born in Babylon, descendant of Babylon | ① "...Shealtiel the father of Zerubbabel" (Matt 1:12) <br> ② He is the third person listed in the third period of Jesus Christ's genealogy (1 Chr 3:19). <br> ③ Zerubbabel's biological father is Pedaiah (1 Chr 3:19), but Shealtiel is recorded as his father in the Matthean genealogy (Matt 1:12). When Shealtiel died without a son, his brother Pedaiah begot a son through his brother's wife to become his brother's heir in accordance with the levirate marriage law (Deut 25:5- 10; <sup>Ref</sup> Matt 22:23-33; Luke 20:28). From this time on, Zerubbabel was called "Zerubbabel the son of Shealtiel" (Ezra 3:2, 8, 5:2; Neh 12:1; Hag 1:1, 12, 14; 2:2, 23; Matt 1:12). <br> ④ He was the main leader of the first return from Babylon and the driving force behind the reconstruction of the temple after the return (Ezra 3:8; 5:2; Hag 1:14; <sup>Ref</sup> Zech 4:6-10). The reconstruction of the temple was halted for 16 years (Ezra 4:4-6, 23-24), but it resumed on the 24th day of the 6th month in 520 BC (King Darius's 2nd year of reign; Hag 1:14-15). Then, it was dedicated on the 3rd day of the 12th month in 516 BC (King Darius's 6th year reign; Ezra 6:15). Thus, Zerubbabel's temple was completed in about 4 years and 5 months. |
| **4th Generation** <br> **Abihud** <br> Ἀβιούδ <br> אֲבִיהוּד <br> <br> Father of glory, father of majesty | ① "Zerubbabel was the father of Abihud ..." (Matt 1:13) <br> ② He is the fourth person listed in the third period of Jesus Christ's genealogy. <br> ③ Zerubbabel had seven sons and one daughter (1 Chr 3:19-20), and all the meanings of the names are about grace, restoration, and fellowship with God. Zerubbabel gave sincere thanks to God for His amazing grace in the process of returning from the Babylonian exile, and thus named his children with the hope that fellowship with God may be restored. <br> ④ Although it states, "Zerubbabel was the father of Abihud ..." (Matt 1:13), the name Abihud does not appear among the names of Zerubbabel's seven sons and one daughter in the Old Testament. Perhaps Abihud was a name that he gave with a hope that the glory may be achieved once again through the reconstruction of the temple (Zech 6:13). |
| **5th Generation** <br> **Eliakim** <br> Ἐλιακίμ <br> אֶלְיָקִים <br> <br> God establishes, God raises up | ① "...Abihud the father of Eliakim ..." (Matt 1:13) <br> ② He is the fifth person listed in the third period of Jesus Christ's genealogy. <br> ③ The meaning of his name contains the confession that only the Almighty God can establish the weak and feeble nation of Israel after the return from the Babylonian exile, especially since the period of the Persian conquest (539–331 BC) had already begun by then. It also shows that there was hope that the strength of the sovereign God would quickly restore the fallen nation. <br> ④ There are three individuals in the Old Testament with the name *Eliakim* (Isa 36:22; 2 Kgs 23:34; Neh 12:41). |

| People | History |
|---|---|
| **6th Generation** <br><br> **Azor** <br><br> Ἀζώρ <br><br> עַזּוּר <br><br> Helpful, helper | ① "...Eliakim the father of Azor" (Matt 1:13) <br><br> ② He is the sixth person listed in the third period of Jesus Christ's genealogy. <br><br> ③ It is presumed that he lived during the Persian era (539–331 BC). The Persian era was a time of severe spiritual corruption; even the priests offered up abominable sacrifices. It is likely that Azor's parents named him with the hope that he may become a man of faith who will assist in God's work of redemption. <br><br> ④ There are three individuals in the Old Testament who are mentioned according to the Hebrew spelling of the name *Azor*, which is עַזּוּר (Jer 28:1; Ezek 11:1-2; Neh 10:17). |
| **7th Generation** <br><br> **Zadok** <br><br> Σαδώκ <br><br> צָדוֹק <br><br> Righteous, righteousness, justice | ① "Azor was the father of Zadok ..." (Matt 1:14) <br><br> ② He is the seventh person listed in the third period of Jesus Christ's genealogy. <br><br> ③ Zadok lived during a period plagued by political conflict and disorder caused by foreign powers, as well as a time of spiritual darkness where righteous people and doers of justice were hard to find. The meaning of his name reveals that Zadok's parents longed for the coming of the Messiah, the righteous and just king. When the Messiah comes, righteousness goes forth like brightness (Isa 62:1). "Righteousness" is the "foundation of God's throne" (Ps 89:14; 97:2). <br><br> ④ There are seven individuals in the Old Testament with the name *Zadok* (2 Sam 19:11; 20:25; 1 Chr 12:28 / 1 Chr 6:10-12 / 2 Chr 27:1 / Neh 3:4; 3:29; Ref Ezra 2:36-37 / Neh 10:21 / Neh 13:13). |
| **8th Generation** <br><br> **Achim** <br><br> Ἀχείμ <br><br> יוֹקִים <br><br> The Lord establishes | ① "...Zadok the father of Achim ..." (Matt 1:14) <br><br> ② He is the eighth person listed in the third period of Jesus Christ's genealogy. <br><br> ③ It is presumed that he lived during the Hellenistic era (331–164 BC). As the Israelites lost their religious freedom and were greatly oppressed under the rule of a powerful nation, they probably hoped that the kingdom of the Messiah would soon be established in accordance with the covenant that God had made with Abraham and David. <br><br> ④ There is only one other person in the Old Testament with the same name—his name was Jokim from the tribe of Judah, a descendant of Shelah (1 Chr 4:21-22). |
| **9th Generation** <br><br> **Eliud** <br><br> Ἐλιούδ <br><br> אֱלִיהוּד <br><br> God is my glory, God of majesty | ① "...Achim the father of Eliud" (Matt 1:14) <br><br> ② He is the ninth person listed in the third period of Jesus Christ's genealogy. <br><br> ③ The name *Eliud* contains hope in God's majesty and glory. <br><br> ④ The word *majesty* refers to an authoritative and solemn attitude or spirit (Ps 21:5; 145:5). This is reminiscent of the dedication of Solomon's temple when the priests could not possibly enter the temple or serve in it, for it was filled with the immense glory of God (1 Kgs 8:11; 2 Chr 7:1-3). |

| People | History |
|---|---|
| **10th Generation**<br>**Eleazar**<br>Ἐλεάζαρ<br>אֶלְעָזָר<br>God has helped, helped by God | ① "Eliud was the father of Eleazar ..." (Matt 1:15)<br>② He is the tenth person listed in the third period of Jesus Christ's genealogy.<br>③ The name *Eleazar* reveals traces of anticipation in the coming of the Messiah as well as hope in God's help during chaotic times under foreign rule when even one safe day was hard to come by.<br>④ There are six persons in the Old Testament with the name *Eleazar* (Exod 6:23 / 1 Sam 7:1 / 2 Sam 23:9; 1 Chr 11:12-14 / 1 Chr 23:21-22, 24:28 / Ezra 8:33; Neh 12:42 / Ezra 10:25). |
| **11th Generation**<br>**Matthan**<br>Ματθάν<br>מַתָּן<br>Gift, offering | ① "... Eleazar the father Matthan ..." (Matt 1:15)<br>② He is the eleventh person listed in the third period of Jesus Christ's genealogy.<br>③ Mattathias, whose name shares the same meaning as the name *Matthan* (meaning "gift"), and his sons led the Maccabean Revolution in order to gain national independence (167–142 BC). The name *Matthan* shows the Israelites' anticipation for God's gift of salvation during their dismal times when there seemed to be no hope of salvation. Many people in the genealogy of Luke have names that mean "God's gift" (Luke 3:24, 25, 26, 29, 31). The only true gift of God is Jesus Christ who will bring the good news of salvation (John 4:10ᵃ; Rom 5:15; Eph 2:8).<br>④ There are two individuals in the Old Testament with the name *Matthan* (2 Kgs 11:18; 2 Chr 23:17 / Jer 38:1). |
| **12th Generation**<br>**Jacob**<br>Ἰακώβ<br>יַעֲקֹב<br>One who takes by the heel, one who supplants | ① "... Matthan the father of Jacob" (Matt 1:15)<br>② He is the twelfth person listed in the third period of Jesus Christ's genealogy.<br>③ He is Joseph's father and Jesus Christ's grandfather. The genealogy in Luke lists Eli as Joseph's father (Luke 3:23).<br>④ Jacob of the Old Testament was the covenantal firstborn to whom the covenant was passed down from Abraham and Isaac; his eleventh son, Joseph, became the spiritual firstborn (1 Chr 5:1-2; Ezek 47:13). In the genealogy in Luke, Eli is listed as Jesus' grandfather in the same generation as Jacob (Matt 1:16; Luke 3:23). |
| **13th Generation**<br>**Joseph**<br>Ἰωσήφ<br>יוֹסֵף<br>The Lord increases, the Lord adds on | ① "Jacob was the father of Joseph the husband of Mary ..." (Matt 1:16)<br>② He is the thirteenth person listed in the third period of Jesus Christ's genealogy.<br>③ Since Joseph was from the family of David (Matt 1:20; Luke 1:27; 2:4), Jesus was from the line of David according to the genealogy (Rom 1:3). However, Jesus is God the Son who was conceived by the Holy Spirit and born of Mary (Matt 1:18, 20; Luke 1:35).<br>④ Joseph, Mary's husband, was a righteous man (Matt 1:19). He immediately obeyed when he received the angel's revelation; by bringing Mary to him and protecting her (Matt 1:20-25; Ref Deut 22:23-24), he became the path for the coming of Jesus Christ to the earth. |

| People | History |
|---|---|
| **14th Generation** <br><br> **Jesus** <br><br> Ἰησοῦς <br><br> יֵשׁוּעַ <br><br> The Lord saves, He who will save His people from their sins | ① "... Mary, by whom Jesus was born, who was called the Messiah" (Matt 1:16) <br><br> ② Jesus Christ is the focus and purpose of the genealogy. He is the fourteenth and last person listed in the third period of the genealogy. He is also the fulfiller of the covenanted promise with Abraham and David. <br><br> ③ According to the genealogy, Jacob was Jesus' grandfather and Joseph was Jesus' father. "As was supposed," He was the son of Joseph (Luke 3:23), but was born of the virgin Mary, by the Holy Spirit (Matt 1:16), in fulfillment of the promise of the "seed of the woman" in Genesis 3:15 (Gal 4:4). <br><br> ④ In accordance with God's administration of redemption, which He had planned since before the beginning of time, Jesus Christ came with the name *Jesus*, the One who "will save His people from their sins" (Matt 1:21), and He brought the good news of great joy which will be for all the people (Luke 2:10). <br><br> ⑤ Only Jesus Christ is the Son of the Most High God who possesses both perfect humanity and perfect divinity (Luke 1:32, 35). He is the only Redeemer who saves His chosen people (John 14:6; Acts 4:12); and He is God Immanuel, the Son who is with us for all eternity (Matt 1:23; John 1:14, 18; Ref John 14:9; 10:30; Phil 2:6-8; Heb 1:1-3). |

# 1st Generation: Jeconiah

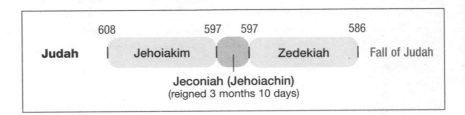

Jeconiah / Ἰεχονίας / יְכָנְיָה

Jehoiachin / Ἰωακιν / יְהוֹיָכִין

The Lord establishes

---

|  | 608 | | 597 | 597 | | 586 |
| --- | --- | --- | --- | --- | --- | --- |
| **Judah** | | Jehoiakim | | | Zedekiah | Fall of Judah |

Jeconiah (Jehoiachin)
(reigned 3 months 10 days)

---

**Order**
Nineteenth king of the southern kingdom of Judah (2 Kgs 24:6-17; 2 Chr 36:9-10)
First person in the third period of Jesus Christ's genealogy (Matt 1:11-12)

**Background**
Matthew 1:11-12 states, ". . . Josiah became the father of **Jeconiah** and his broth-
ers, at the time of the deportation to Babylon. [12] After the deportation to Babylon:
**Jeconiah** became the father of Shealtiel . . . ."
Father: Jehoiakim (18th king of southern kingdom of Judah)
Mother: Nehushta (daughter of Elnathan of Jerusalem; 2 Kgs 24:8)

**Duration of reign**
Jeconiah acceded to the throne at age 18 and reigned 3 months and 10 days (597
BC; 2 Kgs 24:8; 2 Chr 36:9). Second Chronicles 36:9 states, "Jehoiachin was eight
years old when he became king." However, judging by the record that his "wives"
were also taken when Jehoiachin was taken captive to Babylon (2 Kgs 24:15), he
must have been 18 years old when he became king, not 8. The word עָשָׂר ('āśār),
which means "ten/teen" was probably left out by mistake when 2 Chronicles 36:9
was transcribed.

**Evaluation** – evil king (2 Kgs 24:9; 2 Chr 36:9; Jer 22:24-30)

**Active prophet** – Jeremiah (Jer 1:3)

---

Jeconiah (Jehoiachin) succeeded Jehoiakim and became the nineteenth
king of the southern kingdom of Judah. Jehoiachin is יְהוֹיָכִין (yĕhôyākîn)
in Hebrew. The name is a combination of the words יְהוָֹה (yhwh) meaning

"Jehovah" and כּוּן (kûn) meaning "to establish," "to fix," or "to secure." Therefore, the name means, "the Lord establishes."

Jehoiachin's other name, Jeconiah is יְכוֹנְיָה (yĕkônĕyâ) in Hebrew. This name is a combination of יָה (yāh), a shortened form of "Jehovah," and כּוּן (kun), which together render the same meaning as Jehoiachin, "the Lord establishes."

## 1. Jehoiachin did evil in the sight of the Lord.

Jehoiachin was also called Jeconiah (1 Chr 3:16-17; Esth 2:6; Jer 24:1; 27:20; 28:4; Matt 1:11-12) and Coniah (Jer 22:24, 28; 37:1). Though he reigned for a short period of three months and ten days (three months), he did evil in the sight of God according to all that his father had done (2 Kgs 24:9; 2 Chr 36:9). His mother's name Nehushta, נְחֻשְׁתָּא (nĕhuštāʾ), is derived from נְחֹשֶׁת (nĕhōšet), which means "copper," "fetters," "uncleanness," "lust," and "harlotry."

God judged Judah by allowing Nebuchadnezzar, king of Babylon, to besiege it for a second time in the eighth year of his reign (2 Kgs 24:10-12). Although Jehoiachin, along with his mother, his servants, captains, and officials, surrendered to the king of Babylon, the king and all the main leaders of Judah were taken captive to Babylon. Only the poorest people of the land were left (2 Kgs 24:12-16).

Ezekiel 19:5 alluded to Jeconiah as a "young lion." Moreover, verse 6 describes, "he learned to tear his prey; he devoured men," indicating that he disobeyed God and oppressed his people. Ultimately, during the second invasion by Babylon in 597 BC, he was put in "a cage with hooks" and brought to the king of Babylon (Ezek 19:8-9).

## 2. Jehoiachin was released from prison and restored to his throne in the thirty-seventh year of the exile.

King Jehoiachin was released from prison on the twenty-seventh day of the twelfth month in the thirty-seventh year of his exile. This was the year that Nebuchadnezzar's son Evil-merodach became king of Babylon (2 Kgs 25:27, Ref Jer 52:31-34; twenty-fifth day of the twelfth month). The king of Babylon released him from prison and made him change his prison clothes. He also allowed him to have all his meals in the king's presence regularly all the days of his life, and set his throne above the thrones of the kings. He also provided Jehoiachin with everything he needed all the days of his life (2 Kgs 25:27-30; Jer 52:31-34). Second Kings 25:30 states, "And for his allowance, a regular allowance was given him by the king, a portion for each day, all the days of his life." These measures were bestowed upon Jehoiachin in accordance with Jeremiah's prophecy that anyone who surrenders to Babylon will live, but those who resist to the end will be captured and killed (Ref Jer 21:9; 27:8, 11-12, 17; 38:2, 17-21). Jehoiachin was the only one among all the kings of Judah who went to the Babylonian king and surrendered (2 Kgs 24:12).

Jehoiachin, who became king at the age of eighteen, reigned for a mere three months and ten days before he was taken captive to Babylon (2 Kgs 24:8). He was in his mid-fifties when he was restored to his throne. He probably contemplated many things and repented during the thirty-seven years of imprisonment away from his country. It is likely that he realized no one other than God could raise him up again to his position after thirty-seven years of exile. By concluding the book of 2 Kings with the restoration of Jehoiachin, God instilled hope for the people of Judah who were still in exile. He was assuring them that He will restore them if they gain understanding, repent, and persevere to the end.

# 2nd Generation: Shealtiel

---

**Shealtiel / Σαλαθιήλ / שְׁאַלְתִּיאֵל**

I have asked of God

---

**Order**
Second person in the third period of Jesus Christ's genealogy (Matt 1:12)

**Background**
Matthew 1:12 states, ". . . Jeconiah became the father of **Shealtiel**, and **Shealtiel** the father of Zerubbabel."
Father: Jeconiah (Jehoiachin: 19th king of southern kingdom of Judah)
His younger siblings were Malchiram, Pedaiah, Shenazzar, Jekamiah, Hoshama and Nedabiah (1 Chr 3:17-18).

**Remarks**
He was Jeconiah's first son who was born after the deportation to Babylon (Matt 1:12).

---

Shealtiel is שְׁאַלְתִּיאֵל (šĕ'altî'ēl) in Hebrew and Σαλαθιήλ (Salathiēl) in Greek. The name is a compound word composed of שָׁאַל (šā'al), meaning "pray," "plead," or "ask," and אֵל ('ēl), meaning "the Almighty God." Thus, the name means "I have asked of God."

## 1. Shealtiel was in exile with his father Jeconiah (Jehoiachin) in Babylon.

First Chronicles 3:17 states, "The sons of Jeconiah, the prisoner, were Shealtiel his son." Jeconiah was taken to Babylon after a mere three months and ten days on the throne, and his wives were also taken captive (2 Kgs 24:15). Considering that his sons were not included in the list of people taken captive (2 Kgs 24:15), it appears that Shealtiel was born to Jeconiah after he was taken to Babylon. Matthew 1:12 states, "After the deportation to Babylon: Jeconiah became the father of Shealtiel." It should be noted that Jeremiah 22:28 makes mention of the "descendants" of Coniah (Jehoiachin) who have been hurled out to Babylon; however, the word *descendants* (זֶרַע) contextually signifies Coniah's family or his royal household, rather than Coniah's sons. Thus, Shealtiel was born in a distant country during the time of the Babylonian exile. Born and raised in a foreign land, he probably experienced the sorrow and pain of not having a country of his own. If Shealtiel had lived according to the meaning of his name, he would have sought God's help and prayed earnestly when he had no one to depend on.

According to 1 Chronicles 3:17-18, Jeconiah's seven sons born to him during his exile in Babylon were "Shealtiel his son, and Malchiram, Pedaiah, Shenazzar, Jekamiah, Hoshama and Nedabiah." The meaning of each name contains prayer and praise to God. This is evidence that Jeconiah had repented and lived a life of prayer while he was a captive in Babylon. As a result, he received the blessing of being restored to his position thirty-seven years after he was taken into captivity (2 Kgs 25:27-30; Jer 52:31-34).

The meanings of the names of Jeconiah's seven sons are as follows:

① Shealtiel (שְׁאַלְתִּיאֵל) – I have asked of God

② Malchiram (מַלְכִּירָם) – My king is exalted

③ Pedaiah (פְּדָיָה) – God has ransomed

④ Shenazzar (שֶׁנְאַצַּר) – God, protect us

⑤ Jekamiah (יְקַמְיָה) – The Lord will rise

⑥ Hoshama (הוֹשָׁמָע) – The Lord has heard

⑦ Nedabiah (נְדַבְיָה) – The Lord is generous

Even after Jeremiah's proclamation that he would be childless and without descendants, Jeconiah had seven sons including Shealtiel after he was deported to Babylon (Jer 22:30). This can only be explained as God's administration of redemption to "raise up for David a righteous Branch" (Jer 23:5; 33:15) and fulfill the new covenant (Jer 31:31-34). Does this mean that Jeremiah's prophecy about Jeconiah being childless was wrong (Jer 22:30)? The word *childless* used in the verse is עֲרִירִי (*'ărîrî*), which also means "stripped" and describes a state of being stripped of certain honor. Thus, it appears that Jeremiah's prophecy regarding Jeconiah meant that he would not have a son to succeed the royal throne of the Davidic dynasty.

Jeconiah was an unfortunate king who could not pass down the throne to any of his sons even though he had seven sons after he was taken captive to Babylon.

## 2. The genealogy of Jesus Christ records, "Shealtiel the father of Zerubbabel."

A close reading of the Bible will reveal that Zerubbabel was not Shealtiel's biological son. As discussed above, Shealtiel was Jeconiah's first son and Pedaiah was the third son. Also, 1 Chronicles 3:19 states that Zerubbabel was Pedaiah's first son. Hence, Zerubbabel was Shealtiel's nephew, not his son. Then, why does the genealogy of Jesus Christ record Zerubbabel as Shealtiel's son?

The reason lies in the levirate marriage law. The levirate marriage law ensures that the lineage of a family is not cut off when a man dies without a male heir. In such a case, the brother of the deceased man is obligated to take his brother's widowed wife so that she can bear a son to continue his lineage (Deut 25:5-10; Ref Matt 22:23-33; Luke 20:28). Thus, when Shealtiel died without a son to carry on the lineage, his brother Pedaiah took his sister-in-law and bore a son, Zerubbabel. Since then, Zerubbabel was called "Zerubbabel the son of Shealtiel" (Ezra 3:2, 8; 5:2; Neh 12:1; Hag 1:1, 12, 14; 2:2, 23; Matt 1:12). Shealtiel grew up in a foreign land, having to endure all sorts of sorrow and pain, and ultimately died without a son. However, God made Zerubbabel—a great man of faith—his legal son, so wherever the name Zerubbabel was mentioned, it was always recorded as "Zerubbabel the son of Shealtiel."

As reflected by God's work in Shealtiel's life, he probably lived up to the meaning of his name, which denotes constant prayer to God. Psalm 138:3 states, "On the day I called, You answered me; You made me bold with strength in my soul." Calling on God refers to "praying earnestly." We may also be confronted with countless difficulties in this chaotic world today, but God will bless us by drawing close to us when we live a life of calling on God (Deut 4:7; Ps 6:9; 130:2; 145:18).

# 3rd Generation: Zerubbabel

> **Zerubbabel / Ζοροβαβὲλ / זְרֻבָּבֶל**
> Born in Babylon, descendant of Babylon

**Order**
Third person in the third period of Jesus Christ's genealogy (Matt 1:12-13)

**Background**
Matthew 1:12-13 states, ". . . Shealtiel the father of **Zerubbabel**. ¹³**Zerubbabel** was the father of Abihud . . . . "
Zerubbabel's biological father is Pedaiah (1 Chr 3:19).

**Remarks**
He was the leader who led the reconstruction of the temple after the return from the Babylonian exile (Ezra 3:8; 5:2; Hag 1:14; Ref Zech 4:6-10).

The name *Zerubbabel* is זְרֻבָּבֶל (*zĕrubābel*) in Hebrew and Ζοροβαβὲλ (*Zorobabel*) in Greek. In Hebrew, *Zerubbabel* is a compound word composed of זְרַב (*zārab*), meaning "flow" or "be burnt," and בָּבֶל (*bābel*), meaning "Babylon" or "Babel." Hence, the name means, "born in Babylon" or "descendant of Babylon."

## 1. Zerubbabel led the reconstruction of the temple after his return from Babylon.

Although the Israelites were taken captive to Babylon, God promised that they would return after seventy years (Jer 25:11-12; 29:10). In keeping with this promise, God stirred up the spirit of Cyrus the king of Persia and allowed the Israelites to return home from captivity, whereupon they began the reconstruction of the temple (Ezra 1:1-4). In 538 BC Cyrus issued a decree and the Israelites began to return in 537 BC. This was the first return from Babylon.

There were a total of 49,897 people who returned in the first return. Among them the assembly numbered 42,360; their male and female servants numbered 7,337; and the singing men and women numbered 200 (Ezra 2:64-65). There were also eleven leaders who represented them and

Zerubbabel was the first leader mentioned among them (Ezra 2:2).

In the Hebrew manuscript, a *maqqeph* (–) connects the name זְרֻבָּבֶל (*zĕrubābel*) and the word עִם (*'im*), which means "with." This distinguishes Zerubbabel from the other ten leaders, implying that he was the actual chief among the people during the first return from Babylon.

Regarding the participants of the first return, Ezra 1:5 states, "everyone whose spirit God had stirred to go up and rebuild the house of the LORD which is in Jerusalem." They were people who were inspired by God and possessed willing and voluntary faith regarding the reconstruction of the temple.

The fact that there were fewer than 50,000 participants in the first return shows that most of the Jews who were born during the period of captivity were afraid to leave. They did not want to leave behind their livelihood and the positions that they had established thus far and return to the ruins of Jerusalem. However, those who take the lead in doing God's work are always the ones who sacrifice their personal interests and gains in order to follow God's Word (Ref Gen 12:1-4). Zerubbabel possessed the ability and spirituality worthy to represent these exceptional people of faith.

Those who returned to Jerusalem finally began to rebuild the temple in the second month of the second year. Even at this time, the name "Zerubbabel the son of Shealtiel" appears at the forefront (Ezra 3:8). Shortly thereafter, when the adversaries who tried to hinder the construction of the temple approached the leaders of the captives who had returned, Zerubbabel's name appeared at the forefront again (Ezra 4:1-3). It is evident that Zerubbabel was the leader of the people at the time of the return and throughout the entire process of the temple reconstruction. A true leader is faithful and steadfast, devoted to God and His people.

## 2. Zerubbabel was the leader who restarted and completed the construction of the temple, which had been interrupted.

The construction of the temple, which began in 536 BC, came to a halt because of the opposition of the adversaries. Since then, the construction work was neglected for sixteen years, and by this time, it was already 520 BC. It was Zerubbabel who restarted the construction of the temple in obedience to the words proclaimed through the prophets Haggai and Zechariah (Ezra 5:2; Hag 1:14; Ref Zech 4:6-10).

**FIRST, the people obeyed God's Word.**

God rebuked the people through Prophet Haggai saying, "Is it time for you yourselves to dwell in your paneled houses [fancy houses made of cedar] while this house lies desolate?" (Hag 1:4).

Prophet Haggai explained that the people of Judah have sown much, but harvested little; they ate, but there was not enough to be satisfied; they drank, but there was not enough to become drunk; they put on clothing, but no one was warm enough; and they who earned, earned wages to put into a purse with holes. This is all because they have halted the construction of the temple and neglected it (Hag 1:6).

For this reason, God points out in Haggai 1:9, "'You look for much, but behold, it comes to little; when you bring it home, I blow it away. Why?' declares the LORD of hosts, 'Because of My house which lies desolate, while each of you runs to his own house.'"

When the message regarding the construction of the temple was proclaimed through Prophet Haggai, Zerubbabel and all the people obeyed the Word of God (Hag 1:12). Here, the word *obey* is שָׁמַע (*šama'*) and means "to listen" or "to pay attention." They listened closely to God's Word and repented for the lives that they had lived while the construction was on hold.

We may have put ourselves before God until today and lived unsatisfying lives. However, when we obey God's Word and repent, even the most difficult problems will begin to be solved.

**SECOND, the spirit of the people was stirred up.**

Haggai 1:14 states, "So the LORD stirred up the spirit of Zerubbabel the son of Shealtiel, governor of Judah, and the spirit of Joshua the son of Jehozadak, the high priest, and the spirit of all the remnant of the people; and they came and worked on the house of the LORD of hosts, their God."

Here, the word *spirit* is רוּחַ (*rûaḥ*); and the Hebrew word for *stir up* is the hiphil (causative active) stem of עוּר ('ûr), which means "to rouse oneself," "to be awake," "to awaken," or "to incite." Thus, God had awoken the spirits of Zerubbabel, Joshua the high priest, and all the people and caused them to begin the nationwide construction of the temple. It was when God awoke their spirits that the temple construction work, which had been halted for sixteen years, was finally restarted.

**THIRD**, they started the construction immediately.

Prophet Haggai's message regarding the reconstruction of the temple was first proclaimed in the second year of King Darius, on the first day of the sixth month (Hag 1:1). The construction that had been halted was resumed on the twenty-fourth day of the sixth month in the second year of King Darius (Hag 1:14-15), which means the construction began twenty-three days after God's Word was proclaimed. The sixth month was usually the busiest month because preparations for the Feast of the Trumpets, the Day of Atonement, and the Feast of Tabernacles needed to be made. Nonetheless, they were able to prepare and begin the construction work in only twenty-three days, clearly demonstrating how Zerubbabel and the people voluntarily and actively participated in the reconstruction work in order to fulfill God's Word.

The temple construction, which resumed in this manner, was finally completed, and the temple was dedicated to God in the sixth year of King Darius's reign (516 BC), on the third day of the month of Adar (twelfth month; Ezra 6:13-15). For the dedication of the temple, they offered one hundred bulls, two hundred rams, four hundred lambs; and as a sin offering for all Israel twelve male goats, corresponding to the number of the tribes of Israel (Ezra 6:16-17). Then they appointed the priests and the Levites for the service of God in Jerusalem, as it is written in the book of Moses (Ezra 6:18).

God called Zerubbabel His "servant" and "signet ring." Haggai 2:23 states, "'On that day,' declares the LORD of hosts, 'I will take you, Zerubbabel, son of Shealtiel, My servant,' declares the LORD, 'and I will make you like a signet ring, for I have chosen you,' declares the LORD of hosts." Here, the word *signet ring* is חוֹתָם (*ḥôtām*) in Hebrew and means "seal" or "seal ring." In the ancient Near East, the signet ring represented its owner, so the owner always carried it with him. When God said that He would make Zerubbabel like a signet ring, He was promising to be with Zerubbabel and to protect him even until the end. This message was proclaimed on the twenty-fourth day of the ninth month, in the second year of King Darius (Hag 2:10, 18). It was an expression of God's strong desire to complete the construction of the temple through Zerubbabel.

On the twenty-fourth day of the eleventh month in the second year of King Darius, God gave another confirmation through Prophet Zechariah that the construction of the temple would be carried out solely by the work of God's Holy Spirit, not by human strength (Zech 1:7; 4:6). Ultimately, the temple was completed purely by the work of God (Ezra 6:15).

Likewise, even today, God makes His servants like a "signet ring" by the work of the Holy Spirit and builds His house through them. They are endowed with the leading role in the holy work of redemption to complete the kingdom of God (2 Cor 1:22; Eph 1:13; 4:30; Rev 7:2-4; 9:4).

# 4th Generation: **Abihud**

---

**Abihud / Ἀβιούδ / אֲבִיהוּד**

Father of glory, father of majesty

---

**Order**
Fourth person in the third period of Jesus Christ's genealogy (Matt 1:13)

**Background**
Matthew 1:13 states, "Zerubbabel was the father of **Abihud**, **Abihud** the father of Eliakim . . . . "

**Remarks**
Zerubbabel had seven sons and one daughter, but Abihud is not included in the list (1 Chr 3:19-20).

---

The name *Abihud* is אֲבִיהוּד (*'ăbîhûd*) in Hebrew and Ἀβιούδ (*Abioud*) in Greek. In Hebrew, it is a compound word composed of אָב (*'āb*), meaning "father" or "ancestor," and הוֹד (*hôd*), meaning "glory," "majesty," or "splendor." Thus, the name means "father of glory" or "father of majesty."

## 1. The name *Abihud* does not appear among the descendants of Zerubbabel in the Old Testament genealogies.

The names of Zerubbabel's seven sons and one daughter are listed in 1 Chronicles 3:19-20: "And the sons of Zerubbabel were Meshullam and Hananiah, and Shelomith was their sister; and Hashubah, Ohel, Berechiah, Hasadiah and Jushab-hesed, five." Some noteworthy aspects of this genealogy are as follows:

*FIRST*, "Shelomith, their sister" is listed.

The word *sister* is אָחוֹת (*'āḥôt*) in Hebrew. Shelomith was a sister to Zerubbabel's sons, and hence Zerubbabel's daughter. Shelomith's inclusion in the genealogy is unusual because ancient Jews did not list women in their genealogies.

**SECOND, the meanings of his children's names are about restoration, grace, and fellowship with God.**

Zerubbabel was born and raised in Babylon. Later, he became the leader of the return from the Babylonian exile. Throughout these events, he always longed for fellowship with God to be restored and probably named his children seeking God's grace.

The meanings of their names are as follows:

① Meshullam (מְשֻׁלָּם) – friend, fellowship, recovery, reward
② Hananiah (חֲנַנְיָה) – God has favored
③ Shelomith (שְׁלֹמִית) – peaceful
④ Hashubah (חֲשֻׁבָה) – consider, think deeply
⑤ Ohel (אֹהֶל) – tent
⑥ Berechiah (בֶּרֶכְיָה) – the Lord blesses
⑦ Hasadiah (חֲסַדְיָה) – the Lord is kind (goodness of the Lord)
⑧ Jushab-hesed (יוּשַׁב חֶסֶד) – love (grace) will be restored

The meaning of the youngest son's name *Jushab-hesed* is "grace is restored" or "whose love returns." Zerubbabel probably named his youngest son with gratitude toward the grace and love of God who allowed them to return from exile.

**THIRD, Zerubbabel's children are divided into two groups.**

It is uncertain why five children are grouped separately out of the seven sons and one daughter (1 Chr 3:20). However, it can be presumed that the five children had a different mother from the other three—Meshullam, Hananiah, and Shelomith (daughter)—mentioned in the beginning. This would be in accordance with the custom of differentiating people in genealogies when the mothers are different (1 Chr 2:19, 21-24; 3:1-9; 4:5-7).

**FOURTH, Abihud is excluded from this list.**

Zerubbabel had seven sons (1 Chr 3:19-20), but strangely Abihud (Matt 1:13) is not listed as one of the sons. This issue will be discussed in detail in chapter 4 of this book. Clearly, many generations were omitted between Zerubbabel and Abihud, and this reflects God's administration of redemption that is incomprehensible to human reason.

## 2. The name *Abihud* means "father of glory" or "father of majesty."

The name *Abihud* is a combination of the words אָב (*'āb*) and הוֹד (*hôd*), and we must pay special attention to the word *hôd*. This word means "glory," "majesty," and "splendor." It is noteworthy that this word was used to describe the act of glorifying God after the temple was completed.

Zechariah 6:13 states, "Even he shall build the temple of the Lord; and he shall bear the glory, and shall sit and rule upon his throne" (KJV). This message was given in a vision that Zechariah received five months after the reconstruction of the temple had resumed, on the twenty-fourth day of the eleventh month in the second year of King Darius (Zech 1:7).

Zechariah used this message to encourage the ongoing construction work and further proclaimed that Jesus Christ would complete the perfect temple and receive glory. The word *glory* used here was also הוֹד (*hôd*) in Hebrew. Thus, Abihud was probably a name given with earnest hope for the restoration of the Lord's glory.

All glory, honor, and majesty belong to God (Deut 5:24; 1 Chr 29:11; Jude 1:25). We have all been called to give glory, honor, and majesty to God (1 Cor 10:31; Rev 5:12-13). I pray that God is always the "Father of glory" and the "Father of majesty" in our lives.

# 5th Generation: Eliakim

> ## Eliakim / Ἐλιακίμ / אֶלְיָקִים
> God establishes, God raises up

**Order**
Fifth person in the third period of Jesus Christ's genealogy (Matt 1:13)

**Background**
Matthew 1:13 states, "...Abihud the father of **Eliakim**, and **Eliakim** the father of Azor."

**Remarks**
Eliakim's father believed that God is the One who erects what has collapsed and raises the one who has fallen. Thus, he probably named his son with the hope that God would also establish his son's future and raise him up.

The name *Eliakim* is אֶלְיָקִים (*'elyāqîm*) in Hebrew and Ἐλιακίμ (*Eliakim*) in Greek. It is a combination of the words אֵל (*'ēl*), meaning "God," and קוּם (*qûm*), meaning "rise," "raise," or "establish." Hence, the name means, "God establishes" or "God raises up."

## 1. There are three people with the name *Eliakim* in the Old Testament.

The name of Eliakim the son of Abihud does not appear among the descendants of Zerubbabel in 1 Chronicles 3. However, there are three other people with the name *Eliakim* in the Old Testament.

### (1) Eliakim the son of Hilkiah

This Eliakim was the head of the royal household during the reign of King Hezekiah, the thirteenth king of the southern kingdom of Judah. King Hezekiah had sent Eliakim to ask Prophet Isaiah to pray to God when the Assyrians attacked with a great army of 185,000 men (Isa 36:22; 37:1-2). Eliakim was a man of faith favored by the king and he liaised between the king and the prophet.

### (2) Eliakim the son of Josiah

Eliakim, the son of Josiah the sixteenth king of Judah, was actually King Jehoiakim. Pharaoh Neco of Egypt changed his name to Jehoiakim (2 Kgs 23:34; 2 Chr 36:4). He was Josiah's second son (1 Chr 3:15) and became the eighteenth king of Judah at the age of twenty-five; he reigned for eleven years (2 Kgs 23:36; 2 Chr 36:5). He killed Uriah, who spoke the Word of God (Jer 26:20-23) and burned the scrolls of God's Word (Jer 36:21-23). Second Kings 23:37 states that Jehoiakim "did evil in the sight of the LORD, according to all that his fathers had done" (2 Chr 36:5). Consequently, his life became wretched; he was bound with bronze chains and taken to Babylon (2 Chr 36:6).

### (3) Eliakim the priest

The city wall was also destroyed when Nebuchadnezzar king of Babylon besieged and toppled Jerusalem in 586 BC. The wall was restored later in 444 BC after the third return from the Babylonian exile. The people of Israel worked day and night under the extraordinary leadership of Nehemiah who led the third return from the exile and completed the restoration of the wall in just fifty-two days (Neh 4:6, 21-23; 6:15).

The Israelites held a dedication of the wall after it was completed, and Eliakim was one of the priests who participated in the ceremony (Neh 12:27, 41).

## 2. The name Eliakim is a confession that God had raised him up.

Zerubbabel was the leader who not only resumed the reconstruction of the temple that had been halted, but also saw its completion in 516 BC. This was truly the work of God and not of man. Zechariah 4:6 states, "This is the word of the LORD to Zerubbabel saying, 'Not by might nor by power, but by My Spirit,' says the LORD of hosts."

Eliakim's father must have named his son with the hope that God would raise up his son's life and take care of him to the end just as He had raised the temple again through Zerubbabel by His amazing providence. It is presumed that Eliakim's father lived through the Babylonian exile into the time of the Persian rule (539-331 BC). He acknowledged that the Almighty God is the only One who could raise Israel up from the oppressive world powers of the time. Hence, he hoped that his nation would be quickly restored by the absolute sovereign power of the mighty God. If Eliakim did not give up this hope throughout his entire life, then he would certainly have received the grace of God raising him up.

# 6th Generation: Azor

Azor / Ἀζώρ / עַזּוּר
Helpful, helper

**Order**
Sixth person in the third period of Jesus Christ's genealogy (Matt 1:13-14)

**Background**
Matthew 1:13-14 states, "...Eliakim the father of Azor. ¹⁴Azor was the father of Zadok ...."

**Remarks**
There is no special record regarding Azor in the Bible. His name means "helpful" or "helper."

The name *Azor* is עַזּוּר ('*azzûr*) in Hebrew and Ἀζώρ (*Azōr*) in Greek. The Hebrew word is derived from עָזַר ('*āzar*), meaning "to help," "to support," or "to protect."

## 1. There are three people with the name *Azor* in the Old Testament.

The name *Azor* in Matthew 1:13 is pronounced '*azzûr* (עַזּוּר) in Hebrew. The New American Standard Bible transliterates it as "Azzur," and this name is found in three places in the Bible.

### (1) Azzur the father of Hananiah, the false prophet of Gibeon
Jeremiah 28:1 states, "Now in the same year, in the beginning of the reign of Zedekiah king of Judah, in the fourth year, in the fifth month, Hananiah the son of Azzur, the prophet, who was from Gibeon, spoke to me in the house of the Lᴏʀᴅ in the presence of the priests and all the people, saying ...." Hananiah was a false prophet during the reign of King Zedekiah of Judah who opposed the true prophet Jeremiah. He made the false prophecy that God would break the yoke of the king of Babylon and bring the people as well as the vessels of the Lord's house

back from exile; and he died in the seventh month of that same year (Jer 28:17). Azzur was the father of this false prophet.

### (2) Azzur the father of Jaazaniah

Ezekiel 11:1-2 states, "Moreover, the Spirit lifted me up and brought me to the east gate of the LORD's house which faced eastward. And behold, there were twenty-five men at the entrance of the gate, and among them I saw Jaazaniah son of Azzur and Pelatiah son of Benaiah, leaders of the people. He said to me, 'Son of man, these are the men who devise iniquity and give evil advice in this city.'" According to this verse, Azzur was the father of Jaazaniah who devised iniquity and gave evil advice in this city.

### (3) Azzur, the one who placed his name on the sealed document of the covenant

In 444 BC, during the third return from the exile, the city wall of Jerusalem was restored under Nehemiah's leadership, and a spiritual revival in Israel led to the renewal of the covenant. At this time, the leaders stepped forward and placed their names on the sealed document as a sign of their commitment to obey the covenant (Neh 9:38; 10:1). Azzur was one of the names on the sealed document (Neh 10:17).

## 2. The name *Azor* means "helpful" or "a helper."

The name *Azor* or *Azzur* (עַזּוּר) means "helpful" or "a helper" in Hebrew. The name speaks of the hope that he would become a man of exceptional faith who can be of great help to God's work of redemption

Of the three men named Azzur in the Old Testament, Azzur the father of the false prophet Hananiah and Azzur the father of the wicked leader Jaazaniah were not helpful people to God, as is evident in their children's deeds. On the contrary, the other Azzur, who placed his name on the sealed document of the covenant, was helpful to God's work in keeping with the meaning of his name (Neh 10:17). Although they had the same name *Azzur*, some were helpful to God's work while some actually became hindrances.

Azor, the sixth in the fourteen generations of the third period in Jesus Christ's genealogy, was probably helpful to God's work. Likewise, when God gave Eve to Adam as his wife, He made her to be a suitable helper for

Adam (Gen 2:18). Apostle Paul likened the relationship between Adam and Eve to the relationship between Jesus Christ and the Church (Eph 5:31-32). If that is the case, then the Church has to become a suitable helper for Jesus Christ. When we reflect upon our own lives, do we see ourselves being helpful to God's work, or do we see ourselves hindering His work and even harming the Church, the body of Christ?

# 7th Generation: **Zadok**

> **Zadok / Σαδώκ / צָדוֹק**
>
> Righteous, righteousness, justice

**Order**
Seventh person in the third period of Jesus Christ's genealogy (Matt 1:14)

**Background**
Matthew 1:14 states, "Azor was the father of **Zadok**, **Zadok** the father of Achim . . . ."

**Remarks**
There is no special record regarding Zadok in the Bible. His name means "righteous," "righteousness," or "justice."

The name *Zadok* is צָדוֹק *(ṣādôq)* in Hebrew and Σαδώκ *(Sadōk)* in Greek. The Hebrew name צָדוֹק *(ṣādôq)* originates from the word צַדִּיק *(ṣaddîq)*, which means "righteous" and "just," and means "righteousness," "righteous," and "justice."

## 1. There are seven people with the name *Zadok* in the Old Testament.

### (1) Zadok the priest during the time of King David
Zadok served as priest along with Abiathar during the reign of King David (2 Sam 19:11; 20:25). It is known that he was Zadok the "young man mighty of valor" in 1 Chronicles 12:28 who later became a priest. His son was Ahimaaz (1 Chr 6:8).

### (2) There is another priest named Zadok.
First Chronicles 6:12 states, "Ahitub became the father of Zadok, and Zadok became the father of Shallum." Zadok in this verse was the priest who served during the period of the divided kingdom after the time of Solomon (1 Chr 6:10) and before the deportation to Babylon (1 Chr 6:15). Thus, this Zadok is different from Zadok in 1 Chronicles 6:8.

### (3) Zadok, the maternal grandfather of King Jotham of Judah

Second Chronicles 27:1 states, "Jotham was twenty-five years old when he became king, and he reigned sixteen years in Jerusalem. And his mother's name was Jerushah the daughter of Zadok" (2 Kgs 15:32-33). Since this Zadok was the maternal grandfather of King Jotham, the eleventh king of Judah, there is a possibility that he was the one who served as priest during the period of the divided kingdom as recorded in 1 Chronicles 6:12. This, however, is uncertain.

### (4) Zadok who participated in the reconstruction of the city wall

In 444 BC, the reconstruction of the fallen city wall was completed under Nehemiah's leadership, and "Zadok the son of Baana" was in the list of names of those who helped repair the northern wall (Neh 3:4).

### (5) There was another person named Zadok who participated in the rebuilding of the city wall.

Nehemiah 3:29 states, "After them Zadok the son of Immer carried out repairs in front of his house. And after him Shemaiah the son of Shecaniah, the keeper of the East Gate, carried out repairs." This Zadok made repairs on the eastern wall and was a descendant of the priestly family of Immer, who returned from the exile with Zerubbabel (Ezra 2:36-37).

### (6) Zadok who placed his seal on the document of the covenant after the completion of the city wall

In 444 BC, after the construction of the city wall was completed, the leaders of the people stepped forward and committed themselves to obeying the covenant and put their names on the sealed document; Zadok's name was also included (Neh 10:21).

Although it is uncertain, there is a possibility that this Zadok was the "Zadok the son of Baana," who participated in the repairs of the northern wall.

### (7) Zadok the scribe who was appointed over the chambers

Nehemiah chose one person from each of the priests, the scribes, the Levites, and the people of Israel. He then "appointed them over the chambers for the stores, the contributions, the first fruits and the tithes" to gather and distribute them (Neh 12:44-47). Zadok the scribe was among the list of people who were appointed (Neh 13:13).

## (2) The name *Zadok* means "righteous," "righteousness," or "justice."

God used every person named *Zadok* in the Old Testament in great ways. They were used for God's work as a priest, as a laborer for the rebuilding of the city wall, as one who placed his name on the sealed document as a sign of resolve to live according to God's covenant, and as one appointed to oversee the chambers for the stores and tithes.

The parents of Zadok—the seventh of the fourteen generations in the third period of Jesus Christ's genealogy—probably named their son "Zadok" with the hope that he would become like the others in the Old Testament with the same name.

Moreover, it was difficult to find a righteous person practicing justice during a spiritually dark era plagued by political conflict and chaos due to foreign powers. Thus, his name demonstrates the hope that people had in the coming Messiah—the "king who would execute justice and righteousness," the "righteous Branch of David" (Jer 23:5; 33:15). When the Messiah comes, His righteousness will go forth in Zion like brightness (Isa 62:1), and righteousness will be the foundation of His throne (Ps 89:14; 97:2).

The most righteous person on earth is one who has accepted Jesus Christ as Lord, who has been reborn with water and the Holy Spirit, and who lives by faith. Romans 3:22 states, "Even the righteousness of God through faith in Jesus Christ for all those who believe; for there is no distinction." The Scripture continues in Romans 3:24, stating, "Being justified as a gift by His grace through the redemption which is in Christ Jesus." At the end, the bride of the Lamb clothes herself in fine linen, bright and clean, and this linen is the righteous acts of the saints (Rev 19:8). The Greek word for "righteous acts" is δικαίωμα (*dikaiōma*), which means "an action that is right or just" and refers to the "righteousness" bestowed upon us when we believe in Jesus Christ.

The righteousness in us today was given to us through the atoning work of Jesus Christ on the cross (1 Cor 1:30; 6:11; 2 Cor 5:21). Each day we must rely only on Jesus Christ and strive to live as holy instruments who execute the righteousness of God like the people named Zadok in the Bible.

# 8th Generation: **Achim**

---

**Achim / Ἀχείμ / יוֹקִים**

The Lord establishes

---

**Order**
Eighth person in the third period of Jesus Christ's genealogy (Matt 1:14)

**Background**
Matthew 1:14 states, "...Zadok the father of **Achim**, and **Achim** the father of Eliud."

**Remarks**
There is no special record regarding Achim in the Bible. His name means, "the Lord will raise" or "the Lord establishes."

---

The name *Achim* is יוֹקִים (*yôqîm*) in Hebrew and Ἀχείμ (*Acheim*) in Greek. The Hebrew name יוֹקִים (*yôqîm*) is a combination of יָה (*yāh*), a shortened form of *Jehovah*, and the modified form of קוּם (*qûm*), meaning "rise," "raise," or "establish." Hence, the name means, "the Lord establishes."

## 1. There is one person with the name *Achim* (*Jokim*) in the Old Testament.

Jokim (יוֹקִים) appears as a descendant of Shelah, the third son born to Judah by Bath-shua the Canaanitess (1 Chr 2:3; 4:21-22). Jokim worked for the king as a potter. First Chronicles 4:23 states, "These were the potters and the inhabitants of Netaim and Gederah; they lived there with the king for his work." The word *lived* is יָשַׁב (*yāšab*) in Hebrew and means "to dwell" (for an extended period of time), "to stay," "to remain," or "to marry."

The expression "lived there with the king" does not mean that they actually lived with the king for an extended period of time. It means that they managed his land for a long time although they may have dwelt away from the king geographically. It appears that their hearts were always with the king and were acknowledged by the king for their faithfulness.

Wherever we may be working for the Lord today, if we have the faith that the King of kings is always with us, then we will be acknowledged by God and be able to manage that task until the end.

## 2. The name *Achim* (Jokim) means, "The Lord establishes."

Jokim, who appears once in the Old Testament, belongs to the tribe of Judah; and the father of Achim, who appears in the genealogy of Jesus Christ, is also from the tribe of Judah. It appears that there were cases where people of those times chose names for their children from among the names of their forefathers.

As Jokim worked as a potter (1 Chr 4:22-23), he probably realized and experienced that only God establishes our lives, as it is written, "But now, O LORD, You are our Father, we are the clay, and You our potter; and all of us are the work of Your hand" (Isa 64:8). The father of Achim in the genealogy of Jesus Christ probably also realized this and named his son *Achim* ("the Lord establishes") with the earnest hope that God would establish his son's life.

It is presumed that Achim lived during the period of the Greek rule (331–164 BC) in the intertestamental period. Unlike the Persian rulers who were religiously tolerant, the Greeks oppressed religion in their attempt to Hellenize Judah. If Achim lived according to the meaning of his name during times when there was no religious freedom, then he probably hoped earnestly that God would quickly establish the Messianic kingdom through Israel as God had covenanted with Abraham and David. Psalm 127:1-2 states, "Unless the Lord builds the house, they labor in vain who build it; unless the Lord guards the city, the watchman keeps awake in vain. It is vain for you to rise up early, to retire late, to eat the bread of painful labors." God is the beginning and the end of everything (Isa 44:6; 48:12; Rev 1:17; 2:8; 21:6; 22:13). If God does not begin something, establish it, and protect it to the end, then the result will lack substance and all will be in vain. Thus, when we live our lives entrusting everything to God from the beginning to the end without despairing in any difficult situation, then we will receive the blessing of God raising us up and establishing us, as well as our families, our churches, and our businesses.

# 9th Generation: **Eliud**

> **Eliud / 'Ελιούδ / אֱלִיהוּד**
>
> God is my glory, God of majesty

**Order**
Ninth person in the third period of Jesus Christ's genealogy (Matt 1:14-15)

**Background**
Matthew 1:14-15 states, "...Achim the father of **Eliud**. ¹⁵**Eliud** was the father of Eleazar ..."

**Remarks**
There is no special record regarding Eliud in the Bible. His name means "God is my glory" or "God of majesty."

The name *Eliud* is אֱלִיהוּד (*'ĕlîhûd*) in Hebrew and 'Ελιούδ (*Elioud*) in Greek. The Hebrew name אֱלִיהוּד (*'ĕlîhûd*) is composed of אֵל (*'ēl*), meaning "God," and הוֹד (*hôd*), meaning "splendor," "majesty," or "glory." Hence, the name means "God is my glory" or "God of majesty."

The word הוֹד (*hôd*) was used twenty-four times in the Old Testament, and it was mainly used to describe God's glory and majesty.

## 1. The name *Eliud* conveys God's glory.

The word הוֹד (*hôd*), which is a part of the name *Eliud*, was used to describe God's glory.

> **Psalm 8:1** O LORD, our Lord, How majestic is Your name in all the earth, who have displayed Your splendor (הוֹדְךָ, *hôdĕkā*) above the heavens!
>
> **Psalm 148:13** Let them praise the name of the LORD, For His name alone is exalted; His glory (הוֹדוֹ, *hôdô*) is above earth and heaven.

The psalmist declares that the glory of God fills the universe and all creation and that His glory is most splendid, surpassing all other glories in the world.

Although Eliud's parents had to endure the pain of living during a time when they could not worship in the temple, they must have still hoped for the day when God's glory would be revealed. Thus, they probably named their son *Eliud* with the hope that he would live to reveal that glory. Eliud himself probably lived his life without forgetting about God's glory. Whether we eat or drink, we should live for the glory of God (1 Cor 10:31).

## 2. The name *Eliud* conveys God's splendor and majesty.

The word הוֹד (*hôd*), which is a part of the name *Eliud*, was used to describe God's majesty.

> **1 Chronicles 29:11** Yours, O LORD, is the greatness and the power and the glory (וְהַהוֹד, *wĕhahôd*) and the victory and the majesty, indeed everything that is in the heavens and the earth; Yours is the dominion, O LORD, and You exalt Yourself as head over all.
>
> **Job 37:22** Out of the north comes golden splendor; around God is awesome majesty (הוֹד, *hôd*).

A general definition of *majesty* is "supreme greatness or authority." Biblically, however, the word is used to refer to holy fear, splendor, authority, and honor that only God possesses and man dare not approach (Ps 21:5; 145:5). This is reminiscent of the great glory manifested in the form of the cloud that had filled the temple of Solomon during its dedication; the glory-cloud had prevented the priests from entering the temple and from serving in it (1 Kgs 8:11; 2 Chr 7:1-3). Psalm 96:6 states, "Splendor and majesty are before Him, strength and beauty are in His sanctuary."

If Eliud lived according to the meaning of his name, then he probably hoped for the swift restoration of the glorious temple. He would have also stood attentively before God's fearful sovereignty and honor with renewed resolution day by day.

What is the image of a true believer who experiences God's glory and majesty day by day? It is that of a person who gives thanks and praises to God each day. Psalm 104:1 states, "Bless the LORD, O my soul! O LORD my God, You are very great; You are clothed with splendor (הוֹד, *hôd*) and majesty." David also, after proclaiming God's glory and majesty in 1 Chronicles 29:11, confesses in verse 13, "Now therefore, our God, we thank You, and praise Your glorious name." I pray that thanksgiving and praises may also overflow from our lips today and that we may live a life that exalts the splendid glory and majesty of God.

# 10th Generation: Eleazar

---

**Eleazar / Ἐλεάζαρ / אֶלְעָזָר**
God has helped, helped by God

---

**Order**
Tenth person in the third period of Jesus Christ's genealogy (Matt 1:15)

**Background**
Matthew 1:15 states, "Eliud was the father of **Eleazar**, **Eleazar** the father of Matthan . . . . "

**Remarks**
There is no special record regarding Eleazar in the Bible. His name means "God has helped."

---

The name *Eleazar* is אֶלְעָזָר (*'el'āzār*) in Hebrew and Ἐλεάζαρ (*Eleazar*) in Greek. The Hebrew name אֶלְעָזָר (*'el'āzār*) is a combination of אֵל (*'ēl*), meaning "God," and עָזַר (*'āzar*), meaning "to help," "to support," or "to aid." Hence, the name means "God has helped" or "helped by God."

## 1. There are six people with the name *Eleazar* in the Old Testament.

### (1) Aaron's son Eleazar
Eleazar was born to Aaron and Elisheba (Exod 6:23). He was originally the third son, but became Aaron's successor (Num 20:25-28) when his older brothers, Nadab and Abihu, died as a result of offering strange fire before the Lord which God had not commanded them (Lev 10:1-2). Upon entering the land of Canaan, Eleazar, along with Joshua and the heads of the households of the tribes of Israel, apportioned the land to the sons of Israel (Josh 14:1; 17:4; 19:51).

### (2) Abinadab's son Eleazar
The ark of the Lord, taken by the Philistines, was in the land of the Philistines for seven months before it was returned to Beth-shemesh (1 Sam 6:1-16). However, God struck the people of Beth-shemesh with a great

slaughter because they had looked into the ark of the Lord (1 Sam 6:19). The people of Beth-shemesh became fearful of the ark and requested that the ark be moved to Kiriath-jearim. Thus, the people of Kiriath-jearim came and took the ark with them (1 Sam 6:20-21). It was at this time that the people of Kiriath-jearim consecrated Eleazar, Abinadab's son, to keep the ark of the Lord (1 Sam 7:1).

### (3) King David's mighty man Eleazar

Eleazar was one of the thirty chief men who supported David in laying a strong foundation for Israel. He was one of the three mighty men who were the heads of the thirty (2 Sam 23:9-10; 1 Chr 11:10-14). His father was Dodo the Ahohite (2 Sam 23:9; 1 Chr 11:12).

The three mighty men—Jashobeam, Eleazar, and Shammah—fought alongside David when the Philistines gathered to battle, but the men of Israel withdrew in fear (2 Sam 23:9). It was Eleazar who "arose and struck the Philistines until his hand was weary and clung to the sword" (2 Sam 23:10). He was a courageous man who used his last ounce of strength to fight with his sword to the end. The Lord gave them great victory on that day, and the people who had fled followed him from behind for the plunder (2 Sam 23:10).

Eleazar was also with David at Pasdammim when the Philistines gathered there to battle (1 Chr 11:12-13). Even though the people had fled before the Philistines, Eleazar and the other men bravely fought against the Philistines and accomplished the splendid feat of striking them down. This was the work of God, giving "great victory" to Israel (1 Chr 11:14).

Eleazar was one of the "three of the thirty chief men" who went down to the well of Bethlehem by the gate to draw water (2 Sam 23:13-19; 1 Chr 11:15-21). While David was fighting against the Philistines who were camping in the valley of Rephaim, he had a craving for water and said, "Oh that someone would give me water to drink from the well of Bethlehem which is by the gate!" (2 Sam 23:15; 1 Chr 11:17). At this time, the three mighty men among the thirty chief men did not delay in breaking through the camp of the Philistines (2 Sam 23:16; 1 Chr 11:18) and drew water from the well of Bethlehem for David. When David received this water, he said that it was the blood that contained the lives of the three men and poured it all out to the Lord without drinking a drop of it (2 Sam 23:17; 1 Chr 11:19). This was because the water contained the wholehearted devotion, sweat, and tears that the three mighty men (including Eleazar) had shed without the knowledge of others. It contained their faithfulness that did not fear risking their lives.

God does not need a spectator or an eloquent speaker, whose words substitute action. God needs a worker who will exalt Christ in his body whether by life or by death (Phil 1:20-21). What is required of a steward is trustworthiness (1 Cor 4:1-2). One's wholehearted faithfulness and devotion are the holy and living sacrifice acceptable to God (Rom 12:1).

### (4) Mahli's son Eleazar
During Solomon's time, Mahli from the tribe of Levi had two sons, Eleazar and Kish. When Eleazar died without having any sons but only daughters, the sons of their uncle Kish married the daughters so that they may preserve their father's lineage (1 Chr 23:21-22; 24:28, Ref Num 27:1-11; 36:5-12).

### (5) Phinehas' son Eleazar
This Eleazar was one of the people who weighed, numbered, and recorded all the silver, gold, and utensils offered for the house of God when Ezra entrusted them to the hands of Meremoth, the son of Uriah the priest, after the second return from the Babylonian exile (Ezra 8:33-34). The two Levites who assisted Eleazar in this duty were Jozabad (יוֹזָבָד, the Lord has bestowed) the son of Jeshua, and Noadiah (נוֹעַדְיָה, meeting with the Lord) the son of Binnui (Ezra 8:33b).

He is also known to be the same Eleazar who participated when Nehemiah dedicated the city wall after it was rebuilt (Neh 12:27, 42).

### (6) Parosh's son Eleazar
After the second return from the Babylonian exile, Ezra commanded everyone who married foreign wives to confess their sins and separate themselves from their wives. They all replied in a loud voice that they would obey. Eleazar's name was included in the list of men who had married foreign wives (Ezra 10:25).

## 2. The name *Eleazar* means "God has helped."

Most of the people named *Eleazar* in the Old Testament were priests, Levites, or mighty men of God.

Aaron's heir, Eleazar, succeeded Aaron as high priest after his death and became a great leader who led the Israelites into Canaan along with Joshua. Furthermore, his son Phinehas struck Zimri, the leader of the Simeonites, and Cozbi, the Midianite woman, when they committed adultery in Moab, thereby turning away God's wrath (Num 25:6-15). The plague upon Israel was checked after Phinehas killed the two people who committed adultery (Num 25:8). It was after this incident that God made the covenant of a perpetual priesthood with Phinehas and his descendants (Num 25:13). Through this covenant, the lineage of Eleazar and Phinehas succeeded the priesthood almost exclusively.

The name *Eleazar* was probably widely known among the Israelites even around the time when the Eleazar in the genealogy of Jesus Christ was born. His parents probably hoped that their son would become a great son of faith just like the *Eleazars* from the time of Moses and the time of David. They must have hoped that God would help their son in his life. As the world becomes increasingly darker, believers must earnestly ask for God's help. All the help in our lives comes from God (Ps 33:20; 46:1; 115:9-11; 121:1-2; 124:8). "Blessed is he whose help is the God of Jacob and whose hope is in the Lord" (Ps 146:5).

# 11th Generation: **Matthan**

> **Matthan / Ματθάν / מַתָּן**
> Gift, offering

**Order**
Eleventh person in the third period of Jesus Christ's genealogy (Matt 1:15)

**Background**
Matthew 1:15 states, ". . . Eleazar the father of **Matthan**, and **Matthan** the father of Jacob."

**Remarks**
There is no special record regarding Matthan in the Bible. His name means "gift."

The name *Matthan* is מַתָּן (*mattān*) in Hebrew and Ματθάν (*Matthan*) in Greek. The name means "gift" and is derived from נָתַן (*nātan*), which means "to give," "to offer," "to put," or "to place."

## 1. There are two people with the name *Matthan* in the Old Testament.

### (1) Matthan, the high priest of Baal

Athaliah was the daughter born to King Ahab of Israel and Jezebel. She married Jehoram of Judah (2 Kgs 8:18; 2 Chr 21:6). Later, when both her husband King Jehoram and her son King Ahaziah died, she killed all the descendants of the king and made herself king of Judah. "She destroyed all the royal offspring" (2 Kgs 11:1; 2 Chr 22:10), raised up priests for Baal, and led the worship of idols. Hence, Jehoiada the priest killed Athaliah and set Joash, the son of Ahaziah, as king. Matthan, the priest of Baal, was also killed at this time (2 Kgs 11:18; 2 Chr 23:17).

### (2) Matthan, the father of Shephatiah

During the reign of King Zedekiah, the officials who adopted anti-Babylonian policies threw Prophet Jeremiah into a deep cistern in the court of the guardhouse because he, in obedience to God's command, urged the people to surrender to Babylon. Shephatiah the son of Matthan was one of these officials (Jer 38:1-6).

## 2. The name *Matthan* means "gift."

The era of the Maccabean Revolution (167–142 BC) was a time of continuous tumult as the fight for independence continued from the time of Mattathias[20] until the generation of his sons. They fought amidst severe oppression under the rule of Antiochus IV (Epiphanes) of the Seleucid Dynasty.

The name *Matthan*, like the name of Mattathias who led the Maccabean Revolution, means "gift" and indicates the longing for God's gift in the form of total independence for the nation and the emergence of the Messianic kingdom. There are also names that mean "God's gift" in the Lukan genealogy of Jesus Christ: Matthat, Mattathias (two people), Matthat, and Mattatha (Luke 3:24, 25, 26, 29, 31). God's true gift is only One, Jesus Christ the Messiah, who will bring the news of salvation (John 4:10a; Rom 5:15; Eph 2:8).

Matthan's father probably named his son Matthan (gift) because he regarded his child as a gift from God (Ps 127:3). He must have further hoped that his son would live his life worthy of God's grace. If Matthan was a person who lived up to his father's hope, then he probably lived his life giving thanks to God for His grace.

The fact that God has allowed us to be born on this earth is a gift in itself. There is no one who can be born on this earth without the grace of God. The food and drink that we consume on this earth are also considered God's gift (Exod 23:25). Ecclesiastes 3:13 states, "Moreover, that every man who eats and drinks sees good in all his labor—it is the gift of God." Furthermore, God gives us riches and wealth and empowers us to eat from them and to receive our reward and rejoice in our labor. These are all God's gift to us (Ecc 5:19).

Our faith in God is also God's gift (Eph 2:8), and the fact that we have been made ministers of the Gospel to labor for Him is a gift of God's grace (Eph 3:7). For this reason, Apostle Paul confessed, "But by the grace of God I am what I am, and His grace toward me did not prove vain; but I labored even more than all of them, yet not I, but the grace of God with me" (1 Cor 15:10).

We must confess that "every perfect gift" comes from the Father of lights (Jas 1:17) and live our lives seeking the grace of God our Father today.

# 12th Generation: Jacob

---

**Jacob / Ἰακώβ / יַעֲקֹב**

One who takes by the heel, one who supplants

---

**Order**
Twelfth person in the third period of Jesus Christ's genealogy (Matt 1:15-16)

**Background**
Matthew 1:15-16 states, "... Matthan the father of **Jacob**. ¹⁶**Jacob** was the father of Joseph the husband of Mary, by whom Jesus was born, who is called the Messiah."

**Remarks**
According to the Matthean genealogy of Jesus Christ, Jacob was Jesus' grandfather. There is no other special record regarding Jacob. His name means "one who takes by the heel" or "one who supplants."

---

*Jacob*, Jesus' grandfather according to the genealogy of Jesus Christ, is יַעֲקֹב (*ya'ăqōb*) in Hebrew and Ἰακώβ (*Iakōb*) in Greek. The Hebrew name יַעֲקֹב (*ya'ăqōb*) is derived from עָקַב (*'āqab*), which means "to take by the heel" or "to supplant." Thus, the name means "one who takes by the heel" or "one who supplants."

## 1. There is one person with the name *Jacob* in the Old Testament.

The Jacob in the Old Testament is Abraham's grandson and Isaac's son. God acknowledged the faith of the three generations of Abraham, Isaac, and Jacob. Regarding them, God said, "I am the God of Abraham, the God of Isaac, and the God of Jacob" (Exod 3:6, 15; 4:5; Matt 22:32; Mark 12:26; Luke 20:37).

Before his death, Jacob called Joseph's two sons, Ephraim and Manasseh, and placed them in the order of his own sons (Gen 48:5-6). It is not easy to understand why Jacob adopted his two grandsons when he already had twelve sons of his own. However, it was through this episode that Jacob blessed Joseph with the blessing of the firstborn.

According to the law, the firstborn receives a double portion of bless-ings (Deut 21:15-17). Since Joseph's two sons became two independent tribes of Ephraim and Manasseh, in essence they became Joseph's double portion of blessings (1 Chr 5:1-2; Ezek 47:13). Thus, by God's sovereign power, Joseph received the greatest blessing among all the people of Israel.

The Jacob and Joseph in the genealogy of Jesus Christ received the greatest blessing of their time by being recorded as the grandfather and father of Jesus Christ in Matthew 1:16. The relationship between Jacob and Joseph of the Old Testament and of the New Testament seems to have similarities that cannot be overlooked.

## 2. The genealogy in the Gospel of Luke lists *Eli* instead of *Jacob*.

Matthew 1:16 states, "Jacob was the father of Joseph the husband of Mary" while Luke 3:23 states " . . . the son of Joseph, the son of Eli." The Gospel of Matthew records Jacob as Joseph's father while the Gospel of Luke records Eli as Joseph's father. How should this discrepancy be resolved?

The most persuasive answer to this question is that Joseph, who be-came Eli's son-in-law by marrying Mary, legally succeeded his genealogy. According to the Old Testament laws, if a man does not have a son, his inheritance must be given to his daughters. In this case, the daughters must marry men from their own tribe in order to protect their inheritance (Num 27:1-8; 36:1-12).

In Mary's case, she received her father Eli's inheritance because he had no son; and when she married Joseph from the same tribe, he be-came Eli's legal successor and son. The Talmud states that Mary was Eli's daughter, and the Sinaitic-Syriac Manuscripts render Luke 2:4 as follows: "They [both Joseph and Mary] were of the house and lineage of David," thus revealing that Mary was also from the tribe of Judah.[21] Therefore, the view that Matthew recorded the line of Joseph and Luke recorded the line of Mary is most consistent with the content of each Gospel.[22]

It was totally by God's sovereign providence that Jacob received the blessing of becoming the grandfather of Jesus Christ. The name *Jacob* means "one who takes by the heel," "one who deceives," or "one who supplants." Although the name has negative connotations—"one who deceives" or "one who supplants"—it can also connote a positive meaning of someone who obtains blessings through a proactive faith. Even though we were like Jacob in a negative sense, our lives can change and take on the positive meaning of his name when we believe in God and totally rely on Him.

# 13th Generation: Joseph

Joseph / Ἰωσὴφ / יוֹסֵף
The Lord increases, the Lord adds on

**Order**
Thirteenth person in the third period of Jesus Christ's genealogy (Matt 1:16)

**Background**
Matthew 1:16 states, "Jacob was the father of **Joseph** the husband of **Mary**, by whom Jesus was born, who is called the Messiah." Joseph was Jacob's son and Jesus Christ was the Son of Joseph according to the genealogy.

**Remarks**
Joseph emerges as the father of Jesus Christ according to the genealogies of Jesus Christ in the Gospel of Matthew and the Gospel of Luke.

The name *Joseph* is יוֹסֵף (*yôsēp*) in Hebrew and Ἰωσὴφ (*Iōsēph*) in Greek. The Hebrew name יוֹסֵף (*yôsēp*) means "the Lord increases" or "the Lord adds on." It originates from the word יָסַף (*yāsap*), which means "to add," "to increase," "to do again/more," or "he will add on."

Matthew 1:19 states, "And Joseph her husband, being a righteous man." What were the characteristics of Joseph's faith that he was called a righteous man?

## 1. Joseph planned to send Mary away secretly.

According to Jewish tradition, a man and a woman are engaged for about one year before they are officially married and can live together. Mary, who was engaged to Joseph, conceived by the Holy Spirit even before they were married and her belly began to swell (Matt 1:18). Joseph was probably greatly shocked by this unimaginable event and spent many days in agony.

Although he had ultimately decided to break off the engagement, he wanted to put Mary away secretly without publicly revealing her pregnancy, because he deeply loved her (Matt 1:19). Here, the word *secretly* is λάθρα (*lathra*) in Greek and means "without others being aware."

Joseph decided to act this way because Mary would be stoned to death according to the law if her pregnancy became known (Deut 22:23-24), and he wanted to protect her. Through Joseph's actions, God not only protected Mary but also Jesus Christ who was conceived in Mary by the Holy Spirit.

## 2. Joseph had "considered this" and then immediately obeyed the command of the angel of the Lord.

Matthew 1:20 states, "But when he considered this. . . ." The word *this*, ταῦτα (*tauta*) in Greek, is in the plural form meaning "these." It is evident that Joseph contemplated many things until he made the decision to put her away secretly.

The angel appeared to Joseph while he was considering the matter carefully and said, "Joseph, son of David, do not be afraid to take Mary as your wife; for the Child who has been conceived in her is of the Holy Spirit. She will bear a Son; and you shall call His name Jesus, for He will save His people from their sins" (Matt 1:20-21). When Joseph heard this, he obeyed and immediately brought Mary to him (Matt 1:24). From a human perspective, Mary's pregnancy was probably inconceivable since Joseph did not have any relations with her. However, he displayed righteous faith in God when he put aside all his human thoughts and completely obeyed God's Word after he received the revelation.

Matthew 1:25 states, "But kept her a virgin until she gave birth to a Son; and he called His name Jesus." The expression "kept her a virgin" is in the imperfect tense of the word γινώσκω (*ginōskō*) in Greek, meaning that Joseph and Mary did not have relations until Jesus was born. However, after Jesus was born, Mary had relations with Joseph and gave birth to His siblings (Matt 12:46; 13:55).

When Mary gave birth to a son, Joseph named Him *Jesus* (Matt 1:25). This was done in total obedience to the command of the angel of the Lord (Matt 1:21). Joseph was truly a righteous man who sacrificed himself for God's will, and his self-sacrifice became a precious instrument used for the fulfillment of God's administration of redemption. His obedience, however, did not come by his own will but by the grace of God. In keeping with the meaning of his name, "the Lord adds on," this was possible because of the grace added upon God's grace (Ref John 1:16).

# 14th Generation: Jesus

---

**Jesus / Ἰησοῦς / יֵשׁוּעַ**

The Lord saves, He who will save His people from their sins

---

**Order**
Fourteenth person in the third period of Jesus Christ's genealogy (Matt 1:16)

**Background**
Matthew 1:16 states, "Jacob was the father of Joseph the husband of **Mary**, by whom **Jesus** was born, who is called the Messiah." According to the genealogy, Jacob was Jesus' grandfather, and Joseph, His father.

**Remarks**
Jesus was conceived by the Holy Spirit and born through the body of the virgin Mary (Matt 1:18, 20, 23).

---

The name *Jesus* is יֵשׁוּעַ (*yēšûaʿ*) in Hebrew and Ἰησοῦς (*Iēsous*) in Greek. יֵשׁוּעַ (*yēšûaʿ*), meaning "The Lord saves," is a combination of יָהּ (*yāh*), which means "Jehovah," and יָשַׁע (*yāšaʿ*), which means "to save," "to deliver," or "to liberate." Matthew 1:21 states that the name means, "He will save His people from their sins."

## 1. Jesus was conceived by the Holy Spirit and born through the body of Mary.

Matthew 1:16 states, ". . . Mary, by whom Jesus was born, who is called the Messiah." According to the pattern that was repeated throughout the genealogy of Jesus Christ, this verse should read, "Joseph was the father of Jesus." However, Matthew 1:16 breaks from this pattern and records, ". . . Mary, by whom Jesus was born."

It is noteworthy that the expression "was the father of" (or "fathered") appears forty times in Matthew chapter 1. For thirty-nine out of the forty occurrences, it is in the active voice (ἐγέννησεν, *egennēsen*), while the last occurrence, in regard to Jesus, is in the passive voice (ἐγεννήθη, *egennēthē*). The sentence, "Jacob was the father of Joseph the husband of Mary, by whom Jesus was born," clearly reveals that it was by God's sovereign work that Jesus Christ was born through Mary and that it had nothing to do with Joseph's blood lineage or his will.

What is the reason for recording this in such a manner?

**FIRST, it reveals that Jesus was conceived by the Holy Spirit.**

Matthew 1:18 states, ". . . when His mother Mary had been betrothed to Joseph, before they came together she was found to be with child by the Holy Spirit." Matthew 1:20 also states, "Joseph, son of David, do not be afraid to take Mary as your wife; for the Child who had been conceived in her is of the Holy Spirit." Moreover, the angel said to Mary, "The Holy Spirit will come upon you, and the power of the Most High will overshadow you; and for that reason the holy Child shall be called the Son of God" (Luke 1:35).

Therefore, Jesus' birth was the result of the Almighty God's direct work. He was conceived by the Holy Spirit and born through the body of Mary, not as a result of physical relations between Joseph and Mary. As such, there is no biological relationship between Jesus and Joseph.

**SECOND, it reveals that Jesus came as the "seed of the woman."**

Genesis 3:15 states, "And I will put enmity between you and the woman, and between your seed and her seed; He shall bruise you on the head, and you shall bruise him on the heel." This is a covenant that the Messiah would come as a descendant of a woman and destroy Satan (1 John 3:8; Rev 12:9; 20:2). It was fulfilled when Jesus was born of a woman named Mary. Thus, Galatians 4:4 states, "But when the fullness of the time came, God sent forth His Son, born of a woman . . . ."

**THIRD, it reveals that Jesus was born of a virgin.**

Jesus' birth through the virgin Mary was a fulfillment of the prophecy in Isaiah 7:14 which states, "Therefore the Lord Himself will give you a sign: Behold, a virgin will be with child and bear a son, and she will call His name Immanuel." The word *virgin* in this verse is עַלְמָה (*'almâ*). In the Old Testament, it was used to refer to a young unmarried woman or a maiden (Gen 24:43 "maiden"; Exod 2:8 "girl"; Song 1:3 "maidens"; 6:8 "maidens"). Luke 1:27 also describes Mary as a "virgin"; the Greek word for *virgin*, παρθένος (*parthenos*), is used to refer to a mature woman who has never had relations with a man.

Jesus came into this world by being conceived by the Holy Spirit and born of the virgin Mary. This was the fulfillment of the Old Testament prophecy and God's mysterious providence that exceeds all human imagination.

## 2. Jesus is the Christ, the Messiah.

Matthew 1:16 states, ". . . by whom Jesus was born, who is called the Messiah." Jesus is the Christ. Christ in Greek is Χριστός (*Christos*) and means "anointed." In Hebrew, Christ is מָשִׁיחַ (*māšîaḥ*), meaning "Messiah." God anointed Jesus with the Holy Spirit and power (Acts 10:38; Ref Isa 61:1; Luke 4:18). In the Old Testament, three types of people were anointed.

### FIRST, kings were anointed.

A king was called "the Lord's anointed" (1 Sam 2:10; 2 Sam 1:14; Ps 2:2; 18:50; 45:7). King David also was anointed with oil by Prophet Samuel (1 Sam 16:13).

### SECOND, priests were anointed.

A priest was also called an "anointed priest" (Lev 4:3, 5, 16). Exodus 30:30 states, "You shall anoint Aaron and his sons, and consecrate them, that they may minister as priests to Me."

### THIRD, prophets were anointed.

Psalm 105:15 states, "Do not touch My anointed ones, and do My prophets no harm." Here, prophets are described as "My anointed ones."

Jesus is our King of kings (Rev 17:14; 19:16), our High Priest (Heb 2:17; 3:1; 4:14-15; 5:5, 10; 6:20; 7:21, 26-27; 8:1), and the true Prophet (Deut 18:15, 18; Matt 13:57; Luke 13:33; John 4:44; Acts 3:22-24). Thus, the appellation *Christ* shows that Jesus is the incarnate God who fulfills these three offices.

## 3. Jesus is the Savior who will save God's people from their sins.

When Mary conceived Jesus by the Holy Spirit, the angel of the Lord appeared to Joseph in a dream and commanded him, "She will bear a Son; and you shall call His name Jesus, for He will save His people from their sins" (Matt 1:21). The one who can bear the redemptive calling to save His people must first be a person who is without sin so that He can bear the sins of others (Luke 23:41, 47; Rom 8:3; 2 Cor 5:21; Heb 4:15; 7:26; 1 John 3:5). At the same time, He needs to be God who can save by accomplishing the perfect atonement (Rom 9:5; Phil 2:6; 1 John 5:20). Jesus possesses both perfect divinity and perfect humanity, thereby uniquely fulfilling both requirements (Rom 1:3-4).

For this reason, Apostle John wrote of Jesus' birth, "And the Word became flesh, and dwelt among us, and we saw His glory, glory as of the only begotten from the Father, full of grace and truth" (John 1:14). The Greek word for *flesh* is σάρξ (*sarx*) and means "body," "physical body," and "flesh." He became man just like us. He is the Word from the beginning (John 1:1), the Word that was with God (John 1:1-2), and the Word that was God (John 1:1). He is also the Word that created all things (John 1:3), the Word of light, and the Word of life that shines upon all men (John 1:4); and this Word became flesh and dwelt among us as *Immanuel* (Matt 1:23).

The Word became flesh in order to do away with sin and resolve the issue of death. Sin is the cause of pain and death in humankind, for the wages of sin is death (Rom 6:23). Jesus has been manifested once at the consummation of ages in order to put away our sins (Heb 9:26). First John 3:5 also states that He appeared in order to take away our sins. Also, the devil holds the power of death, and Jesus came to destroy the works of the devil (1 John 3:8). Hebrews 2:14-16 explains that He appeared in order to "render powerless him who had the power of death, that is, the devil"; to "free those who through fear of death were subject to slavery all their lives"; and to give "help to the descendant of Abraham." That is why He made propitiation for the sins of the people (Heb 2:17) and gave His life as a ransom for many (Matt 20:28; Mark 10:45). "Ransom" is a payment made by a person to liberate the slave whom he has purchased (1 Tim 2:6; Ref Exod 30:11-16). Jesus, being without sin, bore the cross on behalf of those who rightly deserved punishment for their sins. Thus, we have been redeemed and forgiven by the precious blood that Jesus shed on the cross (Eph 1:7; Col 1:14; 1 Pet 1:18-19; Rev 1:5).

There is no other name besides Jesus by which we must be saved (Acts 4:12). We must receive Jesus in order to become children of God and receive eternal life without perishing (John 1:12; 3:16). Only Jesus Christ is the perfect Son of man, the Son of the Most High (Luke 1:32, 35), the only Redeemer who saves His chosen saints (John 14:6), and God the Son who is with us eternally (Matt 1:23; John 1:14, 18; Ref John 10:30; 14:9; Phil 2:6-7; Heb 1:3). Hallelujah!

# PART FOUR

# The Genealogy of Jesus Christ: Gaps in the Third Period

# The Genealogy of Jesus Christ:
## Gaps in the Third Period

Unlike actual history, the third period of Jesus Christ's genealogy in the first chapter of Matthew omits the records of three kings—Jehoahaz, Jehoiakim, and Zedekiah. They were brothers, and all three kings disobeyed God's Word.

The record in Matthew 1:11 appears as though Josiah begot Jeconiah (Jehoiachin, 2 Kgs 24:6; 2 Chr 36:8), but Jeconiah's father was actually Jehoiakim, and Josiah was his grandfather (1 Chr 3:15-16).

| Actual history (2 Chr 36:1-11) | Josiah | Jehoahaz (3 months) 2 Kgs 23:31 2 Chr 36:2 | Jehoiakim (11 years) 2 Kgs 23:36 2 Chr 36:5 | Jehoiachin (3 months 10 days) 2 Kgs 24:8 2 Chr 36:9 | Zedekiah (11 years) 2 Kgs 24:18 2 Chr 36:11 |
|---|---|---|---|---|---|
| Matthean genealogy (Matt 1:11-12) | Josiah | ——— No record ——→ | | Jeconiah (Jehoiachin) | — No record→ |

In addition, there are generations omitted between Zerubbabel and Abihud in the third period of Jesus Christ's genealogy (Matt 1:13). There are omitted generations also between Abihud and Jesus Christ. Clearly, the genealogy of Jesus Christ is not a genealogy according to the flesh, the purpose of which is to record every generation without omission. Jesus' genealogy is a covenantal genealogy that reveals God's administration in the history of redemption. The following three chapters will closely examine the omissions in the third period of Jesus Christ's genealogy.

Excursus 3

# The 42 Generations in the Genealogy of Jesus Christ at a Glance

**Matt 1:17** Therefore all the generations from Abraham to David are fourteen generations; and from David to the deportation to Babylon fourteen generations; and from the deportation to Babylon to the time of Christ fourteen generations.

Πᾶσαι οὖν αἱ γενεαὶ ἀπὸ ᾽Αβραὰμ ἕως Δαυὶδ γενεαὶ δεκατέσσαρες, καὶ ἀπὸ Δαυὶδ ἕως τῆς μετοικεσίας Βαβυλῶνος γενεαὶ δεκατέσσαρες, καὶ ἀπὸ τῆς μετοικεσίας Βαβυλῶνος ἕως τοῦ Χριστοῦ γενεαὶ δεκατέσσαρες.

| The First Period (1,163 years) | | |
|---|---|---|
| | THE GENEALOGY IN MATTHEW I (14 GENERATIONS FROM ABRAHAM TO DAVID) | THE GENEALOGY IN LUKE 3 (14 GENERATIONS OF THE CORRESPONDING TIME PERIOD) |
| **Period of the Patriarchs** | 1 **Abraham** / אַבְרָהָם / ᾽Αβραάμ (Matt 1:2; 1 Chr 1:27, 34) | 1 Abraham / ᾽Αβραάμ (Luke 3:34) |
| | 2 **Isaac** / יִצְחָק / ᾽Ισαάκ (Matt 1:2; 1 Chr 1:28, 34) | 2 Isaac / ᾽Ισαάκ (Luke 3:34) |
| | 3 **Jacob** / יַעֲקֹב / ᾽Ιακώβ (Matt 1:2; 1 Chr 1:34; 2:1) | 3 Jacob / ᾽Ιακώβ (Luke 3:34) |
| | 4 **Judah** / יְהוּדָה / ᾽Ιούδας (Matt 1:2-3; 1 Chr 2:1) | 4 Judah / ᾽Ιούδας (Luke 3:33) |
| | **By Tamar (Matt 1:3)** | |
| | 5 **Perez** / פֶּרֶץ / Φαρές (Matt 1:3; 1 Chr 2:4; Ruth 4:18) | 5 Perez / Φαρές (Luke 3:33) |
| **Period in Egypt** | 6 **Hezron** / חֶצְרוֹן / ᾽Εσρώμ (Matt 1:3; 1 Chr 2:5; Ruth 4:18-19) | 6 Hezron / ᾽Εσρώμ (Luke 3:33) |
| | 7 **Ram** / רָם / ᾽Αράμ (Matt 1:3-4; 1 Chr 2:9-10; Ruth 4:19) | 7 Ram / ᾽Αράμ (Luke 3:33) Arni (ASV, RSV) |
| | 8 **Amminadab** / עַמִּינָדָב / ᾽Αμιναδάβ (Matt 1:4; 1 Chr 2:10; Ruth 4:19-20) | 8 Amminadab / ᾽Αμιναδάβ (Luke 3:33) |
| Period of the Wilderness Journey and the Conquest of Canaan | 9 **Nahshon** / נַחְשׁוֹן / Ναασσών (Matt 1:4; 1 Chr 2:10-11; Ruth 4:20) | 9 Nahshon / Ναασσών (Luke 3:32) |
| | 10 **Salmon** / שַׂלְמוֹן / Σαλμών (Matt 1:4-5; 1 Chr 2:11; Ruth 4:20-21) | 10 Salmon / Σαλμών (Luke 3:32) |
| **Period of the Judges** | **By Rahab (Matt 1:5)** | |
| | 11 **Boaz** / בֹּעַז / Βοός (Matt 1:5; 1 Chr 2:11-12; Ruth 4:21) | 11 Boaz / Βοός (Luke 3:32) |
| | **By Ruth (Matt 1:5)** | |
| | 12 **Obed** / עוֹבֵד / ᾽Ωβήδ (Matt 1:5; 1 Chr 2:12; Ruth 4:21-22) | 12 Obed / ᾽Ωβήδ (Luke 3:32) |
| | 13 **Jesse** / יִשַׁי / ᾽Ιεσσαί (Matt 1:5-6; 1 Chr 2:12-13; Ruth 4:22) | 13 Jesse / ᾽Ιεσσαι (Luke 3:32) |
| **Period of the United Monarchy** | 14 **King David** / מֶלֶךְ דָּוִד / Δαβίδ Βασιλεύς (Matt 1:6; 1 Chr 2:15; Ruth 4:22) | 14 David / Δαβίδ Βασιλεύς (Luke 3:31) |

*The first and the second periods of the genealogy are distinguished by the two different periods of David's reign—7 years and 6 months in Hebron and 33 years in Jerusalem (2 Sam 5:4-5; 1 Chr 3:4; 29:27; 1 Kgs 2:11).

| The Second Period (406 years) | |
|---|---|
| THE GENEALOGY IN MATTHEW 1 (14 GENERATIONS OF KINGS FROM DAVID TO THE DEPORTATION TO BABYLON) | THE GENEALOGY IN LUKE 3 (14 GENERATIONS OF THE CORRESPONDING TIME PERIOD) |

| | Matthew 1 | | Luke 3 |
|---|---|---|---|
| **Period of the United Monarchy** | 1 | David / דָּוִד / Δαβίδ (Matt 1:6; 1 Chr 2:15; Ruth 4:22) | |
| | **By the wife of Uriah (Matt 1:6)** | | |
| | 2 | Solomon / שְׁלֹמֹה / Σολομών (Matt 1:6-7; 1 Chr 3:5) | 15 Nathan / Ναθάν (Luke 3:31) |
| | 3 | Rehoboam / רְחַבְעָם / 'Ροβοάμ (Matt 1:7; 1 Chr 3:10) | 16 Mattatha / Ματταθά (Luke 3:31) |
| | 4 | Abijah / אֲבִיָּה / 'Αβιά (Matt 1:7; 1 Chr 3:10) | 17 Menna / Μεννά (Luke 3:31) |
| | 5 | Asa / אָסָא / 'Ασά (Matt 1:7-8; 1 Chr 3:10) | 18 Melea / Μελεᾶ (Luke 3:31) |
| | 6 | Jehoshaphat / יְהוֹשָׁפָט / 'Ιωσαφάτ (Matt 1:8; 1 Chr 3:10) | 19 Eliakim / 'Ελιακείμ (Luke 3:30) |
| **Period of the Divided Monarchy** | 7 | Joram / יוֹרָם / 'Ιωράμ (Matt 1:8; 1 Chr 3:11) | 20 Jonam / 'Ιωνάν (Luke 3:30) |
| | **Kings omitted from the genealogy** | | 21 Joseph / 'Ιωσήφ (Luke 3:30) |
| | Ahaziah / אֲחַזְיָה (1 Chr 3:11) Athaliah / עֲתַלְיָה (2 Kgs 11:1-3; 2 Chr 22:12) Joash / יוֹאָשׁ (1 Chr 3:11) Amaziah / אֲמַצְיָה (1 Chr 3:12) | | 22 Judah / 'Ιούδας (Luke 3:30) |
| | | | 23 Simeon / Συμεών (Luke 3:30) |
| | 8 | Uzziah (Azariah) / עֻזִּיָּה / 'Οζίας (Matt 1:8-9; 1 Chr 3:12) | 24 Levi / Λευί (Luke 3:29) |
| | 9 | Jotham / יוֹתָם / 'Ιωθάμ (Matt 1:9; 1 Chr 3:12) | 25 Matthat / Ματθάτ (Luke 3:29) |
| | 10 | Ahaz / אָחָז / 'Αχάζ (Matt 1:9; 1 Chr 3:13) | |
| | 11 | Hezekiah / חִזְקִיָּה / 'Εζεκίας (Matt 1:9-10; 1 Chr 3:13) | 26 Jorim / 'Ιωρείμ (Luke 3:29) |
| | 12 | Manasseh / מְנַשֶּׁה / Μανασσῆς (Matt 1:10; 1 Chr 3:13) | 27 Eliezer / 'Ελιέζερ (Luke 3:29) |
| | 13 | Amon / אָמוֹן / 'Αμώς (Matt 1:10; 1 Chr 3:14) | 28 Joshua / 'Ιησοῦς (Luke 3:29) |
| | 14 | Josiah / יֹאשִׁיָּה / 'Ιωσίας (Matt 1:10-11; 1 Chr 3:14) | 29 Er / "Ηρ (Luke 3:28) |
| | **Kings omitted from the genealogy** | | 30 Elmadam / 'Ελμωδάμ (Luke 3:28) |
| | Jehoahaz (Shallum) / יְהוֹאָחָז (2 Kgs 23:31; 1 Chr 3:15; 2 Chr 36:1-2) Jehoiakim (Eliakim) / יְהוֹיָקִים (2 Kgs 23:34, 36; 1 Chr 3:15; 2 Chr 36:4) | | |

* There may be slight variations in the chronological placement of each generation because it is impossible to figure out the definite years of the 41 figures after Nathan (from Mattatha to Jesus in the Lukan genealogy) since they are mostly people whose deeds are not recorded in the Bible.

| THE GENEALOGY IN MATTHEW 1 (14 GENERATIONS FROM THE DEPORTATION TO BABYLON TO JESUS CHRIST) | THE GENEALOGY IN LUKE 3 (14 GENERATIONS OF THE CORRESPONDING TIME PERIOD) |
|---|---|
| **1** Jeconiah (Jehoiachin) / יְכָנְיָה / Ἰεχονίας (Matt 1:11-12; 1 Chr 3:16) | **31** Cosam / Κωσάμ (Luke 3:28) |
| **King omitted from the genealogy** Zedekiah (Mattaniah) / צִדְקִיָּה (2 Kgs 24:17-18; 1 Chr 3:15-16) | |
| **2** Shealtiel / שְׁאַלְתִּיאֵל / Σαλαθιήλ (Matt 1:12; 1 Chr 3:17) | **32** Addi / Ἀδδί (Luke 3:28) |
| **3** Zerubbabel / זְרֻבָּבֶל / Ζοροβαβέλ (Matt 1:12-13; 1 Chr 3:19) | **33** Melchi / Μελχί (Luke 3:28) |
| → Hananiah (1 Chr 3:21) | **34** Neri / Νηρί (Luke 3:27) |
| → Shecaniah (1 Chr 3:22) a | **35** Shealtiel / Σαλαθιήλ (Luke 3:27) |
| → Shemaiah (1 Chr 3:22) b | **36** Zerubbabel / Ζοροβάβελ (Luke 3:27) |
| → Neariah (1 Chr 3:23) | **37** Rhesa / Ῥησά (Luke 3:27) |
| → Elioenai (1 Chr 3:24) | **38** Joanan / Ἰωαννά (Luke 3:27) |
| **4** Abihud / אֲבִיהוּד / Ἀβιούδ (Matt 1:13) | **39** Joda / Ἰωδά (Luke 3:26) |
| | **40** Josech / Ἰωσὴχ (Luke 3:26) |
| **5** Eliakim / אֶלְיָקִים / Ἐλιακείμ (Matt 1:13) | **41** Semein / Σεμεΐ (Luke 3:26) |
| | **42** Mattathias / Ματταθίας (Luke 3:26) |
| **6** Azor / עַזּוּר / Ἀζώρ (Matt 1:13-14) | **43** Maath / Μάαθ (Luke 3:26) |
| | **44** Naggai / Ναγγαί (Luke 3:25) |
| **7** Zadok / צָדוֹק / Σαδώκ (Matt 1:14) | **45** Hesli / Ἐσλί (Luke 3:25) |
| | **46** Nahum / Ναούμ (Luke 3:25) |
| **8** Achim / יוֹקִים / Ἀχείμ (Matt 1:14) | **47** Amos / Ἀμώς (Luke 3:25) |
| | **48** Mattathias / Ματταθίας (Luke 3:25) |
| **9** Eliud / אֱלִיהוּד / Ἐλιούδ (Matt 1:14-15) | **49** Joseph / Ἰωσήφ (Luke 3:24) |
| | **50** Jannai / Ἰανναί (Luke 3:24) |
| **10** Eleazar / אֶלְעָזָר / Ἐλεάζαρ (Matt 1:15) | **51** Melchi / Μελχί (Luke 3:24) |
| | **52** Levi / Λευί (Luke 3:24) |
| **11** Matthan / מַתָּן / Ματθάν (Matt 1:15) | **53** Matthat / Ματθάτ (Luke 3:24) |
| **12** Jacob / יַעֲקֹב / Ἰακώβ (Matt 1:15-16) | **54** Eli / Ἠλί (Luke 3:23) |
| **Mary's husband** **13** Joseph / יוֹסֵף / Ἰωσὴφ (Matt 1:16) | **55** Joseph / Ἰωσήφ (Luke 3:23) |
| **By Mary** **14** Jesus / יֵשׁוּעַ / Ἰησοῦς (Matt 1:16) | **56** Jesus / Ἰησοῦς (Luke 3:23) |

* The time span of the third period from the time of the deportation to Babylon until the intertestamental period is estimated.
* This chart uses the New American Standard Bible (NASB) for names and verses in English.

Period of the Babylonian captivity

Period of reconstructing the temple and the walls

The inter-testamental period

# Generations Omitted from the First and Second Periods in the Genealogy of Jesus Christ

✳ Systematically Organized and Presented for the First Time in History

The genealogy of Jesus Christ in Matthew 1 is not a consecutive record of all generations without omissions; it actually has many omitted generations. The third book in the History of Redemption series, *The Unquenchable Lamp of the Covenant*, and the fourth book, *God's Profound and Mysterious Providence*, have examined the omitted generations in the first and second periods in Jesus Christ's genealogy. The following is a concise summary.

## 1. Generations omitted from the first period in the genealogy of Jesus Christ

Chronologically, the first period of Jesus Christ's genealogy begins with the birth of Abraham and ends with King David's reign in Hebron, spanning 1,163 years from 2166 BC to 1003 BC.[23]

The following are the omitted generations in this period.

### (1) The period omitted between Ram and Amminadab (most of the 430 years of life in Egypt)

**Matthew 1:4** Ram was the father of Amminadab, Amminadab the father of Nahshon, and Nahshon the father of Salmon.

Most of Israel's 430-year stay in Egypt has been omitted from the first period of the genealogy. The same omission also appears in the Chronicler's genealogies (1 Chr 2:9-10), the genealogy in the book of Ruth (Ruth 4:19-20), and the genealogy of Jesus Christ in Luke 3 (Luke 3:32-33). The evidence is as follows. First, it is evident that Ram is Hezron's son

(Ruth 4:19; Matt 1:3) as 1 Chronicles 2:9 clearly lists the names of Hezron's sons as "Jerahmeel, Ram and Chelubai." Here, Jerahmeel is recorded as the "firstborn of Hezron" in 1 Chronicles 2:25. Thus, it is certain that there is no omission between Hezron and Ram. Since Hezron's name is included among the seventy who migrated to Egypt with Jacob (Gen 46:12), Hezron and his son Ram lived during the early years of the 430-year period in Egypt. Next, Nahshon's father Amminadab is Aaron's father-in-law (Exod 6:23), which places Amminadab in the latter part of the 430-year sojourn in Egypt. In addition, Amminadab's son Nahshon was the leader (i.e., head of the household, chief) of the tribe of Judah during the forty-year wilderness journey after the exodus (Num 1:7; 2:3; 10:14; 1 Chr 2:10).

As examined, Hezron and Ram lived in the early years of the 430-year period in Egypt while Amminadab and Nahshon lived close to the end of the 430-year sojourn. This indicates that there is an omission of most of the period of slavery in Egypt between Ram and Amminadab. God has taken out from the genealogy of Jesus Christ the time in which the Israelites were under slavery in a Gentile nation. Today, we must not chase after the world and become slaves to sin; we must seek after the Word of God and become slaves of obedience, slaves of righteousness, and slaves of God (Rom 6:16, 18-19, 22).

## (2) The period omitted between Salmon and Boaz (about 300 years in the period of the judges)

**Matthew 1:5** Salmon was the father of Boaz by Rahab, Boaz was the father of Obed by Ruth, and Obed the father of Jesse.

Most of the generations in the period of the judges have also been omitted from the first period of Jesus' genealogy between Salmon and Boaz. This omission is also seen in the Chronicler's genealogies (1 Chr 2:11-12), the genealogy in the book of Ruth (Ruth 4:20-21), and the genealogy of Jesus Christ in Luke 3 (Luke 3:32). The evidence is as follows. First, Salmon married Rahab the harlot (Matt 1:5).[24] Rahab lived in the city of Jericho when the Israelites entered Canaan. Since she lived around the time of the Israelites' entry into Canaan, Salmon, who married her, must also have been from that time. However, Boaz lived close to the end of the period of the judges. Boaz married Ruth and fathered Obed. The Bible testifies that Obed is the father of Jesse, the father of

David, which makes Obed David's grandfather (Ruth 4:13-17, 21-22). David was born in 1040 BC (Ref 2 Sam 5:4). Considering that one generation is about twenty-five to thirty years in average, it can be estimated that Obed was born around 1100–1090 BC, which coincides with the time of Judge Jephthah (1104–1099 BC).[25] During the Ammonites' invasion, Jephthah made it clear that it was unjustifiable for the Ammonites to claim the land which had already been occupied by the Israelites for 300 years (from the time of their entry into Canaan; Judg 11:26). Thus, a period of about 300 years, including the sixteen years of the conquest of Canaan, was omitted between Salmon and Boaz. The period of the judges is characterized as a time when "there was no king in Israel" and "every man did what was right in his own eyes" (Judg 17:6; 21:25). God attested to the spiritual darkness of this period by removing it from the genealogy of Jesus Christ (Judg 2:7-10).

## 2. Generations omitted from the second period in the genealogy of Jesus Christ

Chronologically, the second period of Jesus Christ's genealogy starts with the beginning of David's reign in Jerusalem (1003 BC) and ends with Jeconiah's deportation to Babylon (597 BC), spanning about 406 years.[26] Three kings between Joram and Uzziah (Azariah) are omitted from this period.

Matthew 1:8 states, ". . . and Joram the father of Uzziah." But, a comparison with the Chronicler's genealogies reveals that three generations—Ahaziah, Joash, and Amaziah—have been omitted between Joram and Uzziah (Azariah). Uzziah is Azariah's other name (2 Kgs 14:21; 2 Chr 26:1).

> **1 Chronicles 3:11-12** Joram his son, **Ahaziah** his son, **Joash** his son, [12]**Amaziah** his son, **Azariah** his son, Jotham his son.

If we were to include Ahab's daughter Athaliah, who ruled after Ahaziah for six years, then four kings have been omitted from the second period of Jesus' genealogy (2 Kgs 11:3; 2 Chr 22:12). What do these kings have in common?

First, they are all related to Athaliah, who tried to destroy the royal seed (2 Kgs 11:1; 2 Chr 22:10). Ahaziah, Joash, and Amaziah were three generations of Athaliah's descendants. Second, they were evil kings who committed idolatry (2 Kgs 8:27; 11:18; 2 Chr 22:3; 24:17-19; 25:14). Third, they all died wretched deaths (2 Kgs 9:27; 11:13-16; 12:20-21; 14:18-20). By omitting these four kings from the genealogy, God revealed His redemptive administration to judge all the evil powers that seek to quench the lamp of the covenant.[27]

# CHAPTER 9

# Generations Omitted from the Third Period in the Genealogy of Jesus Christ

✳ Systematically Organized and Presented for the First Time in History

Chronologically, the third period of Jesus Christ's genealogy spans about 593 years, from the Israelites' deportation to Babylon during the time of Jeconiah (597 BC) until the birth of Jesus Christ (4 BC). A close study of this period also reveals that many generations have been omitted, as also seen in the first and second periods of the genealogy.

First, three kings around the time of the deportation to Babylon were not recorded in the genealogy. Jehoahaz and Jehoiakim have been omitted from their places in the genealogy which was between Josiah and Jehoiachin (Jeconiah; Matt 1:11). Also, Jehoiachin's (Jeconiah's) successor Zedekiah was omitted. Next, there were generations omitted between Zerubbabel and Abihud (Matt 1:13). We must focus on the name *Abihud* because his name cannot be found in the genealogy of Zerubbabel's descendants in 1 Chronicles chapter 3 (1 Chr 3:19-24). By calculating the years of generations between Abihud and Jesus Christ, we can discover that there are omitted generations there as well.

A systematic study and organization of the generations omitted in the third period of the genealogy of Jesus Christ will lead to a greater insight into God's redemptive administration contained therein.

## 1. Several indications for omissions in the third period

### (1) Evidence from the length of time pertaining to the third period
The third period of Jesus Christ's genealogy consists of 14 generations from Jeconiah to Jesus. Jeconiah was taken to Babylon in 597 BC, and the conservative view on the year of Jesus' birth is 4 BC. Thus, the 14 generations in the third period of the genealogy span 593 years of history. Under the assumption that there is no omitted generation, each genera-

tion in the third period would average about 46 years (593 ÷ 13), which is much longer than the average reckoning of 25 to 30 years per generation. Thus, it is evident that there are a significant number of generations omitted from the third period of Jesus Christ's genealogy.

## (2) Comparison with the Lukan genealogy

Jesus Christ's genealogies in the Gospels of Matthew and Luke diverge after David. The genealogy in Matthew continues with David's son Solomon (Matt 1:6), whereas the genealogy in Luke continues with David's son Nathan (Luke 3:31). In the Matthean genealogy, there are 27 generations from Solomon to Jesus; and in the Lukan genealogy, there are 42 generations from Nathan to Jesus. The two genealogies are records of the two different lineages stemming from David: Matthew 1 traces Jesus' lineage through Joseph, while Luke 3 traces His lineage through Mary. Both of them are based on accurate genealogies that have been carefully preserved until the time of their recordings in the Gospels in order to testify of Jesus Christ.[28] The fact that the portion of the Matthean genealogy contains 15 generations fewer than the corresponding portion of the Lukan genealogy, which covers the same span of time, is clear evidence that there are many generations omitted in the Matthean genealogy.

## (3) Comparison with the Chronicler's genealogies

The genealogy in 1 Chronicles was recorded to implant in the hearts of the returning captives the belief that they are still God's chosen people and that the history of God's elect is perpetual. This genealogy contains a detailed list of Zerubbabel's descendants. According to this genealogy, the lineage of Zerubbabel is as follows: Zerubbabel – Hananiah – Shecaniah – Shemaiah – Neariah – Elioenai – Hodaviah (1 Chr 3:19-24).

Nevertheless, the genealogy of Jesus Christ in Matthew 1 records Abihud immediately after Zerubbabel (Matt 1:13). Interestingly, Abihud does not appear in the genealogy of Zerubbabel's descendants in 1 Chronicles, which is another reason to infer that several generations have been omitted in the Matthean genealogy.

Some might assume that Abihud was Zerubbabel's biological son whose name was simply not recorded in the Chronicler's genealogy. This argument, however, is not convincing since the number and names of Zerubbabel's sons are clearly recorded. The Chronicler's genealogies record that Zerubbabel had a total of seven sons and one daughter: two sons and one daughter (Meshullam, Hananiah, and Shelomith their sister, 1 Chr 3:19) and five others (Hashubah, Ohel, Berechiah, Hasadiah, and Jushab-hesed, 1 Chr 3:20).[29] In the case of Shemaiah, his record states that he had six sons although only five names are mentioned in the genealogy (1 Chr 3:22). Likewise, if Abihud were omitted in this genealogy of Zerubbabel's sons, then the record would have stated that Zerubbabel had six sons not five (1 Chr 3:19).

Considering the precise record of the names as well as the number of Zerubbabel's sons, it is unreasonable to assert that Abihud was Zerubbabel's biological son who happened to have been left out of the Chronicler's genealogy. Moreover, since even the name of Zerubbabel's daughter (Shelomith) was introduced with his descendants (1 Chr 3:19-20), leaving out his son's name would be even more illogical. Henceforth, let us carefully examine each omission in the third period.

## 2. The three kings whose names were not recorded in the genealogy around the time of the deportation to Babylon

Matthew 1:11 states, "Josiah became the father of Jeconiah and his brothers, at the time of the deportation to Babylon." Cross-referencing with the actual genealogy of the kings reveals that Jeconiah (Jehoiachin) was not Josiah's son; in fact, he was Jehoiakim's son (2 Kgs 24:6; 2 Chr 36:8) and thus Josiah's grandson. This indicates that there are kings whose names have been omitted in the genealogy of Jesus Christ around the time of the deportation to Babylon.

### (1) Josiah had four sons: Johanan, Jehoiakim, Zedekiah, and Shallum.

First Chronicles 3:15 states, "The sons of Josiah *were* Johanan the firstborn, and the second was Jehoiakim, the third Zedekiah, the fourth Shallum." Shallum's other name was Jehoahaz (2 Kgs 23:30; 2 Chr 36:1; Jer 22:11). Jehoiakim's mother was Zebidah (daughter of Pedaiah of Rumah; 2 Kgs 23:36), and Jehoahaz and Zedekiah's mother was Hamutal (daughter of Jeremiah of Libnah; 2 Kgs 23:31; 24:18; Jer 52:1).

### (2) The order of accession differs from the order recorded in 1 Chronicles 3:15.

Jehoahaz was twenty-three years old (2 Kgs 23:31; 2 Chr 36:1-2a) when he succeeded Josiah (609b–608 BC) as king. However, he was taken captive to Egypt after only three months into his reign, and Jehoiakim became king in his place (2 Chr 36:2b-4). Jehoiakim became king at the age of twenty-five and ruled for eleven years (608–597 BC; 2 Kgs 23:36; 2 Chr 36:5), and his son Jehoiachin succeeded him (2 Chr 36:6-8). Jehoiachin became king at the age of eighteen (597 BC) and ruled for three months and ten days before he was taken captive to Babylon (2 Kgs 24:8; 2 Chr 36:9-10). King Zedekiah succeeded him at the age of twenty-one (597–586 BC; 2 Kgs 24:18; 2 Chr 36:11; Jer 52:1).

Accordingly, Josiah's oldest son Johanan never became king, but Josiah's other sons—Jehoahaz, Jehoiakim, and Zedekiah—reigned in this order.

### (3) The order of accession differs from the order of birth

In 640 BC, Josiah became king at the age of eight and ruled for thirty-one years (2 Kgs 22:1; 2 Chr 34:1). A calculation of Josiah's age and the birth years of his three sons reveals that Jehoahaz was born in 632 BC, when Josiah was sixteen; Jehoiakim was born in 633 BC, when Josiah was fifteen; and Zedekiah was born in 618 BC, when Josiah was thirty. Thus, Josiah's sons were born in the following order: Johanan, Jehoiakim, Jehoahaz (Shallum), and Zedekiah.

### (4) The kings omitted from the genealogy of Jesus Christ are Jehoahaz, Jehoiakim, and Zedekiah.

A comparison of the above with the genealogy of Jesus Christ in Matthew 1 reveals that Jehoahaz and Jehoiakim were omitted from between Josiah and Jehoiachin, and Zedekiah was omitted after Jehoiachin.

| | | 1 | 2 | 3 | 4 |
|---|---|---|---|---|---|
| Chronicler's Genealogy (1 Chr 3:15) | Josiah | Johanan | Jehoiakim | Zedekiah | Jehoahaz (Shallum) |
| Order of Birth | Josiah | Johanan | Jehoiakim | Jehoahaz (Shallum) | Zedekiah |
| Order of Accession | Josiah | Jehoahaz (Shallum) | Jehoiakim | Jehoiachin | Zedekiah |
| Matthean Genealogy (Matt 1:10-11) | Josiah | Jehoahaz omitted | Jehoiakim omitted | Jeconiah (Jehoiachin) | Zedekiah omitted |

This shows that the genealogy in 1 Chronicles 3:15 was not recorded according to the birth order. In 1 Chronicles 3:15, Zedekiah and

Jehoahaz—brothers from the same mother, Hamutal (2 Kgs 23:31; 24:18)—are recorded together. One reason that the younger brother Zedekiah was recorded before the older brother Jehoahaz was probably because Zedekiah's reign (eleven years) was much longer than that of Jehoahaz (three months).

Although Jehoahaz was the first among Josiah's sons to become king due to active support from the people, the Chronicler listed him last (2 Kgs 23:30). During his short three-month reign, he did evil in the sight of the Lord according to all that his fathers had done (2 Kgs 23:32). Second Kings 23:34 states, "Pharaoh Neco made Eliakim the son of Josiah king in the place of Josiah his father, and changed his name to Jehoiakim. But he took Jehoahaz away and brought him to Egypt, and he died there." By stating that Jehoiakim succeeded Josiah, this verse seems to deny Jehoahaz's kingship. Such a record concerning Jehoahaz is probably related to the reason why he was recorded last in the Chronicler's genealogy despite the fact that he was the first to accede to the throne.

## 3. Generations omitted between Zerubbabel and Abihud

The lineage of Zerubbabel continues after him to Hananiah, Shecaniah, Shemaiah, Neariah, Elioenai, and Hodaviah (1 Chr 3:19-24). We must carefully examine this lineage in 1 Chronicles chapter 3 and its relationship to *Abihud* who succeeded Zerubbabel in Matthew 1:13.

The clue to resolving this conflict between the two genealogies lies in the meaning of the name *Abihud*. The name *Abihud* (Ἀβιούδ) is אֲבִיהוּד (*'ăbîhûd*) in Hebrew. The name is a combination of the word אָב (*'āb*), meaning "father" and the word הוֹד (*hôd*), meaning "majesty" or "glory." Thus, the name means "father of glory," "father is glory," "father of majesty," or "father is majesty."

Interestingly, a name with the same meaning as that of Abihud is found among the descendants of Zerubbabel in 1 Chronicles 3. It is Hodaviah, whose name is הוֹדַוְיָהוּ (*hôdawyāhû*) in Hebrew and means "the majesty of the Lord" and "the glory of the Lord"[30] which is similar to the meaning of Abihud. First Chronicles 3 lists Hodaviah as the last generation among the descendants of Zerubbabel, whereas Jesus Christ's genealogy in Matthew 1 lists Abihud after Zerubbabel. Since the meanings of their names are the same, it is possible to infer that Abihud and Hodaviah were the same person.

First Chronicles 3:19-24 records seven generations including Zerubbabel in the line of Zerubbabel: Zerubbabel, Hananiah, Shecaniah, Shemaiah, Neariah, Elioenai, and Hodaviah. Considering that an average span of each generation is twenty-five years, Hodaviah, the last person in Zerubbabel's lineage in 1 Chronicles 3, is presumed to have lived around 420 BC.[31] According to 1 Chronicles 3:24, Hodaviah had six younger siblings: Eliashib, Pelaiah, Akkub, Johanan, Delaiah, and Anani. Hodaviah's youngest sibling Anani must have been born in the early 400s BC, which is around the time when the book of Chronicles was recorded by its probable author, Prophet Ezra.[32] This important data shows that the Chronicler's genealogies recorded all of the descendants of Zerubbabel without any omission.

| Name | Zerubbabel | Hananiah | Shecaniah | Shemaiah | Neariah | Elioenai | Hodaviah |
|---|---|---|---|---|---|---|---|
| Period (BC) estimated | 570[33] | 545 | 520 | 495 | 470 | 445 | 420 |

* Reckoned with an average of twenty-five years per generation

It is certain that Abihud—Zerubbabel's successor in the Matthean genealogy of Jesus Christ—carried on Zerubbabel's lineage in 1 Chronicles 3. He is most likely the person who resumes the genealogy from where it stops at the end of 1 Chronicles 3. The meaning of the name Hodaviah, the last person in the Chronicler's genealogies (1 Chr 3:24), is the same as the meaning of Abihud, who succeeds Zerubbabel in the Matthean genealogy. Thus, it is possible to deduce that the two people are actually the same person.[34] Matthew Hiller also viewed Hodaviah and Abihud as the same person in his discussion on the omitted generations after Zerubbabel in Jesus Christ's genealogy.[35] Based on the above considerations, we can conclude that Abihud was not Zerubbabel's son and that there were five generations omitted between Zerubbabel and Abihud.

## 4. Generations omitted between Abihud and Jesus Christ

In order to figure out whether or not there are omissions in the generations between Abihud and Jesus Christ, we must first determine whether Shealtiel and Zerubbabel in the Matthean genealogy are the same Shealtiel and Zerubbabel who appear in the Lukan genealogy. The following is a comparison of the records of Shealtiel and Zerubbabel in the two genealogies.

| | | | | | |
|---|---|---|---|---|---|
| **Matthew 1:12-13** | ... | Jeconiah | Shealtiel | Zerubbabel | Abihud |
| **Luke 3:27** | ... | Neri | Shealtiel | Zerubbabel | Rhesa |

Although Shealtiel and Zerubbabel appear in both genealogies, there are many issues that prevent us from concluding that they were the same people.

**FIRST, the Matthean and Lukan genealogies record different persons for Shealtiel's father: Jeconiah and Neri, respectively.**

There are scholars who claim that Shealtiel was originally Neri's son but was later adopted by Jeconiah.[36] This explanation, however, is based on insufficient evidence and contradicts biblical records. First Chronicles 3:17 clearly states, "The sons of Jeconiah, the prisoner, were Shealtiel his son." Thus, there is no foundation for the argument that Shealtiel was originally Neri's son. Furthermore, it is highly unlikely that King Jeconiah adopted Shealtiel when he already had many sons (1 Chr 3:18).

**SECOND, Rhesa, Zerubbabel's son according to the Lukan genealogy, is not found in the Matthean genealogy or the Chronicler's genealogies.**

Rhesa appears neither among the descendants of Zerubbabel in the genealogy in Matthew 1 (Matt 1:13-16) nor in the list of Zerubbabel's sons and descendants in 1 Chronicles 3:19-24.

> **1 Chronicles 3:19-20** The sons of Pedaiah were Zerubbabel and Shimei. And the sons of Zerubbabel were Meshullam and Hananiah, and Shelomith was their sister; [20] and Hashubah, Ohel, Berechiah, Hasadiah and Jushab-hesed, five.

**THIRD, a comparison of the years based on the number of generations in the Matthean and Lukan genealogies leads to the conclusion that they cannot be from the same period.**

If Shealtiel and Zerubbabel in Matthew are the same Shealtiel and Zerubbabel in Luke, then the birth year of Zerubbabel in Luke must also be around 570 BC since Zerubbabel in Matthew was born around 570 BC.

If we assume that the Zerubbabel in Luke was also born around 570 BC, then there would be a span of about 470 years from David (born

1040 BC) to Zerubbabel (born 570 BC) through the line of Nathan in the Lukan genealogy. There are 22 generations in this 470-year time period in the Lukan genealogy. That means there is an average interval of 21 years between each of the generations (470 years ÷ 22 generations). Under the same premise, there would be a span of about 566 years (570 BC – 4 BC) from Zerubbabel to Jesus Christ. Since there are 20 generations for this period in the Lukan genealogy, an average interval between each of the generations would be about 28 years (566 years ÷ 20 generations). Hence, under this premise, the average interval (21 years) between each of the generations from David to Zerubbabel in the Lukan genealogy differ too greatly from the average interval (28 years) between each of the generations from Zerubbabel to Jesus Christ in the same genealogy. Therefore, such a difference provides conclusive evidence that the Zerubbabel in the Lukan genealogy is not the same person as the Zerubbabel in the Matthean genealogy.

In the genealogy in Luke 3, the time from David to Jesus Christ through the line of Nathan is about 1,036 years (1040 BC – 4 BC) with a total of 42 generations. Thus, the average number of years between generations in this period is about 24.7 years (1,036 years ÷ 42 generations). This number is close to 25 years, an average generational interval in the traditional method of reckoning. Therefore, this reveals that there are no omitted generations in the section of the Lukan genealogy corresponding to the second and third periods of the Matthean genealogy.

When we apply the average generational interval of 24.7 years to the 22 generations between David and Zerubbabel in the Lukan genealogy, then we find that Zerubbabel existed about 543 years (24.7 years x 22 generations) after David. That means Zerubbabel was born around 497 BC (1040 BC – 543 years).

**AS A RESULT**, a simple calculation shows that Shealtiel and Zerubbabel in the Lukan genealogy lived about 73 years (570 BC – 497 BC), or about three generations, later than the Shealtiel and Zerubbabel in the Matthean genealogy.

It can be presumed that Neri named his son in remembrance of Shealtiel, a greatly respected ancestor. Shealtiel also named his son in remembrance of Zerubbabel, a prominent leader in history. The Shealtiel in the Matthean genealogy was a successor of the royal lineage of Jeconiah, while the Zerubbabel recorded in the Matthean genealogy was the leader who led the Israelites out of captivity from Babylon and took the lead in the reconstruction of the temple. God's favor upon the ancestors was also an immense glory for the descendants (Ref Luke 1:59). For this reason, the Israelites at the time probably named their children after their ancestors with great anticipation for the Messiah.[37]

The following conclusion can be obtained based on what has been discussed so far.

It is estimated that Abihud, who appears in the third period of the Matthean genealogy, was born around 420 BC.[38] To find his counterpart in the Lukan genealogy, we can count down the generations from David with 24.7 years as the average generational interval. This reckoning will show that *Joda* from the Lukan genealogy is the most likely person who lived around the same time as Abihud (approx. 420 BC) of the Matthean genealogy. There are 25 generations between David and Joda in the Lukan genealogy.

The calculation, then, is as follows. David was born in 1040 BC (Ref 2 Sam 5:4) and Abihud was presumably born around 420 BC. Hence, there are about 620 years between the two individuals (1040 – 420 BC). Dividing the 620 years by 24.7—the average generational interval in the Lukan genealogy—will yield approximately 25 generations. This means that Abihud's counterpart in the Lukan genealogy is 25 generations down from David, and that person is Joda. Hence, Joda lived contemporaneously with Abihud.

Although historical events do not play out exactly like mathematical calculations, basic mathematical values cannot be completely disregarded. There are 18 generations from Joda to Jesus Christ in the Lukan genealogy, whereas there are only 11 from Abihud to Jesus Christ in the Matthean genealogy. This indicates that there is a difference of as many as *seven* generations between the two genealogies.

| | 1040 BC | ... | About 420 BC | ... | 4 BC |
|---|---|---|---|---|---|
| Genealogy in Matthew 1 | David | ... | Abihud | 9 persons | Jesus |
| | | | Total of 11 persons | | |
| Genealogy in Luke 3 | David | ... | Joda | 16 persons | Jesus |
| | | | Total of 18 persons | | |

If there were only 11 generations during the approximate 420-year period from Abihud to Jesus Christ, then the average generational interval would be about 42 years. This value is about 1.7 times greater than the average generational interval for the same period in the Lukan genealogy (i.e., 24.7 years). Therefore, when the Matthean and Lukan genealogies are compared in this manner, it becomes quite evident that there are approximately 7 generations omitted between Abihud and Jesus Christ in the third period of the Matthean genealogy.

Thus far, we have examined the omissions in the third period of the Matthean genealogy. Between Josiah and Jeconiah, Jehoahaz and Jehoiakim have been taken out; and Zedekiah was omitted after Jeconiah. We have also confirmed that five generations (Hananiah, Shecaniah, Shemaiah, Neariah, and Elioenai) were omitted between Zerubbabel and Abihud. The glory of God (Hag 2:7-9), which had appeared when Zerubbabel reconstructed the temple, continues on in the Matthean genealogy through the name *Abihud*, which means "glory of the father." We must also reveal the glory of God by living lives that are centered on the house of God (1 Cor 10:31; Ref Isa 60:7; Zech 6:13).

We also saw that there were about seven generations omitted between Abihud and Jesus Christ. The names of those who lived close to the time of the Messiah's long-awaited coming demonstrate how believers who await the second coming must live: Eliakim ("God establishes"), Azor ("helpful"), Zadok ("righteousness"), Achim ("the Lord establishes"), Eliud ("God is my glory"), Eleazar ("God has helped"), and Matthan ("gift").

We cannot know which persons were omitted from the third period of the genealogy or to which time period they belonged. However, we can be sure that God had omitted them according to His profound providence. God's providence is full of difficult mysteries unfathomable by man (Rom 11:33). Deuteronomy 29:29 states, "The secret things belong to the Lord our God, but the things revealed belong to us and to our sons forever, that we may observe all the words of this law." We must understand God's providence revealed through the genealogies so that we can live our lives observing His Word (Deut 29:29b).

# CHAPTER 10

# The History of the Kings Who were Omitted from the Third Period in the Matthean Genealogy

> ## 1. Jehoahaz (Shallum) / Ἰωαχάς/ יְהוֹאָחָז
> The Lord has grasped

— The seventeenth king of Judah, the southern kingdom (2 Kgs 23:31-34; 2 Chr 36:1-4)
— Omitted from the genealogy of Jesus Christ

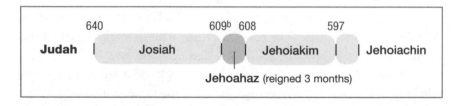

**Background**
– Father: Josiah
– Mother: Hamutal (daughter of Jeremiah of Libnah, 2 Kgs 23:31)

**Evaluation** – evil king (2 Kgs 23:32)

**Active prophet** – Jeremiah (Jer 1:1-3)

**Historical records** – No records

Jehoahaz succeeded Josiah as the seventeenth king of Judah, the southern kingdom. The name Jehoahaz is יְהוֹאָחָז (yěhô'āḥāz) in Hebrew, which is a combination of the word יְהֹוָה (yhwh), meaning "Jehovah" and אָחַז

('*āḥaz*) meaning, "grasp," "take hold," "seize," or "take possession." Thus, the name means, "the Lord has grasped" or "the Lord has seized."

## 1. Jehoahaz was the first to become king ahead of his three brothers.

According to 1 Chronicles 3:15, Josiah had four sons: Johanan was the firstborn; the second was Eliakim (Jehoiakim); the third was Zedekiah (Mattaniah); and the fourth was Shallum (Jehoahaz; Jer 22:11-12). However, the record of Josiah's sons in 1 Chronicles 3:15 is not according to their birth order, which was Johanan, Jehoiakim, Shallum (Jehoahaz), and Zedekiah (2 Kgs 23:31, 36; 24:18). The order in which they succeeded the throne was Jehoahaz (17th king), Jehoiakim (18th king), and Zedekiah (20th king).

Among the four sons, Jehoahaz was the first to become king after his father Josiah (2 Kgs 23:30; 2 Chr 36:1). He probably ascended the throne first because his strength and abilities exceeded those of his brothers, and this was recognized by the people (2 Kgs 23:30). Fundamentally, however, it was the result of God's sovereign work. When the people of Judah specifically chose Jehoahaz from among Josiah's four sons to anoint him as their king, they probably remembered King Josiah. Like David, Josiah had ruled justly (2 Kgs 22:2) for about thirty-one years, and he did not turn aside to the right or to the left. Although the entire nation was immersed in great sorrow due to Josiah's sudden death, the people must have had great expectations when they chose Jehoahaz as their new king—that he would surely succeed his father's faith and establish the nation to become wealthy and strong.

## 2. Jehoahaz was as brutal as a young lion.

Prophet Ezekiel was active during the calamitous period in which the kingdom was about to fall (593–571 BC; Ezek 1:1-3; 29:17). He likened Jehoahaz, who ruled toward the end of the kingdom's history, to a young lion that devoured men (Ref Ezek 19:4b).

> **Ezekiel 19:3** When she brought up one of her cubs, He became a lion, and he learned to tear his prey; He devoured men.

This is a reflection of how he had killed, abused, oppressed, and plundered his own people as soon as he came to power during his short three-month reign.

Although the Bible does not record in detail all of his evil deeds, it sums them up with the statement, "He did evil in the sight of the Lord, according to all that his fathers had done" (2 Kgs 23:32). He made the future of the nation gloomy by doing all the evil that his fathers had done during his short three-month reign. Josephus also described him as "an impious man, and impure in his course of life" (*Ant.* 10.81). Jehoahaz's exceeding strength and abilities earned him the crown before his brothers, but he misused them and did according to all the evil that his fathers had done.

We have been created for good works (Eph 2:10a). Thus, we must live our lives with great faith that pleases God and become His people who are always zealous for good deeds (Eph 2:10b; Titus 2:14).

## 3. Jehoahaz was taken by hooks to Egypt and died there.

Pharaoh Neco the king of Egypt was the second king of the twenty-sixth dynasty of Egypt. He succeeded the throne after his father, Psammetichus I, in 609 BC. After his victory at the battle of Megiddo, he exercised great power over Judah, the southern kingdom. Pharaoh Neco imprisoned Jehoahaz at Riblah just three months into his reign so that Jehoahaz could no longer reign in Jerusalem (2 Kgs 23:33a). He also imposed on Judah a fine of one hundred talents of silver and a talent of gold (2 Kgs 23:33b; 2 Chr 36:3). He then changed Jehoahaz's older brother's name from Eliakim to Jehoiakim and made him king of Judah (2 Kgs 23:34a).

Meanwhile, Jehoahaz was unable to return after he was taken captive to Egypt, and he died there (2 Kgs 23:34b; 2 Chr 36:4) just as Prophet Jeremiah had prophesied.

> Jeremiah 22:10-12 Do not weep for the dead or mourn for him, but weep continually for the one who goes away; for he will never return or see his native land. [11] For thus says the Lord in regard to Shallum the son of Josiah, king of Judah, who became king in the place of Josiah his father, who went forth from this place, "He will never return there; [12] but in the place where they led him captive, there he will die and not see this land again."

Regarding Pharaoh Neco's act of taking Jehoahaz captive to Egypt, Prophet Ezekiel stated, "Then nations heard about him; he was captured in their pit, and they brought him with hooks to the land of Egypt" (Ezek 19:4). The word *hooks* in this verse refers to hooks used to carry or drag fish or wild animals by their gills or nose, and thus depicts the wretched manner in which Jehoahaz was taken captive (2 Kgs 23:34; 2 Chr 36:4; Ref 2 Kgs 19:28; Isa 37:29; Ezek 29:4; 38:4).

Why did Jehoahaz meet such a tragic end? It was because he trusted in his own abilities rather than in God and practiced anti-Egyptian policies. He was proud and did not realize that all his abilities were the result of God's grace. We need to learn from this and must not become self-engrossed, haughty, or arrogant in our hearts even if we may possess abilities that exceed those of others in this world (Jer 43:2; Dan 5:20). An arrogant person will surely commit the sin of standing against God. He will ultimately stumble and be destroyed very suddenly (Prov 16:18; 29:1). Sudden destruction is the fate of the person who is deceived by the arrogance of his heart (Obad 1:3). Therefore, we must realize that any of our abilities that exceed those of others are given to us completely by God's grace and give thanks to Him for them. Furthermore, we must all the more strive to live a life that God upholds (Ps 116:12; 1 Cor 15:10). There is always a path of salvation for those whom God upholds even in the midst of difficulties and sufferings (Ps 119:117; Ref Ps 18:35; 41:3; 94:18).

Shallum (שַׁלּוּם) was Jehoahaz's other name (1 Chr 3:15; Jer 22:11), and it originates from the Hebrew word שָׁלֵם (*šālam*), which means "peaceful" or "secure" (Ref Judg 6:24). If Jehoahaz had lived a peaceful and secure life that God upholds in keeping with the meaning of his name, then the whole nation would have enjoyed great abundance along with the peace that God gives (John 14:27). Nevertheless, he rejected living a life that depends on God and relied on himself. Consequently, he was subjected to the shame of being recorded last in the Chronicler's genealogies even though he was the first among his brothers to become king (1 Chr 3:15).

## 2. Jehoiakim / Ἰωακίμ / יְהוֹיָקִים

The Lord raises up

## (Eliakim) / Ἐλιακίμ / אֶלְיָקִים

God raises up

---

- The eighteenth king of Judah, the southern kingdom (2 Kgs 23:34-24:6; 2 Chr 36:5-8)
- Omitted from the genealogy of Jesus Christ

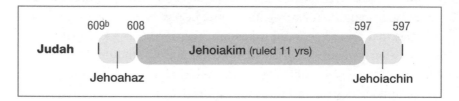

**Background**
- Father: Josiah
- Mother: Zebidah (the daughter of Pedaiah of Rumah; 2 Kgs 23:36)

**Evaluation** – evil king (2 Kgs 23:37; 2 Chr 36:5)

**Active prophets** – Jeremiah (Jer 1:3; 22:18; 25:1; 26:1; 27:1; 35:1; 36:1)
Uriah (Jer 26:20-23), Daniel

**Historical records** – Book of the Chronicles of the Kings of Judah (2 Kgs 24:5; 2 Chr 36:8)

Jehoiakim became the eighteenth king of Judah, the southern kingdom, in place of his younger brother Jehoahaz. Jehoiakim's original name was Eliakim, but Pharaoh Neco changed it to Jehoiakim in order to show that the king of Judah is a subordinate of Egypt.

Eliakim is אֶלְיָקִים (*'elyāqîm*) in Hebrew; it is a combination of the word אֵל (*'ēl*) and קוּם (*qûm*). אֵל (*'ēl*) means "God" and קוּם (*qûm*) means "to rise" or "to raise." Hence, the name *Eliakim* means "God raises up."

Jehoiakim is יְהוֹיָקִים (*yĕhôyāqîm*) in Hebrew. It is a combination of the word יְהֹוָה (*yhwh*), meaning "Jehovah" and קוּם (*qûm*), meaning "to rise" or "to raise." The name thus means "the Lord (Jehovah) raises up."

# 1. Jehoiakim was a tyrant, full of greed.

Jehoiakim exacted silver and gold from the people, each according to his valuation, to give them to Pharaoh as penalty (2 Kgs 23:34-35). The word *exacted* is נָגַשׂ (nāgaś), meaning "to press," "to drive," "to oppress," "to exact," and "to exert demanding pressure." The word describes the force with which Jehoiakim collected the money. Jehoiakim had ruled over the people with coercion in order to collect taxes.

His father, Josiah, did right in the sight of the Lord for thirty-one years. He practiced justice and righteousness and walked in all the way of his father David. Also, he did not turn aside to the right or to the left (2 Kgs 22:1-2; 2 Chr 34:1-2). He cherished the book of the law and trembled before the Word of God (2 Kgs 22:11). He pled for the cause of the afflicted and the needy. As a result, God blessed him with an abundance of food and clothing as well as success in all that he did (Jer 22:15-16).

Contrary to his father, Jehoiakim's eyes and heart were fixed only upon dishonest gain; thus, he practiced oppression and extortion, shedding innocent blood (Jer 22:17). The purpose of Jehoiakim's oppression and extortion of money from the people was not simply to collect taxes for Egypt. After paying off Egypt, he used what remained to build an extravagant palace for himself.

Prophet Jeremiah sharply criticized King Jehoiakim's ambition and vanity in Jeremiah 22:14-16:

> "Who says, 'I will build myself a roomy house with spacious upper rooms, and cut out its windows, paneling it with cedar and painting it bright red.' Do you become a king because you are competing in cedar? Did not your father eat and drink and do justice and righteousness? Then it was well with him. He pled the cause of the afflicted and needy; then it was well. Is not that what it means to know Me? Declares the Lord."

It was a time of national crisis; the nation was on the verge of destruction and had a heavy tribute to pay Egypt. Yet, the king was complacent and caught up in useless extravagance—decorating his palace and boasting of his regal powers. His extravagance was extreme; he built his palace with cedars, the best of materials, and painted his palace walls with rare Egyptian red paint. He believed that he needed to construct many fancy buildings in order to be regarded as a successful king.

The nation flourished and the people enjoyed the blessing of peace during his father's reign as he practiced justice and righteousness, looking after the afflicted and the needy. Nevertheless, Jehoiakim was the exact opposite of his father. He was a selfish king who did not know God and had no regard for securing peace for the people. Even though he was the chief of the nation, he had no interest in saving the nation from destruction or the people from severe distress. He was engrossed only in satisfying his ambition. He reigned for eleven years, and the people probably suffered severe exploitation, oppression, and extortion on top of all kinds of affliction and poverty during that long period of time.

## 2. Jehoiakim was a brutal king who persecuted God's prophet; he cut the scroll of God's Word with a scribe's knife, and burned it.

Jehoiakim tried to kill Prophet Uriah the son of Shemaiah from Kiriath-jearim, who prophesied in the name of the Lord (Jer 26:20). He wanted to kill the prophet because he prophesied about the fall of Jerusalem and the land of Judah, just as Jeremiah had prophesied (Jer 26:20-21). Uriah was afraid and fled to Egypt, but the king sent Elnathan the son of Achbor and certain men with him to bring him back (Jer 26:22). When they captured Uriah and brought him back, King Jehoiakim slew him with the sword and cast his dead body into the burial place of the common people (Jer 26:23; Ref Jer 22:17).

Jeremiah would have lost his life much like Uriah had not some of the elders of the land reminded all the assembly of the people about how Micah of Moresheth had prophesied about the destruction of Jerusalem and the temple in the days of Hezekiah (Jer 26:16-19). Jeremiah was able to escape death, because Ahikam the son of Shaphan protected him and did not hand him over to the people (Jer 26:24).

Shaphan, the father of Ahikam (the one who saved Jeremiah's life), was a scribe during King Josiah's time. He was the scribe who discovered the book of the law during the temple repairs and read it before the presence of the people (2 Kgs 22:3-14; 2 Chr 34:14-21). Ahikam's son Gedaliah also protected Prophet Jeremiah while he was appointed governor of Judah after the fall of Jerusalem (Jer 40:5-6; Ref 2 Kgs 25:22-24). Shaphan, his sons, and his grandsons were part of a godly family that preserved the holy lineage of faith during tragic times—when the nation had been destroyed and its religious leaders had become extremely corrupt.

Shaphan's other son, Gemariah, like his father, was a scribe during Jehoiakim's reign (Jer 36:10). Jeremiah received revelations from God during his days in hiding and had Baruch record and read them. At that time, Gemariah provided accommodations by allowing Baruch to read from the book the words of Jeremiah to all the people from his own chamber (in the upper court, at the entry of the New Gate of the Lord's house; Jer 36:9-10). When Micaiah the son of Gemariah and the grandson of Shaphan heard all the words that Baruch read in his father's chamber, he went to the scribe's chamber and declared all the words to the officials (Jer 36:11-13). Then, all the officials sent Jehudi (יְהוּדִי; Jew) to bring Baruch and the scroll so that they may hear the words directly from him (Jer 36:14-15). After listening to all the words spoken by Baruch, the officials turned to one another in fear and were of one opinion that they should report all these words to the king. After asking Baruch how these words were written, they told him to hide himself with Jeremiah (Jer 36:16-19).

They left the scroll in the chamber of Elishama the scribe and reported all the words to the king. The king then sent Jehudi to get the scroll and to read it to the king and all the officials who stood beside him (Jer 36:20-21). It was the ninth month (Chislev) so the king was sitting in the winter house with a fire burning in the fire pot before him (Jer 36:22).

Jehoiakim did not repent even after hearing the Word of God, but instead committed a cruel act. When Jehudi had read three or four columns, the king cut the scroll with a scribe's knife and threw it into the fire that was in the fire pot (Jer 36:23). He did not hesitate to continue the atrocious act until the whole scroll with the Word of God was consumed in the fire. The king and his servants who heard all these words were not afraid, nor did they rend their garments (Jer 36:24). Elnathan, Delaiah, and Gemariah pleaded with the king not to burn the scroll, but he would not listen to them and continued to burn it without any fear or guilty conscience (Jer 36:25).

As if burning the scroll was not enough, the king commanded Jerahmeel his son, Seraiah the son of Azriel, and Shelemiah the son of Abdeel to seize Baruch the scribe and Jeremiah the prophet (Jer 36:26a). Nevertheless, there was no way to know their whereabouts because the Lord had hidden them and had securely protected their lives (Jer 36:26b).

Jehoiakim defied God by persecuting and killing the prophet whom He sent and by burning the scroll of the Word of God. We must remember that those who defy God will surely perish. Proverbs 13:13 states,

"The one who despises the word will be in debt to it, but the one who fears the commandment will be rewarded."

After Jehoiakim had burned the scroll and the words which Baruch had written at the dictation of Jeremiah, the Word of the Lord came to Jeremiah again. Baruch again wrote at the dictation of Jeremiah the former words that were on the first scroll that was burnt; many similar words were added to them as well (Jer 36:27-28, 32).

The Word of God never disappears no matter how hard people may try to burn and destroy it (Luke 21:33). In fact, God gave more words than He originally gave and pronounced tragic judgment upon Jehoiakim who had burned up the Word (Jer 36:30-31). Judgment ultimately awaits those who persecute and disregard the Word of God, while victory and great rewards await those who hold on to it.

### 3. Jehoiakim was bound in chains and taken to Babylon

In 608 BC, around the time Jehoiakim was about to become king of Judah, the Assyrian Empire had collapsed, and Egypt and Babylon were fighting for supremacy in the former Assyrian territory. Babylon then dominated northern Mesopotamia while Pharaoh Neco of Egypt exerted influence over Palestine. Pharaoh Neco imprisoned Jehoahaz at Riblah in the land of Hamath, that he might not reign in Jerusalem; and he imposed on the land a fine of one hundred talents of silver and a talent of gold. He also changed Eliakim's name to Jehoiakim and made him king (2 Kgs 23:33-34). In 605 BC, Babylon defeated Egypt at the battle of Carchemish and became the most powerful nation of its time (Jer 46:2). After the Babylonian King Nebuchadnezzar secured dominance, he attacked Judah. This was Babylon's first attack upon Judah (2 Kgs 24:1a). It was the third (or the fourth) year of King Jehoiakim's reign (Dan 1:1; Ref Jer 46:2).

Three years later, in 602 BC, Babylon and Egypt battled again. This time, Egypt temporarily gained victory and Nebuchadnezzar returned to Babylon. Jehoiakim seized this opportunity to free himself from Babylon and betrayed King Nebuchadnezzar with the hope that Egypt would come to his aid (2 Kgs 24:1b). However, Egypt was only able to fend off a Babylonian attack; it did not have enough strength to help Judah. Then, Nebuchadnezzar the king of Babylon sent bands of Chaldeans, bands of

Arameans, bands of Moabites, and bands of Ammonites against Judah to destroy it (2 Kgs 24:2-4; Ref Jer 35:11). Nebuchadnezzar took Jehoiakim in bronze chains to Babylon. He also brought some of the articles of the house of the Lord to Babylon and put them in his temple (2 Chr 36:6-7; Ezra 1:7; Dan 1:2).

The Hebrew term for *bronze chains* (נְחֻשְׁתַּיִם, *něhuštayim*) that bound Jehoiakim means "copper," "brass," or "fetter" and is in the dual form, indicating that both of his feet were bound by fetters.[39] Because he relied on worldly powers like Egypt instead of God and cared only for himself, Jehoiakim was bound like a beast and taken to Babylon.

Jehoiakim returned to Jerusalem not long after he was taken captive to Babylon and ruled until 597 BC (eleven-year reign). He did evil in the sight of the Lord (2 Chr 36:5) and died a tragic death at the young age of thirty-six.

## 4. Jehoiakim died miserably just as Jeremiah had prophesied.

Prophet Jeremiah had prophesied that there would be no one to take pity or lament his death (Jer 22:18). He would be dragged off and thrown out beyond the gates of Jerusalem and be buried with a donkey's burial (Jer 22:19), and his dead body would be cast out to the heat of the day and the frost of the night (Jer 36:30). According to tradition, Jehoiakim was killed at the hands of King Nebuchadnezzar's servants in the eighth month of 597 BC and was cast out of the city of Jerusalem just as Jeremiah had prophesied.

King Jehoiakim did not realize that the history of the world throughout all the ages and times is in God's hand (Ps 31:15) and that all power and might lie in His hand (1 Chr 29:12). Had Jehoiakim relied upon God and not upon Egypt, God would have raised up Judah once again.

Isaiah 31:3 states, "Now the Egyptians are men and not God, and their horses are flesh and not spirit; so the Lord will stretch out His hand, and he who helps will stumble and he who is helped will fall, and all of them will come to an end together." As stated, Jehoiakim sought help from Egypt, but it caused him to perish. His reliance upon Egypt became his shame and reproach (Isa 30:1-5; 36:6).

All fear subsides and even the strongest enemy will draw back when a believer relies on God. No great powers of this world can touch those who trust firmly in God (Ps 56:9-11).

### 3. Zedekiah / Σεδεκίας / צִדְקִיָּה

The Lord is righteous

(Matthaniah) / Ματθανια / מַתַּנְיָה

The Lord's gift

- The twentieth king of Judah, the southern kingdom (2 Kgs 24:17-25:7; 2 Chr 36:11-21)
- Omitted from the genealogy of Jesus Christ

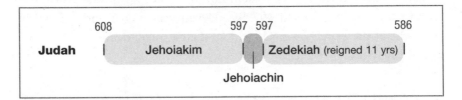

**Background**
– Father: Josiah
– Mother: Hamutal (the daughter of Jeremiah of Libnah; 2 Kgs 24:18)
Zedekiah and Jehoahaz (the seventeenth king of Judah, the southern kingdom) were brothers from the same parents.

**Evaluation** – evil king (2 Kgs 24:19; 2 Chr 36:11-12)

**Active prophets** – Jeremiah (Jer 1: 1-3), Daniel, and Ezekiel

**Historical records** – No record

Zedekiah replaced Jehoiachin to become the twentieth and last king of Judah, the southern kingdom. He was King Josiah's son (Jer 37:1) and Jehoiachin's uncle (2 Kgs 24:17). Zedekiah experienced the tragedy of having the nation completely destroyed during his reign and being taken captive to Babylon. Zedekiah is צִדְקִיָּה (ṣidqiyyâ) in Hebrew and is a combination of the word צֶדֶק (ṣedeq), meaning "righteousness" and "justice" and the word יָה (yāh), a shortened version of יְהוָֹה (yhwh); therefore, it means "the Lord is righteous."

# 1. Zedekiah ignored God's prophecy.

Through Prophet Jeremiah, God warned the people of Israel multiple times that they must surrender to the king of Babylon in order to live. In the ninth year (588 BC) of Zedekiah's reign, King Nebuchadnezzar of the mighty Babylonia attacked Jerusalem (2 Kgs 25:1; Jer 39:1; 52:4). Zedekiah became so anxious during the national crisis that he sent Pashhur the son of Malchijah and Zephaniah the priest, the son of Maaseiah, to ask Prophet Jeremiah to inquire of God on their behalf (Jer 21:1-2).

Through Prophet Jeremiah, God said that the king of Babylon and his army would strike Jerusalem and destroy everything in it, and advised Zedekiah that the people should not resist the Babylonian army, but surrender to them (Jer 21:3-10).

> **Jeremiah 21:9** He who dwells in this city will die by the sword and by famine and by pestilence; but he who goes out and falls away to the Chaldeans who are besieging you will live, and he will have his own life as booty.

Besides this incident, the message to surrender to Babylon was given continuously through Prophet Jeremiah (Jer 38:2, 17). God told Jeremiah, "It will be, that the nation or the kingdom which will not serve him, Nebuchadnezzar king of Babylon, and which will not put its neck under the yoke of the king of Babylon, I will punish that nation with the sword, with famine and with pestilence . . . until I have destroyed it by his hand" (Jer 27:8). With this message, Jeremiah repeatedly warned King Zedekiah, "Bring your necks under the yoke of the king of Babylon and serve him and his people, and live" (Jer 27:12). He also exclaimed, "Serve the king of Babylon, and live! Why should this city become a ruin?" (Jer 27:17).

Meanwhile, false prophets made prophecies that were opposite to Jeremiah's, thus confusing and enticing the leaders and the people (Jer 14:13-15; 27:9-10). The false prophets all tried to drive the true prophet Jeremiah into a corner and Hananiah was the representative of those prophets. He broke the wooden yoke from the neck of Jeremiah and challenged outright what Jeremiah had prophesied, "Even so will I break within two full years the yoke of Nebuchadnezzar king of Babylon from the neck of all the nations" (Jer 28:10-12). Nevertheless, God commanded Jeremiah to make a yoke stronger than the yoke of wood—a yoke of iron (Jer 28:13). Then just as Jeremiah prophesied to Hananiah, "I am about to remove you from the face of the earth. This year you are going to die" (Jer 28:15-16), Hananiah died in the seventh month of that same year (Jer 28:17).

It was probably difficult to accept the appalling reality that their nation had to surrender without putting up any resistance to an enemy that wanted to destroy them. Nevertheless, the best way to secure the nation's welfare and to preserve life was to humbly accept God's judgment for their sins and to entrust the nation's future into God's hand by surrendering to Babylon.

King Zedekiah, however, did not carefully consider the will of God that was proclaimed to him through Prophet Jeremiah. Instead, he disregarded God's Word and betrayed the king of Babylon (2 Kgs 24:20b; 2 Chr 36:13; Jer 52:3b). Zedekiah sent envoys to Pharaoh Hophra of Egypt (Ref Jer 44:30) and requested horses and troops (Ezek 17:15; Ref Ezek 17:7-10). As soon as the Babylonian army heard that the Egyptian army was on their way, they lifted the siege on Jerusalem and retreated temporarily (Jer 37:5, 7, 11). At this time, Zedekiah was probably full of hope that he could totally fend off the Babylonians with the help of the Egyptian power.

Yet, Jeremiah pointed out Zedekiah's vain expectations and self-deceiving heart, saying, "Do not deceive yourselves, saying, 'The Chaldeans will surely go away from us,' for they will not go. For even if you had defeated the entire army of Chaldeans who were fighting against you, and there were only wounded men left among them, each man in his tent, they would rise up and burn this city with fire" (Jer 37:9-10). Indeed, just as Jeremiah had prophesied, Pharaoh's army that had come to help Judah returned to their land in Egypt, and Babylon returned to Judah and besieged the city (Ezek 17:17).

As a result, God allowed the southern kingdom of Judah to be punished for seventy years in Babylon just as Jeremiah prophesied (2 Chr 36:21).

## 2. Zedekiah and his officials ignored God's prophet.

Under very pressing circumstances just before the fall of Jerusalem, Prophet Jeremiah repeatedly proclaimed the following messages of God: "He who goes out to the Chaldeans will live" (Jer 38:2) and "This city will certainly be given into the hand of the army of the king of Babylon and he will capture it" (Jer 38:3). Even after repeatedly hearing God's messages, Zedekiah, the head of the nation, and his high-ranking officials ignored Prophet Jeremiah and completely disbelieved God's Word.

### (1) Jeremiah was put in the stocks at the upper Benjamin Gate

When Pashhur, the chief officer in the house of the Lord, heard Jeremiah's prophecies, even he had Jeremiah beaten and put in the stocks that were at the upper Benjamin Gate (Jer 20:1-2). Despite the obvious signs of the nation's decline and ultimate fall, the people of Israel sought to comfort their anxious hearts with messages of peace that there would be no war and that the city would not be destroyed but would be recovered soon (Jer 28:3-4, 9; 38:4). They were enticed by false prophecies, which led them to destruction by self-deception.

### (2) Jeremiah was imprisoned in the dungeon, a vaulted cell

Until just before the fall of Jerusalem, Prophet Jeremiah cried aloud and proclaimed the message he received from God about the impending violence and destruction upon the people. The people were so wicked that they only listened to the words of the false prophets and closed their ears to the cries of Prophet Jeremiah (Jer 23:25; 27:14-16; 28:15). He was even falsely accused of being a traitor to the nation and was arrested by Irijah, the captain of the guard (Jer 37:13). Irijah did not even give Jeremiah a chance to plea and took him before the officials (Jer 37:14). They beat him and put him in the vaulted cell in a dungeon in the house of Jonathan the scribe, which had been made into a prison (Jer 37:15-16). While preaching the Word of God, Jeremiah was imprisoned in a vaulted cell with no sunlight and lost his freedom as he was kept under strict monitoring. He was oppressed and despised as if he were less than human.

His suffering was so severe that he was afraid that he might die there (Jer 37:20). Then suddenly King Zedekiah sent someone to take Jeremiah out of that place. It was because Jeremiah's prophecy came true (Jer 37:7), and the Babylonian army, which was believed to have retreated, attacked Jerusalem again and the Egyptian army did not help Zedekiah. Zedekiah craftily sent someone to call Jeremiah and secretly asked him if he had received any Word from God. Jeremiah answered without holding anything back, saying, "You will be given into the hand of the king of Babylon" (Jer 37:17). He also appealed to the king regarding the false accusations against him (Jer 37:18) and fiercely protested, "Where then are your prophets who prophesied to you, saying, 'The king of Babylon will not come against you or against this land'?" (Jer 37:19). The king's trusted prophets were the false prophets, and they had hidden their whereabouts once their prophecies were proven wrong.

It was a cruel time when the false prophets were treated well by the royal household while the true prophet, who lived to testify of only God's Word, was ignored and subjected to suffering. King Zedekiah listened to Jeremiah's pleas and protest, and he commanded that Jeremiah be put in the court of the guardhouse and given a loaf of bread each day (Jer 37:21).

### (3) Jeremiah was thrown into Malchijah's cistern in the court of the guardhouse

Nevertheless, Zedekiah and his officials did not cease to oppress Jeremiah. Jeremiah was accused by four of Zedekiah's officials—Shephatiah the son of Mattan, Gedaliah the son of Pashhur, Jucal the son of Shelemiah, and Pashhur the son of Malchijah. They sought to kill the innocent prophet, saying, "Now let this man be put to death, inasmuch as he is discouraging the men of war who are left in this city and all the people, by speaking such words to them; for this man is not seeking the well-being of this people but rather their harm" (Jer 38:1-4). King Zedekiah knew that Jeremiah was God's true prophet, but he feared the officials. Therefore, he placed Jeremiah into their hands and said, "Behold, he is in your hands; for the king can do nothing against you" (Jer 38:5).

The four officials, who had come together for the purpose of killing Jeremiah, threw him into the cistern of Malchijah the king's son (בֵּן; *ben*: descendant), which was in the court of the guardhouse (Jer 38:6). This cistern was made by digging the ground deep and was used as a well among other things. In the cistern into which Jeremiah was thrown, "There was no water but only mud, and Jeremiah sank into the mud" (Jer 38:6b). The word *mud* is טִיט (*ṭîṭ*) and refers to a very sticky type of mud clay (Isa 41:25), and the word *sink* is טָבַע (*ṭāba'*) and refers to a state of drowning deeply (Exod 15:4). Jeremiah's feet and body were buried in the muddy cistern where he was cold and hungry. His entire body was inflicted with severe pain from the earth's pressure pressing down upon his body. He was on the verge of losing his life until Ebed-melech the Ethiopian saved him by pleading with King Zedekiah and taking him out of the cistern (Jer 38:7-13).

During the most dismal time just before the destruction of Judah by the Babylonians, Jeremiah, the prophet of tears, lamented and prophesied about the national destruction out of his sincere love for the nation. Every time Jeremiah received God's Word and cried out, he exposed their violence and proclaimed their destruction. What he received in return was only contempt, persecution, humiliation, mental anguish, physical torment, and wounds (Jer 15:15, 18). Jeremiah confessed, "I have become a laughingstock all day long; everyone mocks me. For each time I speak, I cry aloud; I proclaim violence and destruction, because for me the word of the Lord has resulted in reproach and derision all day long" (Jer 20:7-8). Even his trusted friends watched for his stumbling, saying, "Perhaps he will be deceived, so that we may prevail against him and take our revenge on him" (Jer 20:10). His ministry was truly a trail of tears as he carried out his mission through a thorny path of suffering. Yet Jeremiah could not quit. He bore it all despite the hardship, because as he confessed, "You [Lord] have overcome me and prevailed" (Jer 20:7). It was God's zeal that compelled him and led him all the way.

Despite all kinds of mockery, persecution and severe loneliness, a true minister who proclaims the Word of the living God cannot help but confess, "But if I say, 'I will not remember Him or speak anymore in His name,' then in my heart it becomes like a burning fire shut up in my bones; and I am weary of holding it in, and I cannot endure it" (Jer 20:9). God rewards ultimate victory to those who long for the glory that is to be revealed and endure to the end while fulfilling their duties even in the midst of suffering (Matt 5:10-12; Rom 8:18; Heb 10:36).

## 3. The temple of Jerusalem was destroyed and the southern kingdom of Judah collapsed during Zedekiah's reign.

King Nebuchadnezzar of Babylon attacked Judah and besieged Jerusalem from the tenth day of the tenth month in the ninth year of Zedekiah's reign until the ninth day of the fourth month in the eleventh year of his reign, for about two years and six months (Tishri-to-Tishri calendar; 2 Kgs 25:1-2; Jer 39:1-2; 52:4-7). Jerusalem suffered from a severe famine during this time. As the period of the siege was drawn out, the people even began to boil and eat their own children (Ref Lam 4:10; 5:10). Finally, Jerusalem fell on the ninth day of the fourth month in the eleventh year of King Zedekiah (586 BC).

Zedekiah was captured by the Babylonian soldiers as he was fleeing.

He then had to witness his children being slaughtered before his eyes, after which his own eyes were put out (2 Kgs 25:7). In those days a red-hot iron was used to put out the eyes. After his eyes were put out so brutally, Zedekiah was dragged off to Babylon where he ultimately died (Ezek 17:16).

On the seventh day of the fifth month in the nineteenth year of King Nebuchadnezzar's reign, Nebuzaradan the captain of the guard, a servant of the king of Babylon, came to Jerusalem and burned the house of the Lord, the king's house, all the houses of Jerusalem, and every other great house. All the army of the Chaldeans also broke down the walls around Jerusalem (2 Kgs 25:8-10; 2 Chr 36:19). These things happened because God "gave them all into his hand," the hand of the king of the Chaldeans (2 Chr 36:17). Here, the "king of the Chaldeans" refers to Nebuchadnezzar II of Babylon whom God called "My servant" because He used him as an instrument for the judgment of Judah (Jer 25:9; 27:6; 43:10).

During the first deportation to Babylon (605 BC), they took "some of the vessels of the house of God" (Dan 1:2). Then in the second deportation (597 BC), they carried out "all the treasures of the house of the Lord" and "cut in pieces all the vessels of gold which Solomon king of Israel had made in the temple of the Lord" (2 Kgs 24:13). At this time, the false prophets prophesied falsely as though they were speaking in the name of the Lord saying, "Behold, the vessels of the Lord's house will now shortly be brought again from Babylon" (Jer 27:16). However, rather than bringing them back from Babylon, they lost even the vessels that were left behind.

The third deportation (586 BC) is described in 2 Kings 25:13-16 in the following manner (Ref Jer 27:18-22):

> "The bronze pillars which were in the house of the Lord, and the stands and the bronze sea which were in the house of the Lord, the Chaldeans broke in pieces and carried the bronze to Babylon. They took away the pots, the shovels, the snuffers, the spoons, and all the bronze vessels which were used in temple service. The captain of the guard also took away the firepans and the basins, what was fine gold and what was fine silver. The two pillars, the one sea, and the stands which Solomon had made for the house of the Lord—the bronze of all these vessels was beyond weight."

Nebuzaradan, the Babylonian captain of the guard, carried the remaining articles of the house of God to Babylon (2 Chr 36:18). He also took the rest of the people who were left in the city, and only the poorest of the land were left behind to be vinedressers and plowmen (2 Kgs 25:11-12).

After deporting the people to Babylon, the king of Babylon entrusted the land of Judah to Gedaliah the governor. However, Gedaliah was killed at the hands of a pro-Egyptian supporter named Ishamael and ten of his followers. Those who killed Gedaliah did not obey God's command to "live in the land and serve the king of Babylon" but fled to Egypt (2 Kgs 25:22-26). This plainly portrays the rebelliousness and unbelief of the southern kingdom of Judah, who persistently refused to trust only in God and relied on worldly powers like Egypt.

Zedekiah's original name was Mattaniah (2 Kgs 24:17). *Mattaniah* is מַתַּנְיָה (*mattanyâ*) in Hebrew, a combination of the word מַתָּן (*mattān*), meaning "gift" and the word יָה (*yāh*), which is a shortened version of "Jehovah". Hence, the name *Mattaniah* means "gift of the Lord."

Zedekiah becoming the last king of Judah was a gift from God. It was God's redemptive-historical providence to discipline the southern kingdom of Judah by sending them into Babylonian exile during Zedekiah's reign. Nevertheless, Zedekiah rejected Prophet Jeremiah's advice and fought against Babylon, and as a result he became the unfortunate king who saw the destruction of the nation during his reign.

Ultimately, the history of the southern kingdom of Judah, which began in 930 BC, ended in 586 BC, having lasted 344 years. The rise and fall of a nation rests only in the hands of God (Dan 2:21; 4:17, 35). He is the God of justice who thoroughly punishes sin even that of His chosen people. We must also follow the Word of God, obey, and live lives that overcome sin before God's punishment befalls us.

We have thus far examined the deeds of the fourteen people who appear in the third period of Jesus Christ's genealogy along with the omitted generations. We have especially examined the three kings—Jehoahaz, Jehoiakim, and Zedekiah—who ruled around the time of the deportation to Babylon but were not recorded in the genealogy. These three kings have a few things in common.

**FIRST, each of these three kings did evil according to all that their fathers had done (2 Kgs 23:32, 37; 24:9).**

We must not follow the unbelief or the evil ways of the forefathers.

But we should follow their faith and good deeds. King Josiah the father of the three kings—Jehoahaz, Jehoiakim, and Zedekiah—walked in all the way of his father David and did not turn aside to the right or to the left (2 Kgs 22:2). The three kings, however, did not follow after the uprightness, good deeds, and faith of King Josiah their father and King David.

**SECOND, the three kings did evil in the sight of the Lord (2 Kgs 23:32, 37; 24:9).**

The phrase "in the sight of the Lord" is הֹרִי יְנֵעֶב (bĕʿênê yhwh) in Hebrew and means "in the eyes of the Lord." We may deceive people's eyes, but we cannot deceive God's eyes. The Bible describes God as the One who may seem unknowing but knows everything (1 Sam 16:7; 1 Kgs 8:39; 1 Chr 28:9; 2 Chr 16:9; Ps 7:9; 26:2; 139:23-24; Prov 15:11; Jer 11:20; 17:10; 20:12; Zech 4:10; Acts 1:24; 15:8; Heb 4:13; 1 John 3:20; Rev 2:23). A person's ways may seem pure in his own sight, but it is not so in the eyes of God for He examines the inner thoughts and hearts of the people (Prov 16:2). For this reason, the Bible states that the eyes of the Lord are in every place, watching the evil and the good (Prov 15:3) and that the eyes of the Lord move to and fro throughout the earth (2 Chr 16:9). Job 34:22 states, "There is no darkness or deep shadow where the workers of iniquity may hide themselves." Our lives must never be evil but good in the eyes of God. We have to be zealous in doing good works that are worthy to be presented before God (Eph 2:10; Titus 2:14).

**THIRD, all three kings put their trust in things other than God.**

Jehoahaz, one of Josiah's four sons, was such a capable person that he was the first to become king among his brothers; but he trusted in himself instead of God and was taken captive to Egypt where he died (2 Kgs 23:34). Jehoiakim and Zedekiah did not listen to God's instruction to surrender to Babylon; rather, they put their trust in Egypt and were eventually taken captive to Babylon (2 Kgs 24:1, 7; Jer 27:1-8).

Proverbs 16:20 states, "He who gives attention to the word will find good, and blessed is he who trusts in the Lord." Whenever we face unexpected crises, we must not first seek help from man in whom there is no salvation (Ps 146:3-5). Rather, we must first go to the house of God, and holding fast onto His Word, we must exert great effort in pouring out our hearts in supplication (Ps 62:8). Those who seek the Lord will not lack any good thing (Ps 34:10).

The people of Judah were taken to Babylon in three stages of deportation. The first deportation was in 605 BC, the second in 597 BC, and the third in 586 BC. This was God's punishment and an expression of His indignation toward the southern kingdom of Judah that had sinned, worshipped idols, and despised the Word of God (Ps 85:4; 107:10-11).

Although God left Judah to utter destruction and His people in captivity during King Zedekiah's time, it was not the end of everything. God ceaselessly carried on His redemptive-historical administration by restoring Judah from the Babylonian captivity.

In the next chapter, we will survey the history of this recovery from the Babylonian captivity.

לכל בר דעת דרך המסעות ארבעים שנה במדבר 'והרוחב והאורך של אתך הקדושה מיגר. מ...

עמלק

מדבר צין הוא קדש

ים המלח

הר ההר

מדבר סיני

עיר כרמל

שבט יהוד...

מדבר פארן

מדבר שור

באר שבע

שבט שמעון

שבט

ארץ פלשתם

ארץ גשן

פתם

רעמסס

צען

אלכסנדרי

לות המסעות במדבר
אשר על פה יסעו ועל פי יחנו

| | | |
|---|---|---|
| רז' חר הגדד | טז' רחמה | א' רעמסס |
| ל' ימבתה | טז' רמן פרץ | ב' סכת |
| לא' עברנה | יז' לבנה | ג' אתם |
| לב' עציון גבר | יח' רסה | ד' פי החירת |
| לג' מדבר צין | יט' קהלתה | ה' מרה |
| לד' הר ההר | ד' הר ספר | ו' אילם |
| לה' צלמנה | דא' חרדה | ז' ים סוף |
| לו' פונן | דב' מקהלה | ח' מדבר סין |
| לז' אבת | דג' תחת | ט' רפקה |
| לה' דיבן גר | דד' תרח | וז' אלוש |
| לט' עלמן דבלי' | דה' מתקה | יא' רפידם |
| מ' הרי עברים | דו' חשמנה | יב' מדבר סיני |
| מא' ערבת מואב | דד' מסרות | יג' קברת התאו |
| רח' בני יעקן | דד' חצרת | יד' |

PART FIVE

# The History of the Babylonian Captivity and the Return

# The History of the Babylonian Captivity and the Return

The third period of the genealogy of Jesus Christ records fourteen generations from the deportation to Babylon until the coming of Jesus Christ. The most important events that occurred during this period are the deportation of Judah to Babylon and their return.

God saw the sins of the southern kingdom of Judah becoming pervasive in Jerusalem and throughout Judah. Nevertheless, God bore with them for many years and rebuked them and solemnly admonished them, daily rising early and sending many prophets again and again (2 Chr 36:15-16; Neh 9:29-31, Isa 65:12; Jer 7:13, 24-26; 11:7-8; 25:3-4; 26:5; 29:19; 35:15; 44:4; Hos 11:2; Zech 7:13). The obstinate people of Israel, however, refused to listen until the end, and when their sins had reached their fullness beyond the tipping point, God sentenced them to be punished through the Babylonian captivity.

The southern kingdom of Judah was deported to Babylon on three separate occasions: the first in 605 BC, the second in 597 BC, and the third in 586 BC. Nevertheless, in keeping with His promise to allow them to return after seventy years (Jer 25:11-12; 29:10; Ref 2 Chr 36:21-22; Dan 9:2), God stirred the heart of Cyrus, king of Persia, so that he made a proclamation to free the people from captivity (2 Chr 36:22-23; Ezra 1:1-4). This shows that God will never forsake His people once He has chosen them. He will purify and refine them through punishment such as the captivity, after which He will raise them up and use them again.

The southern kingdom of Judah returned from the Babylonian captivity on three different occasions: the first return in 537 BC, the second in 458 BC, and the third in 444 BC.

The Israelites who returned from the captivity completed the reconstruction of the temple in 516 BC and the rebuilding of the city walls in 444 BC. The rebuilt temple was called Zerubbabel's temple, which served as the center of spiritual life for the Israelites for about five hundred years.

The third period of the genealogy of Jesus Christ includes the era of the Persian rule (539–331 BC), the era of the Greek rule (331–164 BC), the era of the Maccabean Revolution (167–142 BC), the era of the Hasmonean Dynasty (142–63 BC), and the era of the Roman rule (63 BC onwards).

From the time of the completion of the temple and the city walls until the coming of Jesus Christ, prophecies ceased and the Israelites passed through a spiritually dark age, which lasted over four hundred years; nothing from this period was recorded in the Bible. Despite such spiritual darkness, God, in His administration of redemptive history, continued to prepare the coming path of Jesus Christ, the light of redemption for the entire universe (John 1:5; 8:12; 9:5). At last, when the fullness of the time came, He sent forth Jesus Christ, the seed of the woman (Gal 4:4).

By summarizing the history of Israel pertaining to the third period of the genealogy of Jesus Christ, let us discover God's administration of redemption that lies therein.

CHAPTER 11

# The Cause of the Babylonian Captivity

Israel was a weak nation caught between powerful nations such as Assyria and Babylonia to the north and Egypt to the south. During the turbulent transitions of power when Assyria collapsed and the Babylonian empire emerged, Prophet Jeremiah tearfully prophesied about the right path that Israel must take. At that time, the Word that God continuously gave to Prophet Jeremiah to proclaim was that they should surrender to Babylon (Jer 21:8-9; 38:2, 17-21). God said to bear the yoke of Babylon and serve its king (2 Kgs 25:24; Jer 25:11; 27:8-9; 27:12, 17; 28:2, 14; 40:9). From beginning to end, Prophet Jeremiah cried out that the only way for the entire people to survive was to obey the Word of God and surrender to Babylon.

Nevertheless, all of the priests, the prophets, and the people of his time tried to kill Jeremiah, the true prophet. They accused him of being a fraud and a false prophet who lied in the name of the Lord (Jer 26:8-11). In this chapter, we will examine Jeremiah's messages delivered over seven different occasions. In these messages he urged the people of Israel to surrender to Babylon. We will also examine the cause of the Babylonian exile.

## 1. The tragic end of Judah, the southern kingdom

When Pharaoh Neco of Egypt killed King Josiah at Megiddo, the people of Judah enthroned Josiah's third son, Shallum (Jehoahaz, 609b–608 BC; 2 Kgs 23:30-31; Jer 22:11). When the enfeebled kingdom of Judah enthroned Jehoahaz without permission from Pharaoh Neco II of Egypt, he deported the newly crowned king to Egypt and enthroned Josiah's second son, Jehoiakim (608–597 BC), in Jehoahaz's place (2 Kgs 23:34). Under Egypt's oppressive rule over the Palestinian area during those days, Jehoiakim had no choice but to support pro-Egyptian policies. However, when Egypt was defeated in the battle of Carchemish (605 BC) and Babylon became the dominant power in the region, King Jehoiakim became Babylon's vassal and had to pay tribute to Nebuchadnezzar. Three years later, he saw that Egypt successfully defended herself against Babylonian invasions. As a result, Jehoiakim stopped paying tribute to Babylon and supported Egypt again (2 Kgs 24:1; Jer 25:1, 9; 46:2). Then, King Nebuchadnezzar of Babylon realigned his army and sent them to Jerusalem (602 BC). In 597 BC, Nebuchadnezzar sent a second group of Chaldean forces to besiege Jerusalem. Jehoiakim was killed while waiting for assistance from Egypt and was thrown outside the gate of Jerusalem (2 Kgs 24:1-5; Jer 22:18-19).

When Jehoiakim died, his son Coniah (Jehoiachin) succeeded the throne; but he was taken captive to Babylon after only three months and ten days (2 Kgs 24:8; 2 Chr 36:9). Nebuchadnezzar then enthroned Mattaniah (Zedekiah), Josiah's other son and Jehoiachin's uncle (2 Kgs 24:17; 2 Chr 36:10). Not long after he began his reign, King Zedekiah disobeyed God's Word and did not surrender to Babylon. Instead, he rebelled against Babylon and implemented pro-Egyptian policies. As a result, Nebuchadnezzar invaded again in the ninth year of Zedekiah's reign. Once more, Zedekiah foolishly disobeyed God's Word, eagerly awaiting rescue from Egypt until the end. At last, Zedekiah was brought before the king of Babylon; his two sons were killed in his sight and he was bound in chains and taken to Babylon with his eyes put out (2 Kgs 25:5-7). Excruciating humiliation and national tribulation came upon Judah in 586 BC as Jerusalem fell; the temple was destroyed, and countless number of people were deported to Babylon.

## 2. Prophet Jeremiah's tireless plea: "Surrender to Babylon"

Through Prophet Jeremiah, God delivered the message to surrender to Babylon on over seven different occasions. Surrendering to Babylon was the only way to preserve the lives of the Israelites until God's appointed time (Jer 29:5-7, 10-11). God had a grand plan to discipline His people through the seventy years of exile in Babylon, after which He would lead them back to their homeland through His chosen servant, Cyrus the king of Persia (Isa 44:28; Jer 25:11; 29:10; Ref 2 Chr 36:22-23; Ezra 1:1-4). In tears, Prophet Jeremiah urged the Israelites to repent in preparation for the salvation and restoration that God would bring in the future. The book of Jeremiah employs the Hebrew verb שׁוּב(šûb), which literally means "return," ninety-two times to signify repentance. This word foreshadows how the people of Israel would return at the end of their exile in Babylon; simultaneously, it signifies that the people would turn away from their sinful ways and return to the bosom of God. Jeremiah 3:12 states, "Return, faithless Israel," and the word *return* here is also the Hebrew verb, שׁוּב (*šûb*). God also said in Jeremiah 4:1, "If you will return, O Israel," implying that there will always be a path to salvation even in difficult circumstances as long as His people return to God. God pointed out in Jeremiah 2:19, "It is evil and bitter for you to forsake the Lord your God, and the dread of Me is not in you." As long as the people *return* from their rebellious ways, God will wash away their sins and allow them to *return* from their exile in Babylon (Jer 29:11-14).

God thus repeatedly told them—as many as seven times—that they must surrender to Babylon.

### (1) 608 BC (Three years before the first deportation)
In 608 BC—not long after the enthronement of Jehoiakim, the son of Josiah the king of Judah (Jer 27:1; Ref Jer 26:1)—God said, "It will be, *that* the nation or the kingdom which will not serve him, Nebuchadnezzar king of Babylon, and which will not put its neck under the yoke of the king of Babylon, I will punish that nation with the sword, with famine and with pestilence . . . until I have destroyed it by his hand" (Jer 27:8). God also said in Jeremiah 27:17, "serve the king of Babylon, and live! Why should this city become a ruin?"

### (2) 605 BC (At the time of the first deportation)
During the first deportation in 605 BC (Jer 25:1), God said, "Then it will be when seventy years are completed I will punish the king of Babylon and that nation . . . for their iniquity, and the land of the Chaldeans; and I will make it an everlasting desolation" (Jer 25:12). This statement implies that God had decreed the seventy years of the Babylonian exile as the punishment period. Therefore, the people of Judah had to keep their necks under the yoke of the king of Babylon until God's appointed time.

### (3) 597 BC (After the second deportation)
The actual prophecy that "they will return to their land after they serve the king of Babylon for seventy years" was given during the first and second deportations. During the second deportation in 597 BC (Jer 29:2), God said, "When seventy years have been completed for Babylon, I will

visit you and fulfill My good word to you, to bring you back to this place" (Jer 29:10). Afterwards, God showed Prophet Jeremiah two baskets of figs set before the temple of the Lord. Through the parable of the two baskets of figs, He prophesied that they must surrender to Babylon.

The first of the two baskets had very good figs, like first-ripe figs; they referred to the Jews who were carried away captive to Babylon (Jer 24:2-7). The other basket had bad figs which would be thrown away because they cannot be eaten due to rottenness; they referred to the Jews who remained in Judah or those who lived in the land of Egypt (Jer 24:8-10).

### (4) 593 BC (Four years after the second deportation)

Not long after Zedekiah took the throne (Zedekiah's fourth year of reign), God once again delivered the message to "surrender to Babylon" through Prophet Jeremiah (Jer 27:1).[40] In order to deliver this message with full effect, God told Prophet Jeremiah to "make for yourself bonds and yokes and put them on your neck" (Jer 27:2). Furthermore, God commanded Jeremiah to send them to the king of Edom, the king of Moab, the king of the sons of Ammon, the king of Tyre, and the king of Sidon via the messengers that had come to Jerusalem from each of these nations (Jer 27:3). God had not only told Judah to surrender to Babylon, but He also delivered this clear message to the surrounding nations as well. These messengers were special envoys dispatched by each of these nations specifically to conspire an anti-Babylonian alliance. They were in Jerusalem to meet with Zedekiah for this purpose. The fact that they had gathered in Jerusalem leads one to believe that Zedekiah may have been the leader of this conspiratorial effort. However, God clearly stated, "I have given all these lands into the hand of Nebuchadnezzar king of Babylon, My servant, and I have given him also the wild animals of the field to serve him. All the nations shall serve him and his son and his grandson" (Jer 27:6-7). He further told them, in an unequivocal manner, that this alliance to defy Babylon was an exercise in futility which will bring about the sword, famine, and pestilence (Jer 27:4-8). In addition, God warned them not to listen to the false prophets who prophesy, saying, "You will not serve the king of Babylon." He also strongly cautioned them that the lies of these false prophets will "remove you far from your land; and I will drive you out and you will perish" (Jer 27:9-10). Then, God promised that the nation that will "bring its neck under the yoke of the king of Babylon" will remain in their own land, tilling and dwelling in it (Jer 27:11).

In the fifth month of the fourth year of Zedekiah's reign, Hananiah the son of Azzur, the prophet who was from Gibeon, made a false prophecy that God had broken the yoke of the king of Babylon (Jer 28:1-4). However, Prophet Jeremiah put on his neck a wooden yoke ("a wooden bar or frame placed on the head or neck of draft animals to which a cart or a plow is attached for pulling") just as God commanded him (Jer 27:1-2). He then prophesied with his actions that those who do not put their necks under the yoke of the king of Babylon would surely be destroyed (Jer 27:8-9, 11-13; 28:2-4, 10-14). The wooden yoke conveyed a message that even though it would be very difficult, they would live only if they served the king of Babylon. Then, the false prophet Hananiah reacted furiously, taking the wooden yoke from the neck of Jeremiah, and breaking it. At that time, God spoke to Hananiah through Jeremiah, "I have put a yoke of iron on the neck of all these nations, that they may serve Nebuchadnezzar king of Babylon" (Jer 28:13-14).

If the people had just obeyed God's Word to bear the wooden yoke on their necks and surrender to Babylon, irreversible calamities like the iron yoke would not have come upon them. They would have lived in hope and peace (Jer 29:11). Yet, because they disobeyed His Word, Jerusalem was completely destroyed and the temple was burned with fire. The people faced tragic deaths by famine, sword, and pestilence.

Hananiah the prophet also died in the same year in the seventh month—two months after he made the false prophecies (Jer 28:17).

### (5) 588 BC (About two years before the third deportation)

When Nebuchadnezzar of Babylon came up to attack Judah, Zedekiah asked Jeremiah to pray so that Babylon would retreat. Jeremiah replied to Zedekiah, "He who dwells in this city will die by the sword and by famine and by pestilence; but he who goes out and falls away to the Chaldeans who are besieging you will live, and he will have his own life as booty" (Jer 21:9).

The false prophets outright challenged Jeremiah, arguing that the people of Judah would never have to put their necks under the yoke of Nebuchadnezzar the king of Babylon and serve him (Jer 27:9-10, 14-16; 28:2, 4, 11). Their prophecies, however, did not come from God; they were only human schemes (Jer 27:15; 28:15; 29:23, 31). Indeed, everyone wished victory and peace for Jerusalem. Nevertheless, since God had already purposed to execute His *judgment* upon Israel for her sins, yielding to God's plan was the way to life and to salvation.

### (6) 587 BC (One year before the third deportation)

When Jerusalem was under siege by the Babylonian army during the reign of Zedekiah, a captain of the guard whose name was Irijah, the son of Shelemiah the son of Hananiah, arrested Prophet Jeremiah. Irijah said, "You are going over to the Chaldeans!" and brought him to the officials. Then the officials beat Jeremiah and put him into the dungeon, that is, the vaulted cell (Jer 37:11-15).

After many days had passed, Zedekiah sent someone to take Jeremiah out and asked him, "Is there a word from the Lord?" Jeremiah gave the same reply: "You will be given into the hand of the king of Babylon!" (Jer 37:16-17). He then pleaded with the king not to make him return to the jail in the house of Jonathan the scribe, and Zedekiah permitted Jeremiah to remain in the court of the guardhouse and receive a loaf of bread daily (Jer 37:18-21).

### (7) After 586 BC (Immediately after the third deportation)

Through Jeremiah God prophesied to those who remained in Judah, "You should neither go down to Egypt nor be afraid of the king of Babylon. Stay in your land, Canaan. Then, God will be with you and deliver you from the king of Babylon" (Jer 42:7-17). God also said to the exiles in Babylon, "let Jerusalem come to your mind" (Jer 51:50). This was because the land of Babylon would soon perish and disappear (Jer 51:20-64), but the land of Canaan was the land that God "gave to their fathers forever and ever" (Jer 7:7).

## 3. The cause of Israel's captivity in Babylon

From the perspective of the Law, Israel's deportation to Babylon 1,500 km away from their own land signified their expulsion from the land of the covenant. The book of Leviticus describes it as, "the land has spewed out its inhabitants." Leviticus 18:24-25 states, "For by all these the nations which I am casting out before you have become defiled. For the land has become defiled, therefore I have brought its punishment upon it, so the land has spewed out its inhabitants." Also, in Leviticus 18:27-28, God said, ". . . for all these things were done by the people who lived in the land before you, and the land became defiled. And if you defile the land, it will vomit you out as it vomited out the nations that were before you" (NIV).

When God ratified the covenant of the torch with Abraham, He promised that his descendants would return and take over the land of Canaan in the fourth generation. He explained that it was because the iniquity of the Amorites had not yet been complete (Gen 15:16). This implies that a time of judgment for the iniquity of the Amorites, the inhabitants of Canaan, has to be reached before God could give the land of Canaan to Israel, His elect. In other words, the process through which Abraham's descendants come to occupy the land of Canaan is, in a sense, judgment for the iniquity of the Amorites and the inhabitants of Canaan (Lev 18:24-25).

This principle of judgment, however, applied also to Israel, God's chosen people. The people of Israel did not obey the commandments of the Law, which God had given to them through Moses. When they became filled with all kinds of idolatry and harlotry and failed to carry out God's commands for the sabbath and the sabbatical year, God allowed the land to spew out the Israelites so that the land could rest. God had used the Israelites as His instrument to punish the sins of the inhabitants of Canaan; but now, God was using Babylon as His instrument to punish the sins of the Israelites and to spew them out.

Jeremiah 2:13 speaks of two major evils committed by the Israelites during the time of Jeremiah. These two evils became the cause of their exile to Babylon.

> **Jeremiah 2:13** For My people have committed two evils: They have forsaken Me, the fountain of living waters, to hew for themselves cisterns, broken cisterns that can hold no water.

The first evil was that they *forsook God*, the fountain of living waters.

The second evil was that they *hewed for themselves cisterns*. This refers to their idolatry, the sin of serving other gods. God says that He sent Israel away and gave her "a writ of divorce" (Jer 3:8) because Israel was "a harlot" (Jer 3:1, 6). Israel was reproved as a divorced harlot because she forsook God, her true husband (Jer 3:14; NIV), and committed adultery with other lovers.

Even worse, the people of Israel did not even blush while committing such deeds because their hearts had become so hardened (Jer 6:15). Their sins had become so deep, as if the sins had been engraved upon their hearts with an iron stylus or with a diamond point (Jer 17:1). The people became so corrupt that they neglected God's exhortations and despised them as a "reproach" (Jer 6:10). Because they forsook their God, the fountain of living waters, they could not turn from the sins of idolatry and violation of the sabbath day and sabbatical years. As a result, they were destroyed by the Babylonians.

## (1) Sin of idolatry

As a prophet who was active right before the fall of the southern kingdom of Judah, Jeremiah pointed out the sins of the Israelites. He repeatedly warned against their idolatrous ways of forsaking God and walking after gods other than the Lord their God (Jer 1:16; 3:13; 5:19; 7:6, 9, 18; 11:10, 12; 13:10; 16:11, 13; 19:4, 13; 22:9; 25:6-7; 35:15; 44:3, 5, 8, 15, Ref 2 Kgs 22:17; 2 Chr 34:25). They worshiped and served the idols, the molten images that they made (Jer 10:14; 51:17; Ref Isa 2:8). They were engrossed in worshiping idols regardless of where they were, and their gods were as many as their cities (Jer 2:28; 11:13).

As such, God preached His Word by sending all His servants and prophets again and again; He was, "daily rising early and sending them," so that the people could realize the seriousness of their sin of idolatry and repent. Nevertheless, the entire people never heeded His Word but completely ignored it (Jer 7:25; 25:4; 26:5; 29:19; 35:15; 44:4). They even denied the existence of God and took the lead in killing the true prophets who only delivered God's Word by denouncing them as false prophets (Jer 5:12-13).

① **God warned Israel of His judgment through three prohibitions given to Prophet Jeremiah (Jer 16:1-13).**

The three prohibitions given to Jeremiah were related to important matters of life, such as funerals and marriages, all of which symbolically pronounce God's judgment against Judah.

*FIRST,* "**you shall not take a wife for yourself nor have sons or daughters**" **(Jer 16:2-4).**

God commanded Jeremiah not to take a wife or have any children because Judah would be destroyed very soon. God wanted to make the people realize that children or their parents would die without anyone to lament for them or to bury them, and their carcasses would become food for the birds of the sky and for the beasts of the earth (Jer 16:4). Although marriage and childbirth are undoubtedly blessings from God, they can bring great pain in times of national crisis. They would have caused even greater pain and would have been a hindrance for Jeremiah who was ministering before God. Prophet Jeremiah fully obeyed the Word of God, setting a good example of true obedience for the people.

Just as God commanded, Prophet Isaiah named his son *Maher-shalal-hash-baz*, which has a very strange meaning of "swift is booty," prophesying the destruction of Aram and the northern kingdom of Israel (Isa 8:1-4). Furthermore, Isaiah prophesied about the shame of Egypt and Cush by going naked and barefoot for three years (Isa 20:1-6). To awaken the Israelites to the severe wickedness of their idolatry, or spiritual harlotry, Hosea married the adulterous Gomer and endured all kinds of humiliation and misery (Hos 1:1-9). Jeremiah and all these prophets endured realistically unbearable suffering and shame throughout their lives; they painstakingly undertook their mission for their generation by wholly obeying, without adding or taking away from the words that God commanded.

**SECOND**, "do not enter a house of mourning" (Jer 16:5-7).

God told Jeremiah not to enter a house of mourning to lament or to console the people. The prohibition of entering a house of mourning signifies that God would now withdraw His peace, lovingkindness, and compassion from the people of Judah (Jer 16:5). Furthermore, Jeremiah was told to prophesy that both great men and small will die and every house will be mourning, such that they would not be buried or lamented (Jer 16:6).

"Great men" refer to those with power, wealth, and abilities, whereas "small men" refer to those who are powerless in society. Because both great and small men transgressed before God, none of them would be buried nor would their deaths be lamented. Also, since the calamity that fell upon Judah was God's judgment upon them, they were not to enter a house of mourning to comfort the people. Normally, a funeral is a place where a person can most deeply reflect upon life. It provides a solemn hour to remember the lifetime accomplishments of the deceased and to express condolences to the family. However, when severe calamities befall the entire nation so that every household is overwhelmed with countless dead bodies, solemn funerals or mourning are no longer meaningful. This signifies the dreadfulness of the judgment against Judah; wedding ceremonies and funerals—the happiest and the most solemn hour, respectively—would end altogether in Judah.

*THIRD*, "you shall not go into a house of feasting" (Jer 16:8-9).

A house of feasting (a wedding feast) is a place that most explicitly demonstrates the happiness and gladness pursued by all men. The glowing faces of the rejoicing bride and groom as well as the smiling faces of the guests who have come to bless the future of the newlywed probably represent the climax of happiness in life. Furthermore, a marriage builds a family, the primary social unit, and a family is the basis of childbirth that guarantees the existence of the members of society. Hence, when marriages or childbirths disappear, the society will also collapse. Jeremiah's attendance at a wedding feast would imply that the society of Judah would endure, which would then make his message concerning Judah's fall a lie. By prohibiting Jeremiah from entering a house of feasting, God powerfully warned that all happiness and gladness that Israel had enjoyed in the past would be completely gone because of their disobedience to the Word of God.

These three prophetic acts were a strong warning of the most severe punishment that would befall and utterly destroy Israel.

God explained to Jeremiah that the people would protest after hearing the message of the judgment, asking, "For what reason has the Lord declared all this great calamity against us? What is our iniquity, or what is our sin which we have committed against the Lord our God?" (Jer 16:10). Jeremiah was informed to reply with the following answer (Ref Jer 5:19):

> **Jeremiah 16:11-13** Then you are to say to them, 'It is because your forefathers have forsaken Me,' declares the LORD, 'and have followed other gods and served them and bowed down to them; but Me they have forsaken and have not kept My law. [12] You too have done evil, even more than your forefathers; for behold, you are each one walking according to the stubbornness of his own evil heart, without listening to Me. [13] So I will hurl you out of this land into the land which you have not known, neither you nor your fathers; and there you will serve other gods day and night, for I will grant you no favor.'

② **Through the parable of a broken jar (earthenware with a narrow neck), God warned that Israel would surely fall due to their sins of idolatry (Jer 19:1-15; Ref Jer 7:30-34).**

Jeremiah broke a jar in the valley of Ben-hinnom, a place that was used to incinerate garbage or cremate animal carcasses or human corpses. His act was a warning that the calamity upon Judah would be so great that their dead bodies would not have a proper place for burial and would wretchedly become food for the birds and the beasts (Jer 19:11-12; Ref Jer 7:32). Not only that, this was a proclamation of a disaster where their enemies and those who seek their lives would besiege them so that a severe famine would befall them. The famine and distress would be so extreme that they would be driven to eat the flesh of their own sons and daughters (Jer 19:9).

There was a clear reason why Jerusalem, the city of peace, had become a sign for death or a living hell. The Israelites committed sins of idolatry by burning incense to all the hosts of heaven and pouring out drink offerings to other gods. Moreover, they did not repent even after they were given the chance to repent (Jer 19:1, 10-13).

Jeremiah 32:34 states, "But they put their detestable things in the house which is called by My name, to defile it." God was pointing out that Judah had placed the idols even inside the house of the Lord to worship them (2 Kgs 21:1-7; Ezek 8:1-18). Hence, the Israelites had already defiled the temple of God long before it was destroyed by the Babylonians (Ezek 22:4).

## (2) Sin of not keeping the sabbath day and the sabbatical year
### ① Failure in keeping the sabbath day
Whether or not a person has kept the sabbath day determines if he has obeyed or disobeyed the law; it also determines the outcome of blessings or woes (Jer 17:19-27). This is because the sabbath day was given as an eternal sign so that people might know that the Lord is the one who sanctifies His people (Exod 31:13; Ezek 20:12, 20).

Jeremiah stood at all the gates of Jerusalem through which both the kings of Judah and the people came in and went out. There, he proclaimed the teachings and warnings concerning the sabbath day to the kings of Judah, all of Judah, and all inhabitants of Jerusalem who came through those gates (Jer 17:19-20). There were twelve gates in Jerusalem (Ref Neh 3:1-32; 8:1, 3, 16; 12:39; Zech 14:10). Hence, Jeremiah must have proclaimed this message repeatedly—twelve times from all the gates, reflecting clearly how poorly the sabbath day had been kept in those days.

Jeremiah cried out, "Take heed for yourselves, and do not carry any load on the sabbath day or bring anything in through the gates of Jerusalem . . . nor do any work, but keep the sabbath day holy" (Jer 17:21-26). God strictly warned through Jeremiah, "But if you do not listen to Me to keep the sabbath day holy by not carrying a load and coming in through the gates of Jerusalem on the sabbath day, then I will kindle a fire in its gates and it will devour the palaces of Jerusalem and not be quenched" (Jer 17:27).

Just as Jeremiah had prophesied, the southern kingdom of Judah experienced first, second, and third invasions from Babylon, and Solomon's temple and the king's house in Jerusalem were burned with fire (2 Kgs 25:9; 2 Chr 36:19; Jer 39:8; 52:13; Amos 2:5). Likewise, Israel's failure to keep the sabbath day became the direct cause for their exile in Babylon.

Ezekiel chapter 22 proclaims the destruction of the southern kingdom of Judah. Verses 8 and 22 state that the fall resulted because they did not keep the sabbath day. God said in verse 8, "You have . . . profaned My sabbaths" and in verse 26, "they hide their eyes from My sabbaths, and I am profaned among them."

② **Failure in keeping the sabbatical year**
The ordinance of the sabbatical year consists of letting the land rest in the seventh year and setting free their kinsman, the Hebrew slaves, in the seventh year.

**FIRST, they were commanded to sow the land for six years and let it rest on the seventh year (Exod 23:10-11; Lev 25:1-7; 26:34-35).**
After entering Canaan the Promised Land, the Israelites were not supposed to sow the land in the seventh year (Lev 25:2-4); they were not even allowed to reap the grain or the fruit that grows on its own so that the land could rest (Lev 25:5). By allowing the land to rest during the sabbatical year, whatever grew out naturally was to be left as shared food for the landowner, his male and female slaves, his hired man, his foreign residents who lived as aliens with the owner, and even the cattle and animals that were in his land (Lev 25:6-7). In other words, the produce from the sabbatical year was common property to be shared by all in the world of creation. This is because the sabbatical year is a covenant between God and the world of His creation.

God promised that if the Israelites kept the sabbatical year and let the land rest in the seventh year, "then I will so order My blessing for you in the sixth year that it will bring forth the crop for three years" (Lev 25:21). Since God promised that He would provide enough crops for three years in the sixth year, they could eat freely without worrying in the seventh year (the sabbatical year) as well as in the eighth year, and even into the ninth year (Lev 25:22). In this manner, God made the people know that all things belong to God and come from Him (Lev 25:23).

Nonetheless, the people of Israel did not believe in God's Word. They became greedy and did not keep the sabbatical year but sowed in the land even in the seventh year. Because of this, God caused the southern kingdom of Judah to be taken captive to Babylon so that the land could rest. Second Chronicles 36:21 states, "to fulfill the word of the LORD by the mouth of Jeremiah, until the land had enjoyed its sabbaths. All the days of its desolation it kept sabbath until seventy years were complete" (Lev 26:43).

**SECOND, if their slaves were their kinsmen, then they were to work the Hebrew slaves for six years, but let them go free in the seventh year (Exod 21:2-6; Deut 15:12-18).**

The law stipulates that if a male or female slave is a Hebrew, then that slave must be set free in the seventh year of slavery (Exod 21:2; Deut 15:12). Moreover, the freed slave must not be sent away empty-handed; the owner must furnish the slave liberally from his flock, threshing floor, and wine vat, as God has blessed the owner (Deut 15:13-14). It also stipulates that the slave should be released unconditionally as a free man without ransom payment (Exod 21:2). This is because the six years of labor by the purchased slave would be equal to the ransom payment. Deuteronomy 15:18 states, "It shall not seem hard to you when you set him free, for he has given you six years with double the service of a hired man; so the Lord your God will bless you in whatever you do."

After God delivered the Israelites from Egypt, He promised to give them rest (Deut 12:9-10). Nevertheless, the Israelites did not keep the everlasting covenant, that is, the ordinance of the sabbatical year. When the Babylonians invaded the third time and Jerusalem was under siege, the frightened King Zedekiah made a covenant with all the people of Jerusalem and briefly freed their Hebrew slaves (Jer 34:8-10). A while later, however, King Zedekiah and the Israelites took back the servants whom they had set free and brought them into subjection for servitude again (Jer 34:11). Jeremiah 34:14 states, "At the end of seven years each of you shall set free his Hebrew brother who has been sold to you and has served you six years, you shall send him out free from you; but your forefathers did not obey Me or incline their ear to Me." Then comes God's proclamation: "'You have not obeyed Me in proclaiming release each man to his brother and each man to his neighbor. Behold, I am proclaiming a release to you,' declares the Lord, 'to the sword, to the pestilence and to the famine; and I will make you a terror to all the kingdoms of the earth'" (Jer 34:17). Here, the phrase, "I am proclaiming a release to you," means that God would no longer look after or protect the people of Israel.

Because the Israelites violated the ordinance of the sabbatical year and took away the freedom of the servants who had been set free, God also took away their freedom by sending them away into exile to Babylon.

The sins of the people of Judah weighed so heavy that Jerusalem became a bloody city, a pot in which there was a thick layer of rust (Ezek 24:6). There would be no hope for Judah if the filth was not dissolved and washed away (Ezek 22:18-20; 24:6-11). It was in order to give a hopeful future to the people of Judah that God placed them in the furnace of fire called the *seventy years of exile in Babylon*, during which time He poured upon them His wrath and indignation to cleanse away their iniquities (Jer 29:10-11; Ezek 22:21-22; 24:12-14).

God had planned to begin the restoration of Israel through the captives in Babylon. After refining His people in exile for a predetermined period, God would bring them back to Jerusalem. Indeed, this amazing providence abounds with God's endlessly surging love.

Although God sent His people into exile to Babylon, He did not leave them alone in spiritual darkness during the long seventy-year period. God sent His Word for seventy years so that the people could thoroughly repent and become a new people. Hence, Jeremiah did not only proclaim Judah's destruction but also gave them a basis for hope. He proclaimed that Israel could still be delivered by God although they have been scattered as captives. Jeremiah 29:11-14 clearly summarizes this message of hope:

> **Jeremiah 29:11–14** For I know the plans that I have for you . . . plans for welfare and not for calamity to give you a future and a hope. Then you will call upon Me and come and pray to Me, and I will listen to you. You will seek Me and find Me when you search for Me with all your heart. I will be found by you . . . and I will restore your fortunes and will gather you from all the nations and from all the places where I have driven you, and I will bring you back to the place from where I sent you into exile.

God's plan was to purify His people through repentance while enduring the hardship of submitting to Babylon and adapting to life in a foreign land. Eventually, the people would come to understand and believe in God's justice and His administration of redemption.

After the fall of Jerusalem, God continuously sent His prophets to proclaim His Word to the exiles in Babylon. However, God did not proclaim His Word to those who fled to Egypt without surrendering to Babylon. They drowned in the swamp of idolatry in Egypt never to return. They perished for good because they relied on the "crushed reed" of Egypt (Isa 36:6; Ezek 29:6-7).

Sin takes away all the joys of life, both small and big, making all things vain and turning everything into despair. If we do not acknowledge our guilt and thoroughly repent even after numerous warnings against our sins, then peace will vanish from our lives and darkness and death will overshadow us instead.

He who does not keep the sabbath day or does not obey the commandment of tithing according to God's Word is a wicked person. The wicked will never find peace. Isaiah 48:22 states, "'There is no peace for the wicked!' says the Lord" (Isa 57:21). Even in laughter, such a person's heart will be in pain, and the end of joy may be grief (Prov 14:13; Ref Ecc 2:1-2). The laughter of the wicked is filled with the shadow of mourning, grief, and anxiety (Luke 6:25).

Apostle Paul referred to such people as those "who have no hope" (1 Thess 4:13). The hope that is given through the cross and resurrection of Jesus Christ is "living hope" (1 Pet 1:3). Such hope is imperishable, undefiled, and will not fade away. Such hope is reserved for us in heaven (1 Pet 1:4). This hope of glory has now been manifested in Christ Jesus (Col 1:26-27).

CHAPTER 12

# The History of the Babylonian Captivity

The northern kingdom of Israel fell at the hands of Assyria in 722 BC. About 136 years later, in 586 BC, Babylon destroyed the southern kingdom of Judah. God the righteous Judge destroyed these two nations because of their continuous disobedience (2 Kgs 18:9-12; 1 Chr 9:1; 2 Chr 36:15-20).

While Assyrian power began to wane during the reign of King Josiah of the southern kingdom of Judah, Babylon emerged as the new powerhouse of the region. Egypt attempted to assist Assyria in order to keep Babylon in check. However, King Josiah, not wanting to see Assyrian power restored, fought against Pharaoh Neco at Megiddo when Neco was heading north to assist Assyria. Josiah died in the battle (2 Chr 35:20-25). After this, Egypt and Babylon confronted each other at the battle of Carchemish (605 BC). Babylon defeated Egypt and began to dominate the Near East, and Egypt was never to rise again (2 Kgs 24:7).

King Nebuchadnezzar of Babylon attacked Judah in 605 BC during the reign of Jehoiakim. He took the royal family and the nobles, including Daniel, into exile; this was the first deportation. After this, Nebuchadnezzar took more captives to Babylon in the second deportation in 597 BC during the reign of Jehoiachin. Then the third deportation occurred in 586 BC during the reign of Zedekiah.

These three stages of deportation to Babylon were essentially the stages of the destruction of the temple. **During the first deportation to Babylon in 605 BC** (Jer 25:1; 46:2; Dan 1:1), all the articles of the house of the Lord were taken to Babylon. Second Chronicles 36:6-7 records, "Nebuchadnezzar king of Babylon came up against him and bound him with bronze chains to take him to Babylon. Nebuchadnezzar also brought some of the articles of the house of the Lord to Babylon and put them in his temple at Babylon" (Ref Dan 1:2).

**During the second deportation to Babylon in 597 BC** (2 Kgs 24:8, 12), all the treasures of the house of the Lord and of the king's house were carried out, and all the vessels of gold were cut in pieces (2 Kgs 24:10-13). Second Kings 24:13 records, "He carried out from there all the treasures of the house of the Lord, and the treasures of the king's house, and cut in pieces all the vessels of gold which Solomon king of Israel had made in the temple of the Lord, just as the Lord had said."

**During the third deportation to Babylon in 586 BC** (2 Kgs 25:1-2, 8), the temple was burned down (2 Kgs 25:9). The walls around Jerusalem were destroyed (2 Kgs 25:10; 2 Chr 36:19), and the bronze pillars, the stands, and the bronze sea which were in the temple were broken into pieces and carried away to Babylon. The pots, the shovels, the snuffers, the spoons, and all the bronze vessels which were used in temple service were taken away as well (2 Kgs 25:13-17). Seraiah the chief priest and Zephaniah the second priest of the temple were then taken to Riblah, where the king of Babylon struck them down and put them to death (2 Kgs 25:18, 21).

Hence, God thoroughly punished Israel by destroying the cherished temple through the hands of the Babylonians (1 Kgs 9:7-9).

Map 1

# The Routes of the Deportations (1st, 2nd, and 3rd) to Babylon
## as Judah was led away into exile
(2 Kgs 24:1–25:21; 2 Chr 36:6–21; Jer 39:1–10; 52:1–27)

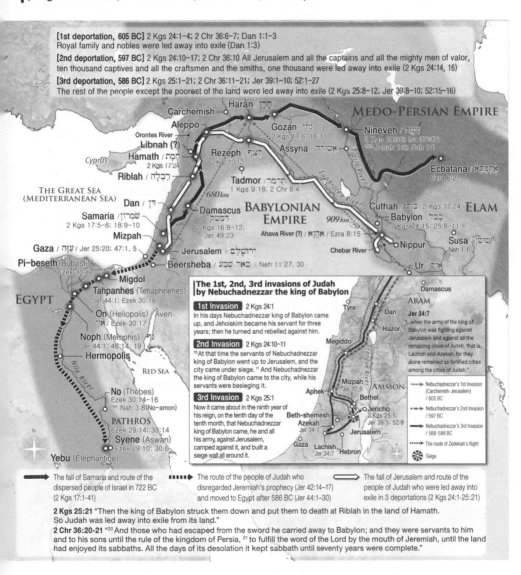

[1st deportation, 605 BC] 2 Kgs 24:1–4; 2 Chr 36:6–7; Dan 1:1–3
Royal family and nobles were led away into exile (Dan 1:3)

[2nd deportation, 597 BC] 2 Kgs 24:10–17; 2 Chr 36:10 All Jerusalem and all the captains and all the mighty men of valor, ten thousand captives and all the craftsmen and the smiths, one thousand were led away into exile (2 Kgs 24:14, 16)

[3rd deportation, 586 BC] 2 Kgs 25:1–21; 2 Chr 36:11–21; Jer 39:1–10; 52:1–27
The rest of the people except the poorest of the land were led away into exile (2 Kgs 25:8–12; Jer 39:8–10; 52:15–16)

Carchemish    Haran / חָרָן    MEDO-PERSIAN EMPIRE
Aleppo    Gozan / גּוֹזָן    Nineveh / נִינְוֵה
Orontes River    2 Kgs 17:6; 18:11    2 Kgs 19:36; Isa 37:37;
Libnah (?)    Assyria / אַשּׁוּר    Jonah 1:2; Nah 1:1
Hamath / חֲמָת    Rezeph / רֶצֶף
2 Kgs 17:24    2 Kgs 19:12    Ecbatana / אַחְמְתָא
Riblah / רִבְלָה    Tadmor / תַּדְמֹר    Ezra 6:2
THE GREAT SEA    1 Kgs 9:18; 2 Chr 8:4
(MEDITERRANEAN SEA)    Dan / דָּן    680km
Samaria / שֹׁמְרוֹן    Damascus    BABYLONIAN    Cuthah / כּוּת / 2 Kgs 17:24    ELAM
2 Kgs 17:5–6; 18:9–10    דַּמֶּשֶׂק    EMPIRE    909km    Babylon / בָּבֶל
Mizpah    2 Kgs 16:9–12;    2 Kgs 24:15; 25:8–11
Jer 49:23    Ahava River (?) / אַהֲוָא / Ezra 8:15    Nippur    Susa / שׁוּשַׁן
Gaza / עַזָּה / Jer 25:20; 47:1, 5    Jerusalem / יְרוּשָׁלַיִם    Neh 1:1
Pi-beseth (Bubastis)    Beersheba / בְּאֵר שֶׁבַע / Neh 11:27, 30    Chebar River    Ur / אוּר
Ezek 30:17
Migdol
Tahpanhes (Tehaphnehes)
Jer 44:1; Ezek 30:18
EGYPT
On (Heliopolis) / Aven
אוֹן / Ezek 30:17
Noph (Memphis) / נֹף
Jer 44:1; 46:14, 19
Hermopolis
RED SEA
No (Thebes)
Ezek 30:14–16
Nah 3:8 (No-amon)
PATHROS
Ezek 29:14; 30:14
Syene (Aswan)
Ezek 29:10; 30:6
Yebu (Elephantine)

**The 1st, 2nd, 3rd invasions of Judah by Nebuchadnezzar the king of Babylon**

**1st Invasion** 2 Kgs 24:1
In his days Nebuchadnezzar king of Babylon came up, and Jehoiakim became his servant for three years; then he turned and rebelled against him.

**2nd Invasion** 2 Kgs 24:10–11
[10] At that time the servants of Nebuchadnezzar king of Babylon went up to Jerusalem, and the city came under siege. [11] And Nebuchadnezzar the king of Babylon came to the city, while his servants were besieging it.

**3rd Invasion** 2 Kgs 25:1
Now it came about in the ninth year of his reign, on the tenth day of the tenth month, that Nebuchadnezzar king of Babylon came, he and all his army, against Jerusalem, camped against it, and built a siege wall all around it.

Damascus    ARAM
Tyre    Dan    Jer 34:7
Hazor    ...when the army of the king of Babylon was fighting against Jerusalem and against all the remaining cities of Judah, that is, Lachish and Azekah, for they alone remained as fortified cities among the cities of Judah."
Megiddo
Mizpah / Jer 17:6    AMMON
Aphek    Jer 41:16    Bethel
Beth-shemesh    Jericho    2 Kgs 25:5;
Azekah    Jer 39:5; 52:8
Jer 34:7    Jerusalem
Gaza    Lachish    Hebron
Jer 34:7

→→→ Nebuchadnezzar's 1st Invasion (Carchemish–Jerusalem) / 605 BC
→•→ Nebuchadnezzar's 2nd Invasion / 597 BC
Nebuchadnezzar's 3rd Invasion / 588–586 BC
✦✦✦ The route of Zedekiah's flight
✹ Siege

The fall of Samaria and route of the dispersed people of Israel in 722 BC (2 Kgs 17:1-41)

The route of the people of Judah who disregarded Jeremiah's prophecy (Jer 42:14–17) and moved to Egypt after 586 BC (Jer 44:1–30)

The fall of Jerusalem and route of the people of Judah who were led away into exile in 3 deportations (2 Kgs 24:1-25:21)

**2 Kgs 25:21** "Then the king of Babylon struck them down and put them to death at Riblah in the land of Hamath. So Judah was led away into exile from its land."

**2 Chr 36:20-21** "[20] And those who had escaped from the sword he carried away to Babylon; and they were servants to him and to his sons until the rule of the kingdom of Persia, [21] to fulfill the word of the Lord by the mouth of Jeremiah, until the land had enjoyed its sabbaths. All the days of its desolation it kept sabbath until seventy years were complete."

**(1) Time of deportation**
  - King of Judah: 3rd (4th) year of Jehoiakim (Jer 25:1; 46:2; Dan 1:1-2)
  - King of Babylon: The 1st year of Nebuchadnezzar (Jer 25:1-3)

**(2) People who were deported**
  - Members of the royal family and nobles including Daniel (Dan 1:1-3)

**(3) Events surrounding the deportation**
  - Nebuchadnezzar king of Babylon invaded the southern kingdom of Judah. He brought some of the articles of the house of the Lord to Babylon and put them in his temple (2 Kgs 24:1; 2 Chr 36:6-7).

  - Three years later (602 BC), bands of Chaldeans, bands of Arameans, bands of Moabites, and bands of Ammonites invaded Judah to destroy it. When King Jehoiakim betrayed the king of Babylon and allied himself with Egypt, he was bound with bronze chains and taken to Babylon (2 Kgs 24:1-2; 2 Chr 36:6). Jehoiakim returned to Jerusalem sometime later.

## 1. The time of the deportation

The southern kingdom of Judah was taken captive in the first deportation in 605 BC during the third year of King Jehoiakim (Dan 1:1). King Nebuchadnezzar had ousted the Egyptian army at the battle of Carchemish and attacked Judah. Daniel 1:1 states, "In the third year of the reign of Jehoiakim king of Judah, Nebuchadnezzar king of Babylon came to Jerusalem and besieged it."

However, Jeremiah 46:2 states, "To Egypt, concerning the army of Pharaoh Neco king of Egypt, which was by the Euphrates River at Carchemish, which Nebuchadnezzar king of Babylon defeated in the fourth year of Jehoiakim the son of Josiah, king of Judah." Here, Jeremiah records the year of the battle of Carchemish (605 BC) as the *fourth year* of Jehoiakim, not the third year, thus differing from the account in Daniel 1:1 by one year.

Jeremiah 25:1 also records the fourth year of Jehoiakim as the first year of King Nebuchadnezzar; the first year of Nebuchadnezzar is 605 BC, the year of his accession. The word *first* from "first year" is רִאשֹׁנִי (*ri'šōnî*) in Hebrew and it originates from the word רֹאשׁ (*rō'š*), which means "head" or "leader." Thus, the first year of Nebuchadnezzar refers to the year 605 BC (accession year) when he became king (head, leader), and this verse differs with the account in Daniel 1:1 by one year as well.

Second Kings 23:34 provides an explanation for this discrepancy.

> **2 Kings 23:34** Pharaoh Neco made Eliakim the son of Josiah king in the place of Josiah his father, and changed his name to Jehoiakim. But he took Jehoahaz away and brought him to Egypt, and he died there.

In this verse, the author of the book of Kings does not state that Jehoiakim became king in place of his younger brother Jehoahaz. Instead, he states that Jehoiakim became king in place of his father Josiah. Historically, the order of reign was Josiah (640–609b BC), Jehoahaz (609b–608 BC), and Jehoiakim (608–597 BC; 2 Kgs 23:30, 34; 2 Chr 36:1-4), but the author of the book of Kings records the order as if Jehoiakim had become king after Josiah. This was done because the author does not acknowledge Jehoahaz as king since he spent his short three-month reign doing evil (2 Kgs 23:31-32).

If we follow the perspective of the book of Kings and reckon 609 BC, the year that Jehoahaz became king, as Jehoiakim's accession year, then the first deportation in 605 BC would become Jehoiakim's fourth regnal year (Jer 25:1; 46:2). The book of Jeremiah also follows this viewpoint in its chronology of the reigns of kings.

## 2. People who were deported and the surrounding events

After his victory at the battle of Carchemish, King Nebuchadnezzar of Babylon headed straight for Jerusalem in order to conquer the southern kingdom of Judah, as it was strategically located at the connecting region between the African continent and southwest Asia. Daniel and the members of the royal family as well as the nobles were taken as captives in the resulting first deportation. Daniel 1:3 states, "Then the king ordered Ashpenaz, the chief of his officials, to bring in some of the sons of Israel, including some of the royal family and of the nobles."

Jehoiakim served Babylon for the first three years, but he again allied himself with Egypt and betrayed King Nebuchadnezzar (2 Kgs 24:1). In 602 BC, King Nebuchadnezzar allied himself with the descendants of Aram, Moab, and Ammon in order to attack Judah (2 Kgs 24:2). He bound Jehoiakim in bronze chains and took him to Babylon; he also took the articles from the house of the Lord and brought them to the land of Shinar in Babylon, into the treasury of his god (Dan 1:1-2; 5:2).

> **2 Chronicles 36:6–7** Nebuchadnezzar king of Babylon came up against him and bound him with bronze *chains* to take him to Babylon. ⁷ Nebuchadnezzar also brought *some* of the articles of the house of the Lord to Babylon and put them in his temple at Babylon.

Jehoiakim was taken captive in 602 BC, but later he returned to Jerusalem and reigned until 597 BC for a total of eleven years until he died. Then, Jehoiachin reigned as king in his place (2 Kgs 24:6).

## 3. The messages of the prophets around the time of the deportation

### (1) Prophet Jeremiah's message

Prophet Jeremiah had proclaimed Jehoiakim's tragic end around the time Judah was taken captive in the first deportation. Jehoiakim had built his house with unrighteousness and his upper rooms with injustice (Jer 22:13). The nation was in a precarious state, and yet he was focused on building himself a roomy house with spacious upper rooms (Jer 22:14). He paneled his house with cedars, the most expensive lumber at the time, and painted it with Egyptian red paint which was difficult to obtain (Jer 22:14). Jeremiah rebuked Jehoiakim's evil deeds, saying that he was after dishonest gain (בֶּצַע, beṣaʻ), shed innocent blood, and practiced oppression and extortion (Jer 22:17).

Prophet Jeremiah prophesied in Jeremiah 22:18-19 regarding the tragic end of the ungodly Jehoiakim. There would be no one among the people of Israel who would take pity on him, feel sorrow, or lament for him. He would be dragged off and thrown out beyond the gates of Jerusalem and be buried with a donkey's burial. In addition, he prophesied, ". . . his dead body shall be cast out to the heat of the day and the frost of the night" (Jer 36:30).

Jehoiakim is known to have returned from captivity in Babylon only to die in battle against Babylon at the end of his reign. And even though there is no specific biblical record of this, it is known that Jehoiakim's body was thrown out of Jerusalem just as Jeremiah had prophesied.[41] Concerning his death, the Jewish historian Josephus also wrote:

"Yet when he [the king of Babylon] was come into the city, he did not observe the covenants he had made; but he slew such as were in the flower of their age, and such as were of the greatest dignity, together with their king Jehoiakim, whom he commanded to be thrown before the walls, without any burial. . . " (*Ant.* 10.97)

### (2) Prophet Daniel's message

Prophet Daniel was taken captive in the first deportation in 605 BC (Dan 1:1-4). He was active past 538 BC, the first year of the Persian King Cyrus (שְׁנַת אֶחָת, *šěnat 'aḥat*: first year) and remained so until Cyrus's third year of reign (536 BC; Dan 1:21; 6:28; 10:1).

Daniel chapters 1 and 2 contain his prophecies regarding the timing of the first deportation to Babylon. During his second year (603 BC) on the throne, King Nebuchadnezzar (605–562 BC) had a dream, but his spirit was troubled and sleep left him because he could not remember the content of his dream (Dan 2:1, 3). He called in the magicians, the conjurers, the sorcerers, and the Chaldeans so that they could tell him his dream (Dan 2:2). They said to the king, "Tell the dream to your servants, and we will declare the interpretation" (Dan 2:4), and the king replied, "If you do not make known to me the dream and its interpretation, you will be torn limb from limb and your houses will be made a rubbish heap" (Dan 2:5). The Chaldeans answered the king and said, "The thing which the king demands is difficult, and there is no one else who could declare it to the king except gods, whose dwelling place is not with mortal flesh," and the king became indignant and very furious and gave orders to destroy all the wise men of Babylon (Dan 2:10-12). The lives of all the wise men of Babylon were in danger, including the lives of Daniel and his friends (Dan 2:13). Arioch, the captain of the king's bodyguard, had gone forth to slay the wise men of Babylon when Daniel asked him with discretion and discernment, "For what reason is the decree from the king so urgent?" After being informed of the matter, Daniel went to the king and calmed his impatient heart by requesting that the king would give him time, in order that he might declare the interpretation to him (Dan 2:14-16).

While Daniel was praying, God revealed to him in a night vision the very dream that King Nebuchadnezzar had dreamt (Dan 2:19-23). Daniel, in turn, told King Nebuchadnezzar everything about his dream

(Dan 2:31-35) and its interpretation (Dan 2:36-45). This dream revealed the future course of world history, which would unfold according to the administration of redemptive history.

A detailed account of King Nebuchadnezzar's dream is as follows:

There was a single great statue that was large and of extraordinary splendor, and its appearance was awesome. "The head of that statue was made of fine gold, its breast and its arms of silver, its belly and its thighs of bronze, its legs of iron, its feet partly of iron and partly of clay" (Dan 2:31-33). There was also a stone cut out without hands and "it struck the statue on its feet of iron and clay and crushed them. Then the iron, the clay, the bronze, the silver and the gold were crushed all at the same time and became like chaff from the summer threshing floors; and the wind carried them away so that not a trace of them was found. But the stone that struck the statue became a great mountain and filled the whole earth" (Dan 2:34-35).

The head of fine gold represents King Nebuchadnezzar of Babylon (Dan 2:38). The breasts and arms of silver represent the kingdom of Persia which would rise after Babylon (Dan 2:39), and the belly and thighs of bronze represent Greece which would later conquer the world (Dan 2:39).The legs of iron represent the fourth kingdom, Rome, which would emerge after Greece (Dan 2:40). The great statue's feet, partly of iron and partly of clay, prophetically describes how this kingdom would be divided (Dan 2:41). After the collapse of the Roman Empire, the world would be divided into various nations; some would be strong and some would be weak ("brittle"; Dan 2:41-42). In actuality, the Roman Empire was divided into the Eastern Roman Empire and the Western Roman Empire in AD 395, and even the influential Western Roman Empire was destroyed at the hands of the Germanic soldier Odoacer in AD 476. When the Western Roman Empire fell, it split into various countries like the various toes of the statue; these countries are England, Germany, France, Switzerland, Portugal, Spain, and Italy of today.

However, the stone cut out without hands struck the great statue and this stone became a great mountain and filled the whole earth (Dan 2:34-35). This stone represents Jesus Christ who is the precious living stone (1 Pet 2:4-5), a stone in Zion (Isa 28:16; Rom 9:33), the spiritual rock (1 Cor 10:4), and the chief corner stone (Ps 118:22; Matt 21:42; Luke 20:17; Acts 4:11). When Jesus Christ, the stone cut out without hands, comes again, the nations of this world will be destroyed just like the great statute described by Prophet Daniel. Then, an eternally indestructible kingdom of God will be established (Dan 2:44-45; Ref Isa 28:16; 1 Pet 2:4).

This dream was true, for it showed what would surely take place in the future (Dan 2:45b). Since Daniel not only made known the content of King Nebuchadnezzar's dream but also interpreted it, he was made ruler over the whole province of Babylon and the chief prefect over all the wise men of Babylon (Dan 2:48). Moreover, at Daniel's request, the king appointed Shadrach, Meshach, and Abed-nego over the administration of the province of Babylon (Dan 2:49).

This event is significant in the history of redemption for the following reasons. First, Daniel, a man of God, was lifted up among the Gentiles. Second, it revealed that Babylon, which took Judah as captives, will one day perish and God's people will surely return. Third, it attested to the fact that the entire history of the world until the second coming of Jesus Christ is progressing according to God's sovereign administration of redemption.

## 1. The time of the deportation

Jehoiakim sinned by ignoring the Word of God and rebelling against Nebuchadnezzar the king of Babylon (2 Kgs 24:1). He also filled Jerusalem with the innocent blood that he had shed. As a result of these sins, he was bound in bronze chains and wretchedly carried away to Babylon (2 Chr 35:5-6; [Ref] Jer 22:18-19; Ezek 19:5-9). After his eleven-year reign, Jehoiakim was succeeded by his son Jehoiachin, who became the nineteenth king of the southern kingdom of Judah (2 Kgs 24:8). At the end of Jehoiachin's reign of three months and ten days, Babylon invaded a second time.

The second deportation of the southern kingdom of Judah occurred in 597 BC (eight years after the first deportation). King Jehoiachin of the southern kingdom of Judah ascended the throne in 597 BC and ruled for three months and ten days before being taken captive to Babylon (2 Kgs 24:8-12; 2 Chr 36:9-10).

According to the *Babylonian Chronicles*, based on the calendar that begins with Tishri (seventh month), it was in the month of Bul (eighth month) in 597 BC when Jehoiachin became king after his father Jehoiakim died. Three months and ten days later, Jehoiachin was removed from the throne, and this was on the second day of the month of Adar (twelfth month) in 597 BC.[42]

Second Kings 24:10-11 states that the servants of King Nebuchadnezzar besieged the city. The word *besieged* used here is the participial form of צוּר (*ṣûr*), meaning that they had besieged it for some time. Babylon had besieged Jerusalem for some time, after which King Nebuchadnezzar came to the city of Jerusalem and finally conquered it in 597 BC, on the second day of the month of Adar (twelfth month). It was at this time that Jehoiachin was removed from the throne; he was then taken captive to Babylon on the tenth day of the month of Nisan (first month) in 597 BC* (Ezek 40:1; 2 Chr 36:10).[43]

## 2. People who were deported and the situation at the time

Nebuchadnezzar king of Babylon arrived after his servants besieged the city. Then the king carried out all the treasures of the house of the Lord and the treasures of the king's house, and cut in pieces all the vessels of gold which Solomon king of Israel had made for the temple of the Lord (2 Kgs 24:10-13; 2 Chr 36:10).

During the second invasion, Babylon not only destroyed the temple and plundered treasures, but also carried away all the important people from the southern kingdom of Judah. In this second deportation to Babylon, the king, the king's mother, the king's wives, his servants, and the leading men of the land were taken captive (2 Kgs 24:12, 15; Ezek 19:8-9). At this time, they led away into exile a total of ten thousand captives including the seven thousand mighty men of valor, all Jerusalem,

---

* The year remains the same since the year does not change when reckoned according to the Tishri-to-Tishri method used in Judah.

all the captains, and one thousand craftsmen and smiths. They were all strong and fit for war (2 Kgs 24:14-16). They took away anyone who could possibly be instrumental in staging an uprising, such as the high officials, (seven thousand) mighty men with both labor and combat power, and (one thousand) skillful craftsmen and smiths (2 Kgs 24:14, 16).

More detail on the people who were deported is as follows:

First, "**all Jerusalem**" were carried away (2 Kgs 24:14). This term does not refer to all the inhabitants of Jerusalem; these people were the central figures who controlled the entire southern kingdom of Judah from its capital, Jerusalem.

Second, "**all the captains**" were carried away (2 Kgs 24:14). The Hebrew word for *captains* is שַׂר (*śar*), which refers to leaders of higher status than the seven thousand mighty men. The word *śar* was translated as commander (Gen 21:22; 26:26), captain (Gen 37:36), master (Exod 1:11), and leaders (Num 21:18).

Third, "**all mighty men of valor**" were carried away (2 Kgs 24:14). The words *mighty men* are גִּבּוֹרֵי הַחַיִל (*gibbôrê haḥayil*), which refers to a vigorous, energetic group of people. Unlike ordinary soldiers, they were officers who received expert training in military leadership. Hence, they were the leading warriors in battle. The Bible repeatedly states that seven thousand warriors were carried away (2 Kgs 24:16).

Fourth, "**one thousand craftsmen and the smiths**" were carried away (2 Kgs 24:16). The Hebrew word for *craftsman* is חָרָשׁ (*ḥārāš*), which refers to an expert who is highly skilled in handling stones, metals, or wooden materials. The Hebrew word for *smiths* is מַסְגֵּר (*masgēr*) and refers to an expert who can make all sorts of weapons. In addition, both the craftsmen and smiths were introduced as "all strong and fit for war" (2 Kgs 24:16). The word *strong* implies strong, vigorous youths among men. This word was also translated as "a mighty one" (Gen 10:8), "warrior" (Ps 120:4), "the strong" (KJV; Ecc 9:11), and "mighty man" (Ps 52:1). Hence, the Bible is repeatedly underscoring the fact that the king of Babylon carried away only the best officials and excellent leaders of Judah during the second deportation.

By taking away all the best leaders and the mighty men of valor fit for war, Babylon completely debilitated the southern kingdom of Judah. This fact was reemphasized with the statement, "None remained except the poorest people of the land" (2 Kgs 24:14). The *poorest people* (דַּלַּת, *dallat*) refers to the lowest social class in Judah, and this expression thus indicates that the southern kingdom of Judah no longer had any power to resist Babylon (Ezek 17:13-14).

The destruction of the house of God and the deportation of all the leaders, warriors, and skilled men were the results of God's stringent punishment, which was the exact fulfillment of His prophecies (Jer 15:13). Isaiah had prophesied to King Hezekiah about one hundred years before the Babylonian invasion that all that was in the palace of Jerusalem would be carried away to Babylon and nothing would be left (Isa 39:6). It was God's warning against Hezekiah who was then consumed with useless boastfulness (2 Kgs 20:17).

Among those who were taken captive during the second deportation were the Prophet Ezekiel and an ancestor of Mordecai, Esther's cousin (Ezek 1:1-3; Esth 2:5-6). King Nebuchadnezzar enthroned Jehoiachin's uncle Mattaniah in his place and changed his name to Zedekiah (2 Kgs 24:17; 2 Chr 36:10). Babylon invaded the southern kingdom of Judah three times and deported the people of Judah. However, they did not take away the entire population. They made Zedekiah king and allowed the royal regime to continue until the complete destruction of Judah (2 Kgs 24:17).

## 3. The messages of the prophets around the time of the second deportation

Prophet Jeremiah proclaimed the following Word of God regarding King Jehoiachin around the time of the second deportation to Babylon.

**FIRST**, Jehoiachin was likened to a "signet ring" and a "despised, shattered jar."

Prophet Jeremiah prophesied about "Coniah the son of Jehoiakim" (Jer 22:24). The name *Coniah* (כָּנְיָ֫הוּ) is the shortened form of *Jeconiah* (יְכָנְיָה) and refers to King Jehoiachin (Jer 37:1; 1 Chr 3:16). Jehoiachin became king at the young age of eighteen and ruled for only three months and ten days, but he did evil in the sight of the Lord according to all that his father had done (2 Kgs 24:8-9).

God said that although Jehoiachin was like a signet ring on His right hand, He will put him off and give him into the hands of King Nebuchadnezzar and into the hands of the Chaldeans (Jer 22:24-25). Signet rings were used as seals on important documents or letters to guarantee a final decision and thus symbolize the holder's honor or authority. However, God declared that He would judge Jehoiachin no matter how important he may be.

In addition, God declared that Jehoiachin's mother, Nehushta, would also be taken captive to Babylon with him and would die (Jer 22:26-27). In accordance with this prophecy, Nehushta was taken captive along with Jehoiachin (2 Kgs 24:15). Jehoiachin was released from prison and was lifted up on the twenty-seventh day of the twelfth month of the year that King Evil-merodach of Babylon ascended the throne, which was thirty-seven years after he was taken captive. Nevertheless, he died in Babylon without being able to return to Jerusalem (2 Kgs 25:27-30; Ref Jer 52:31-34 states the twenty-fifth day of the twelfth month).

God also likened Jehoiachin to a "despised, shattered jar" and pro-claimed that his destruction had already been determined (Jer 22:28). He also prophesied, "Write this man down childless, a man who will not prosper in his days; for no man of his descendants will prosper sitting on the throne of David or ruling again in Judah" (Jer 22:30). In actuality, Jehoiachin had seven sons (Shealtiel, Malchiram, Pedaiah, Shenazzar, Jekamiah, Hoshama and Nedabiah; 1 Chr 3:17-18). Then why does Jeremiah 22:30 state that he would be childless? This was because the southern kingdom of Judah was destroyed and none of Jehoiachin's sons was able to succeed the throne of David.

### SECOND, Jeremiah recounted the vision about the two baskets of figs.

After Jehoiachin was taken captive to Babylon, God showed Jeremiah two baskets of figs set before the temple of the Lord (Jer 24:1). One basket contained very good figs, like first-ripe figs, and the other basket contained very bad figs which could not be eaten (Jer 24:2). Here, the "very good figs" refer to the people of Judah who obeyed the Word of God and were taken captive to Babylon. Jeremiah 24:5 states, "Like these good figs, so I will regard as good the captives of Judah, whom I have sent out of this place into the land of the Chaldeans."

However, the "very bad figs" refer to the people of Judah who refused to become captives of Babylon and either fled to Gentile nations such as Egypt or insisted on remaining in Jerusalem. Jeremiah 24:8 states, "But like the bad figs which cannot be eaten due to rottenness ... so I will abandon Zedekiah king of Judah and his officials, and the remnant of Jerusalem who remain in this land and the ones who dwell in the land of

Egypt." Since it was God's decreed will to punish the southern kingdom of Judah through the Babylonian exile, the good figs were those who followed His will. God had declared His intention to make them repent and allow them to return afterwards (Jer 24:6-7).

God declared His curse upon those who went against His Word by not going into exile in Babylon, "I am sending upon them the sword, famine, and pestilence, and I will make them like split-open figs that cannot be eaten due to rottenness" (Jer 29:17). God's standard for judging between good and evil is whether or not the people obey His will. Since God's Word is living and active and possesses power and might, obeying His Word is actually fulfilling His good will, by which one can experience God's work of salvation (Isa 55:10-11; Heb 4:12). Thus, a person's obedience to the Word is better than sacrifices of the fat of rams and is the shortcut to fulfilling the righteousness of God (1 Sam 15:22-23).

**THIRD**, Jeremiah wrote down the Word of God, which he received, in letters and sent them to the people.

Prophet Jeremiah sent letters to all the elders in captivity who were still alive, as well as to the priests, the prophets, and the rest of the people (Jer 29:1). This took place "after King Jeconiah and the queen mother, the court officials, the princes of Judah and Jerusalem, the craftsmen and the smiths had departed from Jerusalem" (Jer 29:2-3). Zedekiah was ruling over Judah at the time.

The first letter was sent to the people who were taken captive to Babylon. This letter was sent by the hand of Elasah the son of Shaphan and Gemariah the son of Hilkiah, whom King Zedekiah had sent as envoys to Babylon (Jer 29:3). Prophet Jeremiah told the people of Judah to build houses and live in them, and to plant gardens and eat their produce. They were also encouraged to take wives and have children, and to take wives and husbands for their children as well, so that they could multiply. Moreover, Jeremiah told them to "seek the welfare of Babylon" and pray for their welfare because that is how the people of Judah will have welfare as well (Jer 29:4-7). Moreover, Jeremiah explained using God's Word why the people of Judah had to do this. It was because God had promised them, "When seventy years have been completed for Babylon, I will visit you and fulfill My good word to you, to bring you back to this place" (Jer 29:10).

On the other hand, Jeremiah proclaimed that those who did not surrender and remained in Jerusalem would be judged through the sword, famine, and pestilence (Jer 29:15-19). Furthermore, Jeremiah proclaimed that Ahab the son of Kolaiah and Zedekiah the son of Maaseiah, who enticed the people with lies, would be killed by King Nebuchadnezzar (Jer 29:20-23).

All of these prophecies were truly proclamations of God's amazing providence. God had planned to discipline the exiles in Babylon and return them at the appointed time to restart the history of redemption through them. These covenants embody God's endlessly surging love toward His people in exile.

The second letter was sent out to all the captives after Jeremiah heard the content of the letter sent by the false prophet Shemaiah (Jer 29:31). The false prophet Shemaiah sent a letter to all the people in Jerusalem as well as to all the priests including Zephaniah (Jer 29:24-28). In this letter, the false prophet Shemaiah reprimanded Zephaniah the priest for not rebuking Jeremiah of Anathoth. He stated that the priest had not fulfilled his duties as the overseer of the house of the Lord. He said that Jeremiah was a "crazy man who claims to be a prophet" (NLT), so he should be put in "stocks and in the iron collar."

The false prophet Shemaiah directly challenged Jeremiah's prophecy. He asserted that Jeremiah's claim in his letter that "the exile will be long; build houses and live in them and plant gardens and eat their produce" (Jer 29:5) was a madness and a false prophecy (Jer 29:26-28). Shemaiah truly was an ignorant person who did not believe in the Word of God that was proclaimed for the welfare and salvation of his generation.

The Word of the Lord came upon Jeremiah as he listened to the content of Shemaiah's letter from Zephaniah, and Jeremiah sent a letter to the captives again (Jer 29:29-31a). Jeremiah stated that Shemaiah had made the people trust in a lie and that he was a false prophet whom God had not sent. Moreover, Jeremiah prophesied a wretched end for Shemaiah (Jer 29:31b-32).

God proclaimed through Jeremiah that He would punish Shemaiah and his descendants for preaching rebellion and thus he would not see the good (i.e. the return from the Babylonian captivity; Jer 29:32). Jeremiah closed his letter with the phrase "declares the Lord" (Jer 29:32b), emphasizing that what he had spoken would surely be fulfilled because they were the Word of God.

## The Third Deportation (586 BC)

– 11 years after the 2nd deportation / 2 Kgs 25:1-21; 2 Chr 36:11-21; Jer 39:1-10; 52:1-27)

**(1) Time of deportation**
- King of Judah: 11th year of Zedekiah (2 Kgs 25:1-7; Jer 39:1-7; 52:4-11)
- King of Babylon: 19th year of Nebuchadnezzar (2 Kgs 25:8-9; Jer 32:1-5; 52:12-13)

**(2) People who were deported**
- The army of the Chaldeans captured Zedekiah and brought him to the king of Babylon at Riblah. They slaughtered the sons of Zedekiah before his eyes, then put out Zedekiah's eyes, bound him with bronze fetters, and brought him to Babylon. He was put in prison until the day of his death (2 Kgs 25:6-7; Jer 39:4-7; 52:8-11).
- All of the people were carried away into exile except some of the poorest of the land (2 Kgs 25:11-12; Jer 39:9-10).

**(3) Events surrounding the deportation**
- Jerusalem fell under a siege that lasted from the 10th day of the 10th month in the 9th year of Zedekiah's reign (588 BC) until the 9th day of the 4th month in the 11th year of his reign (586 BC). One month later, the army of Nebuzaradan burned the house of the Lord, the king's house, and every great house of Jerusalem. The army of the Chaldeans also broke down the walls surrounding Jerusalem (2 Kgs 25:1-3, 8-10; 2 Chr 36:17-21; Jer 39:1-2, 8; 52:4-6, 12-14).
- The Chaldeans broke in pieces the bronze pillars, the stands, and the bronze sea and carried them to Babylon. They also took away the pots, the shovels, the snuffers, the spoons, and all the bronze vessels that were used in the temple service. The captain of the guard also took away the firepans and the basins, what was fine gold, and what was fine silver. Also taken were the 2 pillars, the 1 sea, and the stands which Solomon had made (2 Kgs 25:13-17; 2 Chr 36:18-19; Jer 52:17-23).
- Nebuzaradan, the captain of the guard, took Seraiah the chief priest and Zephaniah the second priest, along with the 3 officers of the temple. He also took from the city 1 official who was the overseer of the men of war, and 7 (5) of the king's advisers who were found in the city, and the scribe of the commander of the army who mustered the people of the land, and 60 men of the people of the land who were found in the midst of the city. Then the king of Babylon struck them down and put them to death at Riblah (2 Kgs 25:18-21; Jer 52:24-27).

| 4,600 people who were deported in small groups because they did not surrender to Babylon and resisted to the end (Jer 52:28-30) | |
| --- | --- |
| First | In the 7th year of Nebuchadnezzar – 3,023 people (Jer 52:28) |
| Second | In the 18th year of Nebuchadnezzar – 832 people (Jer 52:29) |
| Third | In the 23rd year of Nebuchadnezzar – 745 people (Jer 52:30) |

## 1. The time of the deportation

The southern kingdom of Judah was taken captive in the third deportation in 586 BC (eleven years after the second deportation), in the eleventh year of Zedekiah. Zedekiah was the youngest among Josiah's four sons and ascended the throne at the age of twenty-one and reigned for eleven years (2 Kgs 24:18; 2 Chr 36:11).

Jeremiah clearly proclaimed the Word of God to Zedekiah regarding the path which Judah was to take. Jeremiah advised the king to surrender to Babylon, saying, "Bring your necks under the yoke of the king of Babylon and serve him and his people, and live" (Jer 27:12). Nevertheless, Zedekiah insisted on adhering to the anti-Babylonian policies (2 Kgs 24:20; Jer 27:12-13; 37:2), and as a result, Babylon besieged Jerusalem from the tenth day of the tenth month in the ninth year of Zedekiah (2 Kgs 25:1; Jer 39:1; 52:4; Ref Ezek 24:1-2). Zedekiah asked Egypt for reinforcement (Ezek 17:15), and the Egyptian army set out in order to help Zedekiah (Jer 37:5). The Babylonian army heard this news and temporarily lifted the siege from Jerusalem in fear of Pharaoh's army (Jer 37:5, 11). However, when the Egyptian army heard this news, it immediately retreated back to Egypt, and the Babylonian army attacked Jerusalem once again. From then, the city was under siege until the eleventh year of King Zedekiah's reign (2 Kgs 25:1-2; 2 Chr 36:11-20; Jer 37:7-10; Ezek 17:12-21).

Jerusalem experienced an indescribably miserable famine while it was under siege by the Babylonian army. Even compassionate mothers, unable to fight off the extreme hunger and starvation, would commit the gruesome act of boiling their own children to eat them (Lam 2:20; 4:10; Isa 9:20; Ezek 5:10). This was the result of disobedience to the Word of God, just as Moses, the servant of God, had prophesied (Lev 26:28-29; Deut 28:53-57).

The siege of Jerusalem began in 588 BC, on the tenth day of the tenth month of the ninth year of Zedekiah and continued for about thirty months (based on the Tishri-to-Tishri calendar). The city eventually fell at the hands of Babylon in 586 BC, on the ninth day of the fourth month of the eleventh year of Zedekiah (2 Kgs 25:1-3; Jer 39:1-2; 52:4-6).

At this time, many people died because of the war, famine, starvation, and disease (Lam 2:11-12; 4:9; Jer 14:17-18), and the priests and the prophets were slain in the sanctuary (Lam 2:20). The elderly lay on the ground in the streets and the virgins and the young men fell by the merciless sword (Lam 2:21). Prophet Jeremiah said that tears did not cease day and night, because he saw that the people of Israel were crushed with a mighty blow and with a sorely infected wound (Jer 14:17; Lam 3:48-51). He confessed, "In the street the sword slays; in the house it is like death" (Lam 1:20). Throughout their exile in Babylon, this day—the ninth day of the fourth month of 586 BC in which the southern kingdom of Judah was destroyed and the city of Jerusalem fell—was observed as a day of fasting and mourning by the people of Judah (Zech 7:5; 8:19).

## 2. People who were deported and the surrounding events

When the city of Jerusalem fell on the ninth day of the fourth month of his eleventh year, Zedekiah fled and went out of the city at night by way of the king's garden through the gate between the two walls. He went out toward the Arabah, but the army of the Chaldeans seized him. Zedekiah was taken to Riblah in the land of Hamath where King Nebuchadnezzar was temporarily staying, and there the king of Babylon pronounced judgment upon him. The king of Babylon slaughtered Zedekiah's sons before his eyes and then blinded his eyes. He bound Zedekiah with bronze fetters and imprisoned him until his dying day (2 Kgs 25:4-7; Jer 39:4-7; 52:7-11). This was done according to Ezekiel's prophecies (Ezek 12:8-14).

One month after the fall of Jerusalem, on the tenth day of the fifth month, following Nebuchadnezzar's orders Nebuzaradan methodically led the Chaldean army and burned the house of the Lord, the king's house, all the houses of Jerusalem, and every great house. He also broke down the walls of Jerusalem (2 Kgs 25:8-12; 2 Chr 36:18-19; Jer 39:8-10; 52:12-16). There are two different records of this date. Second Kings 25:8 records it as the seventh day of the fifth month in 586 BC, whereas

Jeremiah 52:12 records it as the tenth day of the fifth month in 586 BC. This variance seems to be due to the difference in the arrival date of the first corps of troops and the last.

Thus, all the cities in Judah were destroyed and made a wasteland (Jer 34:7; Ezek 33:24; Lam 2:1-5). Then, the Chaldeans broke the two bronze pillars (Jachin and Boaz), the stands, and the bronze sea into pieces and carried the bronze to Babylon. They also took away the pots, the shovels, the snuffers, the spoons, and all the bronze vessels which were used in temple service. Moreover, the captain of the guard also took away the fire-pans and the basins; what was of gold he took away for the gold and what was of silver he took away for the silver. Furthermore, they took the two pillars, the one sea, and the stands that Solomon had made for the house of the LORD (2 Kgs 25:13-17; 2 Chr 36:18-19; Jer 52:17-23). Although originally the snuffers and the spoons were made of gold (1 Kgs 7:50), here they are classified with bronze vessels. It is conjectured that this was because the gold vessels of the temple had already been plundered by the Babylonians during the first two invasions. The Babylonian soldiers plundered the bronze vessels in the house of the LORD because in those days bronze was valued as one of the primary spoils of war (2 Sam 8:8; 2 Kgs 25:13-17). Moreover, after having pillaged all the bronze vessels in the temple, the Babylonians soldiers also took "what was made of gold ... for the gold" and "what was made of silver ... for the silver" (NRSV; 2 Kgs 25:15, Jer 52:19). Here, the expression "made of gold" (זָהָב זָהָב, *zāhāb zāhāb*) and "made of silver" (כֶּסֶף כָּסֶף, *kesep kāsep*) in Hebrew repeats the respective words twice thus expressing that the material referenced is of the highest quality. In other words, it literally means "pure gold" and "pure silver" (NASB: "fine gold" and "fine silver"). Seeing that the captain of the guard himself took the gold and silver vessels for their gold and silver (2 Kgs 25:15, Jer 52:19), it is quite evident that they were very valuable items. These things happened as a fulfillment of the prophecy that Prophet Isaiah had declared to King Hezekiah (2 Kgs 20:17; Isa 39:6).

Nebuzaradan the captain of the guard took Seraiah the chief priest and Zephaniah the second priest, as well as the three officers of the temple. He also took from the city one official who was overseer (eunuch; YLT) of the men of war, and seven (five) of the king's advisers who were found in the city. Also taken were the scribe of the commander of the army who mustered the people of the land, and sixty men of the people of the land who were found in the midst of the city. Then the king of Babylon struck them down and put them to death at Riblah (2 Kgs 25:18-21; Jer 52:24-27).

According to Jeremiah 52:28-30, a total of 4,600 people were taken to exile on three occasions. These three occasions, however, were not the three official stages of deportation. These were the deportations of the people who had refused to surrender and resisted deportation until they were finally taken captive in small groups.

First, a group of 3,023 people was taken in the seventh year of Nebuchadnezzar (Jer 52:28).

Second, a group of 832 people was taken in the eighteenth year of Nebuchadnezzar (Jer 52:29).

Third, a group of 745 people was taken in the twenty-third year of Nebuchadnezzar (Jer 52:30).

Israel was gradually disintegrating as all of her people were scattered; some were taken as captives, some were left in the land, and some fled for their lives to nearby nations to escape the calamity. Israel, now torn into pieces, was devastated, but the greatest tragedy of all was that her existence as a national entity had begun to erode.

## 3. The messages of the prophets around the time of the third deportation

God proclaimed His Word through the prophets Jeremiah, Ezekiel, and Daniel around the time of the third deportation to Babylon.

### (1) Prophet Jeremiah's message

Prophet Jeremiah prophesied the following message regarding King Zedekiah at the time of the third deportation to Babylon.

### FIRST, he warned against the false prophet Hananiah.

When crisis and complete chaos engulfed the nation, false prophets ran rampant more than ever before (Jer 14:14-16; 23:25; 27:15; 29:8-9, 21, 23; 34:16). In the fifth month of the fourth year of King Zedekiah, which was around 593 BC, Hananiah the son of Azzur from Gibeon prophesied lies in the house of the Lord in the presence of the priests and all the people (Jer 28:1). He said, "Thus says the Lord of hosts, the God of Israel, 'I have broken the yoke of the king of Babylon. Within two years I am going to bring back to this place all the vessels of the Lord's house ... I am also going to bring back to this place Jeconiah ... king of Judah, and all the exiles of Judah who went to Babylon'" (Jer 28:1-4). The false prophet Hananiah prophesied that God had broken the yoke of the king of Babylon (Jer 28:2), but this was never historically fulfilled. Because all the articles of the house of the Lord had been carried away during the first and second invasions by Babylon (2 Kgs 24:1, 10-13; 2 Chr 36:6-7; Dan 1:2), the people of Israel were greatly interested in when they would be brought back. The false prophets prophesied lies that the vessels of the Lord's house would be brought back from Babylon very soon (Jer 27:16-22).

Hananiah broke the wooden yoke on Prophet Jeremiah's neck (Jer 28:10) and was confident that King Nebuchadnezzar's neck would be broken within two years and Judah would be freed (Jer 28:2-4, 11). However, Prophet Jeremiah proclaimed, "You have broken the yokes of wood, but you have made instead of them yokes of iron" (Jer 28:13). Since "yokes of iron" cannot be broken by human strength, this message meant that nothing could prevent Judah's wretched destruction and deportation to Babylon (Jer 28:14). Then, after Jeremiah proclaimed this prophecy, Hananiah died about two months later, in the seventh month of that year (Jer 28:1, 16-17).

**SECOND, he warned King Zedekiah to surrender to Babylon.**

Zedekiah was King Josiah's son, and he became king of Judah in place of his nephew Jehoiachin. However, he continued to practice anti-Babylonian policies and in defiance of Babylon, Zedekiah allied himself with Edom, Moab, Ammon, Tyre, and Sidon (Jer 27:3). Thus, Babylon summoned King Zedekiah in his fourth year (593 BC; Jer 51:59). After returning to Jerusalem, Zedekiah allied himself with Egypt and rebelled against Babylon.

After the first and second invasions from Babylon, only the poorest people of the land remained in Jerusalem (2 Kgs 24:14), and the entire nation could not find stability even for a moment. Hence, Zedekiah secretly went to Prophet Jeremiah to ask God's will. Jeremiah advised him repeatedly, saying, "Thus says the Lord God of hosts, the God of Israel, 'If you will indeed go out to the officers of the king of Babylon, then you will live, this city will not be burned with fire, and you and your household will survive'" (Jer 38:14-17). Nevertheless, Zedekiah disobeyed and went against God's will.

### Zedekiah's first visit to Jeremiah

In 588 BC, the ninth year of King Zedekiah, King Nebuchadnezzar of Babylon came up to attack him (Jer 52:3b-4). At this critical time, King Zedekiah sent Pashhur and Zephaniah to Prophet Jeremiah, saying, "Please inquire of the Lord on our behalf, for Nebuchadnezzar king of Babylon is warring against us; perhaps the Lord will deal with us according to all His wonderful acts, so that the enemy will withdraw from us" (Jer 21:1-2). He had expected that the God who in the past had given victory against Sennacherib, the king of Assyria, would somehow also destroy King Nebuchadnezzar of Babylon (Ref Isa 37:36-38).

In reply to Zedekiah's request for prayer, Prophet Jeremiah again advised him to surrender to Babylon. He warned that those who surrender would live, but those who remained in the city would be killed by the sword and pestilence. Jeremiah 21:8-9 states, "You shall also say to this people, 'Thus says the Lord, "Behold, I set before you the way of life and the way of death. He who dwells in this city will die by the sword and by famine and by pestilence; but he who goes out and falls away to the Chaldeans who are besieging you will live, and he will have his own life as booty."'" Even in our lives today, God often offers us choices. Those choices are between the way of life and the way of death. If you obey the Word of God, even in situations where you seem to be on the brink of death, the path to life will be opened to you. However, if you get caught up in human reasoning and disobey the Word of God, then that path will become the path of death (Deut 30:15-20).

### Zedekiah's second visit to Jeremiah

When Jeremiah was still coming in and going out among the people, for they had not yet put him in prison, Zedekiah sent Jehucal the son of Shelemiah, and Zephaniah the son of Maaseiah, the priest, to Jeremiah the prophet. They asked him to intercede in prayer for Jerusalem's salvation, saying, "Please pray to the LORD our God on our behalf" (Jer 37:3-4).

Meanwhile, Pharaoh's army had set out from Egypt; and when the Chaldeans who had been besieging Jerusalem heard the report about them, they lifted the siege from Jerusalem (Jer 37:5). At that time, Prophet Jeremiah delivered an even more powerful message: "Behold, Pharaoh's army which has come out for your assistance is going to return to its own land of Egypt. The Chaldeans will also return and fight against this city, and they will capture it and burn it with fire ... Do not deceive yourselves, saying, 'The Chaldeans will surely go away from us,' for they will not go. For even if you had defeated the entire army of Chaldeans who were fighting against you, and there were *only* wounded men left among them, each man in his tent, they would rise up and burn this city with fire" (Jer 37:6-10).

### Zedekiah's third visit to Jeremiah

It was at the time that the army of the Chaldeans had lifted the siege from Jerusalem because of Pharaoh's army (Jer 37:11). When the Babylonian army retreated to the outskirts of Judah, the people who had been suffering from being shut in began to go in and out of the city. Prophet Jeremiah also went out from Jerusalem to go to the land of Benjamin in order to take possession of some property there among the people (Jer 37:12-13). He reached the Gate of Benjamin, also known as the Sheep Gate, which was located on the northeast section of the wall of Jerusalem (Neh 3:1, 32; 12:39). This was the gateway to the land of Benjamin (Jer 38:7). While he was at the Gate of Benjamin, a captain of the guard whose name was Irijah, the son of Shelemiah the son of Hananiah, arrested him (Jer 37:13). He saw Jeremiah as a fugitive who had betrayed his nation and arrested him, saying, "You are going over to the Chaldeans!" (Jer 37:13). This was because Jeremiah had preached that surrendering to Babylon was fully obeying the sovereign will of the Lord (Jer 21:9; 38:2, 17-18). There were many, including Irijah, among the people of Judah who detested this message and Jeremiah was considered a traitor and ostracized. Prophet Jeremiah resolutely explained, "A lie! I am not going over to the Chaldeans"; yet Irijah still arrested Jeremiah and brought him to the officials. Then the officials were angry with Jeremiah and beat him, and they put him in jail in the house of Jonathan the scribe (Jer 37:14-15). After Jeremiah had stayed in the dungeon, that is the vaulted cell, for many days, Zedekiah secretly sent someone to ask him, "Is there a word from the Lord?" Jeremiah's answer was the same: "You will be given into the hand of the king of Babylon!" (Jer 37:16-17). At that time, Jeremiah petitioned to the king not to send him back to the house of Jonathan, and the king gave command to keep Jeremiah in the court of the guardhouse and to give him a loaf of bread daily (Jer 37:18-21).

### Zedekiah's fourth visit to Jeremiah

During the days of Zedekiah, wicked officials (Shephatiah, Gedaliah, Jucal, and Pashhur) cast Jeremiah into the cistern in which there was no water but only mud (Jer 38:1-6). Ebed-melech the Ethiopian, a eunuch, took thirty men and brought up Jeremiah the prophet from the cistern, and Jeremiah stayed in the court of the guardhouse (Jer 38:7-13). Then King Zedekiah sent for Jeremiah again, and he was brought to the king at the third entrance that was in the house of the Lord (Jer 38:14). After saying, "If I give you advice, you will not listen to me" (Jer 38:15), Jeremiah delivered God's message without holding back a single word. He said:

> "Thus says the Lord God of hosts, the God of Israel, 'If you will indeed go out to the officers of the king of Babylon, then you will live, this city will not be burned with fire, and you and your household will survive. But if you will not go out to the officers of the king of Babylon, then this city will be given over to the hand of the Chaldeans; and they will burn it with fire, and you yourself will not escape from their hand.'" (Jer 38:17-18)

Then King Zedekiah replied in fear, "I dread the Jews who have gone over to the Chaldeans, lest they give me over into their hand and they abuse me" (Jer 38:19). However, Jeremiah said, "They will not give you over. Please obey the Lord in what I am saying to you, that it may go well with you and you may live. But if you keep refusing to go out, this is the word which the Lord has shown me" (Jer 38:20-21).

**THIRD, by purchasing the land of Anathoth, he clearly showed that they would return from Babylon.**

The Word of the Lord came upon Prophet Jeremiah in the tenth year of King Zedekiah and the eighteenth year of King Nebuchadnezzar (587 BC; Jer 32:1). This was one year before the southern kingdom of Judah was totally destroyed in 586 BC. Prophet Jeremiah was shut up in the court of the guard at this time (Jer 32:2).

God commanded Jeremiah to purchase the field of Hanamel at Anathoth (Jer 32:7). Jeremiah obeyed this command and bought the field from Hanamel for seventeen shekels of silver. He also prepared two deeds of purchase—one copy was sealed according to the laws and regulations and the other was an open copy. Both were given to Baruch in the sight of Hanamel and other witnesses (Jer 32:9-12). As he gave the deeds to Baruch,

Jeremiah commanded him to put them in an earthenware jar, that they may last a long time in accordance with God's command (Jer 32:13-14).

This event was God's confirmation that although Babylon was taking Judah into captivity, they will surely return to this land. Jeremiah 32:15 also states, "Houses and fields and vineyards will again be bought in this land."

Jeremiah was shut up in the court of the guard, so he had no way to confirm if the field in Anathoth was good or bad or worth the seventeen shekels of silver. Nevertheless, he obeyed God's command and bought the field. This was faith. A person with faith does not calculate but obeys and acts upon the Word as soon as he hears it.

**FOURTH, Jeremiah warned that the city of Jerusalem would be burned at the hands of Babylon and that the cities would become desolate with no inhabitants.**

Jeremiah 34 is a record of Jeremiah's ministry just before the destruction of Jerusalem. Jeremiah 34:1-2 and 22 state that the city of Jerusalem would be burned and destroyed by Babylon and that the cities of Judah would become desolate and without inhabitants.

Only two cities—Lachish and Azekah—remained when the army of the king of Babylon fought against Jerusalem. After being surrounded by enemies on all sides, Zedekiah momentarily appeared to listen to Jeremiah's words and repent. King Zedekiah and the people felt the urgency of the situation when Jerusalem was under siege and about to fall from the Babylonian attack. In an attempt to placate God's anger, they observed the covenant to release their kinsmen, the Hebrews, who had been their servants (Jer 34:8-10; Ref Deut 15:12-18). The officials of Judah, the officials of Jerusalem, the court officers, the priests, and all the people of the land vowed before God to carry out the covenant by passing between the parts of the calf which they had cut in two (Jer 34:18-19).

Not too long afterwards, however, Pharaoh's army set out from Egypt upon receiving Zedekiah's request for assistance. The Babylonian army heard the report about them and they temporarily lifted the siege from Jerusalem (Jer 37:5; Ref Jer 34:21b-22a). King Zedekiah and the people instantly became conceited and took back the servants that they had released (Jer 34:11-16). God had commanded, "If your kinsman, a Hebrew man or woman, is sold to you, then he shall serve you six years, but in the seventh year you shall set him free" (Deut 15:12). God also said, "It shall not seem hard to you when you set him free, for he has given you six years with double the service of a hired man; so the Lord your God will bless you in whatever you do" (Deut 15:18).

However, King Zedekiah did not carry out the sacred covenant but profaned the name of God by turning around and breaking the covenant (Jer 34:16, 18). At this, God proclaimed that a great calamity would fall upon the people of Judah in the future.

First, God said, "'Behold, I am proclaiming a release to you,' declares the Lord, 'to the sword, to the pestilence and to the famine; and I will make you a terror to all the kingdoms of the earth'" (Jer 34:17). Here, the phrase, "I am proclaiming a release to you" means that God will completely remove His hands of protection. As a result, Israel will face the plague of the sword, the pestilence, and the famine. They will be chased out from the land of Canaan and experience the sadness and sorrow of being completely scattered among the nations of the world.

Second, God said that many people will die (Jer 34:18-20). Jeremiah 34:20 states, "I will give them into the hand of their enemies and into the hand of those who seek their life. And their dead bodies will be food for the birds of the sky and the beasts of the earth." This was because "the officials of Judah and the officials of Jerusalem, the court officers and the priests and all the people of the land"—those who passed between the parts of the calf when they entered into the covenant before God—did not keep the covenant (Jer 34:18-19). Cutting the calf in two and passing between its parts meant that those who did not keep the covenant would also be cut in two like the animal and die.

Third, God said that the southern kingdom of Judah will ultimately be destroyed (Jer 34:22). God will again place King Zedekiah and his officials into the hands of their enemies, into the hands of those who seek their life, and into the hands of the army of the king of Babylon, which had temporarily retreated. They will strike the city and burn it, and the cities of Judah will become desolate without inhabitants (Jer 34:21-22). In accordance with this prophecy, the southern kingdom of Judah was completely destroyed on the ninth day of the fourth month in 586 BC, the eleventh year of King Zedekiah (Jer 39:2). Just as the people of Judah recaptured and oppressed the servants they had released, the Babylonian army returned and burned the city and made the cities desolate, making the people of Judah submit to them as their slaves (2 Kgs 25:1-21; 2 Chr 36:11-20; Jer 39:1-10; 52:3-27). The end of King Zedekiah and the southern kingdom of Judah, as well as the tragic calamity proclaimed against the people of Judah, was the inevitable consequence of their breaking of the covenant.

## (2) Prophet Ezekiel's message

While Jeremiah was ministering in his country, Prophet Ezekiel was taken captive to Babylon during the second deportation (597 BC). There, he preached about the impending judgment and at the same time, proclaimed the message of hope (Ezek 1:1). Ezekiel was about thirty years old when God called him (593 BC; five years after King Jehoiachin was captured; Ezek 1:2), which means that he was born around 623 BC. Jeremiah was a youth ("I am a youth"; Jer 1:6) of about fifteen years of age when he received his calling (627 BC; thirteenth year of King Josiah; Jer 1:2), so he was born around 642 BC. Thus, Prophet Jeremiah was a contemporary of Prophet Ezekiel, who was about twenty years younger. They both lived during an unprecedented time of national crisis when they were uncertain of whether Israel would rise again or disappear forever into history. It was during such a period that Prophet Ezekiel proclaimed the following message.

**FIRST, he prophesied through symbolic actions that God would surely judge Israel.**

God used various methods so that Israel would believe in His Word and understand. His last resort was prophesying by symbolic actions rather than by words. God hoped that "they will understand though they are a rebellious house" if He showed them by actual actions and not just by words (Ezek 12:3). This reflects His boundless mercy and endless love for His chosen people. God commanded actions that were seemingly unreasonable, unrealistic, incomprehensible, abnormal, and difficult for people to understand. Yet, Ezekiel performed these actions before the people exactly as God had commanded, without leaving anything out.

Some examples of Ezekiel's prophecies by action included the following:
First, Ezekiel went through the shocking experience of becoming mute just seven days after he received his calling. This was the twelfth

day of the fourth month in the fifth year of King Jehoiachin's captivity (Ezek 1:1-2; 3:16, 26-27). Ezekiel was able to open his mouth and speak again seven years later in the twelfth year of the exile—on the fifth day of the tenth month when he heard that Jerusalem had fallen (Ezek 33:21-22).[44] During this time, Ezekiel spoke only when God opened his mouth; otherwise, he kept silent and lived a secluded life (Ezek 3:27; 24:25-27; Ref 29:21). By making Ezekiel mute and preventing him from publicly prophesying, God showed that what remained for them was no longer forgiveness or compassion but only judgment. God opened Ezekiel's mouth to proclaim the Word only after the tragic news of the fall of Jerusalem and national ruin was delivered (Ezek 33:21-22).

Second, according to God's command, Ezekiel prophesied by acting out the exile. "By day" he acted like a captive by preparing his baggage for exile and bringing it out. "In the evening" he dug a hole through the wall. Then "in the dark," he loaded the baggage on his shoulder and carried it out while covering his face so that he could not see the land, as those going into exile (Ezek 12:3-7). He symbolically enacted all these prophecies "in their sight" according to God's command (Ezek 12:3, 4 (two times), 5, 6, 7). Prophet Ezekiel fervently and desperately acted out these things in front of the largest possible crowd with the hope of enlightening even a single person. Such passion demonstrates God's zeal to uphold and save the collapsing nation.

These symbolic acts were prophecies of the great sorrow and tragedy that would befall the king and his servants as they would have to flee through the wall when the Babylonians invaded. This prophecy was fulfilled in 586 BC during the third Babylonian attack (2 Kgs 25:1-7).

Third, Prophet Ezekiel prophesied by eating his bread with trembling and drinking water with quivering and anxiety (Ezek 12:18-20). This was a prophecy of the tragic situation in which the people would starve to death (Ezek 4:16-17). In actuality, Israel struggled from a bitter famine when they were under siege. They ate with anxious thoughts: "Is this my last meal?," "Will someone come and snatch my food away?," or "Will I be caught while I am eating?" The situation inside the city was truly appalling and dreadful. It is recorded that as the siege was prolonged, the people were so famished that there were fathers among them who ate their sons and sons who ate their fathers (Ezek 5:10; Ref Lam 2:20; 4:10; Isa 9:20).

Fourth, on the tenth day of the tenth month in the ninth year of the exile, Ezekiel used a parable of the "boiling pot" to prophesy that the southern kingdom of Judah—the "rusted pot"—will be destroyed by the fiery invasion of the Babylonians (Ezek 24:1-14). After this prophecy, God forewarned Ezekiel of his wife's death and commanded him not to mourn or weep. That night, Ezekiel's wife died suddenly, and Ezekiel, as God had commanded, suppressed his emotions and did not mourn or weep. Instead, he lamented quietly with a turban on his head and his shoes on his feet. He did not cover his mustache and did not eat the bread of men* (Ezek 24:15-24).

The people saw but did not understand Ezekiel's actions so they asked him what his actions meant for the people of Judah (Ezek 24:19). Ezekiel replied that when Jerusalem falls the Israelites "will rot away in [their] iniquities and [they] will groan to one another" just as Ezekiel had done (Ezek 24:20-24).

Prophet Ezekiel proclaimed, "'It will no longer be delayed, for in your days, O rebellious house, I will speak the word and perform it,' declares the Lord God" (Ezek 12:25). Nevertheless, the people disregarded his prophecies and said, "The vision that he sees is for many years from now, and he prophesies of times far off" (Ezek 12:27). However, none of God's Word was delayed but were all performed exactly as He had spoken (Ezek 12:28).

Even today, we must be aware of false visions (false prophecies that are not based on truth) and flattering divinations (flattering, smooth words that are tempting to the listeners, Ezek 12:24; Jer 8:11; 23:17). The Bible tells us that at the end of the world, many false prophets will arise and distort the Word of God and mislead many people (Matt 24:11; 2 Tim 4:3-4).

### SECOND, he declared that God was waiting for Israel to repent.

From 593 BC until 586 BC, even as the nation was on the verge of collapse, Prophet Ezekiel conveyed the content of God's heart—that He was waiting until the end for Israel to repent. Ezekiel 22:30 states, "I searched for a man among them who would build up the wall and stand in the gap before Me for the land, so that I would not destroy it; but I found no one." There was no one who could subdue God's fiery wrath (Ezek 22:23-31).

---

\* bread of men: money or articles sent to the house of mourning

Lawlessness and violence filled Jerusalem and the iniquities of the people were so great that they provoked God to anger (Ezek 8:17; 9:9). This was the same even within the inner court of the Lord's house, which should be the holiest of all places. There were about twenty-five people practicing idolatry "at the entrance to the temple of the Lord, between the porch and the altar"; they had their backs to the temple of the Lord and were worshipping the sun (Ezek 8:16; Ref Deut 4:19; 17:3-7; 2 Kgs 21:5; 23:11).

It was at this time when Prophet Ezekiel saw a vision from the Lord. God called forth six men holding shattering weapons in order to judge the southern kingdom of Judah. Among them was a man clothed in linen with a writing case at his loins. God commanded him to go through the midst of the city of Jerusalem and put a mark on the foreheads of the men who sigh and groan over all the abominations which are being committed (Ezek 9:1-4; Ref Rev 7:1-4; 9:4). This was the sign of salvation that would allow them to be saved when Jerusalem is judged. God was urging the people of Israel to repent by showing them that there is a way to live even in the midst of fearful judgment (Ezek 18:31-32; 33:11).

**THIRD, he declared that God was continuously with His people in their suffering.**

Prophet Ezekiel saw a vision by the river Chebar in the land of the Chaldeans about 1,000 km from Jerusalem. He said he was among the exiles when "the heavens were opened and I saw visions of God" (Ezek 1:1). "The word of the Lord came expressly" to Prophet Ezekiel "and there the hand of the Lord came upon him" (Ezek 1:3).

The power to open and close the heavens lies in the Word of God (Ref Matt 3:16; John 1:51; Acts 7:56). First Kings 17:1 states, ". . . surely there shall be neither dew nor rain these years, except by my word" (Ref Lev 26:19; Deut 28:23; Luke 4:25). The chosen people of Israel had become captives and were spending days of despair under the sorrow of national ruin and the tyranny of military rule; yet it was at a time like this that the heavens were opened! The Word of God that specifically came upon Ezekiel was unusually powerful, and the hand of the Lord remained upon the prophet's head. Such spiritual phenomena were indeed news of a great joy, like a brilliant stream of light pouring down from within God's administration of redemption. Even when the Israelites were blocked in every direction as a result of God's judgment for their sins, God did not cease even for a moment to carry out the plan of salvation for His people.[45]

There was another special message that God proclaimed to Prophet Ezekiel. It was that God is in the midst of the captives "there" and that He is still working where they are. This is an amazing gospel of hope. In the original Hebrew text of Ezekiel 1:3, the word שָׁם (šām) meaning "there" appears. This portrays how God is with them at the very scene of their suffering in captivity, the scene of great despair.

In the book of Ezekiel, the most dynamic display of God's plan of salvation for His people in captivity was the appearance of the likeness of God's glory, the figures of the four living beings (Ezek 1:4-28). The rims of the four living beings were full of eyes round about (Ezek 1:18), and they represent the all-knowing eyes that watch over Israel as they suffer in their captivity (2 Chr 16:9). This is truly a message of comfort that God is endlessly watching over His beloved people of the covenant with the utmost care. Moreover, it shows that He knows and partakes in all of their pains.

**FOURTH, he delivered the message of hope that Israel would soon be restored and that its former glory would reappear (Ezek 33:1-48:35).**

Ezekiel had resolute faith that all history moves within God's sovereignty. Thus, even as the nation was destroyed, he obeyed the Word of God and never lost hope in restoration. Even when the restoration of Israel looked impossible, he saw the vision of the dried bones coming to life and powerfully testified that the work of God's breath would restore Israel (Ezek 37:1-14).

The last record in the book of Ezekiel is *Jehovah Shammah* (יְהוָה שָׁמָּה), which means "the Lord is there" (Ezek 48:35). This is confirmation that God would save them from the Babylonian oppression and from the shackles of death. It is the promise of hope that the God of salvation would move the people of Israel back to Jerusalem. Hallelujah!

### (3) Prophet Daniel's message

Daniel was taken captive in the first deportation in 605 BC and was chosen to be trained to serve in the king's court (king's personal service; Dan 1:1-7). In the second year of his reign (603 BC), King Nebuchadnezzar had a dream and Daniel interpreted his dream when no one else was able to do so (Dan 2:1, 25-45). At this time, in accordance with Daniel's request to the king, his three friends, Shadrach, Meshach and Abed-nego were placed over the administration of the province of Babylon while Daniel was at the king's court (Dan 2:49).

Afterwards, King Nebuchadnezzar made a great statue that had appeared in his dream on the plain of Dura, the height of which was sixty cubits (approx. 27.4 m) and its width six cubits (approx. 2.7 m; Dan 3:1). He built this statue in order to display his own greatness. It is presumed that he had the statue made just after the third deportation to Babylon in 586 BC after he had completely conquered the southern kingdom of Judah. All the satraps, the prefects, the governors, the counselors, the treasurers, the judges, the magistrates, and all the rulers of the provinces came to the dedication of the image that Nebuchadnezzar the king had set up (Dan 3:2-3). He also proclaimed that "whoever does not fall down and worship shall immediately be cast into the midst of a furnace of blazing fire" (Dan 3:6).

Nevertheless, Daniel's three friends refused to worship the golden image until the end (Dan 3:12). In rage and anger, Nebuchadnezzar called them and tried to appease them, saying, "Now if you are ready, at the moment you hear the sound of the horn, flute, lyre, trigon, psaltery and bagpipe and all kinds of music, to fall down and worship the image that I have made, very well. But if you do not worship, you will immediately be cast into the midst of a furnace of blazing fire; and what god is there who can deliver you out of my hands?" (Dan 3:13-15). At this, Shadrach, Meshach, and Abed-nego boldly replied to the king, "O Nebuchadnezzar, we do not need to give you an answer concerning this matter" (Dan 3:16). They continued, "If it be so, our God whom we serve is able to deliver us from the furnace of blazing fire; and He will deliver us out of your hand, O king. But even if He does not, let it be known to you, O king, that we are not going to serve your gods or worship the golden image that you have set up" (Dan 3:17-18). Then, they were tied up in their trousers, coats, caps, and other clothes and thrown into the blazing furnace. By the king's urgent command, the furnace was made seven times hotter than usual. It was so hot that the men who carried up Shadrach, Meshach, and Abed-nego were burned to death (Dan 3:19-22). Amazingly, although three men—Shadrach, Meshach, and Abed-nego—were thrown into the furnace still tied up (Dan 3:23), there were four men unbound walking about in the midst of the fire unharmed

(Dan 3:24-25). Besides Daniel's three friends, the fourth person had an appearance "like a son of the gods" (Dan 3:25b).

Nebuchadnezzar went near the entrance of the furnace of blazing fire and said, "Shadrach, Meshach and Abed-nego, come out, you servants of the Most High God, and come here," and they came out from the fire (Dan 3:26). By God's mysterious work, Daniel's three friends were unharmed by the fire; not even a single hair was singed, nor were their trousers damaged, nor did they even smell of fire (Dan 3:27). Because of this incident, King Nebuchadnezzar blessed the God of Shadrach, Meshach, and Abed-nego and confessed that there is no other God who can deliver men. He further said that from that time on, anyone who speaks anything offensive against the God of Shadrach, Meshach, and Abed-nego was to be torn limb from limb and his house reduced to a rubbish heap. Then the king caused Shadrach, Meshach, and Abed-nego to prosper in the province of Babylon (Dan 3:28-30).

This incident of the burning furnace occurred just after the southern kingdom of Judah was destroyed during the third deportation to Babylon. It was a demonstration of the fact that the destruction of Judah did not occur because God lacked the ability to save, but that it was done as part of God's redemptive-historical providence to punish the nation. Although the people of Judah were thrown into this furnace-like tribulation of the Babylonian exile, God promised that He will be with them there, and He will deliver them as He had done with Daniel's three friends.

We have just examined the process of Judah's destruction as well as the messages of the prophets who proclaimed the restoration of Israel while holding on to the promise of the eternal covenant. The people of Israel were destroyed because of their iniquities against God, but it was not a total destruction. God was using this extreme disciplinary measure—the destruction of Judah—as a wakeup call to urge the people to awaken and repent. In turn, through the trials and pains of captivity in Babylon the people of Israel came to repent for their sins and seek God.

Psalm 137:1 describes the pain and anguish of the people of Israel in Babylon as, "By the rivers of Babylon, there we sat down and wept, when we remembered Zion." Here, the word *wept* is בָּכָה (*bākâ*), and it does not refer to just crying, but "bewailing," "lamenting," and "shedding tears." The people of Israel had wept with tears and hearts of anguish as they repented before God.

When the seventy years of the Babylonian exile were completed, God allowed them to return to their land as He had promised. This displays the unconditional *agape* love of God who is faithful to His covenant. It was also the fulfillment of the prophecy made through Prophet Jeremiah (Jer 25:11-12; 29:10; 2 Chr 36:21).

## 4. The remnant and the promise of the land

Babylon destroyed the southern kingdom of Judah in 586 BC. Then, the Babylonian army led by Nebuzaradan burned all the buildings in Jerusalem and destroyed the city wall. He also carried away into exile the "rest of the people who were left in the city and the deserters who had deserted to the king of Babylon and the rest of the people" (2 Kgs 25:11; Jer 52:15). The king of Babylon left "some of the poorest of the land" in the land of Judah to be vinedressers and plowmen (2 Kgs 25:12; Jer 39:10; 52:16).

### (1) Gedaliah the governor

The king of Babylon appointed Gedaliah the son of Ahikam, the son of Shaphan, over the people who were left in the land of Judah to rule over them (2 Kgs 25:22). Gedaliah is גְּדַלְיָה (gĕdalyâ) in Hebrew. The word is formed by combining the words גָּדַל (gādal) and יָה (yāh). When combined, the word means "the Lord is great." Gedaliah gathered all the people who had remained and advised them, saying, "Do not be afraid of the servants of the Chaldeans; live in the land and serve the king of Babylon, and it will be well with you" (2 Kgs 25:24).

However, the king's chief officer Ishmael and his followers plotted to kill Gedaliah. When Johanan the son of Kareah came to know of this plot, he went secretly to Gedaliah and said, "Let me go and kill Ishmael the son of Nethaniah, and not a man will know! Why should he take your life, so that all the Jews who are gathered to you would be scattered and the remnant of Judah would perish?" (Jer 40:13-15).

Nevertheless, Gedaliah was careless and did not listen to him (Jer 40:16). Eventually, Ishmael killed him with the sword while he was eating (Jer 41:1-2). It was a pity that Gedaliah was unjustly killed without even being able to partake in the restoration efforts. It was all because he was careless and trusted in man.

## (2) Ishmael

Ishmael was the son of Nethaniah, the son of Elishama, of the royal family and one of the chief officers of the king (Jer 41:1). Here, the word "family" is זֶרַע (zera') and means "descendants." Ishmael was a royal descendant. He had gone to Mizpah along with ten men. While they were eating bread together with Gedaliah, they struck down Gedaliah with the sword (2 Kgs 25:25; Jer 41:1-2). Gedaliah, whom the king of Babylon had appointed as governor, had advised the people to serve the king of Babylon in accordance with the Word of God as delivered by Jeremiah (2 Kgs 25:24). Ishmael, however, was displeased with this and conspired with the Ammonites who practiced anti-Babylonian policies and killed Gedaliah. Ishmael not only killed Gedaliah, but also all the Jews who were with him, as well as the Chaldean (Babylonian) men of war (Jer 41:3).

Ishmael did not stop there. Eighty pilgrims from the region that had formerly been the northern kingdom of Israel came to Jerusalem to mourn the fall of Jerusalem and the destruction of the temple, and to make offerings to God. Ishmael killed seventy of those pilgrims. He went out to meet them, pretending to weep, to lure and kill them. Afterwards, he cast them into the cistern that King Asa had made because of his fear for Baasha, king of Israel (Jer 41:5-9). Then Ishmael sought to capture the king's daughters and all the people who were left in Mizpah, whom Nebuzaradan the captain of the bodyguard had put under the charge of Gedaliah the son of Ahikam, and bring them to Ammon (Jer 41:10). However, he was only able to take eight men with him to the sons of Ammon as he was pursued by Johanan and all the commanders of the forces that were with him (Jer 41:11-15).

## (3) Johanan

Johanan the son of Kareah was one of the captains of the forces after the fall of Jerusalem (2 Kgs 25:23; Jer 40:7-8). Johanan heard about all the evil that Ishmael had done, so he went to fight against Ishmael and found him by the great pool in Gibeon. At this time, all the people whom Ishmael had taken captive from Mizpah rejoiced at seeing Johanan and all the captains of the forces with him. They turned around and came back to Johanan (Jer 41:11-14). Johanan was afraid of the Babylonian army (Jer 41:17-18) so he went and stayed in Geruth Chimham, which was beside Bethlehem, in order to proceed into Egypt.

Johanan asked Prophet Jeremiah to inquire of God regarding where they must go and what they must do (Jer 42:1-6). Ten days later, God replied, saying that they must not go into Egypt but must stay in the land of Judah (Jer 42:7-22). Jeremiah 42:17 states, "So all the men who set their mind to go to Egypt to reside there will die by the sword, by famine and by pestilence; and they will have no survivors or refugees from the calamity that I am going to bring on them."

However, Johanan and the arrogant men with him said that Jeremiah's prophecy was a lie and refused to believe in God's Word (Jer 43:2). They even took Jeremiah and Baruch with them and went to Tahpanhes in the land of Egypt (Jer 43:6-7). At this time, the Word of God came upon Jeremiah again, commanding him to take large stones and to hide them in the brick terrace at the entrance of Pharaoh's palace (Jer 43:9). This symbolic action revealed how the Babylonian king would attack Egypt and set his throne right over these stones. In actuality, King Nebuchadnezzar attacked Egypt in 568 BC and killed many people—including Pharaoh Hophra, the fourth king of the twenty-sixth dynasty—and took captives to Babylon (Jer 43:10-13; 44:30; Ezek 29:17-20; 30:10-26).

### (4) The people of Judah who disregarded Jeremiah's prophecy and moved to Egypt

Jeremiah chapter 44 warns of the judgment against the idolatry of the Jews living in Egypt (Jer 44:27). After the southern kingdom of Judah fell in 586 BC, the people of Judah went down to Egypt and lived in Migdol, Tahpanhes, Memphis, and the land of Pathros (Jer 44:1).

These people ignored Jeremiah's prophecy and moved to Egypt. There, they began to worship once again Ashtoreth the "queen of heaven," which King Josiah had completely eradicated during the religious reformation (Jer 44:17-19; Ref Jer 7:18). This great multitude of Judah that lived in Pathros had said to Jeremiah before entering Egypt, ". . . Whether it is pleasing or displeasing, we will obey the voice of the Lord our God . . . that it may be well with us when we obey the voice of the Lord our God" (Jer 42:5-6). Now, in order to worship Ashtoreth the queen of heaven, they protested to Jeremiah, "We will certainly carry out every word that has proceeded from our mouths" (Jer 44:17). Moreover, they claimed that they had plenty of food, were well-off, and saw no misfortune when they worshiped idols long ago. They complained, however, that ever since they stopped burning incense to the queen of heaven from the time of the

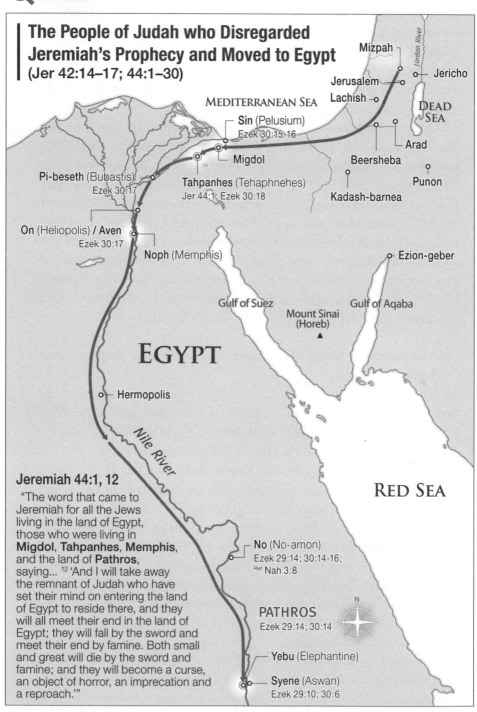

Map 2

# The People of Judah who Disregarded Jeremiah's Prophecy and Moved to Egypt
(Jer 42:14–17; 44:1–30)

MEDITERRANEAN SEA

Mizpah

Jerusalem

Lachish

Jericho

DEAD SEA

Arad

Beersheba

Punon

Kadash-barnea

**Sin** (Pelusium)
Ezek 30:15-16

**Migdol**

Pi-beseth (Bubastis)
Ezek 30:17

**Tahpanhes** (Tehaphnehes)
Jer 44:1; Ezek 30:18

On (Heliopolis) / **Aven**
Ezek 30:17

**Noph** (Memphis)

Ezion-geber

Gulf of Suez

Gulf of Aqaba

Mount Sinai
(Horeb) ▲

# EGYPT

Hermopolis

*Nile River*

## RED SEA

### Jeremiah 44:1, 12

"The word that came to Jeremiah for all the Jews living in the land of Egypt, those who were living in **Migdol, Tahpanhes, Memphis,** and the land of **Pathros,** saying... [12] 'And I will take away the remnant of Judah who have set their mind on entering the land of Egypt to reside there, and they will all meet their end in the land of Egypt; they will fall by the sword and meet their end by famine. Both small and great will die by the sword and famine; and they will become a curse, an object of horror, an imprecation and a reproach.'"

**No** (No-amon)
Ezek 29:14; 30:14-16;
Ref Nah 3:8

N

**PATHROS**
Ezek 29:14; 30:14

**Yebu** (Elephantine)

**Syene** (Aswan)
Ezek 29:10; 30:6

religious reformation by King Josiah, the sixteenth king of the southern kingdom of Judah (640–609 BC; 2 Kgs 23:4-25), they have lacked everything and have met their end by the sword and by famine (Jer 44:18). The women also blatantly retorted that their idolatry would be no problem since they had done it with their husbands' approvals (Jer 44:19).

King Josiah had brought out of the temple of the Lord all the vessels that were made for Baal, for Asherah, and for all the host of heaven and burned them. He had also done away with the idolatrous priests who burned incense in the high places to Baal, to the sun and to the moon and to the constellations, and to all the host of heaven (2 Kgs 23:4-5). Now, Josiah's righteous religious reformation was being harshly criticized by the men of Judah. They were making preposterous statements that the southern kingdom of Judah had collapsed because they did not serve the goddess that they had previously served so well. Their words were even more shocking: "... by burning sacrifices to the queen of heaven and pouring out drink offerings to her, just as we ourselves, our forefathers, our kings and our princes did in the cities of Judah and in the streets of Jerusalem ..." (Jer 44:17). Although they had committed the grave sin of not trusting God and serving idols, they were not penitent at all; rather, they unashamedly boasted that they were simply worshipping the queen of heaven "just as" their forefathers had done. In accordance with Jeremiah's prophecy, God's judgment came upon the entire people of Judah who were engrossed in idolatry in Egypt; they all perished without ever being able to return to their homeland (Jer 44:12-14; Ref Jer 24:8-10; 42:15-17; Ezek 30:1-19). God said that very few of those who had escaped the sword would return to the land of Judah to prove that it was the Word of God—and not theirs—that would stand (Jer 44:26-29).

## (5) The redemptive-historical meaning of the land

God promised that He would give the land of Canaan as an eternal inheritance to the descendants of Abraham. Genesis 17:8 states, "I will give to you and to your descendants after you ... all the land of Canaan, for an everlasting possession." Genesis 48:4 also states, "... and will give this land to your descendants after you for an everlasting possession." However, the southern kingdom of Judah was taken captive to Babylon in 586 BC and Canaan became a deserted land. However, because God promised that He would give the land of Canaan to the descendants of Abraham as an eternal possession, He allowed them to return to the land from Babylon. This promise is confirmed by the following commands.

**FIRST, God commanded Jeremiah to buy the field at Anathoth (Jer 32:7).**

The Word of the Lord came upon Prophet Jeremiah in the tenth year of King Zedekiah and the eighteenth year of King Nebuchadnezzar (587 BC; Jer 32:1). This was one year before the southern kingdom of Judah was totally destroyed in 586 BC. Prophet Jeremiah was shut up in the court of the guard at this time (Jer 32:2).

God commanded Jeremiah to purchase the field of Hanamel at Anathoth (Jer 32:7). Jeremiah obeyed this command and bought the field from Hanamel for seventeen shekels of silver. He also prepared two deeds of purchase—one copy was sealed according to the laws and regulations and the other was an open copy. Both were given to Baruch in the sight of Hanamel and other witnesses (Jer 32:9-12). As he gave the deeds to Baruch, Jeremiah commanded him to put them in an earthenware jar that they may last a long time in accordance with God's command (Jer 32:13-14).

God commanded him to buy land at a time when the nation was on the verge of destruction, because He wanted to instill in the people the conviction that the land would be restored. Nebuzaradan, captain of the bodyguard, freed Jeremiah from the chains that bound his hands. He then told Jeremiah to choose what seems right to him, whether to go with him to Babylon or to stay in the land of Judah, and Jeremiah chose to stay in the land of Judah (Jer 40:1-6).

**SECOND, God commanded those who remained in the land of Judah not to go down to Egypt but to stay in Canaan, their homeland (Jer 42:14-17).**

The remnant of Judah said, ". . . We will not stay in this land . . . No, but we will go to the land of Egypt, where we will not see war or hear the sound of a trumpet or hunger for bread, and we will stay there" (Jer 42:13-14). For them to leave their homeland which God would restore and to go down to Egypt was clearly the sin of disbelief in God's promise.

Thus, Prophet Jeremiah warned, "If you really set your mind to enter Egypt and go in to reside there, then the sword, which you are afraid of, will overtake you there in the land of Egypt; and the famine, about which you are anxious, will follow closely after you there in Egypt, and you will die there. So all the men who set their mind to go to Egypt to reside there will die by the sword, by famine and by pestilence; and they will have no

survivors or refugees from the calamity that I am going to bring on them"
(Jer 42:15-17). Here, Jeremiah said the sword would "overtake" them in
Egypt. The Hebrew uses the imperfect tense of the hiphil (causative) stem
of the verb נָשַׂג (nāśag), which in English is translated as "to overtake."
The word implies that God will order the sword to hunt them down
and overtake them wherever they may flee. Also, in the expression that
the famine "will follow closely after you," the Hebrew word for "follow
closely" is דָּבַק (dābaq), which means "to cleave," "to cling," and "to stick
to." This word is used in describing a state of cleaving to something so
strongly that it cannot be separated (Lam 4:4). Hence, this expression
means that the famine which they had so feared would stick to them and
follow them wherever they go.

Indeed, these words together emphasize the fearful fact that no one
can avoid God's judgment for disobeying His Word, no matter where
they hide. The calamity which they were so afraid of—the sword and
famine and pestilence—was pronounced even to Egypt, the very place
that they had boasted as being the safest place. However, God told them,
"you will die there" (Jer 42:16b) and "they will have no survivors or refugees from the calamity that I am going to bring on them" (Jer 42:17b). As
a fulfillment of those words, every single one of them died tragic deaths,
never again to set foot in their homeland Canaan.

**THIRD**, God commanded the people who were in captivity, "Let
Jerusalem come to your mind" (Jer 51:50).

Jeremiah 51:50 states, "You who have escaped the sword, depart! Do
not stay! Remember the Lord from afar, and let Jerusalem come to your
mind." This is the prophecy that one day Babylon would certainly fall.
Moreover, it is a prophetic warning that when Babylon falls, the remnants
must quickly leave Babylon and return to Jerusalem. This message is similar to King Solomon's prayer to God after the completion of Solomon's
temple and after the ark of the covenant had been laid in its place (1 Kgs
8:46-50).

> **1 Kings 8:33-34** When Your people Israel are defeated before an enemy, be-
> cause they have sinned against You, if they turn to You again and confess
> Your name and pray and make supplication to You in this house, then hear
> in heaven, and forgive the sin of Your people Israel, and bring them back to
> the land which You gave to their fathers.

In accordance with Solomon's prayer and Prophet Jeremiah's prophecy (Jer 29:14; 32:15; 33; 36-44), the southern kingdom of Judah was able to return to Jerusalem after the seventy years of exile in Babylon (2 Chr 36:21-23).

God's Word regarding the land of Canaan was a "promise of the eternal covenant." Thus, God allowing the people of Judah to return to Canaan is a realization of that eternal covenant. For this reason, in Jeremiah 32:37 God announces, "Behold, I will gather them out of all the lands to which I have driven them in My anger, in My wrath and in great indignation; and I will bring them back to this place and make them dwell in safety." God then proclaimed that this was the fulfillment of the eternal covenant. Jeremiah 32:40-41 states, "I will make an everlasting covenant with them . . . and will faithfully plant them in this land with all My heart and with all My soul." In order to keep His promise of the eternal covenant, God took action and brought the people of Judah back to their land from their captivity in Babylon. God is truly faithful to His covenant. Therefore, those who believe in God's promises abide in His administration of redemptive history.

The next chapter will examine the history of the return from the Babylonian captivity in the light of God's redemptive administration in fulfilling His promise regarding the land of Canaan.

# CHAPTER 13

# The History of the Return from the Babylonian Captivity

The people of Israel were taken into captivity on three different occasions in 605 BC, 597 BC, and 586 BC. God, however, bestowed His unconditional grace upon them and brought the people back to Jerusalem, just as He had promised. The Israelites, in their helpless state of despair in captivity, were like the dry bones in the grave. Now, by God's sovereignty and power, they received emancipation from their captivity and returned to their homeland. Their joy was as great as that of the dead being raised to life again (Ref Ezek 37:1-14).

Just as Prophet Isaiah (Isa 44:28; 45:1-3) and Prophet Jeremiah had prophesied (Jer 25:11-12; 29:10, 14), the process of the Israelites' return began when Cyrus king of Persia issued a decree permitting their return from Babylon in 538 BC (2 Chr 36:22-23; Ezra 1:1-4). From this time forward, all the Jewish captives scattered about in the different regions of the Persian Empire ended their years in captivity and returned to Jerusalem on three different occasions. The first return occurred in 537 BC, the second in 458 BC, and the third in 444 BC.

Map 3

# The Routes of the Returns (1st, 2nd and 3rd) from Babylon
(Ezra 1:1–2:70; 7–8; Neh 2; 7:5–72)

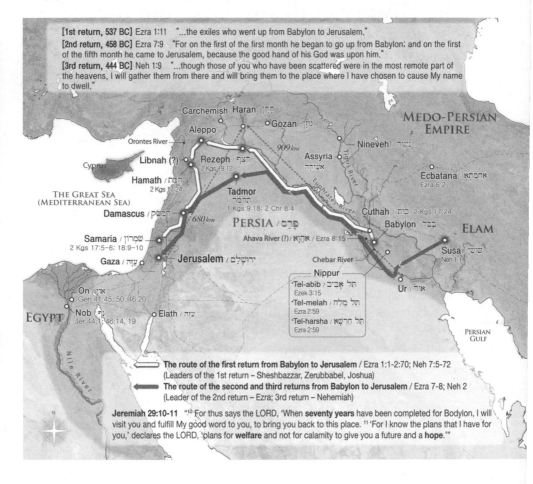

[1st return, 537 BC] Ezra 1:11 "...the exiles who went up from Babylon to Jerusalem."
[2nd return, 458 BC] Ezra 7:9 "For on the first of the first month he began to go up from Babylon; and on the first of the fifth month he came to Jerusalem, because the good hand of his God was upon him."
[3rd return, 444 BC] Neh 1:9 "...though those of you who have been scattered were in the most remote part of the heavens, I will gather them from there and will bring them to the place where I have chosen to cause My name to dwell."

Carchemish  Haran / חָרָן  Gozan / גּוֹזָן  MEDO-PERSIAN EMPIRE
Aleppo
Orontes River  909 km  Nineveh / נִינְוֵה
Cyprus  Libnah (?)  Rezeph / רֶצֶף  Assyria / אַשּׁוּר
2 Kgs 19:12
Hamath / חֲמָת  Ecbatana / אַחְמְתָא
2 Kgs 17:24  Tadmor / תַּדְמֹר  Ezra 6:2
THE GREAT SEA  1 Kgs 9:18; 2 Chr 8:4
(MEDITERRANEAN SEA)  Cuthah / כּוּת / 2 Kgs 17:24
Damascus / דַּמֶּשֶׂק  680 km  PERSIA / פָּרַס  Babylon / בָּבֶל  ELAM
Ahava River (?) / אַהֲוָא / Ezra 8:15
Samaria / שֹׁמְרוֹן  Susa / שׁוּשַׁן
2 Kgs 17:5–6; 18:9–10  Jerusalem / יְרוּשָׁלַיִם  Chebar River  Neh 1:1
Gaza / עַזָּה
Nippur
On / אוֹן  ·Tel-abib / תֵּל אָבִיב  Ur / אוּר
Gen 41:45, 50; 46:20  Ezek 3:15
Nob / נֹב  ·Tel-melah / תֵּל מֶלַח
EGYPT  Jer 44:1; 46:14, 19  Elath / עֵילַת  Ezra 2:59  PERSIAN
·Tel-harsha / תֵּל חַרְשָׁא  GULF
Ezra 2:59

The route of the first return from Babylon to Jerusalem / Ezra 1:1–2:70; Neh 7:5–72
(Leaders of the 1st return – Sheshbazzar, Zerubbabel, Joshua)
The route of the second and third returns from Babylon to Jerusalem / Ezra 7–8; Neh 2
(Leader of the 2nd return – Ezra; 3rd return – Nehemiah)

Jeremiah 29:10-11 "[10] For thus says the LORD, 'When seventy years have been completed for Babylon, I will visit you and fulfill My good word to you, to bring you back to this place. [11] 'For I know the plans that I have for you,' declares the LORD, 'plans for welfare and not for calamity to give you a future and a hope.'"

### Leaders
- Zerubbabel the governor of Judah (meaning: "born in Babylon")
- Jeshua (Joshua) the high priest (meaning: "the Lord saves"; Ezra 2:1-2; Ref Hag 1:1, 14-15)

### King of Persia
- Israel's return was proclaimed in the first year of Cyrus (2 Chr 36:22-23; Ezra 1:1-4)

### The purpose of the return
- The Lord stirred up the spirit of Cyrus king of Persia and commanded him to build the house of God in Jerusalem, which was in Judah (Ezra 1:2-3). Cyrus thus ordered people to give freewill offerings of necessary materials, and the only people who returned were those whose spirit God had stirred to go up and rebuild the house of the Lord which was in Jerusalem (Ezra 1:4-5).

### People who returned: Total 49,897 people
- The whole assembly of 42,360 people (Ezra 2:1-64; Neh 7:5-66)
  - 11 leaders • 15,604 people of Israel (by lineage)
  - 8,540 people of Israel (by region)
  - 4,289 priests • 341 Levites
  - 392 temple servants (Nethinim) and the sons of Solomon's servants
  - 652 people who could not give evidence of their father's households and their descendants
  - 12,531 people not counted
- 7,337 servants (Ezra 2:65; Neh 7:67)
- 200 singing men and women (Ezra 2:65; Neh 7:67 records 245 singers)

### Possessions that were brought out in the return
- Possessions given by King Cyrus
  - He brought out the articles of the house of the Lord, and their numbers were 30 gold dishes, 1,000 silver dishes, 29 knives (KJV), 30 gold bowls, 410 silver bowls of a second kind, and 1,000 other articles (Ezra 1:9-10). Hence, Sheshbazzar returned with a total of 5,400 articles of gold and silver (Ezra 1:11).
  - All those about the Israelites encouraged them with articles of silver, with gold, with goods, with cattle, and with valuables. They also gave freewill offerings to God (Ezra 1:4, 6).
- Animals: They brought out 736 horses, 245 mules, 435 camels, and 6,720 donkeys (Ezra 2:66-67; Neh 7:68-69).

- Offerings from the people in the first return (Neh 7:70-72)
  - Some from among the heads of fathers' households gave to the work.
  - The governor (Zerubbabel) gave the treasury 1,000 gold drachmas (8.4 kg), 50 basins, 530 priests' garments (Neh 7:70).
  - Some of the heads of fathers' households gave into the treasury of the work 20,000 gold drachmas (168 kg) and 2,200 silver minas (1,254 kg) (Neh 7:71).
  - The rest of the people gave 20,000 gold drachmas (168 kg), 2,000 silver minas (1,140 kg), and 67 priests' garments (Neh 7:72).

**Major events surrounding the return**
- They offered burnt offerings morning and evening and celebrated the Feast of Booths (Ezra 3:1-7).
- Reconstruction of the temple began in the 2nd year of their coming to the house of God, in the 2nd month (Ezra 3:8-13), but it was stopped for about 16 years due to the interference of the Samaritans (Ezra 4:1-5).
- Reconstruction of the temple resumed on the 24th day of the 6th month in the 2nd year of King Darius (Hag 1:14-15).
- The temple was completed in *4 years and 5 months*, on the 3rd day of the 12th month in the 6th year of King Darius (Ezra 6:14-15).
- The temple was dedicated, and the priests and Levites were appointed for the service of God (Ezra 6:16-18).
- They observed the Passover on the 14th day of the 1st month in the year in which they finished building the temple. Then, they observed the Feast of Unleavened Bread seven days (Ezra 6:19-22).

# 1. The purpose and the time of the return

### (1) The purpose of the first return

God stirred up the heart of Cyrus king of Persia in his first year (first regnal year: 538 BC) in order to fulfill the Word of the Lord by the mouth of Jeremiah (2 Chr 36:22; Ezra 1:1). The word *stirred* used here is עוּר (*'ûr*) in Hebrew, which means "to rouse," "to excite," or "to awaken." The hiphil (causative) stem of the word *'ûr* was used, indicating that God had compelled King Cyrus's heart to be moved.

In 538 BC, King Cyrus made a proclamation that stated, "The Lord, the God of heaven, has given me all the kingdoms of the earth and He has appointed me to build Him a house in Jerusalem, which is in Judah. Whoever there is among you of all His people, may his God be with him! Let him go up to Jerusalem which is in Judah and rebuild the house of the

Lord, the God of Israel; He is the God who is in Jerusalem" (Ezra 1:2-3; Ref 2 Chr 36:22-23). Then the heads of fathers' households of Judah and Benjamin, the priests, the Levites, and everyone whose spirit was stirred by God arose to go to Jerusalem:

> Ezra 1:5 Then the heads of fathers' *households* of Judah and Benjamin and the priests and the Levites arose, even everyone whose spirit God had stirred to go up and rebuild the house of the Lord which is in Jerusalem.

God stirred up the spirit of Cyrus so that he would command the construction of the house of God "in order to fulfill the word of the Lord by the mouth of Jeremiah" (Ezra 1:1). Prophet Jeremiah prophesied in detail concerning the restoration of the temple, which would consequently restore the worship. He prophesied that God will have "vengeance for His temple" (Jer 50:28; 51:11)—for the temple had been disgraced and trampled by aliens (Jer 51:51)—and there will be offerings brought into the temple again (Jer 33:10-11, 18). The foremost task for those who returned from Babylon was to rebuild the temple and restore their temple-centered worship to God. They would then recover their identity as God's elect.

Just as Prophet Jeremiah had prophesied, the sole purpose of Cyrus's proclamation for the Israelites' return was to build the temple in Jerusalem. Having received God's command, Cyrus sent a proclamation throughout his kingdom and also put it in writing (Ezra 1:1-4). Upon receiving Cyrus's decree to return to Jerusalem, the captives in Babylon must have gathered one by one to join the assembly for the first return—with inspiration and zeal for rebuilding the temple that had been tragically destroyed (Ezra 1:5-6).

## (2) The time of the first return

God foretold through Prophet Jeremiah that the captivity in Babylon would last seventy years (Jer 25:11-12; 29:10). In reference to these seventy years, 2 Chronicles 36:21 states, "to fulfill the word of the LORD by the mouth of Jeremiah, until the land had enjoyed its sabbaths. All the days of its desolation it kept sabbath until seventy years were complete." Just as the cultivation of the land resumes after the sabbatical year ends, the prophecy foretells of the recovery of the land of Judah after the end of the Babylonian exile. The land could not rest because of the Israelites' disobedience; but now it was able to rest as it enjoyed its sabbaths during the days of its desolation. Some scholars reason that the seventy years of rest for the land resulted because the Israelites did not observe seventy sabbatical years (a sabbatical year comes around every seven years) during the 490 years (70 years x 7 years) starting from either the period of the judges or the period of the unified monarchy. In reality, however, the Israelites did not fully keep most of the sabbaths, sabbatical years, or jubilees ever since the time of the exodus. Although it is difficult to determine the precise point in time when they first stopped observing them, it is certain that the Israelites disdained God's law of the sabbatical year and deprived the land of its sabbath rest. Those sabbaths were finally fulfilled when the people who had disobeyed the Word were punished and deported to Babylon.

Based on the time when the people were taken captive and when they returned to start building the temple, we can see that Jeremiah's prophecy of the *seventy years* of captivity was fulfilled precisely.

The first deportation to Babylon took place in the third (fourth) regnal year of Jehoiakim (the first year of King Nebuchadnezzar), which was 605 BC (2 Kgs 24:1; Jer 25:1; Ref Dan 1:1-2). Next, the decree for the Israelites' first return from Babylon was issued in the first regnal year of Cyrus in 538 BC. Cyrus the king of Persia received God's command "to build Him a house in Jerusalem, which is in Judah" (Ezra 1:2) and proclaimed the decree: "Whoever there is among you of all His people, may his God be with him! Let him go up to Jerusalem which is in Judah, and rebuild the house of the LORD, the God of Israel; He is the God who is in Jerusalem" (Ezra 1:3). After the decree was issued, the people of Judah made preparations for some time and finally returned to Jerusalem one year later in 537 BC (Ezra 1:5, 11; 3:1). The actual time when the people of Judah finally began to build the temple after returning to Jerusalem under the decree was in the second month (month of Ziv) of 536 BC (Ezra 3:1, 8). Therefore, counted inclusively, there were exactly seventy years from 605 BC (the year of the first deportation to Babylon) to 536 BC (the year the temple construction began).

## 2. People who returned and the circumstances around the time of the return

### (1) People in the first return

The route of the first return from Babylon is presumed to have been along the River Euphrates, a trade route in those days. It would have passed through Aleppo and Hamath, both located in the northwest region. Then, the route would have turned southward.

Zerubbabel and Jeshua (Joshua), the leaders during the first return, and a total of 49,897 people returned (42,360 people, 7,337 male and female servants, 200 singing men and women; Ezra 2:64-65). Nehemiah recorded that a total of 49,942 people returned, which is forty-five more people than those recorded by Ezra (Neh 7:66-67). This is because Ezra recorded the singing men and women as 200 persons, while Nehemiah recorded them as 245 persons.

Along with a list of those who returned, Ezra and Nehemiah also provided a detailed account of the number of animals that were brought. There were 736 horses, 245 mules, 435 camels, and 6,720 donkeys for a total of 8,136 animals (Ezra 2:66-67; Neh 7:68-69). Horses offered excellent mobility but were the priciest means of transportation. On the contrary, mules—the offspring of a female horse and a male donkey—were less expensive than horses and were more suitable modes of transportation in mountainous regions because they possessed the positive traits of both horses and donkeys. Camels were suitable for long distance travels. Donkeys were small but had strong backs and were most inexpensive, so they were very familiar to the commoners. The ratio of the number of these animals to the "whole assembly" who returned (42,360 people; Ezra 2:64; Neh 7:66) equaled to about one animal for every five persons (one animal per household of five members). The people of Israel possessed so many animals because the natives of Babylon had given them a substantial amount of silver, gold, goods, cattle, and many other treasures and wealth when they left Babylon (Ezra 1:4, 6).

The Israelites had also come out of Egypt "with flocks and herds, a very large number of livestock" (Exod 12:38). God made a distinction between the livestock of Israel and that of Egypt during the fifth plague of pestilence (Exod 9:4). The land of Goshen in which the Israelites resided was set apart during the seventh plague of hail (Exod 9:26). At the time, those among the servants of Pharaoh who feared the Word of God made their servants and livestock come into the houses and avoided the plague (Exod 9:19-20). However, those who disregarded the Word of God left their servants and livestock in the field and could not escape the plague (Exod 9:21-25).

In addition, immediately before the eighth plague of locusts, Moses asked for permission to take all the young and the old, sons and daughters, and all the flocks and herds to go and hold a feast to the Lord (Exod 10:8-9), but Pharaoh refused (Exod 10:10-11). During the ninth plague of the thick darkness, Pharaoh said, ". . . only let your flocks and your herds be detained. Even your little ones may go with you" (Exod 10:24). Nevertheless, Moses answered, ". . . our livestock too shall go with us; not a hoof shall be left behind. . ." (Exod 10:26). Then, during the final plague, the plague of the firstborns, ". . . the Lord struck all the firstborn in the land of Egypt, from the firstborn of Pharaoh who sat on his throne to the firstborn of the captive who was in the dungeon, and all the firstborn of cattle" (Exod 12:29). Only then did Pharaoh surrender, saying, "Take both your flocks and your herds, as you have said, and go, and bless me also" (Exod 12:32). Thus, all the livestock that the Israelites brought out with them were sanctified for use in worshiping God (Ref Exod 3:12, 18; 4:23; 5:3; 7:16; 8:1, 20, 27; 9:1, 13; 10:3, 24-26).

Just one year before the entry into Canaan, in the first month of that year, the Israelites arrived at Kadesh. There, God caused the rock to pour out a great amount of water—enough for both the assembly and their livestock (Num 20:4-11). In this manner, God protected the livestock as well. The water ran down "like rivers" (Ps 78:15-16; 105:41); it was as if the "streams were overflowing" (Ps 78:20) and "like a pool of water" (Ps 114:8). About two million people and a great number of livestock were able to drink until they were satisfied (Ref Ps 114:8; "turned . . . the flint into a fountain of water").

Likewise, during both the exodus and the return from the Babylonian exile, God looked after the people of Israel with His exceeding love. He enabled them to return with a great number of livestock so that they not only had enough for sacrifices and offerings with which to worship God, but also for the necessities of everyday life.

As we have seen thus far, a detailed and precise record of the people as well as the livestock during the return from Babylon reveals God's meticulous care at every stage of the return from their exile. Indeed, God rules over every living creature and all things are by His providence. It is just as Apostle Paul confessed: "For from Him and through Him and to Him are all things. To Him be the glory forever. Amen" (Rom 11:36).

### (2) The possessions that were brought in the first return

When the people of Judah returned, their neighbors as well as all those around them supported them with silver, gold, goods, cattle, and valuables together with a freewill offering for the house of God in accordance with Cyrus's edict (Ezra 1:4, 6). King Cyrus also brought out the articles from the house of the Lord that King Nebuchadnezzar had taken from Jerusalem and placed in the house of his gods (Ezra 1:7). Cyrus the king of Persia had them brought out by the hand of Mithredath the treasurer, and he counted them out to Sheshbazzar, the prince of Judah (Ezra 1:8). Their numbers were 30 gold dishes, 1,000 silver dishes, 29 knives (KJV), 30 gold bowls, 410 silver bowls of a second kind, and 1,000 other articles (Ezra 1:9-10). Hence, Sheshbazzar returned with a total of 5,400 articles of gold and silver (Ezra 1:11). These articles testify that the first returnees, regardless of their status, gave their best effort in dedicating their bodies and souls for the construction of the house of God.

### (3) Circumstances that led to the first return

As a commissioner (NIV – "royal administrator"; KJV – "president") of Persia, the country which dominated the world at the time, Prophet Daniel enjoyed success during the reign of Darius the Mede as well as the reign of Cyrus king of Persia (Dan 6:28). According to the aforementioned passage, we may presume that Daniel had exerted some political influence in establishing the foundations for the Persian Empire.

It was during the first year of the reign of Darius the Mede that Daniel understood the prophecy of Jeremiah, "for the completion of the desolations of Jerusalem, namely, seventy years" (Dan 9:2). Thus, it is presumable that Daniel had an indirect influence on Cyrus, whose spirit God had stirred to proclaim the emancipation of the people of Judah one year before the return from exile (538 BC; Ezra 1:1; 5:13). Also, 2 Chronicles 36:22 records, "Now in the first year of Cyrus king of Persia—in order to fulfill the word of the LORD by the mouth of Jeremiah—the LORD stirred up the spirit of Cyrus king of Persia, so that he sent a proclamation throughout his kingdom, and also *put it* in writing." *The Antiquities of the Jews* also states that Cyrus became aware of his role (as emancipator of the Jews) by reading Isaiah's prophecies concerning himself (Isa 44:28) written 210 years ago (*Ant.* 11.5).

On the other hand, Prophet Daniel was still active in Persia even during the third year of Cyrus (Dan 10:1). Nevertheless, Daniel 1:21 does not record Daniel's final year of activity as the third year of Cyrus. Instead, it says, "Daniel continued until the first year of Cyrus the king." This record sufficiently reflects the extent of Daniel's influence upon Cyrus's proclamation to emancipate the people of Israel in his first year (Ezra 1:1-4).

## (4) The process of the temple construction

The first thing the Israelites did after the exodus was set up the tabernacle on the first day of the first month in the second year of the exodus (Exod 40:17). Likewise, with a burning desire for the temple construction, the exiles returning from Babylon resolved to rebuild the temple at the very place where it had been torn down and burnt.

The people of Israel who returned from exile in 537 BC set up an altar on the foundation where the temple used to be (Ezra 2:68; 3:3). They offered burnt offerings morning and evening, celebrated the Feast of Booths, and prepared for the reconstruction of the temple (Ezra 3:1-7). They finally laid the foundation and began the construction work in the second month of 536 BC (Ezra 3:8-13).

However, the reconstruction work came to a halt due to the relentless interferences by the Samaritans.

> **Ezra 4:5** and [the people of the land] hired counselors against them to frustrate their counsel all the days of Cyrus king of Persia, even until the reign of Darius king of Persia.

Here, the word *counselors* is יָעַץ (*yā'aṣ*) in Hebrew and refers to the king's advisors who at the time received bribes from the Samaritans to slander the Jews. The word *frustrate* is פָּרַר (*pārar*) in Hebrew which means "to thwart," "to crumble," or "to break apart." The passage describes a state in which the sabotage was so severe that the reconstruction effort could not continue.

Thus, the construction of the temple had ceased for about sixteen years (536–520 BC). Then in 520 BC, God raised up the prophets Haggai and Zechariah in order to stir up the spirit of Zerubbabel and Joshua, as well as that of all the people. The reconstruction work then resumed on the twenty-fourth day of the sixth month in the second year of King Darius (Ezra 5:1-2; 6:14; Hag 1:14-15; Ref Zech 4:6-10). The temple was completed in about four years and five months, on the third day of the twelfth month in the sixth year (516 BC) of King Darius (Ezra 6:15).

## (5) The message of the prophets

Prophet Daniel delivered messages that would become the backdrop for the first return from the Babylonian exile. Prophets Haggai (meaning "festival") and Zechariah (meaning "whom the Lord remembers") played pivotal roles in completing the construction of the temple that had been halted for sixteen years after the return (Ezra 5:1-2; 6:14).

① **Prophet Daniel's message**

The people of Judah were deported to Babylon in three different stages, and the first time they returned from Babylon was in 537 BC. Daniel's prophecies, which he received from God, provided the backdrop for this return. The following is a chronological summary of Daniel's messages regarding the first return from exile.

*FIRST*, **the message of the vision of "a tree in the midst of the earth" as shown to King Nebuchadnezzar (thirty-two years before the first return)**

King Nebuchadnezzar (605–562 BC) dreamt about "a great statue" in the second year of his reign (603 BC; Dan 2:31-35). Later, he saw "a tree in the midst of the earth" in his dream (Dan 4:4-18). It is presumed that this took place in about 569 BC, thirty-two years prior to the first return from exile (537 BC). This was when Nebuchadnezzar was "at ease in his house and flourishing in his palace" (Dan 4:4). He was briefly enjoying a period of peace because he had finally conquered Tyre in 573 BC, after a thirteen-year-long siege of the city that had been dominating the seas (Ref Ezek 29:17-18).

Nebuchadnezzar's dream was about "a tree in the midst of the earth." The tree grew large and its height reached to the sky, the beasts of the field found shade under it, and the birds of the sky dwelt in its branches (Dan 4:10-12). Then, a holy one who descended from heaven shouted out and spoke as follows:

> "Chop down the tree and cut off its branches, strip off its foliage and scatter its fruit; let the beasts flee from under it and the birds from its branches. Yet leave the stump with its roots in the ground, but with a band of iron and bronze around it in the new grass of the field; and let him be drenched with the dew of heaven, and let him share with the beasts in the grass of the earth. Let his mind be changed from that of a man and let a beast's mind be given to him, and let seven periods of time pass over him." (Dan 4:13-16)

Daniel explained that the tree in the dream was Nebuchadnezzar. Moreover, he prophesied that the king would be driven away after he has become great and strong, but will be restored after he realizes that God is the ruler over the realm of mankind (Dan 4:22-26).

Twelve months passed since this prophecy was made (Dan 4:29). God had given Nebuchadnezzar a one-year grace period, yet he did not understand and did not repent. One day, after building a luxurious palace in Babylon, he was walking on its rooftop and exuding with pride, he said: "Is this not Babylon the great, which I myself have built as a royal residence by the might of my power and for the glory of my majesty?"(Dan 4:30). While these words were still in his mouth, a voice came from heaven saying, "sovereignty has been removed from you" (Dan 4:31). The voice further declared, "you will be driven away from mankind, and your dwelling place will be with the beasts of the field. You will be given grass to eat like cattle, and seven periods of time will pass over you until you recognize that the Most High is ruler over the realm of mankind and bestows it on whomever He wishes" (Dan 4:32). Immediately, this word concerning Nebuchadnezzar was fulfilled. The king was driven away from mankind and began eating grass like cattle, and his body was drenched with the dew of heaven until his hair had grown like eagles' feathers and his nails like birds' claws. He lived in insanity like a beast (Dan 4:33).

At the end of the days, when the "seven periods of time" (Dan 4:16, 23, 25, 32) had passed, Nebuchadnezzar raised his eyes toward heaven, and his reason returned to him at that very moment. He confessed that his own existence was nothing and God alone is the Most High. Praising God's everlasting dominion and His kingdom which endures from generation to generation, he blessed the absolute Sovereign who does according to His will (Dan 4:34-35). At the same time, his reason returned to him and his majesty and splendor were restored. His counselors and nobles sought him out and reestablished him in his sovereignty; and surpassing greatness was added to him (Dan 4:36). Nebuchadnezzar's overcast countenance became bright, the servants who had left him returned to serve him as king, and he received much more glory and power than he had before.

If we become proud and miss the God-given opportunity to repent (Ref Heb 12:17; Rev 2:21), then from that moment all our honor will disappear and we will live like the beasts (Ref Prov 16:18; 18:12; Ezek 28:12-19). However, if we repent and turn our ways and humbly obey before the Word of God, everything will be restored at that moment, and glory greater than the former will be added on to us (Ref 1 Pet 5:5; Jas 4:6).

King Nebuchadnezzar was able to make a great confession of faith after having experienced the power of God and the state of extreme humility.

> **Daniel 4:37** Now I, Nebuchadnezzar, praise, exalt and honor the King of heaven, for all His works are true and His ways just, and He is able to humble those who walk in pride.

God displayed His absolute sovereignty to the entire world by having the king of the most powerful nation at the time declare that it is God who decides the rise and fall of man. Through this event, God debased Babylon and exalted His people who had become captives, thereby filling the Israelites with eager anticipation of the day when He would set them free.

### SECOND, the message regarding the "four beasts" (fifteen years prior to the first return)

In the first year (בִּשְׁנַת חֲדָה, *bišnat ḥădâ*) of Belshazzar king of Babylon, Daniel saw a vision of four great beasts coming up from the sea (Dan 7:1-3). According to the writings engraved on the clay cylinders discovered in AD 1854, Belshazzar was the firstborn son of King Nabonidus (556–539 BC). Nabonidus allowed his firstborn Belshazzar to rule as co-regent from 553 BC, so the first year of Belshazzar's reign was 552 BC. Thus, Daniel saw the vision of the four great beasts fifteen years prior to the first return from the Babylonian exile. This was approximately the fifty-third year since Daniel was taken captive (605 BC) and about fifty-one years since King Nebuchadnezzar saw the vision regarding the great statue (603 BC; Dan 2:31-35).

Daniel's vision in chapters 2 and 7 are actually the same revelation given in different forms, emphasizing the importance of the revelation as well as confirming that it would surely come to pass. The four great beasts that came from the sea, which Daniel saw in a vision at night, all had different appearances. The first was like a lion, the second like a bear, the third like a leopard, and the fourth was a dreadful and terrifying beast with large iron teeth (Dan 7:3-8). The four great beasts represented four kings that would arise from the earth (Dan 7:17): Babylon, the kingdom that was dominating the world at the time, succeeded by Persia, Greece, and Rome in this order.

King Belshazzar was the most brutal king among the rulers of Babylon, and the people of Judah lived in great fear as captives during his reign. However, by giving this vision of the four great beasts during the first year of his reign, God reassured His people with the great hope that Babylon would certainly fall and that they would be freed to return home from captivity. Furthermore, Daniel saw the vision of God who sat on the throne to judge (Dan 7:9-10) as well as the vision of the Messiah coming with the clouds like a Son of Man (Dan 7:13-14). This vision shows that the rulers of this world will be replaced time after time and all the nations will ultimately face judgment, thus proclaiming that the only eternal ruler is God.

*THIRD*, the message regarding the male ram and the male goat (thirteen years prior to the first return from exile)

Daniel chapters 2 and 7 reveal through history how nations like Babylon, Persia, Greece, and Rome will rule over the world, including the area that encompasses Judah. In Daniel chapter 8, through the vision of the ram and the male goat that Daniel saw by the Ulai Canal, God reveals in detail how His work of redemption will unfold. Daniel received the vision of the ram and the male goat during the third year of the reign of King Belshazzar in 550 BC, thirteen years prior to the first return from exile.

First, Daniel saw a ram with two horns which represent the kings of Media and Persia (Dan 8:3-4, 20). Next, a male goat appeared and broke the two horns of the ram (Dan 8:5-7). This male goat represents the king of Greece, and the conspicuous horn between the two eyes represents Greece's first king, Alexander the Great (Dan 8:21-22). The horn of the male goat was also broken and in its place came up four conspicuous horns, symbolizing how the nation would be divided by four generals after the death of Alexander the Great (Dan 8:8, 22). These four generals were Ptolemy, Seleucus, Lysimachus, and Cassander.

Furthermore, out of one of the four horns came forth another small horn which grew exceedingly great toward the south, toward the east, and toward the Beautiful Land (Dan 8:9). This small horn represents Antiochus IV Epiphanes, a tyrant who would rise from the Seleucid Dynasty. In 167 BC, Antiochus IV put a stop to the daily sacrifices at the temple of Jerusalem and greatly desecrated the temple by erecting a statue of Zeus* there (Dan 9:27).

Through the visions of the ram and the male goat, the great horn, the four conspicuous horns, and the small horn, God revealed that only He holds absolute sovereignty and only He governs the rise and fall of all nations in the world. Thus, He was urging His people in the Babylonian exile to believe in Him alone and rely only on Him.

**FOURTH, the message regarding the writing on the palace wall (two years prior to the first return from exile)**

Nabopolassar established the Neo-Babylonian empire (626 BC) which collapsed about eighty-seven years later, during the reign of its last king, Belshazzar (539 BC). Daniel chapter 5 records the death of Belshazzar, the last king of Babylon (Dan 5:30). Due to Belshazzar's extremely extravagant, hedonistic lifestyle and his reckless reign, the Neo-Babylonian empire received God's judgment and suddenly collapsed. Thereafter, Media and Persia arose as the emerging empire (Dan 5:1-31).

King Belshazzar held a great feast for a thousand of his nobles and drank wine using the vessels of gold and silver taken from the temple of Jerusalem during King Nebuchadnezzar's time. They praised the gods of gold and silver, of bronze, iron, wood, and stone (Dan 5:1-4). Then suddenly, the fingers of a man's hand emerged and began writing opposite the lampstand on the plaster of the wall of the king's palace. The inscription read: "MENĒ, MENĒ, TEKĒL, UPHARSIN" (Dan 5:5, 25). Trembling in great fear, the king called all the conjurers, the Chaldeans, the diviners, and the wise men of Babylon and ordered them to read the inscription and explain its interpretation. Surprisingly, no one could read—let alone interpret—these words written in Aramaic, which was the international language of that time (Dan 5:7-8). Thus, King Belshazzar was greatly alarmed, his face growing even paler; his nobles were perplexed (Dan 5:9).

At this time, the queen entered the banquet hall to comfort King Belshazzar who was immensely perplexed and shaking in fear and anxiety. She suggested that he call upon and inquire of Daniel who had been in the kingdom since the days of Nebuchadnezzar (Dan 5:10-12). The queen spoke of Daniel as the one who has the "spirit of the holy gods" (Dan 5:11), "illumination, insight and wisdom like the wisdom

---

* Zeus: The supreme deity of the ancient Greeks. A being who rules over all phenomena in heaven and earth and upholds politics, law and ethics in human society. He is identified as Jupiter in Roman mythology.

of the gods" (Dan 5:11). She further commented that he possessed "an extraordinary spirit, knowledge and insight, interpretation of dreams, explanation of enigmas and solving of difficult problems" (Dan 5:12). As soon as Daniel walked in, the desperate king promised him a great reward. However, Daniel replied, "Keep your gifts for yourself or give your rewards to someone else; however, I will read the inscription to the king and make the interpretation known to him" (Dan 5:17).

Just as the queen had praised, Daniel—with wisdom from God—clearly read and interpreted every word of the inscription, which no one among the numerous wise men could do. The inscription on the wall was: מְנֵא מְנֵא תְּקֵל וּפַרְסִין ("MENĒ, MENĒ, TEKĒL, UPHARSIN"; Dan 5:25). The word מְנֵא (měnēʾ) means "counted" and thus means, "God has numbered your kingdom and put an end to it" (Dan 5:26). The word תְּקֵל (těqēl) means "to weigh" and thus means, "You have been weighed on the scales and found deficient" (Dan 5:27). The word וּפַרְסִין (ûparsîn) is a combination of the conjunctive particle וּ (û) and the plural form of פְּרַס (pěras: "to divide") meaning, "Your kingdom has been divided and given over to the Medes and Persians" (Dan 5:28).

As prophesied in this inscription, that same night Belshazzar the Chaldean king was slain, and Darius the Mede received the kingdom (Dan 5:30-31). King Darius had allied himself with Cyrus II of Persia (539 BC / 538–530 BC) at this time, so Babylon had essentially fallen at the hands of the allied forces of Media and Persia.

The fall of Babylon had occurred in accordance with God's Word. Babylon fell suddenly at the hands of Media and Persia during Belshazzar's time because of God's sovereign judgment. It was the amazing fulfillment of the history of redemption, which revealed that God's promised visitation—that is, the return of the exiles from Babylon—was at hand (Jer 25:11-12; 29:10).

### FIFTH, the message regarding the seventy weeks (one year prior to the first return)

In the first year (בִּשְׁנַת אַחַת, bišnat ʾaḥat) of Darius's reign, Daniel was reading the book of Jeremiah and came to understand the prophecy that Israel would return from captivity after seventy years. He then fasted and prayed, bearing the sins of the people on his shoulders (538 BC; Dan 9:1-3). Daniel 9:1 states that this was "in the first year of Darius the son of Ahasuerus, of Median descent, who was made king over the kingdom of the Chaldeans." *Darius* here does not refer to Darius I (522–486 BC), Darius II (423–404 BC), or Darius III (336/335–331 BC). He is actually Cyaxares II (539–538 BC), the father-in-law of Cyrus II. Hence, Ahasuerus who appears in this verse is not the Ahasuerus in the book of Esther, but Astyages, the father of Cyaxares II. This was a critical period of great transition in world history. A great power shift was taking place since Babylon—the once glorious empire—had completely collapsed when attacked by the allied forces of Media and Persia. Moreover, the year was 538 BC—one year prior to the first return from exile, which means about sixty-seven years had passed since Daniel was taken captive in 605 BC. Daniel had been taken to Babylon as a young boy (around seventeen years old; Dan 1:1-4) and was now an elderly man of about eighty-four years of age.

This was also around the time when Daniel was serving as one of the three commissioners of the entire empire under the reign of Darius (Dan 6:1-2). Daniel distinguished himself among the commissioners and satraps because he possessed an extraordinary spirit. Then the commissioners and satraps began trying to find a ground of accusation against Daniel; but they could find no ground of accusation or evidence of corruption, inasmuch as he was faithful, and no negligence or corruption was to be found in him (Dan 6:3-4). They then made a vile attempt to entrap Daniel by establishing an injunction (Dan 6:5-9). Being aware that Daniel had been faithfully serving the One and Only God, the God of Israel, they sent out watchers to secretly spy on him. Before long, they found Daniel kneeling on his knees three times a day, praying to his God by the windows open toward Jerusalem; and they reported this to the king (Dan 6:10-13). The king in great distress tried to deliver Daniel, but the wicked men came by agreement to the king and argued that it was a law of the Medes and Persians that no injunction may be changed (Dan 6:14-15). As a result, Daniel was cast into the lions' den according to the king's orders, but he survived miraculously because God's angel had shut the lions' mouth (Dan 6:16-23). The king then gave orders to bring those men who had maliciously accused Daniel, and to cast them, their children, and their wives into the lions' den instead. However, even before they reached the bottom of the den, the lions overpowered them and crushed all their bones (Dan 6:24). Then Darius the king made a decree which stated, ". . . in all the dominion of my kingdom men are to fear and tremble before the God of Daniel; for He is the living God and enduring forever, and His kingdom is one which will not be destroyed, and His dominion will be forever. He delivers and rescues and performs signs and wonders in heaven and on earth, who has also delivered Daniel from the power of the lions" (Dan 6:25-27). Hence, Daniel enjoyed success during the reigns of both Darius and Cyrus the Persian (Dan 6:28).

After these events, Daniel received the revelation of the seventy weeks in Daniel chapter 9 (Dan 9:24-27).

Daniel's revelation regarding the seventy weeks can be divided into three major parts.

**The first part** deals with the seven weeks and the sixty-two weeks. "So you are to know and discern that from the issuing of a decree to restore and rebuild Jerusalem until Messiah the Prince [an anointed one; RSV] there will be seven weeks and sixty-two weeks . . ." (Dan 9:25).

**The second part** deals with the time after the sixty-two weeks when "the Messiah [an anointed one; RSV] will be cut off and have nothing, and the people of the prince who is to come will destroy the city and the sanctuary. And its end will come with a flood; even to the end there will be war; desolations are determined" (Dan 9:26).

**The third part** is the revelation regarding the last week. "And he will make a firm covenant with the many for one week, but in the middle of the week he will put a stop to sacrifice and grain offering; and on the wing of abominations will come one who makes desolate, even until a complete destruction, one that is decreed, is poured out on the one who makes desolate" (Dan 9:27).

This revelation is a prophecy regarding the return from the Babylonian exile and the reconstruction of the temple of Jerusalem. It is also a prophecy about the first coming of Jesus Christ and His death on the cross, as well as the final great tribulation and the end of the world (Ref Matt 24:15).

The period of seventy weeks was a period of God's special providence to be revealed in Israel's history. The revelation of the seventy weeks was God's proclamation that Israel would soon return from the Babylonian exile, just as He had already promised. Moreover, it presented milestones in the history of redemption for each era. Such guidance enables believers to yearn for the day when the Lord returns to finish the transgression, to make an end of sin, to make atonement for iniquity, and to bring in everlasting righteousness. As a result, His saints will be instilled with faith to stay on the alert and be ready (Dan 9:24; RefMatt 24:42-44).

**SIXTH, the message regarding the "great conflict" (one year after the first return)**

After mourning and fasting for three weeks, Daniel was standing by the Tigris River on the twenty-fourth day of the first month. At that time, he saw and understood the vision regarding the great conflict (Dan 10:2-4). This was in the third year of King Cyrus (Dan 10:1). King Cyrus was actually Cyrus II, who had allied with Darius of Media. In 539 BC, he placed Darius at the forefront in destroying Babylon. Then in 538 BC, he consolidated Media into Persia, took over the kingship of Darius and became *de facto* king of Persia. The third year of King Cyrus of Persia refers to 536 BC, the year in which Prophet Daniel was already about eighty-six years old and was at the end of his ministry.

Although the people of Israel could now return to their homeland just as Jeremiah had prophesied, Daniel remained in Persia. He fasted and mourned for three weeks because of his own sins and the sins of his people, as well as for the people's tribulation and suffering. They were in a state of hardship due to the division between the people who returned from the exile and those who chose to remain in Babylon. Hence, Daniel made his petition, embracing the future of the nation that would have to carry on the work of redemption.

Daniel chapter 11 prophesied that even Persia, which just began to rule the world, would also soon fall when a "mighty king" (Alexander the Great) arises (Dan 11:2-3). Then, with the death of Alexander the Great, the empire would be divided into four parts (Dan 11:4); and among them, the Ptolemaic kingdom (southern king) and the Seleucid kingdom (northern king) would fight each other with the chosen people of Israel in the middle (Dan 11:5-20). There is also a detailed prophecy of how Antiochus IV Epiphanes would arise from the Seleucid Dynasty and severely persecute the people of Judah (Dan 11:21-45). He foreshadows the antichrist who will appear at the end of the world. Through the deeds of Antiochus IV, God showed what must take place in the end times, thereby revealing His mysterious providence for salvation.

Lastly, Daniel chapter 12 proclaims the great victory of God's people. It states that there will be a time of distress like never before, but "at that time your people, everyone who is found written in the book, will be rescued" (Dan 12:1). Furthermore, those who have insight will shine brightly like the brightness of the expanse of heaven, and those who lead the many to righteousness, like the stars forever and ever (Dan 12:3). Therefore, what the saints need the most is the faith to endure to the end (Matt 24:13), even in the face of the greatest tribulation in human history (Dan 12:1). For this reason, the book of Daniel concludes with the verses, "How blessed is he who keeps waiting and attains to the 1,335 days! But as for you, go your way to the end; then you will enter into rest and rise again for your allotted portion at the end of the age" (Dan 12:12-13).

Daniel received the last revelation in 536 BC. This year marks the beginning of the reconstruction of the temple that was destroyed during the fall of Jerusalem. Through this revelation, God revitalized the Israelites' reconstruction work of the temple. He also conveyed the message of comfort through the revelation. In the last days, His saints may face unbearable hardships, fall into an inescapable state of despair, or experience tribulation too great to keep the purity of their faith. Nevertheless, God says that His saints are guaranteed to triumph in the end, as long as they trust in God who governs all history, believing and yearning for the coming of His kingdom. If believers do not despair until God completes His work of redemption at the end of the world, and endure to the end by firmly holding on to God's promise of the eternal covenant, then they will enjoy their "allotted portion at the end of the age" (Dan 12:13b).

② **Prophet Haggai's message**
*Haggai* is חַגַּי (*haggay*) in Hebrew and means "festival." Hagggai's messages can be divided into four main parts.

### The first message: Haggai 1:1-15
This message was proclaimed on the first day of the sixth month in the second year of King Darius (Hag 1:1), immediately before the temple reconstruction resumed. Prophet Haggai described the state of the people in three ways.

First, their lives were fruitless. Haggai 1:6 states, "You have sown much, but harvest little; you eat, but there is not enough to be satisfied; you drink, but there is not enough to become drunk; you put on clothing, but no one is warm enough; and he who earns, earns wages to put into a purse with holes." Ever since the reconstruction of the temple had come to a halt, although the people of Judah lived diligently, their lives were always fruitless and futile.

Second, their lives were being blown away. No matter how much we may possess, everything will disappear the moment God blows it all away. Haggai 1:9 states, "'You look for much, but behold, it comes to little; when you bring it home, I blow it away. Why?' declares the Lord of hosts, 'Because of My house which lies desolate, while each of you runs to his own house.'"

Third, their lives were full of calamities. Haggai 1:10-11 describes such lives: "Therefore, because of you the sky has withheld its dew and the earth has withheld its produce. I called for a drought on the land, on the mountains, on the grain, on the new wine, on the oil, on what the ground produces, on men, on cattle, and on all the labor of your hands." This message teaches us that no matter how much people labor, everything will be in vain if God brings on calamity.

What was the cause of this kind of life? It was because the people dwelt in paneled houses while God's house laid desolate (Hag 1:4). This was the sin of halting the reconstruction work and neglecting it. Haggai 1:4 states, "Is it time for you yourselves to dwell in your paneled houses while this house lies desolate?" Here, "paneled houses" refer to fancy houses whose walls and roofs are made of engraved panels or panels of cedar. The people of Judah said that "the time has not come for the house of the Lord to be rebuilt" (Hag 1:2); yet they invested great wealth, time, and effort into decorating their own homes splendidly. Haggai 1:9 describes this state as, "...My house which lies desolate, while each of you runs to his own house." Those who take more interest in their own work rather than the work of the temple will live fruitless lives, no matter how much they labor.

The people of Judah obeyed the voice of the Lord their God and the words of Haggai the prophet (Hag 1:12). They reflected upon their sinful lives when they heard this precise and powerful message that pierced their hearts. At that time, Haggai spoke to the people by the commission of the Lord saying, "'I am with you,' declares the Lord" (Hag 1:13). God stirred up the spirit of Zerubbabel, the governor of Judah, and the spirit of Joshua the high priest, and the spirit of all the remnant of the people, so that they began to rebuild the temple. This was on the twenty-fourth day of the sixth month in the second year of Darius the king (Darius I: 522–486 BC; Hag 1:14-15).

### The second message: Haggai 2:1-9

This message was proclaimed about one month after the reconstruction of the temple resumed, on the twenty-first day of the seventh month in the second year of Darius (Hag 2:1). Although the new temple seemed humble in comparison to the former temple built by Solomon, Prophet Haggai proclaimed a message of encouragement, saying "'. . . but now take courage, Zerubbabel,' declares the Lord" (Hag 2:2-4).

Why? It was because God's Word of the covenant and His Spirit rested in the temple (Hag 2:5). Although the temple may lack in terms of physical appearance, God regarded this temple in which His Word and Spirit dwelt as the greatest and most valuable place in the world.

Moreover, the latter glory of the temple will be greater than its former glory (Hag 2:9) and the wealth of all nations will come into it (Hag 2:7); the wealth of all nations is none other than Jesus Christ (Col 2:2-3). Hence, even the humblest looking temple becomes the most honorable and holy place on this earth if Jesus abides there. Jesus Himself is the spiritual temple (John 1:14; 2:19-22) and the wealth of all nations to which nothing in this world can compare.

### The third message: Haggai 2:10-19

This is a proclamation of blessings for the people who obeyed God's Word and worked on the reconstruction of the temple. This message was given to Haggai on the twenty-fourth day of the ninth month in the second year of King Darius, which was two months after the second message was proclaimed (Hag 2:10). Because the people of Judah were unclean, calamities did not cease to fall upon them (Hag 2:16-17, 19a). Haggai 2:14 states, "Then Haggai said, 'So is this people. And so is this nation before Me,' declares the Lord, 'and so is every work of their hands; and what they offer there is unclean.'"

Why were the people of Judah unclean? They were unclean because they left the temple of God desolate and busily used their hands to build their own houses. They then used those same hands to worship God. People who do their own work before they do God's work are all in an unclean state.

However, the uncleanliness has been lifted and God will pour down

His blessings from the day the Word has been proclaimed. The word "bless" from the phrase "I will bless you" (Hag 2:19b) is the piel (intensive) stem of the Hebrew verb בָּרַךְ (*bārak*) used in the imperfect tense. Thus, the expression signifies that God will greatly and continuously pour His blessings on those who place the house of God above all things.

### The fourth message: Haggai 2:20-23

This fourth message was given on the same day that the third message was given, which was, on the twenty-fourth day of the ninth month in the second year of King Darius (Hag 2:20). God revealed to Prophet Haggai the God who judges the world, and told Haggai to relate the message to Zerubbabel (Hag 2:21-22). He also promised that He would make Zerubbabel as God's signet ring (Hag 2:23). Signet rings at the time were equivalent to a crown or a scepter because they manifested a king's power and authority. God made Zerubbabel like a signet ring to foreshadow how God would give Jesus Christ all authority in heaven and on earth (Matt 28:18) to complete the eschatological salvation and establish the true temple through Him (Rev 21:22).

③ **Prophet Zechariah's message**

The name *Zechariah* (זְכַרְיָה) means "the Lord remembers." The Word of God came to Zechariah in the eighth month in the second year of King Darius (Zech 1:1). This was about two months after Haggai first began to proclaim the Word (Hag 1:1). The construction of the house of God had begun on the twenty-fourth day of the sixth month in the second year of Darius the king (Hag 1:14-15).

The Word of God came to Zechariah again on the twenty-fourth day of the eleventh month (the month of Shebat) in the second year of King Darius (Zech 1:7). This was two months after Prophet Haggai had proclaimed his final message on the twenty-fourth day of the ninth month in the second year of King Darius, the day when the temple of the Lord was founded (Hag 2:18-20). Zechariah proclaimed these messages to encourage the people to finish—without any disruptions—the reconstruction of the temple that they had resumed with great difficulty.

Prophet Zechariah's messages can be divided into three major parts:
The first part includes Zechariah chapters 1 to 6 and contains eight visions about rebuilding the temple. The second part is from chapters 7

to 8 which is about the required attitude for rebuilding the temple. The third part includes chapters 9 to 14 and relate the vision of the messianic kingdom.

### The first message: Zechariah chapters 1-6

This part contains eight visions:

**The first vision** is the vision of four men riding on horses (Zech 1:8-17). There was a man riding on a red horse, and he was standing among the myrtle trees. There were red, sorrel, and white horses behind him (Zech 1:8). The red, sorrel, and white horses were "those whom the Lord has sent to patrol the earth" (Zech 1:10). The "man who was standing among the myrtle trees" was "the angel of the Lord" (Zech 1:11). Here, the word *angel* is מַלְאָךְ (*mal'āk*) in Hebrew, which means "one who was sent" or "messenger." After receiving reports from the angels, the angel of the Lord said, "O Lord of hosts, how long will You have no compassion for Jerusalem and the cities of Judah, with which You have been indignant these seventy years?" Then the Lord answered the angel with "gracious words, comforting words" to give consolation and hope to the Israelites who were discouraged and brokenhearted (Zech 1:12-13). At this time, the angel of the Lord said, "Therefore thus says the Lord, 'I will return to Jerusalem with compassion; My house will be built in it,' declares the Lord of hosts, 'and a measuring line will be stretched over Jerusalem'"(Zech 1:16). These words strongly confirmed that the reconstruction work of the temple, which had begun on the twenty-fourth day of the sixth month in the second year of King Darius (Hag 1:15), would not be interrupted but surely be finished.

**The second vision** is the vision of the four horns and the four craftsmen (Zech 1:18-21).The four horns are "the horns which have scattered Judah, Israel and Jerusalem" (Zech 1:19), referring to the evil forces that fought against Israel. However, the "four craftsmen" come and terrify the "four horns" (Zech 1:20-21). The word *craftsmen* is derived from a Hebrew verb חָרַשׁ (*hāraš*), which means "to cut" or "to engrave," and thus refers to "artisans." These "four craftsmen" are God's instruments that destroy the evil forces. This vision signifies that God will smite the forces that hinder the reconstruction work of the temple, ultimately pointing to the Lord who will destroy Satan at His second coming (Rev 20:10).

**The third vision** is the vision of a man with a measuring line in his hand (Zech 2:1-13). He wanted "to measure Jerusalem, to see how wide it is and how long it is" (Zech 2:2). The measurement of Jerusalem was performed as a confirmation that Jerusalem would be rebuilt. The restoration of Jerusalem is also confirmed in Zechariah 2:12, which states, "the Lord will . . . again choose Jerusalem" (Zech 1:17).

**The fourth vision** is the vision of Joshua being cleansed (Zech 3:1-10). Joshua was clothed with filthy garments (Zech 3:3), but God removed them from him and clothed him with festal robes and put a clean turban on his head (Zech 3:4-5). Since Joshua was the high priest of Israel (Ezra 3:2; 5:2), his restoration reflects the restoration of the entire Israel. This vision further foreshadows the restoration of the saints through the eternal high priest, Jesus Christ.

**The fifth vision** is the vision of a lampstand all of gold and two olive trees (Zech 4:1-14). The lampstand all of gold symbolizes the temple that was being rebuilt at the time (Ref Rev 1:20), and the two olive trees represent Joshua and Zerubbabel, the two leaders in the reconstruction work of the temple (Zech 4:14). Through this vision, God showed that the temple could not be rebuilt by human strength but only by the working of the Holy Spirit. Zechariah 4:6 thus states, "Not by might nor by power, but by My Spirit."

**The sixth vision** is the vision of the flying scroll (Zech 5:1-4). Zechariah 5:3 explains what this scroll is: "This is the curse that is going forth over the face of the whole land; surely everyone who steals will be purged away according to the writing on one side, and everyone who swears will be purged away according to the writing on the other side." Stealing and swearing falsely were widespread sins among the people at the time when the temple was being rebuilt. This vision points out that sins must be purged first in order to rebuild the temple.

**The seventh vision** is the vision of a woman sitting inside the ephah (Zech 5:5-11). Here, the word *ephah* refers to a unit or a tool (container) that is used to measure an amount of grain or liquid. The Bible says that cheating with the *ephah* is wicked (Amos 8:5; Mic 6:10; Ref Lev 19:35-36; Ezek 45:9-12).

This woman sitting inside the ephah is a personification of wickedness. Zechariah 5:8 explains, "This is Wickedness!" This woman would be taken to the land of Shinar and set there (Zech 5:11). Shinar was the very place that God had judged for building the Tower of Babel (Gen 11:1-9). Hence, this vision shows that God certainly judges and punishes wickedness (Ref Rev 20:3, 10).

The **eighth vision** is the vision of the four chariots (Zech 6:1-8). "With the first chariot were red horses, with the second chariot black horses, with the third chariot white horses, and with the fourth chariot strong dappled horses" (Zech 6:2-3). These four chariots are the "four spirits of heaven" (Zech 6:5), and they refer to the angels who execute God's judgment on His behalf (Ref Rev 7:1).

The chariot with the black horses and white horses go forth to the north country (Zech 6:6), and the chariot with dappled horses go forth to the south country (Zech 6:6), while the chariot with strong ones go to patrol the earth (Zech 6:7). The north country represents Babylon and the south country represents Egypt; they show that God will certainly judge the nations that stand against Him. Moreover, the strong horses patrolling the earth signify that there is no place in this world to escape God's judgment.

### The second message: Zechariah chapters 7-8

Zechariah chapters 7 and 8 begin when the Word of the Lord came to Zechariah "on the fourth day of the ninth month, which is Chislev, in the fourth year of King Darius" around 518 BC (Zech 7:1). Beginning with the Bethelites' question about fasting (Zech 7:2-3), these two chapters explain the proper attitude of faith that God's chosen people must have as they rebuild the temple as well as the restoration of Israel in the near future.

Zechariah chapter 7 speaks about the proper attitude of faith.

**The first attitude** is to put away the hypocrisy of formalism. Although the people of Israel had been fasting in the fifth and seventh months for the past seventy years, God said that their fasts were not for Him (Zech 7:5-6). Here, the *seventy years* roughly represent the period (586–518 BC) from the time when the temple was destroyed and fasting began until the fourth regnal year of Darius, who was king at the time. A true saint must fast in order to glorify God, not to seek personal benefit or esteem (Matt 6:16-18; 1 Cor 10:31).

**The second attitude** is to put away disobedience. Israel had been disobeying the Word of God until then. Zechariah 7:10-11 states, "'and do not oppress the widow or the orphan, the stranger or the poor; and do not devise evil in your hearts against one another.' But they refused to pay attention and turned a stubborn shoulder and stopped their ears from hearing." Obeying the Word of God is the fastest way to finish building the true temple.

Zechariah chapter 8 speaks about Israel's restoration, the work they must do, and the glory to come after the restoration. First, Zechariah 8:1-13 speak about Israel's restoration. The restoration takes place when God returns to Zion and dwells in the midst of Jerusalem (Zech 8:3; Ref Isa 52:8). God will save the Israelites who have been scattered and He will bring them back so that they can live in Jerusalem (Zech 8:4-8). There will be peace for the seed (a sowing of peace; RSV), and Israel will become a blessing (Zech 8:9-13). Zechariah 8:14-17 then continues to explain what the restored Israel must do: "'These are the things which you should do: speak the truth to one another; judge with truth and judgment for peace in your gates. Also let none of you devise evil in your heart against another, and do not love perjury; for all these are what I hate,' declares the Lord" (Zech 8:16-17).

Next, Zechariah 8:18-23 describes the glory that Israel will enjoy after her restoration. The period of fasting will become joy, gladness, and cheerful feasts (Zech 8:18-19); and the work of salvation will sweep across the world so that many peoples and mighty nations will come to seek the Lord of hosts in Jerusalem, and to entreat the favor of the Lord (Zech 8:20-23).

### The third message: Zechariah chapters 9-14

This part contains prophetic writings and shows visions of the messianic kingdom. It prophesies that Christ will inaugurate the messianic kingdom at His first coming and consummate it at His second coming. The prophecies in Zechariah chapters 9 through 11 deal mainly with the first coming whereas chapters 12 through 14 prophesy mostly about the second coming. Some of the major prophecies about the Messiah are as follows.

### *FIRST* is the message in Zechariah 9:9.

> **Zechariah 9:9** Rejoice greatly, O daughter of Zion! Shout in triumph, O daughter of Jerusalem! Behold, your king is coming to you; He is just and endowed with salvation, humble, and mounted on a donkey, even on a colt, the foal of a donkey.

Zechariah prophesied that when Jesus Christ the King of kings enters Jerusalem, He will come mounted on a foal of a donkey (Matt 21:7; Mark 11:7; Luke 19:35; John 12:14-15).

**SECOND** is the message in Zechariah 11:12.

> **Zechariah 11:12** "I said to them, 'If it is good in your sight, give me my wages; but if not, never mind!' So they weighed out thirty shekels of silver as my wages."

Here, the word *wages* denotes "compensation or payment for a hireling or laborer." The expression is a prophecy that Jesus will be sold for thirty shekels of silver (Ref Exod 21:32). In accordance with this prophecy, Jesus was sold by Judas Iscariot for thirty shekels of silver (Matt 26:15).

**THIRD** is the message in Zechariah 12:10.

> **Zechariah 12:10** I will pour out on the house of David and on the inhabitants of Jerusalem, the Spirit of grace and of supplication, so that they will look on Me whom they have pierced; and they will mourn for Him, as one mourns for an only son, and they will weep bitterly over Him like the bitter weeping over a firstborn.

Here, the word *pierced* foreshadows that Jesus will be nailed to the cross and His side will be pierced with a spear (John 19:37). The phrase *they will mourn for him* is a prophecy that one day the people of Israel will repent for their sin of killing Jesus on the cross (Rom 11:11, 25).

**FOURTH** is the message in Zechariah 13:1.

> **Zechariah 13:1** In that day a fountain will be opened for the house of David and for the inhabitants of Jerusalem, for sin and for impurity.

Here, the Hebrew word for *fountain* is מָקוֹר (*māqôr*), which means "spring" or "origin." It represents Jesus Christ who is the spring of life that washes away every sin and impurity of fallen mankind (Isa 55:1; John 4:14; 7:37). Revelation 22:17 also says, ". . . And let the one who is thirsty come; let the one who wishes take the water of life without cost." When the Lord returns, the work of eternal life will open up to His people all over the world.

**FIFTH** is the message in Zechariah 14:4.

> **Zechariah 14:4** In that day His feet will stand on the Mount of Olives, which is in front of Jerusalem on the east; and the Mount of Olives will be

split in its middle from east to west by a very large valley, so that half of the mountain will move toward the north and the other half toward the south.

This expression that God's feet will stand on the Mount of Olives is an example of anthropomorphism, which vividly depicts the revelation of Jesus Christ. One of Ezekiel's visions also contains the expression that the Lord will appear at the Mount of Olives. Ezekiel 11:23 says, "The glory of the Lord went up from the midst of the city and stood over the mountain which is east of the city." Hence, the third part of the book of Zechariah portrays the mysterious works of the magnificent kingdom of God that will be completed through the advent of the Messiah.

When the reconstruction of the temple, which had ceased for sixteen years, finally resumed because of the prophecies of Haggai, Prophet Zechariah expounded that the true meaning of rebuilding the temple lies in receiving the coming Messiah and His kingdom. Prophet Zechariah thus encouraged the restoration of proper faith among the people of Judah.

Based on the historical background, we can estimate that Prophet Zechariah was active from around 520 BC when the temple construction began to around 480 BC, long after the temple was finished.[46]

The people of Judah who returned in the first return from exile began to build the temple in 536 BC. However, this work soon came to a halt due to the interference of the Samaritans. The construction ceased for sixteen years thereafter, but resumed in 520 BC, on the twenty-fourth day of the sixth month in the second year of King Darius (Hag 1:15). It was finally completed after about four years and five months, in 516 BC, on the third day of the month of Adar (twelfth month) in the sixth year of King Darius (Zech 6:15). This was seventy years after the temple of Jerusalem was destroyed in 586 BC. Hence, Jeremiah's prophecy that Israel would return after completing seventy years in Babylon was fulfilled without fail (Jer 25:11-12; 29:10).

The driving force behind all this work was the Word of God proclaimed by Prophets Haggai and Zechariah (Ezra 5:1-2; 6:14; Hag 1:12-15). The Word of God is living and active (Heb 4:12). His Word is so powerful that it grows mightily and prevails (Acts 19:20). Hence, the Word of God is the driving force in establishing, reviving, and rebuilding the church, the body of Christ.

**Leader:** Ezra the priest and scribe (meaning: "the Lord helps"; Ezra 7:1-10)

**King of Persia:** 7th year of Artaxerxes I (Ezra 7:7-26)

**The circumstances that led to the return:** 474 BC during the reign of Ahasuerus

Haman plotted to annihilate all the Jews who were dispersed in the 127 provinces of Persia on the 13th day of Adar, the 12th month (Esth 3:7-15). However, the enemies of the Jews were destroyed instead on the 14th and the 15th day of the 12th month. Thus, these days became the Feast of Purim, celebrated throughout the generations by the Jews who had been saved (Esth 9:1-32).

**The purpose of the return**
① Full recovery of the temple-centered community of covenantal faith

② To replenish a great amount of materials that were needed to restore the sacrifices in the temple. Under the leadership of Ezra, the second group of returnees from Babylon brought to the temple of God in Jerusalem the silver and gold, which the king and his counselors had freely offered (Ezra 7:15). They also brought all the silver and gold which they obtained in the whole province of Babylon, along with the freewill offering of the people and of the priests, who offered willingly for the house of their God in Jerusalem (Ezra 7:16-18). In addition, they took utensils for the service of the house of God from the royal treasury and delivered them in full before God (Ezra 7:19-20).

③ For Ezra to teach the laws of God (Ezra 7:25-26)

**People who returned:** About 1,775 males only (Ezra 8:1-20)
 – 2 priests
 – 1 from the royal house of David
 – 1,496 males
 – 15 representatives from each household
 – 38 Levites

**The possessions that were brought in the return**
 – King Artaxerxes gave Ezra up to 100 talents (3,400 kg) of silver, 100 kors (22,000 L) of wheat, 100 baths (2,200 L) of wine, 100 baths of oil, and salt as needed (Ezra 7:22).

- The kings and his counselors and his princes and all Israel present there offered silver, gold, and the utensils for the house of God. Ezra weighed them out to 12 priests and their weights were: 650 talents (22,100 kg) of silver, 100 talents (3,400 kg) of silver utensils, and 100 talents of gold (3,400 kg), 20 gold bowls (1,000 darics, 8.4 kg; 420 g per bowl), two utensils of fine shiny bronze, precious as gold (Ezra 8:25-27; Ref Ezra 7:15-16).

  *Conversion units: 1 talent = 34 kg; 1 kor = 220 L; 1 bath = 22 L; 1 daric = 8.4 kg

- No tax, tribute, or toll was imposed on those who ministered in the house of God (Ezra 7:24).

**Major events surrounding the return**
- They camped for 3 days at the river of Ahava and brought 38 Levites and 220 Nethinim as ministers for the house of God (Ezra 8:15-20).
- As they fasted at the river of Ahava, they sought from God a safe journey for all the returnees, their little ones, and all their possessions (Ezra 8:21).
- They went up from Babylon on the 1st day of the 1st month; they departed from the river of Ahava on the 12th day of the 1st month, and came to Jerusalem on the 1st day of the 5th month (Ezra 7:9; 8:31-32).
- They remained in Jerusalem 3 days, and on the 4th day the silver and the gold and the utensils were numbered and weighed in the house of God, and all the weight was recorded at that time (Ezra 8:32-34). Then the people offered burnt offerings and a sin offering to the Lord (Ezra 8:35).
- When the king's edicts were delivered to the king's satraps and to the governors in the provinces beyond the River, they supported the people and the house of God (Ezra 8:36).
- From the 1st day of the 10th month to the 1st day of the 1st month, they investigated the high priests, the priests, the Levites, the singers, and the Israelites who had married foreign wives and disclosed all their names (Ezra 10:16-44).

# 1. The purpose and the time of the return

The second return took place under the leadership of Ezra the scribe and priest (Ezra 7:11-12, 21; Neh 8:9; 12:26) in 458 BC, which was seventy-nine years after the first return. Although the temple of Jerusalem had already been built, the people of Judah had not yet attained to the proper form of the community of God's elect. At a time like this, the second return brought great relief with work force and material provision. It also brought Ezra's extensive reforms that resolved many spiritual issues among the people of Judah, thereby restoring the people's faith.

### (1) The purpose of the second return

① **Full recovery of a temple-centered community of covenantal faith**
Ezra, the leader of the second return, received permission from King Artaxerxes and gathered all the people who wished to go up to Jerusalem and left Babylon (Ezra 7:7-9). He then assembled the people at the river that runs to Ahava, where they camped for three days, and examined the returnees. However, he did not find any Levites there (Ezra 8:15).

The fact that no Levite had volunteered to return was a serious problem since the Levites played a pivotal role in the temple sacrifices. During the first return, there were 4,289 priests (Ezra 2:36-39; Neh 7:39-42), but only 341 Levites including gatekeepers and singers (or 360; Neh 7:43-45; Ezra 2:40-42). Even if the Levites were to return to Jerusalem, their duties in the temple would have been very difficult with inconsistent and low wages. Thus, they probably preferred to remain in the place of exile where they had already settled for a long time rather than to return to Jerusalem. In order to gather temple ministers, Ezra first selected representatives to be sent to a place called Casiphia. Ezra sent for "Eliezer, Ariel, Shemaiah, Elnathan, Jarib, Elnathan, Nathan, Zechariah and Meshullam, leading men, and for Joiarib and Elnathan, teachers" (Ezra 8:16-17[a]). He then told them what to say to Iddo the leading man at Casiphia and his brothers, the temple servants (Nethinim), so that they can bring ministers for the house of God (Ezra 8:16-17[a]). Then, according to the good hand of God upon them, they brought "a man of insight of the sons of Mahli, the son of Levi, the son of Israel, namely Sherebiah, and his sons and brothers, eighteen men; and Hashabiah and Jeshaiah of the sons of Merari, with his brothers and their sons, twenty men" (Ezra 8:18-19). This way, thirty-eight Levites were obtained. They also brought 220 temple servants for the service of the Levites, and all of them were designated by name (Ezra 8:20).

Much of the record was focused on gathering the Levites and the temple servants to be brought back in the second return. This fact indicates that the ultimate purpose of the second return was to fully restore the community of covenantal faith that would serve God together in His temple.

② **To replenish the great amount of materials needed to restore the temple sacrifices**

Ezra received the silver and gold that the king and his counselors had freely offered to the God of Israel. He also obtained the silver and gold from the whole province of Babylon. Moreover, he received the freewill offering of the people and of the priests, who offered willingly for the house of their God (Ezra 7:15-16).

> **Ezra 8:25–27** and I weighed out to them the silver, the gold and the utensils, the offering for the house of our God which the king and his counselors and his princes and all Israel present *there* had offered. <sup>26</sup>Thus I weighed into their hands 650 talents of silver, and silver utensils *worth* 100 talents, *and* 100 gold talents, <sup>27</sup>and 20 gold bowls *worth* 1,000 darics, and two utensils of fine shiny bronze, precious as gold.

With this money, they purchased animals for various sacrifices and materials needed for their grain offerings and drink offerings to be offered on the altar of the house of God (Ezra 7:17). He also received the necessary utensils for the service of the house of God, along with the amazing permission to provide from the royal treasury whatever else that might be needed for the house of God (Ezra 7:18-20). Then King Artaxerxes said, "Whatever is commanded by the God of heaven, let it be done with zeal for the house of the God of heaven, so that there will not be wrath against the kingdom of the king and his sons." He also prohibited the imposing of taxes, tributes, or tolls on any of the ministers of the house of God (Ezra 7:23-24).

These special measures provided the necessary financial support that enabled the returnees to build a temple-centered community and serve God.

③ **For Ezra to teach the laws of God**

King Artaxerxes appointed Ezra as a religious leader to teach the laws (Ezra 7:25) and as a civil leader with great authority, as that of a king or a magistrate. Ezra 7:26 states, "Whoever will not observe the law of your God and the law of the king, let judgment be executed upon him strictly, whether for death or for banishment or for confiscation of goods or for imprisonment."

Ezra praised God for King Artaxerxes' goodwill, saying, "Blessed be the Lord . . . who has put such a thing as this in the king's heart, to adorn the house of the Lord which is in Jerusalem, and has extended loving-kindness to me before the king and his counselors and before all the king's mighty princes ... " (Ezra 7:27-28). It was entirely by God's grace that Ezra received such proactive support from the king. This enabled him to lead the second return and spur on his reforms according to the Word of God.

### (2) Time of the second return

The people of Israel returned a second time from Babylon under the leadership of Ezra the scribe in 458 BC, during the reign of King Artaxerxes I of Persia (Ezra 7:7-9). This was seventy-nine years after the first return and fifty-eight years after the temple of Jerusalem had been rebuilt in 516 BC.

During these fifty-eight years, the kings of Persia had changed from Cambyses II (530–522 BC), to Bardiya (522 BC), to Darius I (522–486 BC), and then to Ahasuerus (486–465/464 BC). By the time of the second return, Artaxerxes I (464–423 BC) was on the throne.

### (3) Circumstances that led to the second return

The temple of Jerusalem was rebuilt in 516 BC, and about fifty-eight years later, the second return took place in 458 BC. Within this period, there was the Esther incident during the reign of King Ahasuerus (486–465/464 BC). This incident was the result of God's absolute providence to prompt the second return from the Babylonian exile. The following is a summary of the account.

King Ahasuerus promoted Haman, the son of Hammedatha the Agagite, and placed him over all the princes who were with him. All the king's servants who were at the king's gate were to bow down to Haman as the king had instructed. However, Mordecai the Jew neither bowed down to Haman nor paid homage to him, despite the daily urging of the king's servants (Esth 3:1-4). The servants told Haman of the matter and he was filled with rage (Esth 3:5).

When the king's servants told Haman that Mordecai was a Jew, he disdained the idea of laying hands on "Mordecai alone." He also sought to destroy "the people of Mordecai who were throughout the whole kingdom of Ahasuerus" (Esth 3:6). Then they cast the *Pur*, that is the lot, before Haman from day to day and month to month until the month of Adar, the twelfth month, was chosen (Esth 3:7). The lot was cast in the month of Nisan (first month) in the twelfth year of King Ahasuerus. It was the fifth year since Esther was chosen as queen (Esth 1:3; 2:16-17; 3:7).

Haman plotted to kill Queen Esther along with Mordecai, as both were in great favor with the king. He craftily deceived the king by not referring to them as "Jews" but to a "certain people." He brought false charges against the Jews to incite the king to hate them and ultimately destroy them. He said to the king, ". . . their laws are different from those of all other people and they do not observe the king's laws, so it is not in the king's interest to let them remain. If it is pleasing to the king, let it be decreed that they be destroyed . . ." (Esth 3:8-9). Not realizing that the "certain people" were the Jews, the king took off his signet ring and gave it to Haman, allowing him to do as he pleased (Esth 3:10-11).

Upon receiving the king's approval, Haman summoned all the king's scribes on the thirteenth day of the first month and began to write edicts (Esth 3:12-13). The content of the edict was an order "to destroy, to kill and to annihilate all the Jews, both young and old, women and children, in one day, the thirteenth day of the twelfth month, which is the month of Adar, and to seize their possessions as plunder" (Esth 3:13). Haman had also promised King Ahasuerus to put ten thousand talents of silver (340 tons) into the king's treasuries in order to successfully carry out this plan (Esth 3:9).

When Mordecai learned of all that had been done, he tore his clothes, put on sackcloth and ashes, and went out into the city wailing loudly and bitterly. Then the Jews from the other provinces mourned with fasting, weeping, and wailing; many lay on sackcloth and ashes (Esth 4:1-3). When Esther heard the news, she sent Hathach the eunuch to Mordecai to learn the details of the matter and found out that the Jews were at the verge of annihilation (Esth 4:5-9).

At this time, her cousin Mordecai sent word to her, "Do not imagine that you in the king's palace can escape any more than all the Jews. For if you remain silent at this time, relief and deliverance will arise for the Jews from another place and you and your father's house will perish. And who knows whether you have not attained royalty for such a time as this?" (Esth 4:13-14). Mordecai had great conviction in God's providence to protect the Jews living in the kingdom of Persia.

After hearing these words, Esther resolved to fast for three days and asked all the Jews in Susa to fast during these days; her maidens also fasted and prayed with her (Esth 4:15-16).

Esther had not been summoned to the king for the past thirty days (Esth 4:11), and she knew that anyone who comes to the king in the inner court without being summoned would be put to death. Nevertheless, after three days of fasting, Esther went in to the king (Esth 4:16) with the singular resolution, "If I perish, I perish." The king extended the golden scepter to her (Esth 5:1-2). He then asked her, "And what is your request? Even to half of the kingdom it shall be given to you" (Esth 5:3). Esther deferred her request but invited the king and Haman to a banquet instead (Esth 5:4). Then the king quickly summoned Haman and came to the banquet that Esther had prepared. As they drank their wine, the king said to Esther, "What is your petition, for it shall be granted to you. And what is your request? Even to half of the kingdom it shall be done" (Esth 5:5-6). Here, Esther again deferred her answer to the king, requesting that the king and Haman come to the banquet that she would prepare for them the next day (Esth 5:7-8).

Haman left the banquet glad and pleased of heart; but when he saw Mordecai in the king's gate and observed that he did not stand up or tremble before him, Haman was filled with rage against Mordecai. Yet, he controlled himself, went home, and recounted to his friends and his wife Zeresh of his dissatisfaction with Mordecai. At this, they suggested, "Have a gallows fifty cubits (approx. 22.8 m) high made and in the morning, ask the king to have Mordecai hanged on it" (Esth 5:14).

On the night that Esther held the first banquet, the king could not sleep and began to read the book of the chronicles, the records of his reign. He then discovered how Mordecai had reported concerning Bigthan (Bigthana) and Teresh, two of the king's eunuchs who were doorkeepers, who had conspired to assassinate King Ahasuerus (Esth 2:21-23; 6:1-2). The two who had plotted treason were both hanged on the gallows because they were the worst of criminals (Esth 2:23). However, the king only then discovered that five years had passed since then and no reward was given to Mordecai, who had performed the meritorious deed of exposing their treason and thus saving the life of the king of Persia.

The king immediately asked, "Who is in the court?" (Esth 6:4). Haman had just entered the outer court in order to ask the king if he could hang Mordecai on the gallows that he had just built, so he was asked to come in to the king. The king asked Haman, "What is to be done for the man whom the king desires to honor?" and Haman, filled with empty conceit and excitement, said in his heart, "Whom would the king desire to honor more than me?"(Esth 6:6). He answered,

> "For the man whom the king desires to honor, let them bring a royal robe which the king has worn, and the horse on which the king has ridden, and on whose head a royal crown has been placed; and let the robe and the horse be handed over to one of the king's most noble princes and let them array the man who the king desires to honor and lead him on the horseback through the city square. And proclaim before him, 'Thus it shall be done to the man whom the king desires to honor'" (Esth 6:8-9).

Thus, the king said to Haman, "do so for Mordecai the Jew, who is sitting at the king's gate; do not fall short in anything of all that you have said" (Esth 6:10), and Mordecai was greatly honored just as Haman had suggested. Haman had answered the king thinking that he would be honored in this manner, but the exact opposite had occurred.

Now, on the second day of the banquet, as the king drank his wine, he asked for the third time, "What is your petition, Queen Esther? It shall be granted you. And what is your request? Even to half of the kingdom it shall be done" (Esth 7:2; Ref first and second time, Esth 5:3, 6). Then Queen Esther replied, "If I have found favor in your sight, O king, and if it pleases the king, let my life be given me as my petition, and my people as my request; for we have been sold, I and my people, to be destroyed, to be killed and to be annihilated" (Esth 7:3-4). Then the king was enraged and asked, "Who is he, and where is he, who would presume to do thus?" She answered, "A foe and an enemy is this wicked Haman!" (Esth 7:5-6).

The king arose in his anger and went into the palace garden. Meanwhile, Haman desperately begged the queen for his life (Esth 7:7). Just as the king returned from the garden, Haman happened to be falling on the couch where Esther was. The king saw it and said, "Will he even assault the queen with me in the house?" As the word went out of the king's mouth, the people covered Haman's face (Esth 7:8).

Then Harbonah, one of the king's eunuchs (one of the seven eunuchs; Esth 1:10), reported that the fifty-cubit (approx. 22.8 m) gallows which Haman had made for Mordecai stood at Haman's house. The king said, "Hang him on it." Therefore, they hanged Haman on the gallows, and the king's anger subsided (Esth 7:9-10). On that day, King Ahasuerus gave the house of Haman, the enemy of the Jews, to Queen Esther and his signet ring to Mordecai. Esther, in turn, set Mordecai over the house of Haman (Esth 8:1-2).

Esther made a second request to the king saying, ". . . let it be written to revoke the letters devised by Haman, the son of Hammedatha the Agagite, which he wrote to destroy the Jews who are in all the king's provinces" (Esth 8:3-5). On the twenty-third day of the third month (the month of Sivan), King Ahasuerus summoned all of his scribes, and the edict was written according to all that Mordecai commanded (Esth 8:9a). It was written out to the Jews, the satraps, the governors and the princes of the 127 provinces which extended from India to Ethiopia. It was written out to every province according to its script, and to every people according to their language, as well as to the Jews according to their script and their language (Esth 8:9b). Mordecai wrote the edict in the name of King Ahasuerus, sealed it with the king's signet ring, and sent letters by couriers on horses riding on steeds sired by the royal stud (Esth 8:10). This edict granted the Jews who were in each and every city the right to assemble and to defend their lives, to destroy, to kill, and to annihilate the entire army of any people or province which might attack them, including children and women, and to plunder their spoil (Esth 8:11). This was to be done on one day, the thirteenth day of the twelfth month (Adar; Esth 8:12; Ref Esth 3:13). On this day, the Jews assembled in their cities throughout all the provinces of King Ahasuerus to lay hands on those who sought their harm; and no one could stand before them, for the dread of them had fallen on all the peoples (Esth 9:1-2). Even all the princes of the provinces, the satraps, the governors, and those who were doing the king's business assisted the Jews, because the dread of Mordecai had fallen on them. Indeed, Mordecai was great in the king's house, and his fame spread throughout all the provinces; Mordecai was becoming more and more powerful (Esth 9:3-4).

At last, on the thirteenth day of the twelfth month, the Jews struck all their enemies with the sword, killing and destroying them; they did as they pleased to those who hated them. Five hundred people were killed in Susa alone (Esth 9:5-6). In addition, Haman's ten sons were killed all at once. The names of the ten sons were Parshandatha, Dalphon, Aspatha, Poratha, Adalia, Aridatha, Parmashta, Arisai, Aridai, and Vaizatha (Esth 9:7-10).

On that day the number (500 people) of those who were killed at the citadel in Susa was reported to the king. Then the king said to Queen Esther, ". . . Now what is your petition? It shall even be granted you. And what is your further request? It shall also be done." Esther requested the king to allow the Jews in Susa to carry out the edict of this day (the thirteenth day of the twelfth month) on the next day (the fourteenth day of the twelfth month) as well. She further requested that the dead bodies of Haman's sons be hanged on the gallows (Esth 9:11-13). Therefore, the king commanded that this be done. An edict was issued in Susa on the fourteenth day of the twelfth month, and Haman's ten sons were hanged (Esth 9:14). This hanging was a declaration of the annihilation of the household of Haman the Agagite, the enemy of the Jews (Esth 3:1), and a stern warning against those who hated the Jews (Ref Deut 21:22-23; 1 Sam 31:10; Ezra 6:11).

On the fourteenth day of the twelfth month, another three hundred men were killed in Susa, and the rest of the Jews in the other provinces also assembled to defend their lives and rid themselves of their enemies. They killed 75,000 of those who hated them; but they did not lay their hands on the plunder (Esth 9:15-16).

Indeed, the thirteenth and fourteenth days of the twelfth month were not the final days for the Jews, but the final days for the enemies of the Jews. These were the days of utter destruction of the enemies' power, and the days of boundless glory and gladness for the Jews. The Jews rested on the fourteenth day and made it a day of feasting and rejoicing. In Susa, however, because their enemies were annihilated over two days (from the thirteenth to the fourteenth day of the twelfth month), they rested on the fifteenth day and made it a day of feasting and rejoicing (Esth 9:17-18). Therefore, the rural Jews who lived in villages made the fourteenth day of the twelfth month a holiday for rejoicing and feasting and sending portions of food to one another (Esth 9:19).

Then Mordecai sent letters to all the Jews who were in all the provinces of King Ahasuerus, obliging them to celebrate the fourteenth and fifteenth days of the twelfth month annually (Esth 9:20-22). These two days were called פּוּרִים (purîm) after the word פּוּר (pûr), which refers to the lot that was cast to destroy the Jews on a single day (Esth 9:23-26). These days were to be remembered and celebrated by every Jew throughout every province and every city (Esth 9:27), and their memory and celebration were to never fade from their descendants (Esth 9:21-22, 26-28).

All these events occurred in 474 BC, during the twelfth year of King Ahasuerus (Esth 3:7). Sixteen years passed thereafter and the second return from the exile took place in 458 BC. The second return came seventy-nine years after the first return. The hearts of every Jew who were scattered across the 127 provinces of Persia trembled in great fear of being annihilated on a single day. However, they were miraculously saved by God's absolute and sovereign providence, and this incident must have played a crucial role in triggering the second return from exile.

## 2. People who returned and the circumstances around the time of the return

### (1) People in the second return

The king granted all that Ezra had requested (Ezra 7:6); because of this, he could have been escorted by king's troops or horsemen. Yet he refused all these and sought only the *favorable hand of God*; thus, he succeeded in returning safely (Ezra 8:21-23). The people who came back in the second return were 1,496 males, 38 Levites, and 220 servants—about 1,775 people in total (Ezra 8:1-20).

Large groups among the people who gathered for the second return came from the sons of Shecaniah, 300 males; the sons of Joab, 218 males; the sons of Pahath-moab, 200 males; and the sons of Shecaniah, 150 males (Ezra 8:3-5, 9-10). Furthermore, the descendants from seven families—whose ancestors had already returned to Jerusalem in the first return, came forth determined to join the second return. Ezra chapter 2 records the number of the first returnees. The numbers of the first and second returnees from these seven families were as follows:

| Classification | The sons of Adin | The sons of Elam | The sons of Shephatiah | The sons of Bebai | The sons of Azgad | The sons of Adonikam | The sons of Bigvai |
|---|---|---|---|---|---|---|---|
| Number of the First Returnees | 454 | 1,254 | 372 | 623 | 1,222 | 666 | 2,056 |
| Number of the Second Returnees | 50 | 70 | 80 | 28 | 110 | 60 | 70 |
| 1st + 2nd | 504 | 1,324 | 452 | 651 | 1,332 | 726 | 2,126 |

The copy of the decree from King Artaxerxes proclaimed, ". . . any of the people of Israel and their priests and the Levites in my kingdom who are willing to go to Jerusalem, may go with you" (Ezra 7:13). The king strengthened Ezra's authority through this decree by writing, "you are sent by the king and his seven counselors," so that Ezra could successfully inquire concerning Judah and Jerusalem (Ezra 7:14).

### (2) The possessions that were brought in the second return

The people in the second return fasted at the river of Ahava and sought from God a safe journey for themselves, their children, and all their possessions (Ezra 8:21). After their fasting prayer by the river of Ahava, Ezra set apart twelve of the leading priests, and weighted out to them the silver, the gold and the utensils, the offering for the house of God which the king and his counselors and his princes and all Israel in Persia had offered. He then had the priests and the Levites bring them to Jerusalem to the house of God (Ezra 8:24-25; 28-30). There were 650 talents (22,100 kg) of silver, 100 talents (3,400 kg) of silver utensils, and 100 talents (3,400 kg) of gold, 20 gold bowls (1,000 darics, 8.4 kg; 420 g per bowl), two utensils of fine shiny bronze, precious as gold (Ezra 8:26-27; Ref Ezra 7:15-16).

They then departed from the river of Ahava on the twelfth day of the first month (Ezra 8:31) and at last arrived in Jerusalem. Since they went up from Babylon on the first day of the first month and came to Jerusalem on the first day of the fifth month, their journey had taken about four months (Ezra 7:9). It was a rough journey with the actual traveling distance being over 1,500 km. However, God's good hand was upon those who were returning, and He delivered them from the hands of the enemies and from ambushes on the way (Ezra 8:31).

After they arrived in Jerusalem, they remained there three days. On the fourth day, the silver and the gold and the utensils were weighed out in the house of God into the hand of Meremoth the priest, and all the weight was recorded at that time (Ezra 8:32-34). The exiles who had come from captivity offered burnt offerings to God (12 bulls, 96 rams, and 77 lambs) and a sin offering (12 male goats; Ezra 8:35). Then they delivered the king's edicts to the king's satraps and to the governors in the provinces beyond the River, and they supported the people and the house of God (Ezra 8:36).

## (3) Ezra's reforms
### ① Ezra the scribe and the priest
Ezra (עֶזְרָא) was the leader of the second return from the exile and his name means "the Lord helps." As a descendant of the high priest Aaron (Ezra 7:1-6; Ref 1 Chr 6:3-15, 49-53), he was a priest as well as a scribe and leader (Ezra 7:6, 11, 12, 21; 10:10, 16; Neh 8:1, 2, 4, 5, 9, 13; 12:26).

The Scripture comments regarding Ezra, ". . . in the reign of Artaxerxes king of Persia, there went up Ezra . . . " (Ezra 7:1a). The Bible also states, ". . . and the king granted him all he requested because the hand of the Lord his God was upon him" (Ezra 7:6b). Considering such records, it can be presumed that Ezra probably began his ministry in 464 BC, the year that King Artaxerxes ascended to the throne. In addition, Nehemiah 12:26 instructs us that Ezra was active "in the days of Joiakim the son of Jeshua, the son of Jozadak" as well as in the days of Nehemiah the governor. The high priest Joiakim was Jeshua's (Joshua) son (Neh 12:10, 26), and Joshua was Jehozadak's son (Hag 1:1, 12, 14; 2:2, 4; Zech 6:11), and Jehozadak was the son of Seraiah who was the high priest during the fall of the southern kingdom of Judah in 586 BC (2 Kgs 25:18-20; 1 Chr 6:14-15).

Ezra, who was born in Babylon, resolved to forsake all of his vested rights in Babylon. He was a scribe skilled in the law and was determined "to study the law of the Lord and to practice it, and to teach His statutes and ordinances in Israel" (Ezra 7:6, 10). The word *skilled* is מָהִיר (*māhîr*) in Hebrew, which means "quick" or "experienced," and points to Ezra's competence and mastery of the law of God. Hence, this word reflects Ezra's unparalleled ability to quickly find the law from any part of the book, as well as his promptness in practicing them. As both scribe and priest during a period of extreme national turmoil, Ezra was a great pioneer who ignited the first flames of transformation in Jewish history.

Moreover, the word *scribe* is a participial form of the Hebrew word סָפַר (*sāpar*) which means "to write." The nominative means "the one who writes," which is "a scribe." The scribes in Ezra's time studied the laws of Moses and taught them to the people who had returned from exile. They focused on removing the idolatry of foreign gods and restoring the people's faith in the Lord. Indeed, teaching the Word of God must become a lifelong duty of the ministers of the Lord. Like Ezra, they must teach while setting their hearts to "study" and "practice" the Word of God first.

## ② Ezra's reforms

Ezra's reforms were carried out in various ways. The people, the priests, and the Levites intermarried with foreigners, and the princes and the rulers had been most active in intermingling with the people of the land. When Ezra learned about this, he bore their sins on his shoulders and made confession. At that time, many people also wept bitterly and resolved to make a covenant with God to put away their foreign wives and their children, in hopes that God's wrath would subside (Ezra 9:1-15; 10:1-14). For three months, from the first day of the tenth month to the first day of the first month, all men who had married foreign wives were investigated from among the high priest, the priests, the Levites, the singers, and the people; and all their names were fully disclosed (Ezra 10:16-44).

**FIRST, they confessed their sins and prayed with tears before the temple of the Lord.**

All reforms must begin with prayer and repentance. Upon his arrival at Jerusalem, Ezra discovered that the people of Israel had been intermarrying foreign women for the past fifty-eight years since the temple was rebuilt. Ezra tore his garment and robe, pulled some of the hair on his head and beard, and sat down appalled (Ezra 9:1-3). At the evening offering, he arose, even with his garment and robe torn, and bowed down before the house of God, praying and weeping as he made confessions for their iniquities (Ezra 9:5-15). While he was praying, a very large assembly gathered about him also weeping bitterly (Ezra 10:1). Shecanaiah came forth first from among the people to Ezra determined to repent and to obey the law (Ezra 10:2-3). A reform without prayer and repentance is not a true reform; a reform can only be triumphant through repentance and prayer.

**SECOND, Shecaniah resolved to repent and the people took an oath.**

While Ezra was making confessions for the iniquities of the people, Shecaniah the son of Jehiel, one of the sons of Elam, confessed his sins and repented saying, "We have been unfaithful to our God and have married foreign women from the people of the land" (Ezra 10:2). He declared that they would "put away all the wives and their children" that they took from foreign lands (Ezra 10:3). He also encouraged Ezra saying, "Arise! For this matter is your responsibility, but we will be with you; be courageous and act" (Ezra 10:4). At this, Ezra rose and made the leading priests, the Levites, and all Israel take an oath that they would do according to this proposal; thus, they took the oath (Ezra 10:5).

**THIRD, the assembly of Israel was summoned.**

Ezra rose from the house of God and went into the chamber of Jehohanan the son of Eliashib. Ezra neither ate bread nor drank water, for he was mourning over the unfaithfulness of the exiles (Ezra 10:6). He summoned an assembly of Israel in Jerusalem and made a powerful proclamation that whoever does not come within three days, all his possessions would be forfeited* and he himself excluded from the assembly of the chosen people (Ezra 10:7-8).

All the people assembled within three days, on the twentieth day of the ninth month. Heavy rain fell so that the people could not stand in the open square, and this caused their hearts to tremble greatly because of their sins (Ezra 10:9, 13). Ezra proclaimed, "Now therefore, make confession to the Lord God of your fathers and do His will; and separate yourselves from the peoples of the land and from the foreign wives" (Ezra 10:11). The assembly replied in a loud voice, "That's right! As you have said, so it is our duty to do" (Ezra 10:12).

Nevertheless, this was not an issue that could be resolved in one or two days. Thus, there were suggestions to appoint leaders for this matter and set appointed times, so that those who had married foreign wives may resolve the matter with the elders and judges of each city within the appointed time. Only Jonathan and Jahzeiah opposed this, whereas Meshullam and Shabbethai the Levite supported them (Ezra 10:13-15). Ezra appointed heads for each of their father's households, all of them by name. Then, on the first day of the tenth month, they began to investigate the matter of men who had married foreign wives; they completed the detailed and careful investigation after three months, on the first day of the first month of the following year (Ezra 10:16-17).

**FOURTH, the list of those who intermarried with foreign wives was disclosed.**

Ezra 10 records in detail the list compiled during the three months of investigation of those who married foreign wives. There were a total of

---

* The sinner's entire possession was confiscated and even his family members were punished.

114 people, five from the house of the high priest (v. 18), thirteen from the house of priests (vv. 20-22), ten from the Levites (vv. 23-24), and eighty-six from among the commoners (vv. 25-43). According to this list, the leaders had been foremost in this unfaithfulness (Ezra 9:2). According to Ezra chapter 2, the priests only made up about ten percent of the total number of people in the first return from exile, and yet they made up fifteen percent of the total number of people who married foreign wives. This shows that the leaders were at the forefront in committing this sin.

Ezra 10:44 also states, ". . . some of them had wives by whom they had children." In other words, through this reform, there were many who had to bear the bitter pain of separating themselves not only from their wives but also from their children. A reform that takes place according to the will of the Word, in order to fulfill the administration of God's redemption, must endure and overcome even the pain of severing family ties (Matt 10:37).

As seen from above, the people of Judah were spiritually stagnant for the fifty-eight years following the completion of the temple reconstruction. This was when God prepared the spiritual foundation for their second return through Mordecai and Esther.

Following the first return, God's people were walking the path of corruption even after they had finished rebuilding the temple amidst great hardship. To save His own, God called Ezra the priest and scribe to Jerusalem in the second return from Babylon (Ezra 7:6-9). God awakened His people to repentance through Ezra, and this was His great mercy and love to restore the purity of their faith.

**Leader:** Nehemiah (meaning: "whom the Lord comforts")
- The cupbearer to Artaxerxes king of Persia (Neh 1:1, 11)
- Governor of Judah for 12 years from the 20th to the 32nd year of Artaxerxes (Neh 2:1-10; 5:14; 13:6)

**King of Persia:** 20th year of Artaxerxes I (Neh 1:1; 2:1)

**The circumstances that led to the return**
- In the month of Chislev in the 20th year of Artaxerxes (444 BC), Nehemiah heard the news that the wall of Jerusalem had been broken down and its gates burned with fire (Neh 1:1-3). Then, Nehemiah fasted and prayed as he wept and mourned for his country and people for 4 months, until the month of Nisan in the 20th year of Artaxerxes (Neh 1:4-2:2). At last, by the help of the good hand of God (Neh 2:8, 18), Nehemiah was appointed by Artaxerxes as the governor of the land of Judah, so that he could go to Jerusalem and rebuild the city wall.

**The purpose of the return**
- It was to appoint Nehemiah as the governor of Judah in order to rebuild the wall of Jerusalem and to establish an orderly community of Judah (Neh 2:5-8; 5:14; 13:6).

**People who returned:** Only 1 person, Nehemiah, was recorded (Neh 2:1-11).

**Possessions brought in the return**
- King Artaxerxes of Persia had previously stopped the reconstruction of the city wall of Jerusalem (Ezra 4:7-24). However, after hearing Nehemiah's request, he granted the reconstruction and even provided building materials (Neh 2:1-9). This was because the good hand of God had helped Nehemiah (Neh 2:8, 18).

**Major events surrounding the return**
- Presumably, Nehemiah departed immediately after the king granted his request in the 20th year of King Artaxerxes (Neh 2:1). He probably took about 4 months to reach Jerusalem as the people of the second return had done; he most likely arrived on the 1st day of the 5th month (Neh 2:11; 6:15; Ref Ezra 7:9).
- Sanballat, Tobiah, and Geshem's interferences were fierce (Neh 4:1-14).

> - The wall was completed in 52 days on the 25th of Elul, the 6th month, (Neh 6:15). Ezra taught the law (Neh 8:1-12), the people celebrated the Feast of Booths in the 7th month (Neh 8:13-18), and they gathered to repent and place seals on the document of the covenant on the 24th day of the 7th month (Neh 9:1-38; 10:1-27). Afterwards, they celebrated the dedication of the wall (Neh 12:27-43).
> - They excluded all foreigners from Israel (Neh 13:1-3).

## 1. The purpose and the time of the return

### (1) The purpose of the return

During the first return from exile, God restored the people of Judah as the central figures in redemptive history by allowing them to reconstruct the temple. During the second return, God restored the people's faith internally through the reforms of Prophet Ezra. Now, in the third return, God blocked off external attacks by erecting the city walls, thereby restoring the purity of the chosen people of God through reformation and revival.

The first and second returns from Babylonian captivity bore fruit through the construction of the city walls and the reform movements that occurred during the third return. As a result, Judah was able to possess the appearance of God's elect as the main figures in the history of redemption.

### (2) The time of the third return

The third return occurred in 444 BC, the twentieth year of King Artaxerxes. In the ninth month (Chislev) of the twentieth year of King Artaxerxes, Nehemiah heard the report that the wall of Jerusalem had been broken down and its gates had been burned with fire (Neh 1:1-3). In the first month (Nisan) of the twentieth year of King Artaxerxes, Nehemiah entreated the king to allow him to rebuild the walls of Jerusalem (Neh 2:1). Nehemiah fasted and prayed as he wept and mourned for his country and people for four months, from the ninth month (Chislev) to the first month (Nisan). The people of Judah from the first and second returns had rebuilt the temple in Jerusalem and they had started anew. However, the foreigners had greatly humiliated them and now Jerusalem lay in ruins with its gates burnt down. The moment Nehemiah heard this heartbreaking news, he could not help but pray before God.

On the other hand, from a chronological perspective, we should note that the "first month (Nisan)" in Nehemiah 2:1 should be the first month of the following year, which is the *twenty-first* year of King Artaxerxes. This is because, according to the calendrical order, the ninth month (Chislev) is followed by the tenth, the eleventh, the twelfth and the first month of the following year. However, the book of Nehemiah states that the first month (Nisan) was *still* in the "*twentieth year* of King Artaxerxes," not the twenty-first, because it uses the Tishri-to-Tishri reckoning method. This indicates that Nehemiah reckoned the regnal years according to Jewish reckoning methods, although King Artaxerxes was a foreign king.

Then, why did Nehemiah date the regnal years of a Persian king according to the Tishri-to-Tishri reckoning method, when the custom in Persia was to reckon the year from Nisan-to-Nisan? He lived in Persia but did not follow the Persian methods when he referred to the regnal chronology of Persia. This is possibly because Nehemiah was following the customary Jewish practice in the spirit of intense patriotism.[47] This is supported by evidence from the Aramaic papyri from Elephantine of the fifth-century BC. These documents also dated the reigns of Persian kings according to the Tishri-cycle used in Judah rather than the Nisan-cycle used in Persia.[48] Therefore, since Artaxerxes became king in 464 BC, his twentieth year would be 444 BC, which was about fourteen years after the second return from the exile in 458 BC.

There is, however, one seemingly strange chronological record. Ezra 7:7 states that the second return occurred "in the seventh year of King Artaxerxes." Since Artaxerxes became king in 464 BC, his twentieth year would be 444 BC and his seventh year would be 457 BC. However, the second return was in 458 BC (i.e., the sixth year), not 457 BC. Where does the one-year discrepancy come from? The difference comes from the fact that Nehemiah used the Tishri-to-Tishri calendar while Ezra used the Nisan-to-Nisan calendar. As we have examined in the fourth book of The History of Redemption series, the Tishri and Nisan-based calendars differ by one year for six months out of the year.

If so, what proof is there that the book of Ezra had used the Nisan calendar?

In order to resolve this issue, we must first decide which calendar was used in the book of Haggai in the Old Testament. It is evident that Haggai used the Nisan-to-Nisan reckoning method. After the first return from the Babylonian exile, the people began building the temple but were interrupted. Then the construction resumed and that day was recorded as "the twenty-fourth day of the sixth month in the second year of Darius the king" (Hag 1:15). Three months later, God's Word came upon Haggai, and this day was recorded as "the twenty-fourth day of the ninth month in the second year of Darius" (Hag 2:10). If the Tishri-to-Tishri calendar was used in the book of Haggai, then the twenty-fourth day of the sixth month should have been recorded as the *first year* of King Darius, for this month falls before the new regnal year begins in the month Tishri (the seventh month). However, the twenty-fourth day of the sixth month was recorded as "the second year of Darius the king," and hence testifies that Haggai reckoned the regnal years based on the Nisan-to-Nisan calendar.

Likewise, Ezra also recorded the time when the temple construction resumed (Hag 1:14-15) as "the *second* year of the reign of Darius" not his *first* year (Ezra 4:24). This is clear evidence that the book of Ezra in the Old Testament also used the Nisan-to-Nisan calendar.

According to Ezra 7:7-9, the people leaving Babylon in the second return departed on the first day of the first month in the *seventh* year of King Artaxerxes and arrived in Jerusalem on the first day of the fifth month. However, since this period was reckoned based on the Nisan-to-Nisan calendar, if converted to the Tishri-cycle calendar, then it would be the *sixth* year of King Artaxerxes. Just as 444 BC, the year of the third return from exile, was reckoned based on the Tishri-to-Tishri calendar, the second return from exile should also be reckoned based on the Tishri-to-Tishri calendar. Doing so, the year of the second return would not be 457 BC, but 458 BC, the sixth year of King Artaxerxes.

Fourteen years passed since the second return in 458 BC. It was now 444 BC, and the Israelites had been trying hard to build the walls of Jerusalem during these fourteen years. Israel would be able to obtain the physical form of a nation and free herself from the influences of her enemies only when the walls were fully repaired. However, the Israelites' efforts to build the city walls were interrupted by adversaries such as Rehum the commander and Shimshai the scribe. They conspired against the people of Judah by telling the king that the people will stop paying taxes and rebel against the king once they rebuild the city walls. Thus, they received a decree from King Artaxerxes to stop building the walls.

Empowered with this authority, they put a halt on God's work (Ezra 4:7-23).

In 444 BC, however, King Artaxerxes listened to Nehemiah's entreaty and granted the third return from exile. It was indeed the help of God's good hand that led the king to issue a decree so that Nehemiah could return to Jerusalem and rebuild the city walls (Neh 2:8, 18).

## 2. People who returned and the circumstances around the time of the return

### (1) People in the third return

There is no explicit record of how many people participated in the third return from exile. The Scripture makes mention of only one person, Nehemiah, whom Artaxerxes the king of Persia had appointed governor of Judah and sent to Jerusalem (Neh 2:5-8; 5:14). Nehemiah was a cupbearer to King Artaxerxes (Neh 1:11) as well as governor of Judah for twelve years, from the twentieth year to the thirty-second year of the king's reign (Neh 2:1; 5:14; 13:6). During this period, he dwelt with the people of Israel and demonstrated powerful leadership in helping the people settle down and reform their faith. He did not cease to pray for Israel's restoration (Neh 1:4-11; 13:14, 22, 29-31). The name *Nehemiah* means "the Lord comforts." As reflected in his name, Nehemiah was a great leader who gave true comfort and hope to the returning exiles through the Word of God.

### (2) Events that led to the third return

The city walls were completed only after long years of hardship (142 years = 586 BC – 444 BC) due to intense external opposition. At the time, Judah was still under the jurisdiction of governors sent by the Persian Empire. Hence, building a city wall could be easily misconstrued as preparation for an uprising in order to gain independence. This was why Rehum the commander (a governor of Samaria) and Shimshai the scribe, along with Artaxerxes' servants in the provinces beyond the River, wrote a letter against Jerusalem to King Artaxerxes (Ezra 4:17). In the copy of the letter, they stated that the Israelites would not pay tribute, custom, or toll, and it would decrease the revenue of the kings (Ezra 4:13). They further wrote, "that city is a rebellious city and damaging to kings and provinces, and they have incited revolt within it in past days; therefore, that city was laid waste" (Ezra 4:15, 19).

After receiving the complaint letter from Rehum the commander and Shimshai the scribe, King Artaxerxes put a halt to the construction of the walls of Jerusalem. Ezra 4:21-22 states, "So, now issue a decree to make these men stop work, that this city may not be rebuilt until a decree is issued by me. And beware of being negligent in carrying out this matter; why should damage increase to the detriment of the kings?" As soon as the copy of King Artaxerxes' document was read before Rehum, Shimshai the scribe, and their colleagues, they went in haste to Jerusalem to the Jews and stopped the construction by force of arms (Ezra 4:23). It is most likely that the adversaries tore down the partially erected walls and burned them down during this time.

Nehemiah heard that his countrymen, the people of Judah, were in great distress and reproach, and that the wall of Jerusalem had been torn down and its gates were also burned with fire. When he heard the news, he sat down and wept and mourned for days, fasting and praying before God (Neh 1:2-11). When Nehemiah had been praying for his country in great distress and contrition for four months (Neh 2:1), he appeared as though he were sick in the eyes of King Artaxerxes. Therefore, the king asked him, "Why is your face sad?" (Neh 2:2). Nehemiah became very afraid (Neh 2:2b) that he could make matters worse by telling the king about Jerusalem because Artaxerxes had strictly forbidden the rebuilding of the wall of Jerusalem (Ezra 4:17-23). To Nehemiah's surprise, however, the king not only permitted him to return to Jerusalem after hearing his entreaty but also proactively assisted the rebuilding of the city wall. He also issued letters for the governors of the provinces beyond the River, and a letter to Asaph the keeper of the king's forest to provide him with timber (Neh 2:3-8).

It is hard to believe that the king, who had vehemently opposed the reconstruction of the walls earlier, was now granting Nehemiah's request. King Artaxerxes had issued an order to stop the construction of the city walls (Ezra 4:21-23) after seeing the complaint letter from Rehum the commander and Shimshai the scribe (Ezra 4:8). Not long after that, however, he issued another decree to grant Nehemiah permission to rebuild the city wall (Neh 2:1-9). According to Persian royal tradition, a king's edict cannot be changed or revoked once it has been issued (Ezra 6:11-12; Esth 1:19; Dan 6:8, 15). Without God's amazing providence, it would have been impossible for the king to issue an edict, revoke it, and then reissue one that overturns the content of the previous one. Indeed, it was by God's good hand upon Nehemiah that the king granted his request (Neh 2:18).

> **Nehemiah 2:8** and a letter to Asaph the keeper of the king's forest, that he may give me timber to make beams for the gates of the fortress which is by the temple, for the wall of the city, and for the house to which I will go. And the king granted them to me because the good hand of my God was on me.

God controls and moves man's heart as He wishes. He even governs the heart of the king, the supreme ruler of a nation (Prov 21:1). God may raise up a king or He may dethrone him. He rules over the realm of humankind according to His will (Dan 5:21). In every generation, the rise and fall of all nations of the world, as well as the success and failure of an individual, depend solely on God's sovereignty. Therefore, even if we face the greatest of hardships in our lives, we will experience God's grace of prosperity in all things when we completely rely on the help of God's sovereign hand.

### (3) Endless opposition against the rebuilding of the city walls

Nehemiah began the reconstruction of the city walls after the third return from exile, but this work did not prove easy. Enemies like Sanballat and Tobiah prevented the construction from progressing through continuous opposition and threats (Neh 4:1-3, 7-8).

For the people of Judah who had just returned from exile, rebuilding and restoring the collapsed city wall was truly a burdensome task. Their dangerous situation worsened as their adversaries began to threaten them aggressively for even making plans for the reconstruction.

① **Interruptions from within the community of returnees**
*FIRST*, **the Tekoite nobles did not support the work.**

Reconstruction of the walls required strenuous labor involving the transport of heavy rocks, timbers, or dirt either on one's back or on a cart. This is well reflected in the words such as "support," "burden bearers," and "took their load," which appear frequently in the description of the rebuilding process (Neh 3:5; 4:10, 17). The phrase *burden bearer* in Nehemiah 4:10 is סַבָּל (*sabbāl*) in Hebrew, which means "transporter" or "bearer of burden." The phrase *took their load* in Nehemiah 4:17 is עָמַס (*'āmas*) in Hebrew, which is used in the qal stem of the verb in its masculine plural participial form; it means "to carry a load." These words reflect the strenuous nature of the labor, which was performed by everyone regardless of rank. Everyone had to carry the heavy loads of rocks, timber, and dirt throughout the fifty-two days of construction work. However, the scriptural record points out that some Jewish nobles who lived in Tekoa did not bear the burdens of building the wall of Jerusalem.

> **Nehemiah 3:5** Moreover, next to him the Tekoites made repairs, but their nobles did not support the work of their masters.

The expression *did not support* is לֹא־הֵבִיאוּ צַוָּרָם (lōʾ-hēbîʾû sawwāram) in Hebrew. The word הֵבִיאוּ (hēbîʾû) is the hiphil (causative) stem of the participial form of בּוֹא (bôʾ), which means "to come." In this conjugation, the verb can be rendered to mean "to bring" weighty objects such as an ark or loads (1 Chr 12:40; 13:5; 2 Chr 5:7). Also, the root word for צַוָּרָם (sawwārām) is צַוָּאר (sawwāʾr), which refers to the shoulder or neck of a human or an animal. Hence, this verse can be literally translated as, "the nobles did not carry anything on their necks or shoulders." In fact, other versions of the Bible have translated this verse more literally. The New King James Version translates, ". . . but their nobles did not put their shoulders to the work . . . ," and the Revised Standard Version translates, ". . . but their nobles did not put their necks to the work . . . ." The Jewish nobles in Tekoa regarded the work of carrying heavy loads as inappropriate or too lowly for people of their status. This was a critical moment in history when God's work of redemption was about to be fulfilled. It was crucial for everyone to come together in one will. Moreover, with such fierce external opposition, everyone took great pains to finish the Lord's work together. At such a critical juncture, these nobles were only concerned about saving their face and salvaging their honor. Apostle Paul also rebuked such lazy people who only looked after their own work and neglected the work of the Lord. In Philippians 2:21 he said, "For they all seek after their own interests, not those of Christ Jesus."

**SECOND**, some returnees who lived near Jerusalem did not participate in rebuilding the city wall.

People came from near and far to participate in rebuilding the city walls. This work force did not only consist of the inhabitants of Jerusalem. People proactively came to participate under the leadership of various regional leaders. There were people who dedicated themselves to the end without ever leaving their work areas. They were the men of Jericho (Neh 3:2), the Tekoites (Neh 3:5, 27), the men of Gibeon (Neh 3:7), the men of Mizpah (Neh 3:7, 19), the people from the district of Beth-haccherem (Neh 3:14), the people from the district of Beth-zur (Neh 3:16), and the people from both districts of Keilah (Neh 3:17-18).

Nevertheless, there were returnees who did not participate in rebuilding the city wall although they lived close to Jerusalem. These men and their descendants were threatened persistently by Sanballat and his men. These Jews who were filled with extreme fear and anxiety came to the construction site and told the men ten times, "They will come up against us from every place where you may turn," in an attempt to bring their people back to their homes. Nehemiah 4:12 records, "When the Jews who lived near them came and told us ten times, 'They will come up against us from every place where you may turn . . . . '" This verse shows that these Jews did not participate in the reconstruction work although they lived near the city wall, and that they only sought after their own safety.

On the contrary, the people who participated in rebuilding the wall stood firmly in one faith with Nehemiah. They did not waver even after receiving urgent requests over ten different occasions from the Jews who lived nearby. Not a single person responded to those requests, and everyone devoted themselves even more to rebuilding the wall.

② **Opposition from the adversaries: beginning phase of the reconstruction of the wall**

The Bible provides detailed records of the adversaries' continuous efforts to sabotage the construction work, which started from the moment the Israelites began the construction until its completion.

Sanballat and the rest of the enemies mocked the Jews when Nehemiah methodically divided the entire wall into forty-two sections, and the people of Israel mustered up the power to participate in the construction in a systematic manner (Neh 3:1-32).

Nehemiah 4:1-2 states, "Now it came about that when Sanballat heard that we were rebuilding the wall, he became furious and very angry and mocked the Jews. He spoke in the presence of his brothers and the wealthy men of Samaria and said, 'What are these feeble Jews doing? Are they going to restore it for themselves? Can they offer sacrifices? Can they finish in a day? Can they revive the stones from the dusty rubble even the burned ones?'"

Sanballat was a Horonite and the governor of Samaria at that time. *Horon* refers to a city named Beth-horon, which belonged to the tribe of Ephraim (Josh 16:3, 5). It is conjectured that Sanballat was a descendant of an interracial marriage between an Israelite and a Gentile; such racial mixing was a policy promoted by the Assyrians. Morever, Tobiah the Ammonite who was standing near Sanballat said, "Even what they are building—if a fox should jump on it, he would break their stone wall down!" (Neh 4:3).

The adversaries looked down on the frail people of Judah and cursed at them (Neh 4:4). Despite outright humiliation and interference, Nehemiah endured it all in silence and prayed, "Hear, O our God, how we are despised! Return their reproach on their own heads and give them up for plunder in a land of captivity" (Neh 4:4).

③ **Opposition from the adversaries: midway through the construction of the wall (Neh 4:6-23)**

With the Samaritan governor Sanballat the Horonite at the center, the adversaries mocked the people by saying that Israel did not have the strength to rebuild the wall, and even if they were to do so, the wall would be so weak that it would soon collapse (Neh 4:1-3). However, the construction was rapidly progressing as the entire wall was joined together to half its height. Nehemiah 4:6 explains, "So we built the wall and the whole wall was joined together to half its height, for the people had a mind to work."

Here, the expression "the whole wall was joined together" means that the sections of the wall that had been under construction separately were all coming together at some point in time. The people must have been deeply moved as they witnessed the sections of the walls that various groups had rebuilt being connected together into one wall (Ref Eph 4:1-7, 16).

According to Nehemiah 4:8, the adversaries not only mocked and threatened to interrupt the rebuilding of the wall of Jerusalem, but they also utilized military force. They planned to unite themselves for an ambush against Jerusalem while the people of Israel were unaware, so that they can kill them and put a stop to the work (Neh 4:11).

While the adversaries had mocked and frustrated them with words, the people did not waver in their work even though the labor was strenuous. However, when they were faced with a sudden, serious crisis, they became dispirited. The people of Judah were discouraged and said, "The strength of the burden bearers is failing, yet there is much rubbish; and we ourselves are unable to rebuild the wall" (Neh 4:10). Indeed, the sabotage against the reconstruction of the wall was becoming so dangerous that people wanted to give up the work, even after they had already made much progress. Here, the word *rubbish* is וְהֶעָפָר (*wĕhe'āpār*) in Hebrew, which means "and the dust." There were still heaps of rubble and mounds of demolished remains around the wall of Jerusalem from the time Jerusalem was destroyed by the Babylonians in 586 BC. They faced the threat of the enemy's military attacks in addition to the already heavy burden of physical labor. Thus, the burden of the reconstruction of the wall must have felt unbearably heavy, making their hearts cower.

④ **Nehemiah's meticulous strategy (airtight defense in parallel with the wall reconstruction)**

As the adversary's threat became more definite and direct, Nehemiah set up a meticulous plan and quickly implemented it.

**FIRST, weapons were prepared for battle while the construction work continued.**

Nehemiah commanded half of the servants to carry out the construction work while the other half stood guard holding spears, shields, bows, and breastplates; and the captains were behind the whole house of Judah (Neh 4:16). Those who were rebuilding the wall took their load with one hand doing the work and the other holding a weapon (Neh 4:17). There was also an armory where weapons were kept in the city of Jerusalem (Neh 3:19).

**SECOND, a trumpeter stood near Nehemiah in order to notify of the enemy's attack and to mobilize the soldiers when a battle started (Neh 4:18).**

The wall of Jerusalem was divided into forty-two sections which were rebuilt simultaneously. Nehemiah thus said, "The work is great and extensive, and we are separated on the wall far from one another" (Neh 4:19). Since everyone was in charge of his section and all forty-two sections were under construction simultaneously, the people were apart from one another as they worked. Hence, Nehemiah ensured that a trumpet could be blown loudly when danger drew near so that the people could be instantly mobilized as troops to counter the enemy's attacks and defend Jerusalem (Neh 4:20). Thus, half of them kept guard with weapons "from dawn until the stars appeared," while the other half continued with all their might to rebuild the city walls (Neh 4:21).

**THIRD**, each man with his servant had to spend the night within Jerusalem (Neh 4:22).

Here, the word *servant* is נַעַר (*na'ar*) in Hebrew and refers to the servants brought by the people who participated in the work (Ref Ezra 2:65; Neh 7:67). The inhabitants of Jerusalem were not the only people who participated in rebuilding the wall. There were the men of Jericho (Neh 3:2), the Tekoites (Neh 3:5), the men of Gibeon (Neh 3:7), the people from Beth-haccherem (Neh 3:14), the people from Mizpah (Neh 3:15), the people from Beth-zur (Neh 3:16), and the people from Keilah (Neh 3:17-18). All those who participated in the reconstruction of the wall— even those who lived far away—could not return to their homes for fifty-two days and kept to their duty stations in the city until the very end.

**FOURTH**, Nehemiah, his close associates, and the men of the guard who followed him did not remove their clothes and held their weapons even when they went to sleep (Neh 4:23).

Nehemiah and the men of the guard who followed him worked together as one, never easing up on their airtight defense for even a single day while they rebuilt the city wall. Due to such impregnable defense around the entire wall, the adversaries could neither attack Jerusalem nor interrupt the construction of the wall.

⑤ **The adversaries' final sabotage attempt: the plot to assassinate Nehemiah**

At last, the wall was completed with only doors in the gates left to be installed (Neh 6:1-14). Nehemiah 6:1 relates, "Now when it was reported to Sanballat, Tobiah, to Geshem the Arab and to the rest of our enemies that I had rebuilt the wall, and that no breach remained in it, although at that time I had not set up the doors in the gates." Once the adversaries saw that the Jews had finished rebuilding the wall much faster than expected, and that the wall had been rebuilt securely, they plotted to kill Nehemiah, the leader in the reconstruction effort (Neh 6:2). In order to entice Nehemiah out of the city to murder him, they repeatedly requested a meeting in the plain of Ono, which was about 16 km east of Joppa. Nevertheless, Nehemiah avoided the encounter, saying, "I am doing a great work and I cannot come down" (Neh 6:2-4). When Nehemiah refused the meeting, Sanballat made a fifth request for a meeting in which he sent his servant with an open letter. In it he threatened Nehemiah saying that the king would soon hear the rumor that Nehemiah was planning to rebel and become king. Hence, he suggested that Nehemiah should meet and confer with him (Neh 6:6-7).

When all his attempts had failed due to Nehemiah's firm resolve, Sanballat came up with a strange plan. He bribed the priest Shemaiah, who was able to enter the temple freely, so that he may make a false prophecy to Nehemiah. Shemaiah confined himself at home in order to receive Nehemiah's attention and lure him into his home. Shemaiah made the false prophecy to Nehemiah saying, "Let us meet together in the house of God, within the temple, and let us close the doors of the temple, for they [Sanballat's men] are coming to kill you, and they are coming to kill you at night" (Neh 6:10). This prophecy was a plot to harm Nehemiah under the disguise of protection (Neh 6:13). If Nehemiah had gone into the temple in accordance with this false prophecy, the people would remember Nehemiah as a cowardly leader. Moreover, Nehemiah would have transgressed the law that prohibited a non-priest from entering the temple. Nehemiah firmly refused, saying, "I will not go in" (Neh 6:11). When he realized that Shemaiah was making this false prophecy after Sanballat and Tobiah had bribed him (Neh 6:12), Nehemiah prayed, "Remember, O my God, Tobiah and Sanballat according to these works of theirs, and also Noadiah the prophetess and the rest of the prophets who were trying to frighten me" (Neh 6:14).

## (4) The miraculous completion of the city wall and its dedication ceremony

① **The wall of Jerusalem was completed in fifty-two days, on the twenty-fifth day of the sixth (Elul) month (Neh 6:15).**

The completion of the wall signified that the people of Judah had now been granted the genuine appearance of a nation in accordance with God's administration in redemptive history. Walls are erected to protect the city from external attacks and to maintain their purity as the chosen people of God. On the third night after his arrival in Jerusalem, Nehemiah arose secretly and inspected the wall of Jerusalem that had been broken down. He made a detailed plan and thorough preparations to rebuild the wall (Neh 2:11-16). He then encouraged the people of Judah, the priests and princes, and all the other workers to put their hands to the good work (Neh 2:17-18).

The construction of the wall began on the fourth day of the fifth month (Av) and ended fifty-two days later, on the twenty-fifth day of the sixth month (Elul). Nehemiah had petitioned the king to allow him to go to Jerusalem in the first month (Nisan; Neh 2:1-5) and he departed as soon as he was granted permission (Neh 2:6-9). He finally arrived in Jerusalem to find its walls destroyed and its gates burned with fire. After a careful inspection, he was firmly resolved to rebuild the city wall and to never experience this reproach again. The reconstruction began as he had the people put their hands to work from the fourth day of the fifth month (Neh 2:13-18).

Against much opposition and schemes, the construction of the city wall was thoroughly completed in only fifty-two days in 444 BC, on the twenty-fifth day of the sixth month (Elul) in the twentieth year of King Artaxerxes (Neh 6:15).

② **Ezra read from the book of the law, and the Feast of Booths was observed.**

The people of Judah who had finished building the wall asked Ezra to read from the law, and everyone repented in tears (Neh 8:1-12). They also observed the Feast of Booths; they observed it on such a grand scale that such a celebration was never seen since the days of Joshua. There was great rejoicing among the sons of Israel (Neh 8:13-18).

③ **The covenant was sealed.**

On the twenty-fourth of the seventh month, all the sons of Israel assembled with fasting, in sackcloth and with dirt upon them. Having separated from all foreigners, they stood and confessed their sins and the iniquities of their fathers. While they stood in their place, they read from the book of the law for a fourth of the day; for another fourth, they worshipped God (Neh 9:1-3). They also renewed the covenant by making an agreement in writing (sure covenant, KJV) and all the leaders, the Levites, and the priests sealed it (Neh 9:38). Although the Israelites had returned to their homeland from Babylon, they were still under the influence of Persia and their lives were no different from those of foreigners. With the city walls rebuilt, however, they could truly start anew as God's covenanted community.

④ **The city wall was dedicated.**

After the third return, the wall was fully rebuilt on the twenty-fifth day of the sixth month (Elul; Neh 6:15), but its dedication was performed much later (Neh 12:27-43). The dedication of the wall was repeatedly delayed because the number of the inhabitants in Jerusalem was too small. After the city was rebuilt, Nehemiah reassigned the living areas for the people of Israel by having the people cast lots to bring one out of ten to live in Jerusalem, while nine-tenths remained in the other cities (Neh 11:1). The leaders of the people, the one-tenth who were chosen by lot, as well as those who volunteered, now inhabited Jerusalem (Neh 11:2). Then, he recorded every name of the leaders who lived in Jerusalem (Neh 11:3-24). He introduced them in the following order: the families and the numbers of the sons of Judah and the sons of Benjamin who lived in Jerusalem (Neh 11:3-9, Ref 1 Chr 9:3-9), the priests (Neh 11:10-14, Ref 1 Chr 9:10-13), the Levites (Neh 11:15-18, Ref 1 Chr 9:14-16), the gatekeepers (Neh 11:19; Ref 1 Chr 9:17-27), and the singers (Neh 11:22-23; Ref 1 Chr 9:33).

Nehemiah proceeded with the dedication of the wall only after the city of Jerusalem was repopulated through his prudent policy. Nehemiah sought out the Levites from all their places in order to bring them to Jerusalem so that they might celebrate the dedication with gladness, with hymns of thanksgiving and with songs to the accompaniment of cymbals, harps and lyres (Neh 12:27). At this time, the sons of the singers were assembled as well, and these singers had built themselves villages around Jerusalem (Neh 12:28-29).

For the dedication of the wall, the priests and the Levites first purified themselves, and then they purified the people, the gates, and the city. Then Nehemiah appointed two great choirs. The first, led by Ezra, proceeded to the right on top of the wall; the other proceeded to the left, led by Nehemiah. These two choirs performed a unique celebration by proceeding in opposite directions as they walked on top of the wall while praising and giving thanks.

**The choir that followed Ezra** consisted of Hoshaiah and half of the leaders of Judah. There were also Azariah, Ezra, Meshullam, Judah, Benjamin, Shemaiah, and Jeremiah (Neh 12:32-34). Some of the sons of the priests held trumpets, and they were: Zechariah, Shemaiah, Azarel, Milalai, Gilalai, Maai, Nethanel, Judah, and Hanani (Neh 12:35-36). They proceeded on the wall from the Tower of Furnaces to the Broad

# Dedication of the Wall
(Neh 12:27–43)

**Fish Gate** / שַׁעַר הַדָּגִים
Neh 12:39

**Old Gate**
שַׁעַר הַיְשָׁנָה
Neh 12:39

**Gate of Ephraim**
שַׁעַר אֶפְרַיִם
Neh 12:39

**Tower of the Hundred**
100 cubits (45.6m) in height
Neh 12:39

**Sheep Gate**
**(Benjamin Gate)**
שַׁעַר הַצֹּאן
Neh 12:39

**Tower of Hananel**
Neh 12:39

**Temple**

**Broad Wall**
Neh 3:8; Ref Jer 51:58

**Inspection Gate**
**(Gate of the Guard)**
שַׁעַר הַמִּפְקָד
Neh 12:39

**Choir led by Nehemiah**
Neh 12:38–40

**Choir led by Ezra**
Neh 12:31–37

**Tower of Furnaces**
Neh 12:38

**Nehemiah 12:38–40**
"The second choir proceeded to the left, while I (Nehemiah) followed them with half of the people **on the wall, above the Tower of Furnaces, to the Broad Wall**, [39] and **above the Gate** of **Ephraim**, by the **Old Gate**, by the **Fish Gate**, the **Tower of Hananel**, and the **Tower of the Hundred**, as far as the **Sheep Gate**, and they stopped at the **Gate of the Guard**. [40] Then the two choirs took their stand in the **house of God**. So did I and half of the officials with me;"

**Nehemiah 12:31; 36–37**
"Then I had the leaders of Judah come up **on top of the wall,** and I appointed two great choirs, the first proceeding to the right on top of the wall... [36] ...Ezra the scribe went before them. [37] And at the **Fountain Gate** they went directly up the **steps of the city of David** by the stairway of the way above the house of David to the **Water Gate** on the east."

**Water Gate** / שַׁעַר הַמַּיִם
Neh 12:37

**Refuse Gate**
שַׁעַר הָאַשְׁפֹּת
Neh 12:31

**Fountain Gate** / שַׁעַר הָעַיִן
(gate by the king's garden)
Neh 12:37

Wall, over the Gate of Ephraim, past the Old Gate, the Fish Gate, the Tower of Hananel and the Tower of the Hundred, as far as the Sheep Gate; and they stopped at the Gate of the Guard (Neh 12:38-39).

Also, in **the choir that followed Nehemiah**, the priests who held the trumpets were Eliakim, Maaseiah, Miniamin, Micaiah, Elioenai, Zechariah, and Hananiah; with them were Maaseiah, Shemaiah, Eleazar, Uzzi, Jehohanan, Malchijah, Elam, and Ezer (Neh 12:41-42a). The singers sang loudly, with Jezrahiah as their leader (Neh 12:42b). Then the two choirs ("the companies which gave thanks," KJV and RSV), Nehemiah, and half of the officials with him took their stand in the house of God (Neh 12:40). The dedication of the wall ended on the same day after the people gathered at the temple again and offered great sacrifices to God. At that time, the people rejoiced greatly, and even the women and children rejoiced, so that the joy of Jerusalem was heard from afar (Neh 12:43b).

On the day of the dedication of the wall, the book of Moses was read aloud in the hearing of the people. Upon hearing the law (Deut 23:3-6), they excluded all foreigners from Israel and renewed the covenant community (Neh 13:1-3).

### (5) Nehemiah's second return and his reforms
The Jews became corrupt again after Nehemiah returned to Persia following his twelve-year term as governor (444–433 BC). Therefore, he returned to Jerusalem one year later (432 BC) and carried out a series of reforms (Neh 13:4-31).

① **Nehemiah expelled Tobiah (Neh 13:4-9).**
Tobiah used his relationship with Eliashib the priest who was appointed over the chambers of the temple to obtain a large room for his own use. This room had formerly been used to store tithes, offerings, and other various articles (Neh 13:4-5). Tobiah's dwelling place within the temple became a foothold for evil through which the entire nation of Israel became corrupt. As soon as Nehemiah arrived in Jerusalem, he threw all of Tobiah's household goods out of the room and cleansed the room. He then returned the utensils of the house of God with the grain offerings and the frankincense to the room (Neh 13:7-9).

② **Nehemiah restored the Levites who had forsaken their posts and left their service (Neh 13:10-13).**

The Levites had left their posts because their livelihood was threatened as the people stopped offering tithes. Nehemiah thus reprimanded the officials and appointed treasurers (KJV) to be in charge of the storehouses. Additional persons were appointed as assistants, so that they could oversee the tithes and distribute them (Neh 13:10-13).

③ **Nehemiah made the people observe the sabbath properly (Neh 13:15-22).**

When Nehemiah returned, the people were still eager to engage in business and make money on the sabbath. Therefore, he closed the city gates as it grew dark on the day before the sabbath and did not open them again until the sabbath was over. He commanded the Levites to purify themselves and come as gatekeepers to sanctify the sabbath day (Neh 13:22).

④ **Nehemiah rebuked those who intermarried with foreign women and drove them away (Neh 13:23-28).**

The Jews at the time took women from Ashdod, Ammon, and Moab as their wives. Nehemiah struck some of them, pulled out their hair, and made them swear by God that they would never again allow their children to intermarry with foreigners (Neh 13:23-25). Nehemiah also drove away one of the sons of Joiada, the son of Eliashib the high priest, because he became the son-in-law of Sanballat the Horonite (Neh 13:28). Nehemiah concluded his reforms with the final prayer, "Remember me, O my God, for good" (Neh 13:31). Nehemiah's reforms, along with the reforms of Prophet Malachi, were the last reforms in the Bible. In truth, Nehemiah was a great leader whose heart burned with faith. With God's zeal, he forcefully urged repentance from the hearts of the Israelites. However, Nehemiah's reform was the final reform before Israel transitioned into a spiritual dark age called the intertestamental period.

## (6) Prophet Malachi's message

*Malachi* (מַלְאָכִי) means "My messenger" in Hebrew. The book of Malachi consists of messages delivered around 432 BC, after the three stages of return from the Babylonian exile (537 BC, 458 BC, and 444 BC) as well as after the reconstruction of the temple and the city wall. Although they had returned from exile, they were still under Persian oppression, and the messianic kingdom was not yet established. It was during this time that Prophet Malachi proclaimed the six discourses to awaken the people to recognize their formalistic faith and immoral sins.

**The first discourse** is in Malachi 1:2-5. As the advent of the glorious messianic kingdom seemed to tarry, the Israelites began to doubt whether God really loved them. Thus, God confirmed His love for Israel by comparing Esau and Jacob. Malachi 1:2-3 states, "'I have loved you,' says the Lord. But you say, 'How have You loved us?' 'Was not Esau Jacob's brother?' declares the Lord. 'Yet I have loved Jacob; but I have hated Esau, and I have made his mountains a desolation and appointed his inheritance for the jackals of the wilderness.'"

**The second discourse** is in Malachi 1:6-2:9. Here, Prophet Malachi proclaimed the wickedness of the priests and the curse that was to befall them. First, the priests' sin was in despising God. Malachi 1:6 states, "O priests who despise My name." They presented defiled food and animals with blemishes—the blind, the lame, the sick, and what was taken by robbery—as sacrifices to God (Mal 1:7-8, 13-14). Offering sacrifices to God was tiresome to them, and they disdainfully sniffed at it (Mal 1:13). Second, the curse was pronounced on the priests: "Behold, I am going to rebuke your offspring, and I will spread refuse on your faces, the refuse of your feasts; and you will be taken away with it" (Mal 2:3). They received this curse because they had corrupted "the covenant of Levi" (Mal 2:8).

**The third discourse** is in Malachi 2:10-16. Prophet Malachi rebuked wrongful marriages among the people of Israel. First, he denigrated marriages with foreign women. Malachi 2:11 states, ". . . for Judah has profaned the sanctuary of the Lord which He loves and has married the daughter of a foreign god." Secondly, he denigrated divorcing one's wife. The people of Israel sinned by mistreating and abandoning their wives. Malachi 2:14 states, "Yet you say, 'For what reason?' Because the Lord has been a witness between you and the wife of your youth, against whom you have dealt treacherously, though she is your companion and your wife by covenant."

**The fourth discourse** is in Malachi 2:17-3:6. After rebuking the sins of the priests and the people in the first three discourses, the fourth discourse prophesies the coming of the Messiah who will judge those sins. Malachi 3:1 describes the Messiah as "the Lord" and "the messenger of the covenant." In particular, "the messenger of the covenant" is an expression for Jesus Christ who will come as the Mediator of the new covenant (Heb 12:24). Since this Messiah will come to judge, it is written, "I will draw near to you for judgment" (Mal 3:5).

The fifth discourse is in Malachi 3:7-12. At this time, Prophet Malachi points to a way through which the people of Israel could build a right relationship with God. Although Israel had turned aside from God and had not kept His statutes until then, God said, "Return to Me, and I will return to you" (Mal 3:7). The way to return is by repenting for robbing what belongs to God and bringing again the whole tithe and offerings (Mal 3:8). God will open for such a person the windows of heaven and pour out for him a blessing until it overflows (Mal 3:10).

The sixth discourse is in Malachi 3:13-4:3. In his final discourse, Prophet Malachi revealed what the end would be like for the righteous and for the unrighteous. In those days, some people thought that it was vain to serve God (Mal 3:14) since the wicked and the arrogant who tested God were more blessed than they were (Mal 3:15). God declared to such people that the righteous and the unrighteous would certainly face different ends. Those who fear the Lord and esteem His name will be written in the book of remembrance (Mal 3:16). They will become God's own possession and receive the blessing of being spared by God (Mal 3:17). Therefore, there will be a clear distinction between the righteous and the wicked, between one who serves God and one who does not serve Him (Mal 3:18).

On that day, the arrogant and every evildoer will be chaff and ashes under the soles of their feet (Mal 4:1, 3). However, those who fear the name of God will have the sun of righteousness rise with healing in its wings; and they will "go forth and skip about like calves from the stall" (Mal 4:2).

All of this will be accomplished at the coming of the Messiah. Finally, Malachi proclaimed that the day of the Messiah's coming is "the great and terrible day of the Lord" and that Elijah will come before the coming of that day (Mal 4:5). When Elijah comes, he will restore the hearts of the fathers to their children and the hearts of the children to their fathers. Elijah's ministry will thus restore the relationship between God and the people of Israel, which had been severed due to grave sins like those of the days of Malachi. As the final prophet who closes out the history of the Old Testament, Malachi concludes by introducing Elijah as the one who will bridge the Old Testament to the central figure of the New Testament—Jesus Christ (Ref Matt 11:14; Luke 1:17).

## Conclusion: The redemptive-historical administration of the return from Babylonian captivity

The entire process of the return from Babylonian captivity was the result of the help of God's good hand. The following points display how the return from Babylonian captivity manifests God's redemptive-historical administration.

### 1. The return signifies the end of God's wrath toward the iniquities of Judah.

The fact that the chosen people were taken into captivity in the godless gentile nation of Babylon was, indeed, a great and humiliating tragedy that resulted from God's wrath. It was the execution of God's punishment and the expression of His wrath toward their sins of worshiping idols, failing to observe the sabbaths and the sabbatical years, rebelling against God's Word, and despising His divine counsel (2 Chr 36:21; Ref Jer 34:8-16). Regarding this, Psalm 107:10-11 comments, "There were those who dwelt in darkness and in the shadow of death, prisoners in misery and chains, because they had rebelled against the words of God and spurned the counsel of the Most High."

As a result of God's punishment, they lost the blessed land of Canaan and were forcibly deported to Babylon where they became wretched slaves deprived of their freedom. God's wrath was truly frightening and painful. They ate unclean foods and could not worship in Babylon. They spent days of despair with no prospect of returning to their homeland. Psalm 137:1 states, "By the rivers of Babylon, there we sat down and wept, when we remembered Zion."

The Babylonians mocked and insulted the Jews in their miserable state, demanding them to play instruments and to sing one of the songs of Zion for their merriment (Ps 137:3). This was the Babylonians' way of mocking God. The people of Judah, however, could not play the instruments that were used to praise God in order to amuse the Babylonians. They hung their harps on the willows by the rivers of Babylon so that they would not be able to play them at all (Ps 137:2). They made up their minds and refused the Babylonians' requests, saying, "How can we sing the Lord's song in a foreign land? If I forget you, O Jerusalem, may my right hand forget her skill. May my tongue cling to the roof of my mouth if I do not remember you, if I do not exalt Jerusalem above my chief joy" (Ps 137:5-6). All prospect of freedom disappeared as the Babylonian oppression worsened daily. Their sufferings had reached extremes causing their appetites to fade; they were indeed on the verge of death (Ps 107:18). Psalm 107 emphasizes many times that "they cried out to the Lord in their trouble" (Ps 107:19; Ref Ps 107:6, 13, 28).

The word *trouble* originates from the word צָרַר (*ṣārar*) meaning "to besiege" or "to bind," and thus it means "narrow" or "sealed tightly." When the Israelites spent 430 years of wretched slavery under the pharaoh's oppression, the Scripture comments, "the sons of Israel sighed because of the bondage, and they cried out; and their cry for help because of their bondage rose up to God" (Exod 2:23). Likewise, God did not turn away from the prayers of the Jews when they cried out in their trouble, but He redeemed them from the hands of the adversary (Ps 107:2; Ref Exod 2:24-25; Jer 31:11).

At last, He shattered Babylon's seemingly indestructible bronze gates and cut the iron bars (Ps 107:16). By God's sovereign work, Babylon, the most powerful nation at the time, fell at the hands of the allied forces of Media and Persia (Ref Jer 50:3, 9; 41-46; 51). Then, God stirred the heart of King Cyrus of Persia so that he would proclaim the edict allowing the Israelites to return to their land (2 Chr 36:22-23; Ezra 1:1-4). He found the path to life for those who were lost and led them to a city where they could live (Ps 107:7). Psalm 107:20 states, "He sent His word and healed them, and delivered them from their destructions."

Even today, God sends His Word so that providence directs every one of our movements. He is still at work now, running full speed ahead toward our redemption (Ps 147:15; 2 Thess 3:1).

For the people of Judah who had been oppressed and confined for so long, their miraculous, newfound freedom was like an unbelievable dream. In Psalm 126:1, the psalmist expresses this feeling by singing, "When the Lord brought back the captive ones of Zion, we were like those who dream."

Throughout their days in captivity, nostalgia flooded the hearts of the Jews as they longed for the restoration of Jerusalem (Ps 137:5-6). When God's sovereign power brought freedom for them, their laughter was restored. They were able to laugh and sing praises to their hearts' content (Ps 126:2). Thus, the psalmist erupted with emotion, confessing repeatedly, "Let them give thanks to the Lord for His lovingkindness, and for

His wonders to the sons of men" (Ps 107:8, 15, 21, 31).

From the moment they were taken far from the house of God, they were deprived of the freedom to worship and were forced to take meals of indignity. Now that all this had come to an end, they were able to return to Jerusalem which they had so longed for. On their way back, they emoted in song, singing repeatedly, "The Lord has done great things for us; we are glad" (Ps 126:3). Even the Gentiles who did not know God could not contain their amazement at God's sovereignty and great work of salvation (Ref Isa 45:14; 52:10). They confessed, "The Lord has done great things for them" (Ps 126:2b).

All of this resulted because God had curtailed His wrath and bestowed grace upon His land. He forgave and covered the sins of His people (Ps 85:1-2). The people were afflicted because of their rebellious ways and iniquities (Ps 107:17), but with His immense mercy and love, God did not find fault but covered them as if they never existed.

Now, God's anger toward the people of Judah had ceased. Psalm 85:3-4 states, "You withdrew all Your fury; You turned away from Your burning anger. Restore us, O God of our salvation, and cause Your indignation toward us to cease."

How great and many are our sins! Even though our sins are unforgivable, God knows our weaknesses and is pleased to cover up our shamefulness and faults. God heals the brokenhearted, preaches the gospel to the poor, gives liberty to the captives and the oppressed, and grants freedom to the prisoners. He is truly the God of boundless mercy and love (Isa 61:1; Luke 4:18).

## 2. The return attests to the certainty of the future eschatological salvation.

God saved the people of Judah from their captivity in Babylon. Psalm 107 described the state of captivity in Babylon mainly in four ways.

First, their souls were weary from the wandering, hunger, and thirst (Ps 107:4-5). Second, they were bound in misery and chains while dwelling in darkness and the shadow of death (Ps 107:10, 14). Third, they were at their wits' end, staggering like a drunken man because they rose up to the heavens and went down to the depths (Ps 107:26-27). Fourth, they were as men afflicted at sea because of a storm (Ps 107:29). The people of Judah cried out to the Lord in their trouble, and He delivered them out of their distresses (Ps 107:6, 13, 19, 28). He led them to their desired haven (Ps 107:30).

All this work of salvation was completely by God's grace. Psalm 85:1 states, "O Lord, You showed favor to Your land; You restored the captivity of Jacob." Psalm 85:11 states, ". . . righteousness looks down from heaven." The people of Judah were taken captive to Babylon as sinners, and when they returned, righteousness was restored to them because righteousness had looked down from heaven. This is similar to how God saw the cruelty of the Egyptians and the affliction of the Israelites, heard their cries, and was aware of their sufferings. He then personally came down to deliver them from Egypt (Exod 3:7-10).

Believers in the end times must also be saved from captivity in Babylon, the great city. "And he cried out with a mighty voice, saying, 'Fallen, fallen is Babylon the great! She has become a dwelling place of demons and a prison of every unclean spirit, and a prison of every unclean and hateful bird. . .' I heard another voice from heaven, saying, 'Come out of her, my people, so that you will not participate in her sins and receive of her plagues'" (Rev 18:2-4). The God who saved the people of Judah from captivity in Babylon will surely save His saints from Babylon, the great city of sin.

## 3. The return shows that there will be a remnant.

Prophet Isaiah prophesied that although Judah will be taken captive to Babylon, there will certainly be a remnant that returns. Isaiah 11:11-12 states, "Then it will happen on that day that the Lord will again recover the second time with His hand the remnant of His people, who will remain, from Assyria, Egypt, Pathros, Cush, Elam, Shinar, Hamath, and from the islands of the sea. And He will lift up a standard for the nations and assemble the banished ones of Israel, and will gather the dispersed of Judah from the four corners of the earth" (cf. Jer 31:7-8).

Even the name of Isaiah's son *Shear-jashub* is שְׁאָר יָשׁוּב (*šĕ'ār yāšûb*) in Hebrew, which means, "a remnant shall return." Prophet Isaiah took his son Shear-jashub to King Ahaz in order to deliver a message to the king who was in serious danger from invasions by the Arameans and the northern kingdom of Israel. It was a warning that the few who trust in the Lord will survive, but those who do not trust Him will be destroyed, never to return. Prophet Amos described the remnant as "a kernel" (Amos

9:9) while Prophet Isaiah described it as a "stump" (Isa 6:13).

The people of Israel returned to Jerusalem from the Babylonian exile in three stages (537 BC, 458 BC, and 444 BC), fulfilling God's Word that there will be a remnant. The return of the remnant teaches us four major lessons.

### (1)  It teaches us that there is a remnant for every generation in the history of redemption.

Whenever God's history of redemption faced the risk of termination due to man's unbelief and rebellion, God spared His holy people at every generation. God's providence thus ensured the continuous progression of His redemptive history from its inception to its conclusion.

Adam, in the book of Genesis, fell after eating from the tree of the knowledge of good and evil. Nevertheless, after being promised the seed of the woman (Gen 3:15) and receiving the garments of skin (Gen 3:21), he went on to teach the Word of God to his descendants even outside the garden of Eden (Ref Gen 5:28-29). By doing so, Adam fulfilled his role as the remnant who carries on God's history of redemption.

Noah was also a remnant who survived the flood, which was God's judgment against the wickedness that filled the earth. Genesis 7:23 states, "Thus He blotted out every living thing that was upon the face of the land, from man to animals to creeping things and to birds of the sky, and they were blotted out from the earth; and only Noah was left, together with those that were with him in the ark."

Abraham was also a remnant who was rescued from the idolatrous Ur of the Chaldeans and taken to the land of Canaan (Gen 11:31; 12:1-4; Acts 7:3-4). The people of Israel including Joshua were a remnant of the history of redemption; they came out of Egypt after overcoming the suffering of oppression, went through the forty years of training in the wilderness, and finally entered Canaan alive (Num 14:29-30). The people who returned from the Babylonian exile were also a remnant in the history of redemption.

Now, as the history of redemption is moving on from the New Testament era (Rom 9:27; 11:5), there will also be a remnant in the end time. They are the rest of the children of the "woman clothed with the sun" (Rev 12:1); and they are the ones who keep the commandments of God and hold on to the testimony of Jesus (Rev 12:17). We must also become God's remnant—the central figures that will carry on His history of redemption. We cannot do this by our own strength; it will be done only by God's absolute sovereignty and unconditional grace (Rom 9:8; 11:5; Jer 31:7).

**(2) It teaches us that there will certainly be a remnant who will return to Jesus Christ in the last days.**

Isaiah 10:21 states, "A remnant will return, the remnant of Jacob, to the mighty God." Here the expression *a remnant will return* is שְׁאָר יָשׁוּב (šě'ār yāšûb), which contains the same words as the name of Prophet Isaiah's son, Shear-jashub. God had already shown that although Judah was taken captive to Babylon, there would be a remnant that would return. They were the people who truly relied on the Lord, the Holy One of Israel (Isa 10:20). Furthermore, the expression *the mighty God* in Isaiah 10:21 is אֵל גִּבּוֹר ('ēl gibbôr) in Hebrew. This is the same expression used to refer to Jesus Christ the Messiah in Isaiah 9:6. Through the return of the remnant from the Babylonian exile, we are assured that there will also be a remnant that will return to Jesus Christ in the last days.

Apostle Paul said in Romans 9:27, "Isaiah cries out concerning Israel, 'THOUGH THE NUMBER OF THE SONS OF ISRAEL BE LIKE THE SAND OF THE SEA, IT IS THE REMNANT THAT WILL BE SAVED.'" He further stated in Romans 11:5, "In the same way then, there has also come to be at the present time a remnant according to God's gracious choice." Jesus also said that when He returns, He will send forth His angels to gather together His elect from the four winds, from one end of the sky to the other (Matt 24:31). God will gather His elect and unite them in the spiritual Zion, namely, the universal Church of Jesus Christ where His promise dwells.

**(3) It teaches us that there are blessings that the remnant will enjoy.**

① **The remnant's sins will be pardoned.**

Micah 7:18 states, ". . . passes over the rebellious act of the remnant . . . ." Here, the words *passes over* is עָבַר ('ābar) in Hebrew, meaning "go away," "do away," or "take away." (Job 7:21; Zech 3:4). Micah 7:19 also states, ". . . He will tread our iniquities under foot. Yes, You will cast all their sins into the depths of the sea."

② **The remnant will flourish.**

Prophet Micah said that the remnant will flourish as the "sheep in the fold" ("the sheep of Bozrah"; KJV) or "a flock in the midst of its pasture" (Mic 2:12). Jeremiah prophesied that the remnant that returns from Babylonian exile will thrive. He relayed God's promise, saying, "Then I Myself will gather the remnant of My flock out of all the countries where I have driven them and bring them back to their pasture, and they will be fruitful and multiply" (Jer 23:3). Here, the words *fruitful* and *multiply* are the translations of the Hebrew verbs פָּרָה (*pārâ*) and רָבָה (*rābâ*). These same words were used in the creation account (Gen 1:28) as well as in the postdiluvian command to Noah, "Be fruitful and multiply" (Gen 9:1; [Ref] Exod 1:7). This shows that the return of the remnant is the work of new creation, and they will be endowed with exceedingly abundant blessings both spiritually and physically.

Prophet Zechariah also stated in Zechariah 8:11-12: "'But now I will not treat the remnant of this people as in the former days,' declares the LORD of hosts. 'For there will be peace for the seed: the vine will yield its fruit, the land will yield its produce and the heavens will give their dew; and I will cause the remnant of this people to inherit all these things.'" This prophecy was proclaimed primarily for the people who had returned from the Babylonian exile and were building the temple; but this ultimately refers to the remnant who has become God's people in Jesus Christ. The expression *to inherit* in Zechariah 8:12 is נָחַל (*nāhal*) in Hebrew, which means "to receive as possession or inheritance." In other words, the remnant will be blessed not only with material blessings but also with the everlasting inheritance in the kingdom of heaven.

③ **The remnant will become a strong nation.**

Micah 4:7 states, "I will make the lame a remnant and the outcasts a strong nation, and the LORD will reign over them in Mount Zion from now on and forever." Here, the *remnant* was originally "the lame (the weak; NLT)" and "the outcasts." However, God promises that He will make them a strong nation. This *strong nation* is the kingdom that God will rule over from now and forever. These words confirm that the remnant will be under God's reign forever in His kingdom.

**(4) It teaches us what kind of people is God's remnant.**

① **The remnant is chosen by God.**

Isaiah 10:22-23 states, "For though your people, O Israel, may be like the sand of the sea, only a remnant within them will return; a destruction is determined, overflowing with righteousness. For a complete destruction, one that is decreed, the Lord GOD of hosts will execute in the midst of the whole land." Here, the words *determined* and *decreed* are used in relation to the return of the remnant. Romans 11:5 also states, ". . . there has also come to be at the present time a remnant according to God's gracious choice." Here, the expression *at the present time* is καὶ ἐν τῷ νῦν καιρῷ (*kai en tō nyn kairō*) in Greek, and it uses the word καιρός (*kairos*) to signify *God's time*. Hence, these words together emphasize that the work of salvation for the remnant will take place, not in man's time, but in God's time.

② **The remnant is upright.**

Zephaniah 3:13 states, "The remnant of Israel will do no wrong and tell no lies, nor will a deceitful tongue be found in their mouths; for they will feed and lie down with no one to make them tremble" (cf. Amos 5:15; Isa 1:9). Such accounts of the remnant calls to mind the 144,000 in the book of Revelation. The Scripture also describes the 144,000 as having "no lie . . . in their mouth" (Rev 14:5).

③ **The remnant relies only on God.**

Micah 5:7 states, "Then the remnant of Jacob will be among many peoples like dew from the LORD, like showers on vegetation which do not wait for man or delay for the sons of men." Zephaniah 3:12 states, "But I will leave among you a humble and lowly people, and they will take refuge in the name of the LORD." Isaiah 10:20 also states, "Now in that day the remnant of Israel ... will truly rely on the LORD, the Holy One of Israel." Here the word *truly* is בֶּאֱמֶת (*be'ĕmet*) in Hebrew, which means "in truth." The Word of God is the truth (Ps 119:43, 160; Prov 22:21; Ecc 12:10; John 17:17; 2 Cor 6:7; Col 1:5; 2 Tim 2:15; Jas 1:18). The remnant abides in God's Word and relies on Him only. Jeremiah 42:15 states, "...listen to the word of the LORD, O remnant of Judah" (Isa 46:3).

Jeremiah 23:3 states, "Then I Myself will gather the remnant of My flock out of all the countries where I have driven them and bring them back to their pasture ..." (Neh 1:9). Here, the phrase *bring them back* uses the hiphil stem in the perfect tense of the Hebrew verb שׁוּב (šûb), implying that God will make them return by His resolute will and sovereign power. This resolute will and sovereign power of God are manifested when He stretches forth His hand. Isaiah 11:11 explains, "Then it will happen on that day that the Lord will again recover the second time with His hand the remnant of His people, who will remain, from Assyria, Egypt, Pathros, Cush, Elam, Shinar, Hamath, and from the islands of the sea" (Exod 13:3). They are also manifested through God's zeal. Isaiah 37:32 states, "For out of Jerusalem will go forth a remnant and out of Mount Zion survivors. The zeal of the LORD of hosts will perform this."

God will prepare a *highway* for the remnant at Christ's second coming. This highway will open up miraculously just as the dry land appeared when God parted the Red Sea (Exod 14:21). Isaiah 11:16 states, "And there will be a highway from Assyria for the remnant of His people who will be left, just as there was for Israel in the day that they came up out of the land of Egypt." Therefore, today's saints must become the remnant for this generation by firmly believing that the highway will open up when God stretches out His hand with zeal. Therefore, we must rely solely on Him. The true remnant of the last days is the saints who rely only on God and thereby carry on the magnificent history of redemption with uncompromising precision.

## 4. The return from captivity manifests the fulfillment of God's Word.

God spoke through Prophet Jeremiah that captivity in Babylon would last seventy years (Jer 25:10-11; 29:10). Second Chronicles 36:21 describes these seventy years as, " . . . until the land had enjoyed its sabbaths. All the days of its desolation it kept sabbath until seventy years were complete." This means that just as cultivation begins again when the sabbatical year is over, the land of Judah would be restored once the years in captivity are completed.

When reckoned from a temple-centered, redemptive-historical perspective, Jeremiah's prophecy was fulfilled in seventy years. The temple of Jerusalem was destroyed in 586 BC during the third deportation to Babylon and was rebuilt seventy years later, in 516 BC. Moreover, the prophecy was also fulfilled in seventy years when reckoned from the first deportation. The first deportation was in 605 BC; and the first return from captivity, resulting from King Cyrus's edict, was in 537 BC. However, they actually began building the temple one year later, in 536 BC, which is the seventieth year from 605 BC, when counted inclusively. Hence, the return from captivity and the reconstruction of the temple signified the fulfillment of God's Word. As a result, the people of Judah, now reestablished as God's people, were able to regain the form of a nation, ready to manifest His glory to all the nations.

God restored His people through various leaders and prophets so that they could carry on His administration in the history of redemption. In order to do this, the destroyed temple, the city, and the city wall had to be rebuilt, and the remnant in exile had to return. For this reason, the psalmist prayed in Psalm 126:4, "Restore our captivity, O Lord, as the streams in the South." The word *South* (*negeb*) originates from a word that means "parched" and refers to the wilderness in southern Palestine (Ref Gen 20:1; Judg 1:15). During the rainy season, however, the streams in this parched land overflow with water so that the land is filled with life once again. Hence, the people prayed that the path from Babylon back to Jerusalem would also be filled with the captives of Zion like the overflowing streams of the South. Israel, who had sinned in the past, was punished and their homes became desolate with no inhabitants. Nevertheless, as Jeremiah prophesied, the days have finally come when God will "sow the house of Israel and the house of Judah with the seed of man and with the seed of beast" (Jer 31:27).

Such a great task as this requires blood, sweat, and tears, along with self-sacrifice and service. The psalmist pointed this out, by saying, "Those who sow in tears shall reap with joyful shouting. He who goes to and fro weeping, carrying his bag of seed, shall indeed come again with a shout of joy, bringing his sheaves with him" (Ps 126:5-6). They were in the worst of situations—they would sow but could not reap. Furthermore, their present time was the bleakest and there was no visible future. Nevertheless, according to the psalm, they should not accept and settle or despair at the reality; they should still go out to the field and sow. This was indeed a confession full of conviction that God would certainly allow them to reap sheaves of joy in the end. In accordance with the psalmist's conviction, God allowed His people to rebuild the temple in 516 BC. Then, seventy-nine years after the first return in 537 BC, God again called them out of Babylon for the second time in 458 BC and led a nationwide religious reformation. Finally, the third return took place in 444 BC when God enabled Nehemiah to rebuild the walls of Jerusalem.

Today, we may also repeatedly encounter situations resulting in despair. Nevertheless, we must be confident that God's sovereign grace will surely triumph according to His redemptive-historical administration and providence. If we do not lose hope and sow seeds of sacrifice and dedication for the gospel by becoming like a grain of wheat, we will ultimately reap great joy and an abundance of the good and righteous fruits (John 12:24). God keeps an account of all the tears and sweat we shed while we seek to fulfill our calling for the gospel, and He will repay us accordingly (Matt 16:27; Rom 2:6; 2 Tim 4:14; Ref 2 Cor 9:6; Gal 6:7). The sufferings of this present time are not worthy to be compared with the glory that is to be revealed to us (Rom 8:18).

It was God's sovereign providence that carried forward the entire course of history of the return from the Babylonian exile. After God's sovereign providence freed them from Babylon, spiritual revivals took place at the urging of the men of God, such as Ezra and Nehemiah. These revivals led to reforms that sought to restore the purity of their lineage, which had been defiled through intermarriages with foreigners. As time passed, however, the people of Judah again became spiritually indolent and corrupt as they intermingled with the Gentiles. It was during such a time that Nehemiah offered up his final prayer, "Remember me, O my God, for good." Nehemiah, having fully realized the limitations of human beings, offered this humble confession for himself while entrusting his fellow Jews to God. This was truly a mournful petition for God's mercy (Neh 13:31). This prayer is the final prayer and the conclusion to the Old Testament historical books, which began with the book of Joshua. It was an expression of great anticipation and earnest longing for Jesus Christ the true Savior.

God continued to fulfill His covenant to save His chosen people by preserving the descendants of David. He called forth the descendants of David who were suffering in the foreign land of Babylon and restored them to the Promised Land. It was part of His ceaseless work to carry out His administration in redemptive history to usher in the messianic kingdom.

The final prayer of the Old Testament saint Nehemiah certainly did not fall to the ground. That prayer was fulfilled through God's redeemed saints and the Church founded by the Holy Spirit, all because Christ came, lived, died, and rose again to ascend into heaven. Now, we are yearning for the glorious kingdom of the Messiah. This kingdom, which our returning Lord will establish through the remnant of the last days, is the consummation of redemptive history. As we await its glorious arrival, may we all, by faith, run full speed ahead toward the kingdom of heaven.

לכל בר דעת דרך המסעות ארבעים שנה במדבר והרוחב והאורך של ארץ הקדושה מנהר מ

מדבר צין הוא קדש

עמלק

ים המלח

ירד

מדבר סיני

שבט

מדבר פארן

מדבר שור

באר שבע

שבט

שמעון

ארץ פלשתם

ארכב גשן

פתם

שרה

צען

אלכסנדרי

לוח המסעות במדבר
אשר על פי יסעו ועל פי יחנו

| | | |
|---|---|---|
| א׳ רעמסס | טו׳ רתמה | לז׳ ההרהגדגד |
| ב׳ סכת | טז׳ רמן פרץ | ל׳ ייטבתה |
| ג׳ אתם | יז׳ לבנה | לא׳ עברנה |
| ד׳ פיהחירת | יח׳ רסה | לב׳ עציןגבר |
| ה׳ מרה | יט׳ קהלתה | לג׳ מדברצין |
| ו׳ אילם | ך׳ הרספר | לד׳ ההרההר |
| ז׳ ים סוף | כא׳ חרדה | לה׳ צלמנה |
| ח׳ מדברסין | כב׳ מקהלת | לו׳ פונן |
| ט׳ דפקה | כג׳ התחת | לז׳ אבת |
| יו׳ אלוש | כד׳ תרח | לה׳ דיבןגד |
| יא׳ רפידם | כה׳ מתקה | לט׳ עלמן דבלי׳ |
| יב׳ מדברסיני | כו׳ חשמנה | מ׳ הרי עברים |
| יג׳ קברתהתאו | כז׳ מסרות | מד׳ ערבתמואב |
| יד׳ חצרות | | רה׳ בני יעקב |

PART SIX

# The History of the Postexilic Period until Jesus Christ

# The History of the Postexilic Period
## until Jesus Christ

The final return of the Jewish people from Babylonian captivity took place in 444 BC. At this time, Nehemiah spurred on the people and rebuilt the city wall (Neh 6:15). He also carried on a reform movement until 432 BC. However, the Bible omits about four hundred years of history thereafter until the coming of Jesus Christ. Some call this period the "four hundred silent years." Nevertheless, no silent years can exist in God's history of redemption. Historically, it was a period of utter darkness, but God's history of redemption advanced even more rapidly and powerfully like rapids rushing torrentially through the neck of a river. During these four hundred years, the rise and fall of world powers progressed rapidly, all according to God's prophecies..

God foresees the beginning, the progression, and the end of all history; He guides them in His sovereign providence (Ref Num 12:6; Isa 42:9; 46:9-10; Hos 12:10; 2 Pet 1:21). He governed and directed the history of all nations and powerful monarchs in order to fulfill His plan for the redemption of His people. Even today, in His sovereignty, God intervenes in all the events that occur in this world and actively works within them (Deut 32:8; Dan 2:21; 4:17, 34-35; Acts 17:26).

The Old Testament book of Daniel clearly shows that world history progresses according to God's sovereign will. God had shown to Daniel the revelations about the great statue in chapter 2 (Dan 2:31), the four beasts in chapter 7 (Dan 7:3), the ram and the male goat in chapter 8 (Dan 8:3-14), the seventy weeks in chapter 9 (Dan 9:24-27), and the war between the Seleucid kingdom in Syria (king of the North) and the Ptolemaic kingdom in Egypt (king of the South) in chapter 11. These were all accurate prophecies of events that would occur in world history. The heated rivalry between the world powers starting with Assyria, Babylon, Persia, Greece, and finally Rome proceeded in accordance with God's prophecies through Daniel.

History is certainly not a series of random events. History is a great panorama that advances toward the fulfillment of the eternal covenant. It proceeds without even the slightest deviation from God's redemptive-historical administration within His profound providence. Just as all history has proceeded according to God's prophecies, the future will also carry on according to His Word.

The book of Daniel is ultimately a prophecy concerning the end of world history. As Jesus spoke about the end, He said, "Therefore when you see the abomination of desolation which was spoken of through Daniel the prophet, standing in the holy place (let the reader understand)" (Matt 24:15; Mark 13:14). Every teaching in the Bible was written as instruction and warning for all believers upon whom the ends of the ages have come (1 Cor 10:11; Ref Isa 46:10). When we illuminate world history with the light of God's redemptive history, we will attain the wisdom to overcome—with the courage of faith and the conviction of victory—any tempest of tribulation in the end times (Dan 8:17, 19; 10:14; 12:4, 13; 1 Cor 10:11-13).

The time from the postexilic era until the coming of Jesus Christ can be divided into five historical periods. They are:

① the period of Persian domination after Nehemiah's reforms (432–331 BC)
② the period of Hellenistic rule (331–164 BC)
③ the period of the Maccabean Revolution (167–142 BC)
④ the period of the Hasmonean Dynasty (142–63 BC)
⑤ the period of Roman domination (63–4 BC; Jesus Christ born in 4 BC).

The following survey of the history from the postexilic era to Jesus Christ will prove that these historical periods also proceeded according to God's Word.

# CHAPTER 14

# The Period of Persian Domination (432–331 BC) After the Time of Nehemiah

The southern kingdom of Judah fell to the Babylonians in 586 BC. In 538 BC, Cyrus the king of Persia issued a decree to free the people of Judah from Babylonian captivity, and Judah was placed under Persian rule thereafter. This continued even after 432 BC, when Nehemiah carried out the last religious reformation.

From the time the northern kingdom of Israel collapsed at the hands of Assyria in 722 BC until the end of Persian domination over Judah, the history of the world has seen the successive rise and fall of Assyria, Babylon, and Persia. Before we examine the period of Persian domination, we will first examine the history of Assyria and Babylon.

## 1. The golden age of Assyria and its fall

Assyria was a city-state that was established in the upper regions of the Tigris River at around 3000 BC. The actual emergence of Assyria as an imperial power on the world stage was in the reign of Tiglath-pileser I (1115–1076 BC). Moreover, the empire went into a period of decline after his death. About three hundred years later, Assyria began to thrive again and reached its golden age during the reign of Tiglath-pileser III. The names of the kings who reigned after Tiglath-pileser III are often mentioned in the Bible.

### (1) Tiglath-pileser III (745–727 BC)
The Bible refers to Tiglath-pileser III as "Pul, king of Assyria" (2 Kgs 15:19). Menahem, the king of Israel at the time, was defeated by Tiglath-pileser III in battle and gave "Pul, the king of Assyria" a thousand talents of silver so that he returned to his own land (2 Kgs 15:19-20).

During the reign of Ahaz (743 BC [731 BC]–715 BC), the twelfth king of the southern kingdom of Judah, Rezin king of Aram and Pekah king of Israel became allies and attacked Jerusalem (2 Kgs 16:5). At that time, Rezin king of Aram attacked Elath, chased out the people of Judah, and allowed the Arameans to live there (2 Kgs 16:6). Then, Ahaz sought deliverance from Tiglath-pileser III by sending the gold and silver that were in the house of God and in the treasuries of the king's house as a present to the Assyrian king (2 Kgs 16:7-8). Then, Tiglath-pileser III listened to his petition; he attacked the northern kingdom of Israel and took their people as captives. He also killed Rezin king of Aram (2 Kgs 15:29; 16:9).

Tiglath-pileser III arrived in Judah, the southern kingdom, after he had attacked Aram and Israel. Rather than helping Judah, which was being cornered by attacks from the Edomites and the Philistines, he afflicted them (2 Chr 28:20). Although Ahaz had given great wealth to the king of Assyria, it did not help him (2 Chr 28:21). Ahaz was in distress, and yet instead of relying on God, he sinned even more by sacrificing to the gods of Damascus (2 Chr 28:22-23).

First Chronicles 5:6 states, "Beerah his son, whom Tilgath-pilneser king of Assyria carried away into exile; he was leader of the Reubenites." First Chronicles 5:26 also states, "So the God of Israel stirred up the spirit of Pul, king of Assyria, even the spirit of Tilgath-pilneser king of Assyria, and he carried them away into exile, namely the Reubenites, the Gadites and the half-tribe of Manasseh, and brought them to Halah, Habor, Hara and to the river of Gozan, to this day." Thus, the genealogy in 1 Chronicles 5 supports the historicity of Tiglath-pileser III (alternate spelling: Tiglath-pilneser).

### (2) Shalmaneser V (727/726 BC–722 BC)

Hoshea, the last king of Israel, became king after he killed Pekah with the help of Assyria. At first, he submitted to Assyria, but later instituted anti-Assyrian policies. At this, Shalmaneser V attacked Israel and besieged Samaria for three years (2 Kgs 17:3-5; 18:9-10).

### (3) Sargon II (722 BC/721–705 BC)

While Shalmaneser V was besieging Samaria and destroying it, his younger brother Sargon II usurped his throne and then, destroyed the northern kingdom of Israel (2 Kgs 17:6; 18:11; Isa 20:1).

### (4) Sennacherib (705 BC/704–681 BC)

In the fourteenth year of King Hezekiah, the thirteenth king of the southern kingdom of Judah, Sennacherib seized all the fortified cities of Judah, and King Hezekiah paid tribute to the king of Assyria (2 Kgs 18:13-16). Sennacherib had attacked Judah in accordance with the prophecies made through Prophet Isaiah (Isa 7:17).

Sennacherib attacked a second time (2 Kgs 18:17-37; 2 Chr 32:1-19), but the angel of the Lord went to the camp of the Assyrians and struck down 185,000, including all the mighty warriors, commanders, and officers, so that when they rose early in the morning, all of them were dead (2 Kgs 19:35; Isa 37:36).

Sennacherib returned home in shame (בְּבֹשֶׁת פָּנִים, *bĕbōšet pānîm*: "shamefaced" or "a flush of embarrassment on his face"). He then went into the house of Nisroch (the Assyrian god of fire) his god and was killed with the sword by his own sons Adrammelech and Sharezer (2 Kgs 19:36-37; 2 Chr 32:21; Isa 37:37-38). The tragedy of his murder at the hands of his own sons occurred according to Isaiah's prophecy (2 Kgs 19:7; Isa 37:6-7).

Sennacherib had first attacked Judah in 701 BC, in the fourteenth year of King Hezekiah (2 Kgs 18:13); then he attacked a second time. Since Sennacherib died in 681 BC, it means that he did not die immediately after his failure to conquer the southern kingdom of Judah. He must have remained on the throne for nearly twenty years before he was killed. However, the account in 2 Chronicles 32:21 makes it appear as if he were killed immediately after he returned from the debacle of the second attack. The Scripture records these events in this way in order to emphasize the tragic fate of those who defile God's name as well as to show that all has been fulfilled according to God's Word.

### (5) Esarhaddon (681–669 BC)

After killing King Sennacherib their father, Adrammelech and Sharezer had to flee to Ararat because of their crime. Esarhaddon, their brother, became king in Sennacherib's place (2 Kgs 19:36-37; Isa 37:37-38). Adrammelech and Sharezer, who killed Sennacherib, were his sons, along with Esarhaddon (Isa 37:38), and the land of Ararat to which they fled was the region of Armenia located in the upper regions of the Tigris and the Euphrates Rivers.

After Esarhaddon became king, he continued his father's unfinished military campaigns, and Assyria prospered greatly. He either took the enemies of Judah and Benjamin as captives or forced them to migrate (Ezra 4:2). According to historical records, Esarhaddon raised funds and materials needed for the great construction projects in the Assyrian empire by commanding the twenty-two vassal kings to supply them, and the name of King Manasseh, the fourteenth king of Judah, was on the list of vassal kings. Esarhaddon, who had afflicted God's chosen people of Israel, died of a disease while trying to suppress a rebellion within the land of Egypt, and Ashurbanipal succeeded him on the throne.

### (6) Ashurbanipal (669 BC/668–632 BC) or Osnappar (Ezra 4:10)

Manasseh reigned in Judah (696–642 BC) during the reigns of Assyrian kings Esarhaddon, son of Sennacherib (681–669 BC), and Ashurbanipal, son of Esarhaddon (669 BC/668–632 BC). Ashurbanipal the Assyrian King mentioned in the Bible is presumed to have been the king who had bound Manasseh in chains and took him to Babylon (2 Chr 33:10-11). According to an Assyrian epitaph, Assyria attacked Judah in 648 BC, and it appears that this was when Manasseh was taken to Assyria. He was deported at the age of sixty in 648 BC, which was the forty-ninth year of his reign.

King Hezekiah, Manasseh's father and the thirteenth king of Judah, had adhered to anti-Assyrian policies, but Manasseh followed the ways of his grandfather Ahaz and implemented pro-Assyrian policies. Manasseh's name was even on the list of vassals who helped Ashurbanipal when he went on a military campaign to Egypt. Even though Manasseh had so closely cooperated with Assyria, when he repeatedly disobeyed God's Word, God stirred the heart of the Assyrian king to capture Manasseh, bind him in chains, and take him to Babylon (2 Chr 33:10-11). The commanders of the king of Assyria took Manasseh to Babylon, and not to Assyria, which indicates that Babylon was under Assyrian rule at the time.

When Manasseh was in distress, however, he entreated the Lord with great humility and prayed to the God of his fathers. Then, God was moved by his entreaty and heard his supplication; He restored him again to Jerusalem and to his kingdom (2 Chr 33:12-13). Manasseh finally came to his senses and realized that the Lord was God (2 Chr 33:13b). From this time forward, he built the outer wall from the valley on the west side of Gihon until the entrance of the Fish Gate. He also put army commanders in all the fortified cities in Judah. Furthermore, he removed the foreign gods and the idols from the house of God. He also took the altars, which he had built on the mountain of the house of the Lord and in Jerusalem, and threw them outside the city. He then set up an altar of the Lord and sacrificed offerings on them. Then, he ordered the people to serve only God (2 Chr 33:14-16).

Ezra 4:10 states, ". . . great and honorable Osnappar deported and settled in the city of Samaria, and in the rest of the region beyond the River." Here, Ashurbanipal is referred to as the "great and honorable Osnappar" (אָסְנַפַּר רַבָּא וְיַקִּירָא, *ʾāsnappar rabbā wěyaqqîrā*). The Hebrew expression *rabbā wěyaqqîrā* means "great and famous," indicating Ashurbanipal's superior military and political prowess. After Assyria destroyed the northern kingdom of Israel, Ashurbanipal continued his predecessor's (Esarhaddon) policy to forcibly settle the people from other nations in Samaria (2 Kgs 17:24-26; Ezra 4:2).

In order to disrupt the rebuilding of the walls of Jerusalem, there were people who brought charges against the Israelites to Artaxerxes king of Persia (Ezra 4:7-10). It was Ashurbanipal who had brought these people by force to Samaria.

### (7) Ashur-etil-ilani (632–628 BC)
Ashurbanipal had two sons and the kingship was given to Ashur-etil-ilani. Ashurbanipal's other son, Sinsharishkun, became king of Babylon after the rebellion was suppressed in Babylon. There, he confronted Ashur-etil-ilani, ultimately killed him, and took the throne of the Assyrian empire.

### (8) Sinsharishkun (628–612 BC)
Assyria's national power began to wane rapidly after the reign of Ashurbanipal. Nineveh, the capital of Assyria (2 Kgs 19:36; Isa 37:37), was captured by the allied forces of Babylon and Media in 612 BC, and Sinsharishkun was also killed at this time.

### (9) Ashur-uballit II (612–608 BC)
After Nineveh was captured in 612 BC, Assyria was forced to retreat toward the region of Haran, and the nation was on the verge of collapse. In 609 BC, Egypt's Pharaoh Neco went up north to Carchemish on the banks of the Euphrates in order to assist what was left of the Assyrian Empire and to crush the newly emerging powerhouse Neo-Babylonia. King Josiah, the sixteenth king of Judah at the time, did not want to see

the recovery of Assyria nor did he want to see Egypt exert its influence over the Palestinian region. Thus, in 609 BC, he confronted Pharaoh Neco in battle as he was heading north to Carchemish in order to aid Assyria.

At this time, Pharaoh Neco warned King Josiah saying that it was God's command to strike Babylon so he should not interfere with God's will by fighting against Egypt (2 Chr 35:21). King Josiah, however, not realizing that Pharaoh's words were from the mouth of God, insisted on fighting and was ultimately wounded by the enemy's arrow during the battle in the valley of Megiddo. His servant drove his body in a chariot and brought him to Jerusalem, but unfortunately, he died (2 Kgs 23:29-30; 2 Chr 35:20-25).

Afterward, in 608 BC, when Ashur-uballit II (612–608 BC) was in power, Assyria was totally destroyed at the hands of Babylon's Nabopolassar. This was sometime between the end of the reign of King Jehoahaz and the beginning of the reign of King Jehoiakim of Judah (Ref 2 Kgs 23:34). The fall of Assyria occurred in accordance with the sovereignty of God who is the Lord of all history; it was an exact fulfillment of God's prophecy spoken through the prophets Nahum and Zephaniah (Nah 1:1; 2:8-13; 3:7-19; Zeph 2:13-15).[49]

Nineveh, the capital of Assyria, was a great city (Jonah 1:2; 3:2-3) with one hundred and twenty thousand children "who do not know the difference between their right and left hand" (Jonah 4:11) and six hundred thousand total inhabitants including all the adults. Long ago, when Prophet Jonah had proclaimed the message of God's judgment (Jonah 3:4), the king of Nineveh, the people, and even the animals fasted. They put on sackcloth in repentance and turned from their evil ways. At this, God showed great mercy and the calamity did not fall upon them (Jonah 3:5-10). Even though God may have planned for judgment, if we repent from the depths of our hearts and turn from our ways, then He will forgive our sins and save us (Matt 12:41; Luke 11:30).

It is presumed that Prophet Jonah proclaimed his message to Nineveh around the time when the solar eclipse occurred on the fifteenth day of the sixth month in 763 BC. Hence, it is conjectured that he was active between 780–763 BC.[50]

Nineveh was a proud and exultant city that ruled over the whole world such that it boasted, "there is no one besides me" (Zeph 2:15). However, the city that had boasted of its mighty power was destroyed one hundred fifty years after Jonah's message was proclaimed. The city that had received forgiveness after repenting was destroyed overnight because it committed the evil of shedding the blood of neighboring nations and for its trickery, violence, pillaging, harlotries, sorceries, and idolatry (Nah 3:1-4).

Assyria's destruction is a stern lesson from history. A city or a nation may have repented at one point in its history; it will, however, eventually be destroyed if it does not continue to obey the Word of God to the very end but contends against God and worships idols.

## 2. The rise and fall of the Neo-Babylonian Empire

Babylon is located in the southern plains of Mesopotamia between the Tigris and the Euphrates Rivers. It was also called "the land of Shinar" (Gen 10:10; 11:2; Isa 11:11) as well as "the land of the Chaldeans" (Jer 24:5; 25:12; Ezek 12:13). The most famous king during the first Babylonian dynasty was Hammurabi (1792–1750 BC), the promulgator of the codes of law. Afterward, it was ruled by the Hittites, the Kassites, the Assyrians, and the Elamites until the reign of Nebuchadnezzar I (1124–1103 BC) through whom Babylon maintained the status of an independent nation as it ushered in the Middle Babylonian period.

As the Assyrian Empire became powerful, Babylon remained under its domination until the reign of Nabopolassar (626–605 BC). Babylon did enjoy a brief respite of independence during the reign of King Merodach-baladan (722–710 BC; 704–703 BC). Babylon had long been under the influence of Assyria until it finally defeated Assyria in 608 BC and gained independence to establish the Neo-Babylonian Empire. In order to strike Egypt, Nabopolassar sent the then army commander Nebuchadnezzar to Carchemish (605 BC). They completely destroyed Pharaoh Neco's army, which had been stationed there, and attained world dominance (Jer 46:2).

Prophet Habakkuk (period of ministry: 642–627 BC) prophesied in detail about how Assyrian power would wane as the Neo-Babylonian Empire emerges. Habakkuk 1:5-6 states, "Look among the nations! Observe! Be astonished! Wonder! Because I am doing something in your days—You would not believe if you were told. For behold, I am raising up the Chaldeans, that fierce and impetuous people who march throughout the earth to seize dwelling places which are not theirs." Here, God says that He is "doing something in your days" in order to accomplish His redemptive will, and that is "raising up the Chaldeans." Here the word *raising* is the participial form of the Hebrew word קוּם (*qûm*) in its hiphil stem. Therefore, it means that this is not a past event but an imminent future event. Although the event had not occurred, it is imminent and at the same time, it is a great, amazing, and an unforeseen event. God was raising up the Chaldeans, that is the Neo-Babylonian Empire, so that He can use them to discipline His people. In other words, God was warning through Prophet Habakkuk that He has already prepared the means to destroy the southern kingdom of Judah as a disciplinary measure.

The following Babylonian kings are mentioned in the Bible.

### (1) Merodach-baladan (722–710 BC; 704–703 BC)

Merodach-baladan was also called Berodach-baladan (2 Kgs 20:12). In some historical records, he was also referred to as Mardokempados or Marduk-apla-iddina II.

As soon as Merodach-baladan heard that the Assyrian king Shalmaneser V had died, he sought military assistance from Elam and rebelled against the Assyrian monarchy. Thus, Babylon enjoyed independence from 722–710 BC, but it was again conquered by King Sargon II of Assyria. However, as soon as Sargon II died and Sennacherib became king of Assyria, Merodach-baladan claimed independence for Babylon, which lasted for about seven to nine months from 704 BC to 703 BC. Later, he was expelled by Sennacherib and died during his exile in Nagitu, west of Elam.

The Bible records that Merodach-baladan sent letters and presents to King Hezekiah after he heard of Hezekiah's sickness and subsequent recovery (2 Kgs 20:12; Isa 39:1, Ref 2 Chr 32:31). This was around 701 BC when Hezekiah had already recovered from his illness, and Merodach-baladan had already lost the throne to Assyria. Babylon, at the time, was being ruled by Bel-ibni (presumed to be Merodach-baladan's family member) who was placed on the throne by Assyria (702–700 BC).[51] However, it appears that Merodach-baladan was still powerful and continued to fight against Assyria to gain independence for Babylon.[52] Thus, the reason Merodach-baladan had sent ambassadors to Hezekiah was to gain Hezekiah as an anti-Assyrian ally.

## (2) Nebuchadnezzar II (605–562 BC)

(2 Kgs 24-25; 2 Chr 36; Jer 21:1-7; 25:1-12; ch. 52; Dan 1-4)

Nebuchadnezzar II had assisted his father King Nabopolassar (626–605 BC), the founder of the Neo-Babylonian Empire, in conquering Nineveh. Nineveh was the capital of Assyria, which was the most powerful nation at the time. Nebuchadnezzar II went on to succeed his father as the second king of the Neo-Babylonian Empire. He defeated Pharaoh Neco of Egypt at the battle of Carchemish in 605 BC. With this victory, he was the king of what was now worthy to be called the most powerful nation in the world. In 609 BC, Pharaoh Neco defeated King Josiah in battle and took Carchemish as the base of operations for the attack against Babylon. However, he was utterly defeated in 605 BC by Nebuchadnezzar II's army. After this, Nebuchadnezzar II took the kings of Judah—Jehoiakim, Jehoiachin, and Zedekiah—as captives to Babylon one after another (2 Kgs 24:1-25:7). He also destroyed Jerusalem in 586 BC (2 Kgs 25:1-17; 2 Chr 36:17-21). However, in accordance with the prophecy in Daniel 4, he suffered from mental illness and was dethroned for seven periods of time (Dan 4:25, 32-33).

## (3) Evil-merodach (562 BC/561–560 BC)

Evil-merodach succeeded his father, Nebuchadnezzar II, as king. The first year of his reign coincided with the thirty-seventh year of the exile of Jehoiachin king of Judah (2 Kgs 25:27). Jehoiachin was captured in the eighth year of the reign of Nebuchadnezzar (2 Kgs 24:12), which was 597 BC, so the thirty-seventh year of the exile of Jehoiachin was 561 BC. The year that Evil-merodach became king was בִּשְׁנַת מָלְכוֹ (bišnat mālkô) and a close translation of the original Hebrew would read, "The year he began to reign as king." Thus, Evil-merodach succeeded Nebuchadnezzar II as king in 562 BC, and 561 BC was the first year of his reign. Evil-merodach released Jehoiachin from prison in the thirty-seventh year of his exile (561 BC). He allowed Jehoiachin to have his meals in the king's presence regularly and gave him a daily allowance all the days of his life (2 Kgs 25:27-30; Jer 52:31-34).

## (4) Nergal-sar-ezer (560–556 BC)

Nergal-sar-ezer was King Nebuchadnezzar's son-in-law and he held a high position as the Rab-mag (chief soothsayer/magician) during Nebuchadnezzar's reign (Jer 39:3, 13). In 560 BC, he assassinated his brother-in-law Evil-merodach and ruled for about four years.

The following biblical records reveal Nergal-sar-ezer's deeds before he became king.

The southern kingdom of Judah was destroyed by Babylon on the ninth day of the fourth month of Zedekiah's eleventh year of reign (2 Kgs 25:2-3; Jer 39:1-2; 52:5-6). That year was 586 BC, the nineteenth year of the reign of Nebuchadnezzar (2 Kgs 25:8; Ref Jer 32:1). As soon as Jerusalem was destroyed, all the officials, Babylon's powerful elites, came in and sat down at the Middle Gate of Jerusalem (Jer 39:3). The Middle Gate was considered the heart of Jerusalem as well as the passageway that divided the city of Jerusalem into two sections. The high officials of Babylon sat there in order to boast that Jerusalem had completely fallen into Babylon's hands. Among the high officials present were Nebuzaradan the captain of the guard, Samgar-nebu, Sar-sekim the Rab-saris, Nergal-sar-ezer the Rab-mag, and all the rest of the officials (2 Kgs 25:8; Jer 39:3).

In addition, Nebuchadnezzar gave orders to Nebuzaradan the captain of the guard, to release Jeremiah who had been imprisoned and to look after him (Jer 39:11-12). All the officials participated in carrying out this order, and Nergal-sar-ezer the Rab-mag was also present (Jer 39:13-14a). The officials, including Nergal-sar-ezer, dealt kindly with Jeremiah by entrusting him to Gedaliah (the grandson of Shaphan and son of Ahikam) to take him home. Hence, Jeremiah was able to stay in the land among the people without being taken into captivity (Jer 39:14b; 40:1-6).

## (5) Nabonidus (556–539 BC) and Belshazzar (553–539 BC)

Labashi-Marduk succeeded (556 BC) Nergal-sar-ezer but was dethroned by the priests after only nine months. Then, Nabonidus became king. In 553 BC, Nabonidus fell ill during battle and had to recover in Lebanon, so he allowed his first son Belshazzar to rule as coregent. In the first year of Belshazzar, Daniel received the vision of the four beasts coming out of the sea (Dan 7:1-3), and the vision of the ram and the male goat in the third year of his reign (Dan 8:1-14). Belshazzar held a feast for a thousand of his nobles and drank wine out of the vessels taken from the temple of Jerusalem. At that time, the fingers of a man's hand emerged and began writing on the plaster of the wall of the king's palace (Dan 5:1-5). The writing on the wall was "MENĒ, MENĒ, TEKĒL, UPHARSIN" (מְנֵא מְנֵא תְּקֵל וּפַרְסִין; Dan 5:25). It means, "God has numbered your kingdom and put an end to it" (MENĒ), "you have been weighed on the scales and found deficient" (TEKĒL), and "your kingdom has been divided and given over to the Medes and Persians" (PERĒS; Dan 5:26-28). In accordance with the writing on the plaster wall, Belshazzar the king of Babylon was suddenly killed that night, and Babylon fell. Then, Darius the Mede received the kingdom (Dan 5:30-31).

The Neo-Babylonian Empire corresponds to the head of gold of the great statue that Nebuchadnezzar saw in Daniel 2 (Dan 2:31-32, 38). The Bible also referred to Babylon as the "golden cup" of the ancient world (Jer 51:7). The Neo-Babylonian Empire also corresponds to the first beast, the lion, in the vision of the four beasts in Daniel 7 (Dan 7:2-4; Jer 4:7; 49:19; 50:44). Such interpretations are bolstered by the many artifacts of winged lions that were found in the various Babylonian ruins. The vision in which the lion's wings are plucked so that it was made to stand on two feet (Dan 7:4) is a foreboding of how the nation's power would slowly wane after King Nebuchadnezzar's death and would ultimately be destroyed at the hands of the Medes and Persians.

## 3. The rise and fall of the Persian Empire

King Darius of Media (Cyaxares II: 539–538 BC) and Cyrus II of Persia (539 BC/538–530 BC) united to kill King Belshazzar of Babylon and destroyed the nation. When Babylon was destroyed, Cyrus II of Persia honored his uncle King Darius by conceding to him the throne of the united empire of the Medes and the Persians. That is why Daniel 5:30-31 states that after King Belshazzar died, Darius the Mede received the kingdom (Dan 9:1; 11:1).

Darius appointed one hundred and twenty satraps as he desired and put them in charge of the entire kingdom. He also established three commissioners over them, and Daniel was one of the commissioners (Dan 6:1-2). The two years of Darius's reign were a period of transition, and the empire he ruled over was known as the Medo-Persian empire (Dan 5:28; 6:8, 15, 28). The transitional empire of Medo-Persia rose to power in fulfillment of the prophecy, "When seventy years have been completed for Babylon, I will visit you and fulfill My good word to you, to bring you back to this place" (Jer 29:10; Ref Jer 25:11-12; 2 Chr 36:21). God used the Medo-Persian Empire to fulfill His prophecy and His administration of redemption.

In the second year of Darius's reign, Cyrus, the *de facto* ruler, had Darius officially transfer his kingship to him. He also annexed Media into Persia and officially took the throne of the new Persian Empire in 538 BC.

Cambyses I (600–559 BC) of Persia married Mandane, the daughter of Astyages, the fourth king of Media, for political reasons. Cyrus II was the son born between them. Cyrus II's birth through the marriage of Cambyses I and Mandane was part of God's redemptive-historical administration to save Israel. This is evident from Prophet Isaiah's prophecies which detailed Cyrus's name and his deeds about one hundred and fifty years prior to his birth (Isa 44:28; 45:1-8).

The name *Cyrus* means "sun" in the Old Persian language and also designates an "anointed one" (Isa 45:1) in the Bible. Cyrus proclaimed to the people of Judah scattered across Persia to return to their homeland and rebuild the temple (2 Chr 36:22-23; Ezra 1:1-4; Ref Isa 44:28; 45:13). The reconstruction work began in 536 BC (Ezra 3:8-13) but was halted for about sixteen years until 520 BC because of interference from the Samaritans (Ezra 4:1-6). The work resumed on the twenty-fourth day of the sixth month of the second year of Darius (520 BC), and it was completed about four years and five months later, on the third day of the twelfth month of the sixth year of Darius (516 BC; Hag 1:14-15; Ezra 6:15).

It certainly was no coincidence that Cyrus suddenly rose to power to liberate the hopeless Jews from captivity; it was all part of God's providence for His beloved people. Around 700 BC, when Babylon was destroyed, God spoke to Prophet Isaiah and referred to Cyrus as "the man of My purpose from a far country." God said, "Truly I have spoken; truly I will bring it to pass. I have planned it, surely I will do it" (Isa 46:11). The life of King Cyrus helps us to see the universal reign of God as He governs the history of all mankind including that of Israel. Moreover, His absolute sovereignty is displayed as He fulfills His Word exactly and entirely.

The various kings of Persia recorded in the Bible are as follows.

## (1) Darius I (522–486 BC)

Three kings emerged after the death of Cyrus II: Cambyses II (530–522 BC), Bardiya (522 BC), and Darius I (522–486 BC). Daniel 11:2 prophesied regarding these three kings, "And now I will tell you the truth. Behold, three more kings are going to arise in Persia . . . ." While Cambyses was away on his campaign in Egypt, of the three kings, Bardiya seized the throne by deceiving the people saying that he was Smerdis, Cambyses' younger brother; thus, he was called Pseudo-Smerdis.

Darius I was the king who allowed the reconstruction of the temple to resume in 520 BC. The reconstruction work had been halted for sixteen years since it began in 536 BC after the first return from Babylonian exile (Ezra 4:24; 5:6-6:15; Hag 1:14-15; 2:10; Zech 1:7; 7:1).

### (2) Ahasuerus (Xerxes I: 486–465 BC/464 BC)

King Ahasuerus deposed Queen Vashti and granted the queenship to Esther (Esth 2:17). Daniel 11:2 states, "Behold, three more kings are going to arise in Persia. Then a fourth will gain far more riches than all of them . . . ." This "fourth" king was King Ahasuerus. Ahasuerus' three predecessors had successfully conquered Lydia, Babylon, and Egypt. In conjunction with these conquests, Darius's strict taxation policy allowed Ahasuerus to accumulate great wealth.

In the third year of his reign, he threw a banquet for all his princes and attendants. The banquet lasted for 180 days during which he "displayed the riches of his royal glory and the splendor of his great majesty" (Esth 1:4). This record is a glimpse into the greatness of his wealth. As he increasingly grew in strength through his wealth, he was able to stir up everyone to fight against Greece (Dan 11:2b).

In 474 BC, when Ahasuerus discovered Haman's plot to kill all the Jews living throughout the 127 provinces of the Persian Empire, he had Haman and his family killed instead (Esth 7:10; 9:10). At first, King Ahasuerus was blinded by Haman's gifts and clever speech so that he took off his signet ring and gave it to Haman (Esth 3:10-11). From this time, Haman went about freely advancing his plan to kill Mordecai and to annihilate all the Jews (Esth 3:12-15). However, one night, King Ahasuerus could not fall asleep so he read the book of records, the chronicles. There, he read the excerpt that documented how Mordecai had discovered and prevented a plot to kill the king (Ref Esth 2:19-23). Thus, he rewarded Mordecai whom Haman wanted to kill (Esth 6:1-11). Ultimately, Ahasuerus learned all about Haman's schemes through Queen Esther, and Haman was hanged on the gallows, which he had built to kill Mordecai (Esth 7:10). Ahasuerus issued another edict to kill anyone who sought to annihilate the Jews (Esth 8:9-14). Moreover, Haman's ten sons (Parshandatha, Dalphon, Aspatha, Poratha, Adalia, Aridatha, Parmashta,

Arisai, Aridai, and Vaizatha) were killed (Esth 9:7-10) and their bodies were hung on the gallows (Esth 9:13-14).

In 474 BC, God foiled Haman's plot to annihilate the Jews through His special work of providence through King Ahasuerus. As a result, sixteen years later, in 458 BC, the second return from captivity with Ezra as the leader proceeded safely.

### (3) Artaxerxes I (Longimanus: 464–423 BC)

King Ahasuerus' third son, Artaxerxes I killed Artabanus, who had murdered his father, and ascended the throne. He granted the people of Judah their second return from captivity under Ezra's leadership (Ezra 7:1-8). Previously, he had ordered the rebuilding of the city walls to be stopped after reading a malicious letter from Bishlam, Mithredath, Tabeel, and the rest of his colleagues (Ezra 4:7-23). However, in 444 BC, he granted the third return from captivity so that Nehemiah could return and rebuild the city walls (Neh 1:1; 2:1-8). Finally, the walls of Jerusalem were completed in fifty-two days (Neh 6:15).

The following kings ruled Persia after this time:

> Darius II (Nothus: 423–404 BC)
> Artaxerxes II (Mnemon: 404–359 BC)
> Artaxerxes III (Ochus: 359/358–338/337 BC)
> Artaxerxes IV (Arses: 338/337–336/335 BC)
> Darius III (Codommanus: 336/335–331 BC)

Persia was represented by the silver breasts and arms of the great statue that appears in Daniel 2 (Dan 2:32, 39). Regarding the silver, Persia was the first nation to institute a tax collection system in the form of silver coins. Persia was also described as the beast resembling a bear in Daniel 7 (Ref Isa 13:17-18; Jer 51:28). The body of this bear was raised up on one side (Dan 7:5). This is a prophecy of how the kingdom was at first united as the Medo-Persian Empire, but later one side (Persia) would become superior and would annex the other nation under its dominion. Three ribs were in its mouth between its teeth (Dan 7:5), and this represented the nation's greed. In actuality, Persia devoured three nations, which pertain to these three ribs: Lydia (546 BC), Babylon (539 BC), and Egypt (525 BC) in sequence.

Daniel chapter 8 describes the Persian Empire as the ram. Daniel 8:3-4 states:

"Then I lifted my eyes and looked, and behold, a ram which had two horns was standing in front of the canal. Now the two horns were long, but one was longer than the other, with the longer one coming up last. I saw the ram butting westward, northward, and southward, and no other beasts could stand before him nor was there anyone to rescue from his power, but he did as he pleased and magnified himself."

Here, "a ram which had two horns" represents Medo-Persia. Daniel 8:20 clarifies, "The ram which you saw with the two horns represents the kings of Media and Persia." One horn was longer than the other, because although Media and Persia were a united empire, Persia would become increasingly stronger and would dominate Media. The ram also butted westward, northward, and southward. This was the prophecy that Persia, which originated from the east, would spread out to all three directions with its great appetite for conquest. In fact, Persia conquered Babylon, Syria, and Asia Minor to the west, Egypt to the south, and Armenia and the nations near the Caspian Sea to the north.[53]

The Persian Empire was able to conquer such a vast area because of what God had spoken through Prophet Isaiah. Isaiah 45:1-2 states:

"Thus says the Lord to Cyrus His anointed, whom I have taken by the right hand, to subdue nations before him and to loose the loins of kings; to open doors before him so that gates will not be shut: 'I will go before you and make the rough places smooth; I will shatter the doors of bronze and cut through their iron bars.'"

At one time, Persia was renowned as a powerful empire. After the reign of Artaxerxes II (404–359 BC), however, continuous internal conflicts and useless wars took their toll, and the empire went into decline. The Persian Empire finally fell in 331 BC when King Darius III was defeated by Alexander the king of Greece in the battle of Gaugamela.

Persia exercised a lenient religious policy in the nations it had conquered. Therefore, the Jews under the Persian rule were able to practice their religion autonomously under the leadership of their high priest.

CHAPTER 15

# The Hellenistic Period (331–164 BC)

Daniel 11 contains detailed and factual accounts of the historical events that would take place about two hundred years after the fall of the great Persian Empire. Although there are many prophecies in the Bible, detailed prophecies of historical events such as the ones in Daniel 11 are not common. Daniel 11:2 states, "And now I will tell you the truth . . . ." Here, the word *truth* is אֱמֶת (*'ĕmet*) and means "firmness," "truly," "truth," or "truthful." This is a clear proclamation that the prophecies that follow are true and that they will surely be fulfilled. Daniel received this vision in 536 BC, "the third year of Cyrus," by the bank of the Tigris River while he was fasting and praying for three weeks (Dan 10:1-6).

Daniel 11 contains prophecies about the conqueror Alexander the Great's powerful reign over Greece and its subsequent division into the four dynasties. The chapter also details the various events and wars between the southern dynasty (Ptolemy)—which occupied Palestine, including Israel, and the regions of Egypt—and the northern dynasty (Seleucus) which occupied Syria. The account in Daniel 11 also prophesies about the persecution of the Jews by Antiochus IV (Epiphanes) and his eventual miserable fate.

It is truly amazing to read such factual, accurate, and detailed prophecies of the rise of these forthcoming kings and their roles. Although seemingly complicated, history clearly confirms that God unfolds the history of the powerful monarchs and the nations according to His decreed administration in order to fulfill His plan of redemption.

## 1. Alexander the Great and the division of his empire (331–320 BC)

In 331 BC, Alexander the Great defeated Darius III of Persia in their final battle (battle of Gaugamela) and became a mighty conqueror who ruled over the world. Regarding Alexander, Daniel 11:3 states, "a mighty king will arise, and he will rule with great authority and do as he pleases."

Alexander died suddenly in June of 323 BC at the age of thirty-two.[54] Immediately, the Greek Empire faced extreme political turmoil. It was at this time that Antigonus, who had been ruling over Syria, took over most of the Greek Empire. Many generals opposed this and joined forces to challenge Antigonus. Ultimately, the various generals who sought to become Alexander the Great's successor (*Diadochi*) vied for power through fierce battles. This time period was called the period of the Diadochi (323–301 BC).

After the death of Antigonus in the battle of Ipsus in 301 BC, the period of the Diadochi came to an end, and the Greek Empire was divided up by the four generals. General Seleucus occupied northern Syria and the regions of Mesopotamia; General Ptolemy occupied Egypt, Palestine, and the regions of southern Syria; General Lysimachus occupied Asia Minor; and General Cassander occupied Greece proper (Macedonia and Greece). The Bible already prophesied of these historical events numerous times.

According to the prophecy of the great statue in Daniel chapter 2, Greece is portrayed as the kingdom of bronze that rules the whole world (Dan 2:32, 39). In actuality, the ancient Greeks excelled in their copper smelting technology.

In the vision of the four beasts in Daniel chapter 7, Greece is described as the beast that resembles a leopard. Daniel 7:6 states, "After this I kept looking, and behold, another one, like a leopard, which had on its back four wings of a bird; the beast also had four heads, and dominion was given to it." In actuality, Greece, led by Alexander the Great, conquered the whole world with the speed of a leopard. The great feat was achieved between the years 336 BC to 323 BC (Ref Jer 5:6; Hos 13:7; Hab 1:8).

The four wings of a bird on the leopard's back represent the speed of his conquests. In addition, the four heads of the beasts reveal how four people would divide his territory after his death at the age of thirty-two. Indeed, a fierce battle for succession ensued after Alexander's untimely death, after which his empire was divided into four kingdoms.

These events are portrayed again in the vision in Daniel chapter 8 where the male goat strikes the ram and makes it fall (Dan 8:5-8). This male goat represents Greece, which would destroy Persia and rule the world. Historically, the male goat had symbolized the Greek Empire, and thus the Greeks were called *the goat people*. Daniel 8:21 states, "The shaggy goat represents the kingdom of Greece . . . ." Daniel 8:5 states that this male goat came from the west over the surface of the whole earth without touching the ground. This is a description of how Alexander the Great would swiftly conquer the world in a short time.

This male goat had a conspicuous horn between his eyes (Dan 8:5), and this large horn was Greece's first (Dan 8:21) and most powerful king, Alexander the Great. However, this large horn was broken and four horns arose in its place toward all sides of the heavens. This is again the prophecy of how the kingdom would be divided into four after Alexander the Great (Dan 8:22). Daniel chapter 11 describes Alexander the Great as "a mighty king" (Dan 11:3). Moreover, the prophecy describes the division that would occur after his death with the kingdom being "broken up and parceled out toward the four points of the compass" (Dan 11:4).

In keeping with this prophecy, Greece went through the period of the Diadochi after Alexander's death after which the kingdom was divided up by four dynasties (Ptolemaic Dynasty, Seleucid Dynasty, Lysimachus Dynasty, and Cassander Dynasty). Among these four the Lysimachus and the Cassander Dynasties did not last as long as the other two dynasties. Lysimachus had taken control of Asia Minor, but he died in battle against Seleucus in 281 BC. Cassander became king over Macedonia and Greece. He also founded Thessalonica in 315 BC. However, his kingdom was annexed by Rome in 167 BC.

The Ptolemaic and Seleucid dynasties endured for a long time as they intensely battled over the regions around Palestine where the Jews lived. The two dynasties battled one another on various occasions in order to conquer the land of Israel. The Jews were ruled by the Ptolemaic Dynasty from 320 BC and then by the Seleucid Dynasty from 198 BC.

Of the four dynasties that divided the Greek Empire, the Ptolemaic and Seleucid dynasties are directly connected to the rule of Palestine. The king of the South mentioned in Daniel 11:5 is the king of the Ptolemaic Dynasty (Egypt) and the king of the North is the king of the Seleucid Dynasty (Syria). Historically, there was a series of six wars between the Ptolemaic and Seleucid dynasties known as the Syrian Wars. Daniel chapter 11 contains detailed prophecies of the third to the sixth Syrian Wars.

- **First Syrian War** (274–271 BC)
- **Second Syrian War** (260–253 BC)
- **Third Syrian War** (246–241 BC; Dan 11:7-8)
- **Fourth Syrian War** (221–217 BC; Dan 11:10-12)
- **Fifth Syrian War** (202–195 BC; Dan 11:13-17)
- **Sixth Syrian War** (170–168 BC; Dan 11:22-30a)
  ① First War: Ptolemy VI attacks Antiochus IV (Dan 11:22-24)
  ② Second War: Antiochus IV's first campaign to Egypt (Dan 11:25-28)
  ③ Third War: Antiochus IV's second campaign to Egypt (Dan 11:29-30a)

## 2. The period of the Ptolemaic Reign (320–198 BC)

After the death of Alexander the Great in 323 BC, the various generals were embroiled in fierce battles. At that time Ptolemy I conquered Jerusalem, and thus began the reign of the Ptolemaic Dynasty in 320 BC. Ptolemy I was tolerant of foreign religions and allowed the migration and settlement of many Jews in Alexandria (capital of the kingdom located on the northern coast of Africa on the Mediterranean Sea). By God's providence, the Jews who lived there at the time received support from Ptolemy II to translate the Hebrew Bible (Old Testament) into Greek— the *de facto* official language of the world at the time. This translation was called the *Septuagint* (LXX; seventy-two persons took part in the translation work). The Jews flourished during the Ptolemaic reign and enjoyed autonomy under the leadership of the high priest.

The kings of the Ptolemaic Dynasty who appear in the Bible are as follows.

### (1) Ptolemy I (323–285 BC)
Daniel 11:5 describes him saying, "Then the king of the South will grow strong . . . ." The king referenced here is Ptolemy I who ruled Egypt. He was the most competent and powerful king among the four generals who divided the kingdom after the death of Alexander the Great.

### (2) Ptolemy II (285–246 BC)
Daniel 11:6 states, "After some years they will form an alliance, and the daughter of the king of the South will come to the king of the North to

carry out a peaceful arrangement. But she will not retain her position of power, nor will he remain with his power, but she will be given up, along with those who brought her in and the one who sired her as well as he who supported her in those times."

Here, the phrase "after some years" shows that a lot of time had passed since Ptolemy I and Seleucus I obtained dominion and proclaimed themselves as kings in Daniel 11:5. The king of the South in the above passage is Ptolemy II, the son of Ptolemy I. He had sought to enter into friendly relations with the Seleucid Dynasty by giving his daughter Berenice in marriage to Antiochus II. In turn, Antiochus II divorced his wife Laodice and married Ptolemy II's daughter Berenice hoping to forge an alliance with the king of the South. As soon as Ptolemy II died in 246 BC, Antiochus II again acknowledged his first wife Laodice as his lawful wife and named her son Seleucus II his successor. Not long after this, Laodice killed Berenice, her son, and even Antiochus II; then, she made her son Seleucus II king.

### (3) Ptolemy III (246–221 BC)

The description in Daniel 11:7, which states, "one of the descendants of her line," refers to Ptolemy II's son and Princess Berenice's younger brother Ptolemy III. As soon as Ptolemy III ascended the throne, he attacked the Seleucid kingdom in order to avenge the death of his sister Berenice, and this became the third Syrian War (246–241 BC). Ptolemy III killed Laodice, invaded the fortress of the king of the North, and defeated them. Then he took "their gods with their metal images and their precious vessels of silver and gold" from Seleucus II, Laodice's son, and brought them to Egypt (Dan 11:8). Jerome commented that Ptolemy III took 40,000 talents of silver and precious vessels, 2,500 gods, and other spoils.[55] The Scripture states, ". . . he on his part will refrain from attacking the king of the North for some years" (Dan 11:8b).

### (4) Ptolemy IV (221–203 BC)

Daniel 11:10-12 describes the fourth Syrian War. Seleucus II, the king of the North attacked Ptolemy III, the king of the South, but returned home without achieving his purpose (Dan 11:9). Then his sons, Seleucus III and Antiochus III, began preparations for war (Dan 11:10a). Between the two sons, the firstborn Seleucus III ascended the throne first in 223 BC. However, after he died in battle in Asia Minor, his younger brother

# The Ptolemaic and Seleucid Dynasties

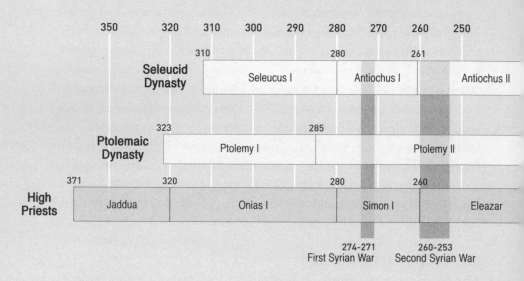

Antiochus III succeeded the throne. Antiochus III mobilized a multitude of great forces and advanced like a flood against Ptolemy III's oldest son, Ptolemy IV. Thus, Antiochus III captured the strong fortress (Dan 11:10). However, Ptolemy IV counterattacked Antiochus III, and recovered a great amount of lost territory. This occurred during the battle of Raphia (located near Gaza in the Palestinian region) at the end of the fourth Syrian War in 217 BC. Daniel 11:11 comments on this event as follows: "The king of the South will be enraged and go forth and fight with the king of the North. Then the latter will raise a great multitude, but that multitude will be given into the hand of the former."

Ptolemy IV was victorious in battle against Antiochus III. Consequently, his heart was lifted up because he saw that he held in his hands enough power to kill tens of thousands of people. Becoming proud, he entered into the holy of holies, which only the high priest could enter, and defiled the temple. Ptolemy IV's success was short lived as he died of an unknown disease in 203 BC (Dan 11:12).

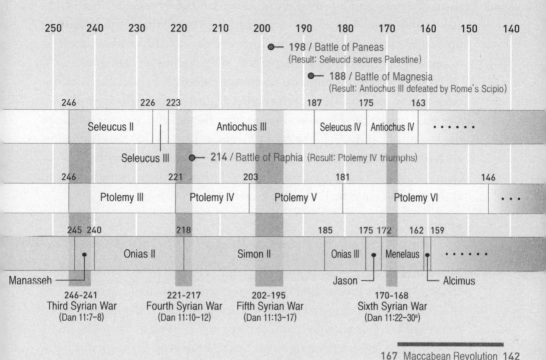

| 250 | 240 | 230 | 220 | 210 | 200 | 190 | 180 | 170 | 160 | 150 | 140 |
|---|---|---|---|---|---|---|---|---|---|---|---|

●— 198 / Battle of Paneas
(Result: Seleucid secures Palestine)

●— 188 / Battle of Magnesia
(Result: Antiochus III defeated by Rome's Scipio)

246        226  223                    187      175      163

| Seleucus II | | Antiochus III | Seleucus IV | Antiochus IV | • • • • • • |

Seleucus III   ●— 214 / Battle of Raphia (Result: Ptolemy IV triumphs)

246              221        203              181                        146

| Ptolemy III | Ptolemy IV | Ptolemy V | Ptolemy VI | • • • |

245 240              218                185    175 172    162 159

| Onias II | Simon II | Onias III | • | Menelaus | • | • • • • • • |

Manasseh ——

Jason ——                                          —— Alcimus

246-241
Third Syrian War
(Dan 11:7-8)

221-217
Fourth Syrian War
(Dan 11:10-12)

202-195
Fifth Syrian War
(Dan 11:13-17)

170-168
Sixth Syrian War
(Dan 11:22-30ᵃ)

167 Maccabean Revolution 142

## (5) Ptolemy V (203–181 BC)

Daniel 11:13-17 deals with the fifth Syrian War. When Ptolemy IV died and his young son Ptolemy V ascended the throne, various neighboring nations joined forces to attack the Ptolemaic kingdom. Daniel 11:14 alludes to this, saying, "Now in those times many will rise up against the king of the South."

During this time, some Jews sought to enlist the help of the Seleucid Dynasty in order to gain independence for Judah. Daniel 11:14 describes such people as "the violent ones." The word *violent* in Hebrew is פְּרִיץ (*pĕrîṣ*), which means "one who breaks." Thus, these were haughty people (i.e., they "lifted themselves up") who broke God's laws. They had no regard for God and used human trickery to embroil the Seleucid Dynasty into their visions for Judean independence (Dan 11:14). Because of this, however, the severe and oppressive rule of the Seleucid Dynasty replaced the relatively lenient rule of the Ptolemaic Dynasty ("but they will fall down"; Dan 11:14).

In 198 BC, Antiochus III was victorious against Ptolemy V in the battle of Paneas and captured the beautiful land of Jerusalem (Dan 11:15-16). At this time, Antiochus III attacked the king of the South by casting up a siege ramp, and neither the forces of the South nor their choicest troops (elite forces) had the strength to withstand him (Dan 11:15).

From this time, Seleucus began to rule Palestine. Daniel 11:16 elaborates on this, saying, "But he who comes against him will do as he pleases, and no one will be able to withstand him; he will also stay for a time in the Beautiful Land . . . . " The *Beautiful Land* (Dan 11:16) that Antiochus III captured is אֶרֶץ־הַצְּבִי (*'ereṣ-haṣṣĕbî*) and means "land of beauty" or "land of glory." The expression refers to the land of Israel with Jerusalem at its center (Dan 8:9; 11:45; Ezek 20:6, 15).

## 3. The period of the Seleucid Reign (198–164 BC)

Antiochus III, the most powerful ruler in the Seleucid Dynasty, often clashed with the Ptolemaic Dynasty over the Palestinian region. In 198 BC, Antiochus III defeated Ptolemy V in the battle of Paneas and seized control of the Palestinian region.

While the Jews were being ruled by the Ptolemaic Dynasty until 198 BC, the following kings ruled the Seleucid Dynasty.

Seleucus I*: 312–280 BC (Dan 8:8, 22; 11:5)
Antiochus I: 280–261 BC
Antiochus II: 261–246 BC (Dan 11:6)
Seleucus II: 246–226 BC (Dan 11:7-9)
Seleucus III: 226–223 BC (Dan 11:10)

While the Ptolemaic Dynasty was tolerant of Jewish customs and traditions, the Seleucid Dynasty forced the Jews to adopt the Hellenistic culture. They also taxed the Jews heavily and looted the temple treasures.

The following kings of the Seleucid Dynasty ruled over the Jews.

---

* Daniel 11:5 refers to him as "one of his princes." Seleucus I was one of the generals of the Ptolemaic Dynasty during the era of the divided kingdom, but as he grew strong, he declared independence and established the Seleucid Dynasty.

## (1) Antiochus III (223–187 BC)

After defeating Ptolemy V and capturing the beautiful land of Jerusalem in 198 BC, Antiochus III, the king of the North, mobilized the strength of his entire kingdom to conquer the Ptolemaic kingdom. However, he later changed his policy to one of peace and amity: he married his daughter Cleopatra I to Ptolemy V (Dan 11:17a). This was his attempt to put Rome in check as it was rising as a powerhouse at the time. It was also an attempt to use his daughter to place the Ptolemaic Dynasty under his control. However, after her marriage to Ptolemy V, Cleopatra I fell in love with her husband and devoted herself to the good of the Ptolemaic Dynasty by pledging her loyalty to the Ptolemaic kingdom. Then, she had her husband forge an alliance with Rome. Antiochus III's plans had failed completely. This was in accordance with the prophecy in Daniel 11:17, which stated, ". . . he will also give him the daughter of women to ruin it. But she will not take a stand for him or be on his side."

Afterward, Antiochus III attacked and captured many islands in the Mediterranean Sea (Dan 11:18a). In fulfillment of Daniel's prophesy, "a commander" (Dan 11:18) from Rome named Lucius Scipio was sent to check Antiochus III's maritime advance. Antiochus scorned him severely. However, Lucius Scipio put a stop to this scorn, and in fact, he turned the scorn back upon Antiochus III (Dan 11:18b). This happened at the battle of Magnesia (190–188 BC). In this battle, Lucius Scipio, with an army of thirty thousand men, destroyed Antiochus III's army of seventy thousand men. He also took Antiochus IV, Antiochus III's son, and around twenty others as hostages back to Rome. He forced Antiochus III to pay an enormous war indemnity to Rome each year.

After his great defeat to Rome, Antiochus III returned to his own land. In regard to this, Daniel 11:19 states, "So he will turn his face toward the fortresses of his own land . . . ." He tried to restore his fallen honor by preparing for his comeback with an expansion of armaments. However, the rebel forces killed him just as it was prophesied, "he will stumble and fall and be found no more" (Daniel 11:19b). His elaborate plans had instantly failed.

## (2) Seleucus IV (187–175 BC)

Seleucus IV ascended the throne in place of his father Antiochus III, but he overtaxed the people in order to repay the war indemnity that he inherited because of Antiochus III's defeat against Rome. The word *oppressor* in Daniel 11:20 is נָגַשׂ (*nāgaś*) and refers to one who imposes taxes. He sent Heliodorus, his finance minister, through Palestine the "Jewel of his kingdom" and collected taxes by coercion (Dan 11:20a; Ref 2 Macc 3:7-40).

Then, Daniel 11:20b prophesied, ". . . yet within a few days he will be shattered, though not in anger nor in battle." Seleucus IV was killed in battle by Heliodorus, a man whom he had appointed.

### (3) Antiochus IV Epiphanes (175–163 BC)

Antiochus IV succeeded his older brother, Seleucus IV. Regarding Antiochus IV Daniel 11:21 states, "In his place a despicable person will arise, on whom the honor of kingship has not been conferred." The word *despicable* in the phrase "a despicable person" is written with the passive Hebrew verb בָּזָה (*bāzâ*) which means "to despise" or "to hold in contempt." The term refers to someone who is despised or a person who is rightly held in contempt. This meant that Antiochus IV would never become a great figure who can be acknowledged as king. He was a despicable person who could not become king because he was taken as a hostage of war to Rome when his father, Antiochus III, was defeated in battle. He schemed so that Demetrius, who would succeed the throne as Seleucus IV's firstborn, was taken hostage to Rome in his place. He also sent his lieutenant Andronicus to kill Seleucus IV's second son Antiochus under the pretense of protecting him. Then, he killed Andronicus because he was afraid that the truth might be discovered. He also punished Heliodorus who had killed his older brother Seleucus IV.

Daniel 11:21b sums up the situation aptly, saying, "but he will come in a time of tranquility and seize the kingdom by intrigue." Here, the word *intrigue* means "to deceive in a skillful and cunning manner" or "to deceive in a bizarre manner." On the outside, Antiochus IV possessed a peaceful visage as if nothing was happening, but he had been devising all sorts of deceit and sly trickery to establish himself as king.

Antiochus IV warred against Ptolemy VI on three occasions. The description of the first war is written in Daniel 11:22-24, the second war in Daniel 11:25-28, and the third war in Daniel 11:29-30.

#### First War: Ptolemy VI attacks Antiochus IV

Ptolemy VI attacked Antiochus IV with "overflowing forces" but was defeated (Dan 11:22). The prophecy describes Antiochus IV's tactics as follows: "After an alliance is made with him he will practice deception, and he will go up and gain power with a small force of people" (Dan 11:23). Thus, Antiochus IV made the neighboring nations put their guard down by entering into alliances with them while gradually expanding into a powerful nation with a small force.

Daniel 11:24 states, "In a time of tranquility he will enter the richest parts of the realm, and he will accomplish what his fathers never did, nor his ancestors; he will distribute plunder, booty and possessions among them, and he will devise his schemes against strongholds, but only for a time." Antiochus IV achieved what no one else had previously achieved by attacking the richest lands of the Ptolemaic Dynasty. Then, he distributed the plunder and booty of the Ptolemaic Dynasty among the troops who went to fight. He did this in order to gain favor from his soldiers so that he may "devise his schemes against strongholds (מִבְצָר, mibṣār; "fortress" or "fortified city"), but only for a time." However, the phrase, "but only for a time," reveals that his policy of benevolence will end and his true colors as a tyrant will emerge.

### Second War: Antiochus IV's first campaign to Egypt

In 170 BC, Antiochus IV attacked Ptolemy VI. This became his first campaign to Egypt during the sixth Syrian War (170–169 BC; Dan 11:25-28). Ptolemy VI fought with an extremely large and mighty army, but he could not hold them off. His army was scattered and many were slain; and he was taken captive (Dan 11:25). Ptolemy VI was defeated despite his extremely large and mighty army because Antiochus IV had bribed Ptolemy VI's closest subjects who ate his choice food. Antiochus IV had devised schemes with them so that they would betray their king (Dan 11:25b-26).

Ptolemy VI, who was taken captive, suggested to Antiochus IV that they become allies and so they sat at the same table. Regarding this Daniel 11:27 states, "As for both kings, their hearts will be intent on evil, and they will speak lies to each other at the same table." Antiochus IV told Ptolemy VI that he would restore his throne, but in reality, he sought to place the Ptolemaic kingdom under his rule. Moreover, Ptolemy VI entered into a false treaty promising allegiance in order to escape captivity and regain his throne. Ptolemy VI again fought against Antiochus IV after he was restored to his throne. The prophecy in Daniel 11:27 states, ". . . but it will not succeed, for the end is still to come at the appointed time." As such, the treaty between the two kings was never carried out. When God's appointed time came, their true colors were revealed and the treaty was completely shattered.

After his campaign to Egypt, Antiochus IV, the king of the North, returned to his land with a great amount of plunder, but his heart was filled with pride. He set his heart against the holy covenant and did as he pleased (Dan 11:28). Antiochus IV stopped by Judah on the way back to Syria and seized a great amount of wealth and treasures. In his arrogance, he entered the temple, which was forbidden for Gentiles. He, then, destroyed the golden altar and the lampstand, causing great sorrow all over Israel, and the rulers and the elders groaned in lament (Ref 1 Macc 1:20-28).

### Third War: Antiochus IV's second campaign to Egypt

Daniel 11:29 states, "At the appointed time he will return and come into the South, but this last time it will not turn out the way it did before." This was his second campaign to Egypt during the end of sixth Syrian War (168 BC; Dan 11:29-30a). The phrase, "the appointed time," reveals that even Antiochus IV's second attack will also occur within God's providence. However, Antiochus IV's campaign to Egypt was not as successful as the last one. As soon as he attacked the Ptolemaic kingdom, the Romans mobilized the ships of Kittim (the Macedonian fleet), and Antiochus IV had to withdraw from the Ptolemaic kingdom (Dan 11:30).

Antiochus IV vented his anger from his defeat against the Ptolemaic kingdom by heightening his persecution of Jerusalem. He returned home in despair after his defeat and became enraged at the holy covenant and did as he pleased (Dan 11:30). The word *enraged* is זָעַם (zāʿam) and means "to denounce," "to curse," or "to express indignation." This expression bears the same connotation as the phrase "be set against the holy covenant" in Daniel 11:28.

When Antiochus IV returned, he showed regard for those who forsook the holy covenant and gave them power, strength, and great wealth. Regarding this, Daniel 11:30 states that he would "show regard for those who forsake the holy covenant."

Antiochus IV also mobilized the army to desecrate the "sanctuary fortress" (Dan 11:31ᵃ). In 167 BC, he did away with the regular sacrifice in the temple. Then, on December 8th (fifteenth day of Chislev), he erected the statue of Zeus ("the abomination of desolation") on the temple altar and made the people worship it (Dan 11:31; Ref 1 Macc 1:54; 2 Macc 5:1; 6:2). He also sent envoys to Jerusalem and to the various cities in Judah and proclaimed the edict forbidding circumcision and the observance of the Sabbath (Ref 1 Macc 1:41-50). Furthermore, anyone observing the laws were put to death. He also forced the Jews to kill a pig, which they abhorred, and offer it on the altar on the twenty-fifth day of each month to commemorate the king's birthday (Ref 1 Macc 1:54-64; 2 Macc 6:7).

His wickedness intensified with each passing day to an extent that the Jews could no longer withstand it. The Gentiles engaged in all sorts of lewd and debaucherous acts inside the temple; they had relations with prostitutes and preyed on women within the temple precincts (Ref 2 Macc 6:3-4). Furthermore, he magnified himself and placed himself above the gods, forcing the people to worship him (Dan 11:37). Antiochus IV deified himself by calling himself "Epiphanes," which means "God manifest."

Daniel 8 describes Antiochus IV as the small horn that came forth from one of the four horns (Dan 8:8-9). It states that this small horn will attack the Beautiful Land of Jerusalem (Dan 8:9). Furthermore, it will strike the people of Israel—the host of heaven—so that some of the stars, the leaders, will fall to the earth (Dan 8:10). He will magnify himself to be equal with God, the Commander of the host. He will also remove the regular sacrifice from Him and throw down His sanctuary (Dan 8:11).

It was prophesied that it would take 2,300 evenings and mornings for the desecrated holy place to be properly restored (Dan 8:14). Historically, about 2,300 evenings and mornings had actually passed since Antiochus IV began his policy to obliterate the Jewish religion in 170 BC until the temple was restored through the Maccabean Revolution in December of 164 BC (twenty-fifth day of Chislev; Ref 1 Macc 4:52). Antiochus IV's deeds prefigure the works of the antichrist, which will appear in the end times to contend with God (Rev 13:5-7).

Concerning the end of Antiochus IV (Epiphanes), Daniel 8:25 prophesies: "And through his shrewdness he will cause deceit to succeed by his influence; and he will magnify himself in his heart, and he will destroy many while they are at ease. He will even oppose the Prince of princes, but he will be broken without human agency" (Ref Job 5:12). In addition, Daniel 11:45 states, ". . . yet he will come to his end, and no one will help him." For the sin of conquering Jerusalem and profaning the temple, his intestines rotted; he suffered from this long, drawn-out illness until he finally died the most absurd and pathetic death. Such historical facts demonstrate that any worldly nation that contends with God will ultimately be destroyed no matter how powerful it may be.

On the other hand, ". . . the people who know their God will display strength and take action" (Dan 11:32b). Daniel 11:35 also states, "Some of those who have insight will fall, in order to refine, purge and make them pure until the end time; because it is still to come at the appointed time."

No matter how powerfully the forces of the antichrist may oppose the people of God, their time of activity is under God's decree and within the sphere of His providence. Moreover, God's people will display courage despite the persecutions of the antichrist. They will be purged and purified; they will persevere to the end and ultimately triumph (Matt 24:13; Luke 21:19; John 16:33; 2 Thess 1:4; Rev 13:10; 14:12).

# CHAPTER 16

# The Maccabean Revolution
# (167–142 BC)

The Jews were divided into two groups during the time of Antiochus IV (Epiphanes). The first group consisted of those who betrayed the covenant and committed evil. The second group consisted of those who were wise among the people and knew their God (Dan 11:32). Antiochus IV's blasphemies against the temple ultimately stirred up the emotions of the Jews and sparked a revolt for independence. The officials of the Seleucid Dynasty commanded Mattathias the priest to place detestable idols in the holy sanctuary and to make sacrifices there. The revolution began when Mattathias and his family (the Maccabees) resisted and fought against them.

The prophecy in Daniel was most likely a sufficient impetus for the Maccabean Revolution, since he prophesied about the destruction of Greece (Dan 8:23-25; 11:40-45). The pious people of God who believed in His Word given through Prophet Daniel must have held conviction in the fall of Antiochus IV and the imminence of their own salvation. They fought with firm faith, risking their lives in order to achieve the predestined victory.

## 1. Mattathias (167–166 BC)

In 167 BC, the priest Mattathias took his five sons (John, Simon, Judas, Eleazar, and Jonathan) to Modein, which was located 39 km from Jerusalem. They, then, tore down the pagan altars and started the revolution. Mattathias fled to the mountains in order to battle against the Seleucid forces using guerrilla warfare tactics. Many of the *Hasidims* (means "pious") joined him at this time. Mattathias, however, died at the beginning of the revolution and was buried in the tomb of his ancestors at Modein (Ref 1 Macc 2:70).

## 2. Judas Maccabeus (166–160 BC)

When Mattathias died, his third son Judas Maccabeus (means "hammer") succeeded his father as the leader of the Jews (Ref 1 Macc 3:1). Judas Maccabeus, with his superior leadership, was able to recover Jerusalem on the twenty-fifth of Chislev (ninth month of the Jewish calendar, December in the solar calendar) in 164 BC (Ref 1 Macc 4:52). He purified the temple according to the regulations of the law and did away with all the idols. After the purification of the temple, he held a dedication celebration known as *Hanukkah* (חֲנֻכָּה; means "dedication"; Neh 12:27) or the Feast of the Dedication (John 10:22); this marked the beginning of the Jewish celebration called the Festival of Lights.

Judas Maccabeus died during the battle of Elasa fought against the Seleucid Dynasty in 160 BC. Mattathias' other sons Eleazar and John died in 163 BC and 161 BC, respectively.

## 3. Jonathan Apphus (160–142 BC)

The youngest son, Jonathan, assumed leadership after Judas Maccabeus died. Jonathan reorganized the revolution and was triumphant against the Seleucid forces. He conquered the northeast regions of Israel and the Transjordan (a high plateau on the east side of the Jordan River). The Seleucid Dynasty wanted to win his favor and made him the new high priest in 152 BC. However, in 142 BC, Jonathan was killed by General Trypho, an adversary of the Seleucid Dynasty.

## 4. Simon III Thassi (142–134 BC)

Simon was Mattathias' last surviving son. When he assumed the leadership role after Jonathan in 143 BC, he did not fight head on against the Seleucid Dynasty as his other brothers had done. Instead, he used diplomacy to negotiate with them. Ultimately, in 142 BC, the Jews were able to drive out the Seleucid Dynasty completely. They were finally free from the yoke of the Gentiles (Ref 1 Macc 13:41). From this time on, the Jews secured full independence and the period of the Hasmonean Dynasty began.

The Maccabean Revolution was the fulfillment of God's Word that prophesied the end of Antiochus IV (Dan 8:25; 11:45). It showed the victory of those who followed and believed in the Word: "but the people who know their God will display strength and take action" (Dan 11:32b).

CHAPTER 17

# The Period of the Hasmonean Dynasty (142–63 BC)

The period of the Hasmonean dynasty refers to the time from 142 BC, when Simon secured independence for Judea, until 63 BC, when the Romans conquered Jerusalem. The Maccabean family was also known as the Hasmonean dynasty. Some scholars believe that the name *Hasmonean* originated from the name of the region that the family came from. On the other hand, there are others who believe that the name derives from *Asamonaeus* (*Ant.* 12.265), an ancestor of the Maccabees who was part of the Jehoiarib division (first division) of the priestly line (1 Macc 2:1; 1 Chr 9:10, 24:7).[56]

## 1. John Hyrcanus I (134–104 BC)

Simon, who actually began the Hasmonean period, was killed by his own son-in-law in 134 BC. Then, Simon's son Hyrcanus I became king. He encouraged circumcision and adhered to the observance of the laws; his goal was to restore the Davidic kingdom. He had secured the largest territory since King Solomon. However, as his territory expanded and his powers strengthened, he became increasingly corrupt and began to Hellenize the names of his children as well as the royal family culture.

## 2. Aristobulus I (104–103 BC)

Hyrcanus I died and his firstborn Aristobulus I became king. He expanded his territory to northern Lebanon and called himself king. When Aristobulus I died, his wife, Salome Alexandra made his brother Alexander Jannaeus king and became his wife.

### 3. Alexander Jannaeus (103–76 BC)

Alexander Jannaeus ascended the throne after his brother Aristobulus I died in 103 BC. He enforced a policy of violence and oppression in order to persecute the Pharisees who opposed the performance of the high priestly duties by the Hasmonean royal family. Thus, the Pharisees often involved the Seleucid Dynasty in order to revolt. Alexander Jannaeus captured eight hundred of the masterminds behind this scheme and crucified them on the cross.

### 4. Salome Alexandra (76–67 BC)

When Alexander Jannaeus died, his wife, Salome Alexandra took the throne. In an attempt to restore the relationship with the Pharisees, she again established them as members of the Sanhedrin, and her firstborn son Hyrcanus II, who was the high priest, received their support.

### 5. Aristobulus II (67–63 BC)

A fierce struggle for power ensued following the death of Salome Alexandra. Ultimately, the second son Aristobulus II emerged victorious and drove out his older brother Hyrcanus II. Thus, Aristobulus II became the high priest as well as king.

While Judea was struggling with internal conflicts, Pompey of Rome came to the land of Judea with his Roman forces and conquered it without any difficulty.

# CHAPTER 18

# The Period of Roman Domination
# (63 BC–4 BC, the Birth of Jesus Christ)

Rome corresponds to the legs of iron in the vision of the great statue in Daniel chapter 2 (Dan 2:33, 40). Rome was an empire as strong as iron and was often referred to as "the iron monarchy of Rome."

Rome emerges as the fourth beast in the vision of the four beasts in Daniel chapter 7. It is described as "dreadful and terrifying and extremely strong; and it had large iron teeth." The ten horns on the head of this fourth beast represent the ten kings who will appear in this world after the collapse of Rome (Dan 7:7, 24). The little horn, which will appear among the ten horns, represents the antichrist which will oppose the Most High God and persecute the believers (Dan 7:8, 24-26).

The following is a brief summary of Roman history.

During the eighth century BC, Rome was a small nation under the rule of the Etruscans (the ancient people of Etruria) near the Tiber River valley in the southern Italian peninsula. Around 270 BC, Rome emerged as a powerhouse that would unite the entire Italian peninsula. Afterward, Rome was victorious in the Punic Wars, a series of three wars against Carthage (262–146 BC). She was also triumphant in the Macedonian Wars, a series of four wars against the kingdom of Macedonia (214–148 BC). As a result, Rome seized control over the entire the Mediterranean region.

After conquering the Syrian region in 64 BC, Rome finally annexed the Seleucid kingdom in 63 BC and then turned the Ptolemaic kingdom into a province of Rome in 30 BC. Politically, Julius Caesar, Pompey, and Crassus ruled as the First Triumvirate from 60 BC to 45 BC. However, when Crassus was killed during the battle of Carrhae against Parthia in 53 BC, Julius Caesar and Pompey struggled to seize power. Between 45–44 BC, Julius Caesar fought off the influence of the Senate (a political institution in ancient Rome) and assumed sole control of the government. In 44 BC, however, Julius Caesar was assassinated by the aristocrats of the Roman Republic who opposed him. Immediately after this, Octavian, Antony, and Lepidus divided up the territory and ruled as the Second Triumvirate (43-31 BC). Octavian and Antony, both wanting to seize sole control, overthrew Lepidus and fought fiercely against each other. In 31 BC, Octavian defeated the joint forces of Antony and Cleopatra VII, the last queen of the Ptolemaic Dynasty, at the battle of Actium and secured sole control. In 27 BC, he received the name Augustus ("His Reverence") and became the first Roman emperor. He ruled until AD 14.

The Judean territories were ruled by the Roman Empire in the following manner.

## 1. John Hyrcanus II (63–40 BC)

Hyrcanus II, always dissatisfied after losing the throne to his younger brother Aristobulus II, enlisted the help of the Roman General Pompey. Pompey conquered Jerusalem in 63 BC. Pompey eliminated Aristobulus II, who was opposed to Rome, and established Hyrcanus II as the high priest of Judea, which was now a vassal of Rome.

Meanwhile, there was an ambitious upstart named Antipater, who was the son of Antipas the governor of Idumaea (Edom). Idumea had been annexed by Judea during the time of Hyrcanus I. Since Antipater had always supported Rome during the revolts in Jerusalem, he had earned Rome's trust and was appointed governor of Judea in 55 BC. Antipater thus became the unofficial ruler of Judea. Then, in 47 BC, when Julius Caesar was struggling in his battle against Ptolemy in Alexandria, Antipater and Hyrcanus II came to his support. After Julius Caesar gained victory, he allowed Hyrcanus II to use the title "king" and appointed Antipater as the Roman procurator of Judea. However, Julius Caesar was assassinated in 44 BC and Antipater was also poisoned to death by a Zealot named Malichus.

## 2. Antigonus (40–37 BC)

In 40 BC, Antigonus, the son of Aristobulus II, rebelled against Rome and conquered Jerusalem. He ruled over Judea until 37 BC. He mutilated his uncle Hyrcanus II's ears so that he would be ineligible for the priesthood, and sent him into exile. Of Antipater's two sons, Phasael, who was the governor of Judea, struck his own head against the rocks while he was bound in chains and committed suicide. Meanwhile, Antipater's other son Herod, who was the governor of Galilee, fled to Rome.

## 3. Herod the Great (37–4 BC)

In 37 BC Herod, who had escaped to Rome, returned with the help of the Roman army and seized control of Jerusalem, which had hitherto been under Antigonus' control. Herod, then, became king of Judea. At this time, Herod executed Antigonus and many of the Sadducees at Antioch. In order to win the favor of the Jews, Herod the Great began the reconstruction of the temple in Jerusalem in 20 BC.

Herod was a brutal and cruel tyrant who possessed the superior ability to protect his regal powers. Herod saw that Aristobulus III, the high priest and his brother-in-law, had gained popularity among the people. He became jealous and saw him as a threat to his power, so he had him drowned in the ponds within the palace complex. He also made false charges against Hyrcanus II and had him killed. He even killed his own wife Mariamne, and after her death, he went on to kill her mother (his mother-in-law), Alexandra as well. Deceived by the slander and schemes of his servants, he even killed his own children. When baby Jesus was born in Bethlehem, he ordered all the male babies under the age of two born in Bethlehem and its vicinity to be killed (Matt 2:16).

The life of Herod the tyrant, who had shed so much innocent blood, ended tragically. He died while suffering from a long, drawn-out disease. Josephus' historical records state:

> After this, the distemper seized upon his whole body, and greatly disordered all its parts with various symptoms; for there was a gentle fever upon him, and an intolerable itching over all the surface of his body, and continual pains in his colon, and dropsical turnouts about his feet, and an inflammation of the abdomen, and a putrefaction of his privy member, that produced worms. Besides which he had a difficulty of breathing upon him, and could not breathe but when he sat upright, and had a convulsion of all his members . . . (*Wars*. 1. 656).

Herod's disease was God's fearful wrath and punishment for his sins.

When Herod died from illness in 4 BC, Israel was divided among his three sons. Herod Archelaus (4 BC – AD 6) became the tetrarch of Judea, Samaria, and Idumaea (Matt 2:22); Herod Antipas (4 BC – AD 39) became tetrarch of Galilee and Perea (Matt 14:1-12; Mark 6:14-29; Luke 9:7-9; 23:5-15); and Herod Philip II (4 BC – AD 34) became tetrarch of Ituraea and Trachonitis (Luke 3:1).

Jesus was born toward the end of Herod the Great's reign. When the magi came to Herod and asked, "Where is He who has been born King of the Jews?" (Matt 2:2), his heart was violently shaken, and he and all Jerusalem were troubled (Matt 2:3). Ultimately, he ordered a bloody massacre of all male babies under the age of two in Bethlehem and its vicinity (Matt 2:16).

Politically, Herod's tyrannical rule reached its peak and all the people shook in fear. Spiritual darkness deepened as faith in God became a mere formality. Hellenism became deeply embedded into the Jewish society, and the chosen people of Israel became extremely secularized. It was at this time that "the fullness of the time came" (Gal 4:4), and the promised seed of the woman, Jesus Christ, came upon this earth (Gen 3:15). Here, the phrase "the fullness of the time" is ὅτε δὲ ἦλθεν τὸ πλήρωμα τοῦ χρόνου (*hote de ēlthen to plērōma tou chronou*) in Greek. A literal rendering of this phrase means, "However, when came the fullness of the time." Here, *time* is χρόνος (*chronos*) and refers to general time, but Galatians 4:2 expresses it as "the date set by the father," referring to a special time appointed by God. Here, the word *set* is προθεσμίος (*prothesmios*) and means "appointed beforehand" or "determined."

God had predetermined the time to send Jesus Christ to save His people from the bondage of death and the law that resulted from sin. Moreover, Christ also came to free us from all sorts of oppressions in this world. In other words, Jesus Christ came according to God's eternal decree. Thus, this *time* was the most perfect and appropriate time within God's administration of redemption; it was the time when God poured out His immense love for His people. The coming of Jesus Christ was the light of hope that ended the four-hundred-year long era of spiritual darkness in Judah. Furthermore, it was the eternal light of life for all humankind who had been living as slaves of sin under the dark shadows of death (John 1:4-5, 9; 8:12; 9:4-5).

Thus far, we have surveyed the portions of world history that are related to Israel. Our survey has covered the period from the time the people of Judah returned from Babylonian exile to the coming of Jesus Christ, the seed of the woman, who came at the fullness of time.

In the last book of the Old Testament, Malachi 4:5-6, it states, "Behold, I am going to send you Elijah the prophet before the coming of the great and terrible day of the Lord. He will restore the hearts of the fathers to their children and the hearts of the children to their fathers, so that I will not come and smite the land with a curse." Here, "the great and dreadful day of the Lord" refers to the day that the Messiah the Savior comes. This day not only refers to the first coming of Jesus Christ, but ultimately makes us look forward to the day of the second coming when He will at last judge all the forces of evil. Thus, the Old Testament concludes with a message of anticipation for the Savior as well as an expectation for Prophet Elijah who would prepare the path for the coming of the Messiah (Ref Matt 11:14; 17:10-13; Luke 1:17).

In addition, the Gospel of Matthew, the first book in the New Testament opens with the words, "The record of the genealogy of Jesus the Messiah . . ." (Matt 1:1). This reveals that the focus of the Old and New Testaments is Jesus Christ and that He is the bridge that connects the two testaments. Furthermore, this is a proclamation that Jesus Christ is the Messiah (Savior), the ultimate fulfiller of the administration of redemption. He is the One the Israelites had longed and hoped for from the time they returned from the Babylonian captivity and while they were enduring indescribable oppression at the hands of Persia, Greece, and Rome.

Map 4

# Territories of the Four Great Empires
# (Neo-Babylonia, Persia, Greece, and Rome)

**Neo-Babylonia** / Era of Nebuchadnezzar II (605–562 BC)

**Persia** / Era of Artaxerxes I (464–423 BC)

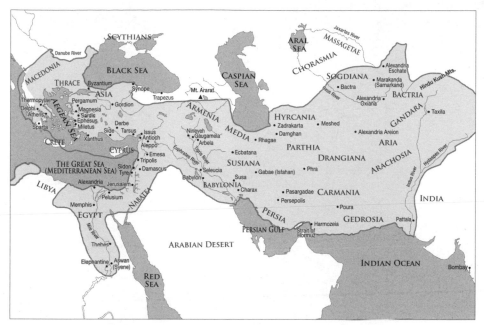

**Greece** / Era of Alexander the Great (336–323 BC)

**Rome** / Era of Augustus (31 BC–AD 14)

לכל בר דעת דרך המסעות ארבעים שנה במדבר 'והרוחב והאורך של אתן הקדושה מנהר מ

עמלק

מדבר צין הוא קדש

ים המלח

עתר

מקדה

עיר כרמל

השור שבט

באר שבע

שבט שמעון

מדבר סיני

מדבר פארן

מדבר שור

ארץ פלשתם

ארץ גשן

פתם

צען

אלכסנדרי

לוח המסעות במדבר
אשר על פי היסעו ועל פי היחנו

| א' רעמסס | טו' רתמה | טז' חרהגדגד |
| ב' סכת | טז' רמן פרץ | ל' יטבתה |
| ג' אתם | יז' לבנה | לא' עברנה |
| ד' פיהחירת | יח' רסה | לב' עציןגבר |
| ה' מרה | יט' קהלתה | לג' מדבר צין |
| ו' אילם | כ' הרספר | לד' הרההר |
| ז' ים סוף | כא' חרדה | לה' צלמנה |
| ח' מדבר סין | כב' מקהלת | לו' פונן |
| ט' דפקה | כג' תחת | לז' אבת |
| יו' אלוש | כד' תרה | לח' דיבןגד |
| יא' רפידם | כה' מתקה | לט' עלמן דבל' |
| יב' מדבר סיני | כו' חשמנה | מ' הרי עברים |
| יג' קברת התאוה | כז' מסרות | מא' ערבה מואב |
| יד' חצרות | כח' בני יעקן | |

# Jesus Christ, the Fulfiller of the Administration of Redemptive History, and the Promise of the Eternal Covenant

# Jesus Christ, the Fulfiller of the Administration of Redemptive History, and the Promise of the Eternal Covenant

The history of redemption progresses according to God's predestined decrees and unfolds according to His administration. The genealogy of Jesus Christ is the epitome of God's marvelous administration in redemptive history. The entire history of the Old Testament is summarized in the genealogy of Jesus Christ, and the history of the New Testament begins with the genealogy of Jesus Christ. The genealogy of Jesus Christ clearly proclaims that the entire history of the Old and New Testaments focus on Jesus Christ who stands at the heart of redemptive history.

As we bring to a close our study of the genealogy of Jesus Christ in light of God's administration in the history of redemption, I hope now to draw a conclusion to all that we have examined thus far.

First, we will examine the relationship between the promise of the "seed of the woman," which is the starting point of all covenants, and the genealogy of Jesus Christ. Next, we will compare the genealogy of Jesus Christ in Matthew and Luke from the redemptive-historical perspective. Then, we will consider Jesus Christ, the fulfiller of the administration of redemption.

Finally, we will discuss what the proper attitude of the believers who have received the promise of the eternal covenant should be.

## 1. The promise of the "seed of the woman" and the genealogy of Jesus Christ

The ultimate goal of all the covenants in the Bible is the completion of the history of redemption through Jesus Christ.

Genesis 3:15 promised that the Messiah, who would come as the seed of the woman, will crush the serpent's head. This promise was ultimately fulfilled at the coming of Jesus Christ, the seed of the woman and the hope of salvation for all mankind.

The history contained in the genealogy of Jesus Christ in Matthew 1 shows the process in which the promise of the seed of the woman is fulfilled. The genealogy also reveals the fulfillment of the other covenants that advanced this initial promise. Furthermore, the genealogy of Jesus Christ boldly proclaims that Jesus Christ has come as the One who fulfills the promise of the "seed of the woman."

**FIRST, Jesus Christ was born of the "virgin Mary."**

| ex | hēs | egennēthē | Iēsous | ho | legomenos | Christos |
|---|---|---|---|---|---|---|
| ἐξ | ἧς | ἐγεννήθη | Ἰησοῦς | ὁ | λεγόμενος | Χριστός |
| from | whom | was born | Jesus | who | is called | Christ |

The genealogy begins with Abraham, passes through David, and continues on to Jesus Christ. Matthew 1:16 states, ". . . Mary, by whom Jesus was born, who is called the Messiah." This passage regarding the birth of Jesus is recorded in a manner different from the rest. If it had followed the pattern of, "Abraham was the father of Isaac, Isaac the father of Jacob," then it should have been written, "Joseph was the father of Jesus." However, it states, ". . . Mary, by whom Jesus was born, who is called the Messiah." The passage sounds as if Jesus does not have a father. This connects Jesus Christ directly to Mary and shows how Jesus fulfills the promise in Genesis 3:15 that the Messiah would come as the "seed of the woman." Galatians 4:4 states, "God sent forth His Son, born of a woman." Jesus Christ came to this earth in order to crush the serpent's head and destroy Satan as promised. For this reason, Hebrews 2:14 states, ". . . He Himself likewise also partook of the same, that through death He might render powerless him who had the power of death, that is, the devil" (Ref 1 John 3:8).

**SECOND, Jesus Christ was conceived by the Holy Spirit.**

In the genealogy in Matthew 1, the phrase, ". . . became the father of . . . ," was repeatedly used for all forty persons of the genealogy, from Abraham to Mary's husband Joseph, throughout its fifteen verses (Matt 1:2-16). Thirty-nine instances use the predicate ἐγέννησεν (egennēsen), the active voice of the word γεννάω (gennao) meaning "to beget." However, to describe the birth of Jesus Christ, the predicate "was born" was employed, which is ἐγεννήθη (egennēthē), the divine passive of the word gennao (Matt 1:16).

This shows that Mary did not give birth to Jesus by her own strength. The birth of Jesus Christ had nothing to do with man's will or with Joseph's blood lineage. Jesus was conceived in the body of the virgin Mary by God's sovereign work of the Holy Spirit (Matt 1:18, 20; Luke 1:35).

Since the conception through the Holy Spirit was possible through God's mighty and direct intervention, it was an event beyond the rational understanding of man. However, true faith transcends all rationality by believing that God's Word will surely be fulfilled just as He has spoken. It is about hoping for what cannot be hoped for and believing in what cannot be believed (Heb 11:1; Rom 4:18).

When the angel Gabriel announced to Mary that she would conceive through the Holy Spirit, she answered, "May it be done to me according to your word" (Luke 1:38). Mary could have been sent away by Joseph to whom she had been engaged to marry; she could have been stoned to death by the people (Deut 22:23-24). Yet, she accepted both possibilities with faith and risked her life to obey. She believed that the Word of God is able to create something out of nothing. Thus, she also believed, without a doubt, that if this same Word was at work, then it would be possible to conceive through the Holy Spirit (John 1:3, 10).

In addition, when the angel Gabriel told her that she had conceived (Luke 1:32-33), she believed that the Davidic covenant was being fulfilled through her. This is why Elizabeth, the mother of John the Baptist, said to Mary, "And blessed is she who believed that there would be a fulfillment of what had been spoken to her by the Lord" (Luke 1:45). Thus, Mary's conception through the Holy Spirit is a clear testimony that the promise of the "seed of the woman" in Genesis 3:15 has been fulfilled in Jesus Christ.

**THIRD**, Jesus Christ was, as was supposed, the son of Joseph.

Luke 3:23 states, "When He began His ministry, Jesus Himself was about thirty years of age, being, as was supposed, the son of Joseph, the son of Eli." This verse clarifies that although people generally knew Jesus as Joseph's son, He was actually the Son of God, who had been conceived by the Holy Spirit and born of the virgin Mary. This truth is confirmed again as the ascending genealogy of Jesus traces back all the way up to God (Luke 3:38).

The genealogies in Matthew and Luke differ in their structures, the number of generations, and the number of persons included. Nevertheless, they are united in their objective to bring to light how the promise of the "seed of the woman" in Genesis 3:15 was fulfilled in redemptive history. In this singular effort, they, together, testify of the One—Jesus Christ.

## 2. The convergence of the genealogies in the Gospel of Matthew and the Gospel of Luke

The genealogy in Matthew 1 is the genealogy of the line of Joseph, while the genealogy in Luke 3 is the genealogy of the line of Mary, Jesus' mother.[57] The genealogy in Matthew lists Jacob as Joseph's father, while the genealogy in Luke lists Eli as his father (Matt 1:16; Luke 3:23).

A reading of the Lukan genealogy in Greek reveals something very unusual. The definite article τοῦ (*tou*) precedes each name in the long genealogy except that of Joseph; only Joseph does not have the definite article before his name. This reflects that this genealogy does not belong to Joseph but to Eli. Joseph, in reality, was not part of Eli's genealogy. Joseph was the son of Eli, but he was a legal son, not a biological son.

| v.23: ... | υἱός,  | ὡς | ἐνομίζετο, | (missing) | Ἰωσὴφ | τοῦ | Ἠλὶ | | |
|---|---|---|---|---|---|---|---|---|---|
| | son | as | was supposed | ---- | of Joseph | the | of Eli | | |

| v.24: | τοῦ | Μαθθὰτ | τοῦ | Λευὶ | τοῦ | Μελχὶ | τοῦ | Ἰανναὶ | τοῦ | Ἰωσὴφ |
|---|---|---|---|---|---|---|---|---|---|---|
| | the | of Matthat | the | of Levi | the | of Melchi | the | of Jannai | the | of Joseph |

The absence of this article certainly places Joseph's name in a special position in the series of names. It leads us to suppose that the relationship between Joseph and Eli was different from the rest, and thus Eli was not Joseph's biological father but a legal father.[58]

Then how did Joseph become Eli's legal son?

Eli was Mary's father and he most likely did not have a male heir. According to family inheritance laws, the daughter receives the inheritance when there is no apparent male heir (Num 27:8; 36:6-9). Joseph, Eli's son-in-law, most likely became Eli's adopted son after Mary and Joseph were married.[59]

Hence, Joseph was Jacob's biological son (Matt 1:16) and at the same time, an heir of Eli, Mary's father (Luke 3:23). By this profound mystery, the two genealogies (genealogies of Jacob and Eli) converge into one at Joseph and in Jesus Christ.

The genealogy of Jesus Christ in Matthew 1 and Luke 3 list the same people from Abraham to King David. After King David, however, the Matthean genealogy continues with Solomon (Matt 1:6) while the Lukan genealogy continues with Nathan (Luke 3:31). Solomon and Nathan are brothers. First Chronicles 3:5 lists the four sons born to David by Bathshua (Bathsheba), and they are Shimea (Shammua), Shobab, Nathan, and Solomon (2 Sam 5:14; 1 Chr 14:4).

The Matthean genealogy records Solomon after King David and continues on to Joseph, the father of Jesus Christ according to the genealogy (Matt 1:16). On the other hand, the Lukan genealogy records Nathan after King David, continues to Eli the father of Mary, and then to Joseph, Eli's legal son (Luke 3:23-31). Thus, it is truly a mysterious and profound providence that these two genealogies, which took two very different paths after King David, converged with Joseph.

What is more amazing is that the family of Jacob, Joseph's biological father, and the family of Eli, Joseph's legal father (i.e., Mary's father), are both descendants of David. God promised that the Messiah would come as the seed of the woman and as a son of David. In order to fulfill this promise, He preserved the two lineages of David (Solomon and Nathan). At last, God joined these two lineages together again through Joseph and Mary's marriage. Furthermore, He sent forth Jesus through His conception by the Holy Spirit inside Mary's body so that He would be born as the seed of the woman, thereby accomplishing His administration in redemptive history. The genealogy of Jesus Christ is truly the encapsulation of the history of redemption and the epitome of the fulfillment of redemption. All the covenants and promises of the covenants established within God's redemptive administrations are fulfilled in Jesus' genealogy.

After God promised that the Messiah would come as the seed of the woman in Genesis 3:15, He preserved the lineage of Jesus Christ until He came to fulfill that promise. Those years were, indeed, the years of long-suffering for God who had been waiting for the coming of the seed of the woman.

They were the years of heartbroken tears for God as He preserved the people of the covenant despite their unbelief, so that they could continue the lineage of Jesus Christ for the ultimate fulfillment of His covenant.

They were the years of God's love and unending forbearance even in the midst of the continuous cycle of mankind's rebellion and God's punishment.

They were the years of God's constant and painstaking care to ensure the continuous and unrelenting march of the history of redemption.

They were the years of God's holy war that He fought with all His might against Satan's schemes to destroy God's covenant.

They were the years of God's zealous labor as He actively searched to find the *virgin* Mary and the *righteous* Joseph through whom the seed of the woman would come as promised.

The seed of the woman came at the "fullness of the time" (Gal 4:4). The "seed of the woman" came without even the slightest deviation from God's foreordained plan of redemption. Jesus Christ, who is fully God, came into this world fully human so that He may save the fallen man (Rom 1:3-4). Thus, the genealogy of Jesus Christ proclaims to the entire universe that Jesus—who came as the "seed of the woman"—is the true Savior for in Him dwells the fullness of divinity as well as the fullness of humanity.

## 3. Jesus Christ, the fulfiller of the administration of redemptive history

God's first promise of salvation after the fall of Adam and Eve in the garden of Eden was the promise of the "seed of the woman" in Genesis 3:15. This promise took concrete shape through the promise that Jesus Christ would come as a son of Abraham. The genealogy that we have examined thus far is redemptive-historically significant because it records the fulfilling process of the promises of the "seed of the woman" and "the son of David, the son of Abraham." Thus, we come to meet in the genealogy, Jesus Christ—the fulfiller of the administration of redemptive history.

### (1) Jesus Christ, the true son of Abraham

The Matthean genealogy, which connects the Old and the New Testaments, opens with Matthew 1:1 by stating, "The record of the genealogy of Jesus the Messiah, the son of David, the son of Abraham." The fact that Jesus Christ came as the son of Abraham is the fulfillment of the covenant that God made with Abraham. Moreover, this fact becomes the most important link that connects the Old and the New Testaments.

### ① Covenant with Abraham

The Abrahamic covenants in the Old Testament already revealed many times the promise that the Messiah would come as the son of Abraham. Thus, Jesus Christ's coming as a descendant of Abraham is a fulfillment of the Old Testament covenants.

Genesis 12:3 states, "And in you all the families of the earth will be blessed." This verse has a deeper meaning than the mere fact that all the families of the earth will be blessed because of Abraham. Here, the phrase *in you* is בְּךָ (*bĕkā*) in Hebrew and this ultimately signifies that all the families of the earth will be blessed through *the* son of Abraham, Jesus Christ. All the families of the earth cannot be blessed in a mere human being. All the families of the earth can only be blessed in Jesus Christ.

Genesis 13:15 states, "For all the land which you see, I will give it to you and to your descendants forever." God had promised on many occasions that He would give the land to Abraham and his descendants (Gen 15:18; 26:3-4; 28:13-14; 35:12). Here, "your descendants" primarily refer to Isaac and his descendants. However, we must take note of the word "forever." No human being can possess land on the earth forever. In fact, even the physical descendants of Abraham were not able to possess the land of Canaan continuously. They lost possession of it when they were taken captive to Babylon and also after AD 70 when Jerusalem was destroyed by Rome. Thus, only Jesus Christ can possess the land forever; therefore, "your descendant" ultimately refers to Jesus (Gal 3:16).

Genesis 18:18 states, ". . . since Abraham will surely become a great and mighty nation, and in him all the nations of the earth will be blessed." Here, the phrase "in him" is בוֹ (*bô*). Once again, the promise is that all the nations of the earth will be blessed in Abraham, which ultimately points to the fact that all the spiritual descendants of Abraham will be blessed in Jesus Christ the Messiah, *the* son of Abraham (Gal 3:7-9, 29). Accordingly, Abraham had the duty to command and educate his children and his household after him to keep the way of the Lord by doing righteousness and justice so that his descendants may receive Jesus Christ (Gen 18:19).

In addition, Genesis 22:18 states, "In your seed all the nations of the earth shall be blessed, because you have obeyed My voice." Here, the phrase, "in your seed" is בְזַרְעֲךָ (*bĕzarʿăkā*). This means "in a seed," which ultimately refers to Jesus Christ, since only God—and not man— can bless all the nations of the earth.

As we have examined thus far, the "seed" which appears in God's covenant with Abraham ultimately refers to Jesus Christ. In this light, the "seed" that God promised to Abraham was only One—Jesus Christ (Gal 3:16, 19).

② **Jesus Christ, the singular seed**
In Galatians 3:16, Apostle Paul says, "Now the promises were spoken to Abraham and to his seed. He does not say, 'And to seeds,' as referring to many, but rather to one, 'And to your seed,' that is, Christ." According to this, no matter how numerous the descendants of Abraham may be, the only One that God acknowledges as the true seed of Abraham is Jesus Christ. Thus, even the physical descendants of Abraham (Isa 41:8; John 8:33, 39) cannot be acknowledged as Abraham's descendants unless they believe in Jesus Christ, the true seed of Abraham.

Regardless of whether one is a physical Jew or a Gentile, only those who believe in Jesus Christ can become the spiritual descendant of Abraham (Gal 3:14). Galatians 3:7 states, "Therefore, be sure that it is those who are of faith who are sons of Abraham." Also, Galatians 3:29 states, "And if you belong to Christ, then you are Abraham's descendants, heirs according to promise." The Matthean genealogy powerfully proclaims to all nations of the world that Jesus Christ is the Messiah who came as the son of Abraham (Matt 1:1). Jesus Christ is the promised seed (Gal 3:19), and we become Abraham's spiritual descendants by believing in Christ. All the people of the world will become descendants of Abraham by belonging to Jesus Christ, and they will be blessed with Abraham (Gal 3:9).

**(2) The blessings of the spiritual descendants of Abraham**
We, who have become descendants of Abraham through faith in Jesus Christ, receive the following blessings with Abraham.

*FIRST*, we are freed from all curses.
Galatians 3:13 states, "Christ redeemed us from the curse of the Law,

having become a curse for us—for it is written, 'Cursed is everyone who hangs on a tree.'" Those who boast that they are saved by the deeds of the law will be placed under the curse of the law. Galatians 3:10 states, "For as many as are of the works of the Law are under a curse; for it is written, 'Cursed is everyone who does not abide by all things written in the book of the law, to perform them.'" Here, the word "under" is ὑπὸ (hypo) and is used in Galatians to refer to the state of being shackled like a slave or a servant (Gal 3:22, 25).

Thus, those who have not become spiritual descendants of Abraham are all slaves under the curse. Jesus, however, has redeemed us on the cross by receiving the curse on behalf of all humankind (Gal 3:13).

In Galatians 3:22, Apostle Paul described the state of being "under the curse" as being "shut up under sin." Here, the word *shut* is συγκλείω (synkleiō) and refers to a state where one is "confined on all sides" or "surrounded completely." We were placed under the curse of sin and death, but Jesus has redeemed us by the blood of the cross; thus, we have been freed completely from all curses (Rom 8:2).

### SECOND, we receive God's righteousness as a gift.

We receive God's righteousness as a gift when we believe in Jesus Christ. Romans 3:22 states, ". . . even the righteousness of God through faith in Jesus Christ for all those who believe; for there is no distinction." Galatians 3:24 also states, ". . . so that we may be justified by faith."

This is the doctrine of *justification by faith*. It teaches us that salvation does not come through man's good works; salvation comes by faith and through God's grace.

> **Romans 3:28** For we maintain that a man is justified by faith apart from works of the Law.

> **Galatians 2:16** Nevertheless knowing that a man is not justified by the works of the Law but through faith in Christ Jesus, even we have believed in Christ Jesus, so that we may be justified by faith in Christ and not by the works of the Law; since by the works of the Law no flesh will be justified.

### THIRD, we become children of God.

Those who believe in Jesus Christ not only become righteous, but they also become sons of God (Gal 3:26) by *adoption*. In the Bible, an adopted son is one who has become a child of God through redemption by the precious blood of Jesus Christ. It is the process where the people—

who were by nature children of wrath, children of darkness, and children of Satan (Eph 2:3; John 8:44)—become children of blessings, children of the light, and children of God (Isa 65:23; John 1:12; 12:36; Eph 5:8; Phil 2:15; 1 Thess 5:5; 1 John 3:1; Ref Rom 8:14, 16-17). An adopted son receives the status and privileges of a son and can call God, "Abba, Father" (Rom 8:15; Gal 4:5-6; Ref WCF 12:1, WSC Question 34). God's children become one in Jesus Christ (Gal 3:28) and are heirs according to the promise (Gal 3:29).

Galatians 4:7 states, "Therefore you are no longer a slave, but a son; and if a son, then an heir through God." Here, the word "heir" is κληρονόμος (klēronomos) and means "one who receives his allotted possession by right of sonship." Conceptually speaking, this is the opposite of a slave. The heir possesses all the glory, blessings, and privileges, which he will enjoy in the kingdom of God. An heir is a true son who calls God, "Abba, Father" (Rom 8:15; Gal 4:6).

Today, all the descendants of Abraham who believe in Jesus Christ have been freed from all curses resulting from sin and have been made righteous. As heirs of His kingdom, they are God's children who call Him "Abba, Father."

### FOURTH, we are enabled to live by faith.

Galatians 3:11 states, "Now it is evident that no one is justified before God by the law, for 'The righteous shall live by faith'" (ESV).

What kind of person lives by faith?

A person who lives by faith is one who has been crucified on the cross with Jesus Christ (Gal 2:20). People who belong to Jesus Christ have crucified the flesh with its passions and desires (Gal 5:24).

Why must we die on the cross with Jesus?

First, when our old self is crucified on the cross, our body of sin is destroyed, and we no longer live as slaves to sin (Rom 6:6). We do not let our bodies obey its lusts (Rom 6:12). Nor do we lend the members of our body to sin as instruments of unrighteousness; rather, we present ourselves to God as instruments of righteousness (Rom 6:13). To whomever we may present ourselves as slaves for obedience, we become slaves of the one whom we obey—either of sin resulting in death or of obedience resulting in righteousness (Rom 6:16-19).

Next, by dying on the cross with Jesus, we shall also live with Him

(Rom 6:8). Romans 6:5 states, "For if we have become united with Him in the likeness of His death, certainly we shall also be in the likeness of His resurrection." Therefore, those who have been crucified and raised with Jesus walk in newness of life (Rom 6:4). They live everyday with God in the newness of life. I pray that we will savor eternal life everyday with Christ as we walk with Him all the way now and forever. May it be just like the lyrics of the hymn "Lately the life of Christ":

> Lately the life of Christ burst out alive in me!
> Old things have passed away, even myself is new.
> His life floods through me, like rivers towards the sea,
> His love shines on me like sun shining on the dew.
> With Christ I'll savor life unending everyday;
> now and forever I'll walk with Him all the way.

### (3) Jesus Christ, the true son of David

The genealogy in Matthew 1 is a summary of the redemptive-historical process through which Jesus Christ came as the "seed of the woman" and as "the son of Abraham." Jesus Christ's coming as "the son of David" is also a fulfillment of the promise of the eternal covenant in the Old Testament.

① **The promises concerning the son of David in the Old Testament**
God promised a descendant through the Davidic covenant. Second Samuel 7:12-13 states, "When your days are complete and you lie down with your fathers, I will raise up your descendant after you, who will come forth from you, and I will establish his kingdom. He shall build a house for My name, and I will establish the throne of his kingdom forever." God promised to raise up a descendant who will "come forth from" David and to establish the said descendant's throne forever (1 Chr 17:11-14).

Primarily, the phrase "who will come forth from you" refers to David's son, King Solomon. However, a person's throne cannot be established forever; thus, this promise has to be viewed as one regarding the Messiah who will establish God's eternal kingdom. In addition, the word "descendant" used here is in the singular form and is different from the Hebrew word בֵּן (bēn) used to refer to a son. This verse uses the Hebrew word זֶרַע (zeraʿ) referring to a "seed" or a "descendant." This is the same word used in the phrase "seed of the woman" prophesied in Genesis 3:15. Therefore, the descendant "who will come forth from" David must be the Messiah who will come as the "seed of the woman."

The promise of the one "descendant" in the Davidic covenant is continually renewed throughout the Old Testament. Even Psalm 132:11-12 states, "The Lord has sworn to David a truth from which He will not turn back: 'Of the fruit of your body I will set upon your throne. If your sons will keep My covenant and My testimony which I will teach them, their sons also shall sit upon your throne forever.'" Psalm 89:4 also states, "I will establish your seed forever and build up your throne to all generations."

② **Different expressions for the *son of David***

The Old Testament uses a variety of expressions for the *son of David* referring to the Messiah. Isaiah 9:7 describes Him as the One who will "establish it [the throne of David] and to uphold it with justice and righteousness from then on and forevermore." According to Isaiah 9:6, He is "a child" and "a son" and is called "Wonderful Counselor, Mighty God, Eternal Father, Prince of Peace."

Daniel 7:13-14 portrays the one who will reign over an indestructible kingdom with everlasting dominion as "One like a Son of Man" coming with the clouds of heaven.

Ezekiel 37:25 contains the promise, "David My servant will be their prince forever." Ezekiel was a prophet who was taken captive to Babylon during the reign of King Jehoiachin (Ezek 1:1-2). King David was already dead and gone at the time he made this prophecy. Thus, "David My servant" here refers to the Messiah. In Ezekiel 37:24, "My servant David" is referred to as "one shepherd," and this shepherd also refers to the Messiah who will become the eternal king (John 10:11, 14; 1 Pet 5:4; Ref Heb 13:20; Rev 7:17). Thus, the various expressions for the true son of David as used in the Old Testament all describe the Messiah who is the eternal King of the everlasting kingdom.

③ **Jesus Christ who came as the son of David**

Jesus Christ is the Messiah who came as the fulfillment of the covenant regarding the descendant of David. In Luke 1:32-33, the angel Gabriel announced to Mary that she will conceive through the power of the Holy Spirit. Then, he said, ". . . the Lord God will give Him the throne of His father David; and He will reign over the house of Jacob forever, and His kingdom will have no end" (Ref Acts 2:29-31).

The sick who wanted to be healed by Jesus called Him the "Son of David" (Matt 9:27, 15:22, 20:30-31, etc.). When Jesus entered Jerusalem, the people and the children who longed for the Messiah also called Him the "Son of David" (Matt 21:9, 15).

Jesus' coming as the "Son of David" is a fulfillment of all the covenants in the Old Testament. Not only did the Word become flesh, but His coming as the "Son of David" reveals His eternal messianic kingship with dominion like that of King David. Jesus who came as the eternal king of heaven in the first coming became the redeeming Lord on the cross. Now, when Jesus returns, the promise that the "Son of David" will become the eternal king of the kingdom of God will be fully realized. For this reason Revelation 22:16 describes the second coming Christ, who will come as the bright morning star, as the "root and the descendant of David."

The genealogy of Jesus Christ in Matthew 1 proclaims Jesus as the "son of David" (Matt 1:1). By so doing, it reveals to all nations of the world that He is the Messiah, the eternal prince (Ezek 37:24-28), who came according to the promises and covenants of the Old Testament. Furthermore, it teaches us that He will fully consummate all promises and covenants at His second coming.

## 4. The outlook on the promise of the eternal covenant

### (1) Attitude toward the promise of the eternal covenant

All the eternal covenants in the Bible are fulfilled in Jesus Christ, and we give glory to God when we say "Amen" to those promises. Second Corinthians 1:20 states, "For as many as are the promises of God, in Him they are yes; therefore also through Him is our Amen to the glory of God through us."

Saying "Amen" to a promise attests to a life of believing in the promise. Galatians 3:22 refers to this as the "promise by faith." Thus, we take part in God's promise when we are fully assured (Rom 4:21) that He is more than able to fulfill His promise of the eternal covenant.

Hebrews 11:39-40 states, "And all these, having gained approval through their faith, did not receive what was promised, because God had provided something better for us, so that apart from us they would not be made perfect." Here, receiving "what was promised" is expressed as being "something better." Believers who receive the promise of God's eternal covenant are those who receive the gift of "something better."

There are many believers in this world. Moreover, there are believers who understand this promise of the eternal covenant and live by faith in the promise; however, there are believers who are not even aware of such a promise. I pray that today we will become believers and a church endowed with the promise of the eternal covenant, the gift of "something better."

A saint who cherishes this promise of the eternal covenant is one who "perseveres." A saint needs perseverance to endure all kinds of persecutions and difficulties until the end when God's eternal promise is completely fulfilled at Christ's second coming.

Hebrews 10:36 states, "You need to persevere so that when you have done the will of God, you will receive what he has promised" (NIV). Hebrews 6:15 also states, "And so, having patiently waited, he obtained the promise" (Heb 6:12; Ref Matt 24:13). God's administration of redemption and providence to fulfill His eternal promise will advance forward each day despite any disturbances by evil forces; and what God has promised, He will fulfill (Job 23:13-14; Isa 46:10; Hab 2:3-4). I hope that we will all be victorious through faith by persevering until the end when all of God's promises of the eternal covenant are fulfilled.

## (2) The promise of the eternal covenant and the blood

The Scriptures are a book of promise. The Bible consists of the Old Testament (old covenant) and the New Testament (new covenant), which can also be rendered as the old promise and the new promise. The entire Bible is made up of the promise of the eternal covenant.

What is the essence of this promise of the eternal covenant? It is the blood.

The essence of the old covenant was the blood. During the ratification of the covenant on Mount Sinai, Moses took the blood of the sacrifice and sprinkled it on the people. Then he said, "Behold the blood of the covenant, which the Lord has made with you in accordance with all these words" (Exod 24:8). Hebrews 9:19 states that the blood was sprinkled on the book of the covenant as well as on all the people. Thus, that blood became the "blood of the covenant" (Heb 9:20). This blood foreshadows the blood of Jesus Christ that would be shed on the cross. During the Last Supper, Jesus Christ, the mediator of the new covenant (Heb 8:6; 9:15; 12:24), called the wine, which symbolized His blood, the "blood of the covenant" (Matt 26:28; Mark 14:24). Thus, the blood that was sprinkled upon the old covenant foreshadows the blood of Jesus Christ that will be shed on the cross for the fulfillment of the new covenant.

This blood accomplishes eternal redemption once and for all (Heb 9:12). It is the blood of Christ, who through the eternal Spirit offered Himself without blemish to God (Heb 9:14). Thus, we are strengthened by this blood of the eternal covenant and obtain the confidence to enter the holy place (Heb 10:19-20).

Ultimately, if the essence of the eternal covenant is the blood, then the genealogy of Jesus Christ, which proclaims the fulfillment of the eternal covenant, also testifies of the blood of the cross.

> The blood of the cross is the fulfillment of all eternal covenants.
> The blood of the cross is the execution of all eternal promises.
> The blood of the cross puts an end to all curses.
> The blood of the cross has blotted out all sin and death.
> The blood of the cross is the power of all salvation.
> The blood of the cross is the conclusion to the administration of redemptive history that runs through all genealogies.
> The blood of the cross guarantees eternal life and happiness.
> The blood of the cross is the end of all defeats and the beginning of eternal victory.
> The blood of the cross is the end of all darkness and the beginning of light.
> The blood of the cross is the focus and the pinnacle of the administration of redemption.
> The blood of the cross is the judgment of all the powers of evil and the ultimate victory for believers.

Therefore, we must know nothing but the cross (1 Cor 2:2) and boast only in the cross all throughout our lives. In Galatians 6:14, Apostle Paul says, "But may it never be that I would boast, except in the cross of our Lord Jesus Christ, through which the world has been crucified to me, and I to the world."

We must also crucify our passions and desires on the cross (Gal 5:24) so that only Christ lives and works in us (Gal 2:20). We must fill up in ourselves what is lacking in Christ's afflictions for the sake of His body, the Church (Col 1:24). We must live a life that is filled with the brand-marks of Christ, both in our flesh and in our souls (Gal 6:17).

The God of peace brought up Jesus Christ from the dead through the blood of the eternal covenant (Heb 13:20). This God of peace equips us in every good thing (Heb 13:21) and will preserve us complete so that our soul and body may be without blame at the coming of our Lord Jesus Christ (1 Thess 5:23).

Now I earnestly hope that the blood of the eternal covenant, which God accomplished on the cross, will be sprinkled on the entire world, the universe, and the nations. Through the life that is in the blood of the eternal covenant, all the dead will repent and come alive again to become an exceedingly great army of the Lord (Ezek 37:10). Then, a new work of revival will sweep across the entire world.

Until the day when all the promises of the eternal covenant within God's mysterious providence are completely fulfilled, may only Jesus Christ be exalted in the remaining days of our lives (Phil 1:20). Hallelujah!

# Commentaries

Rev. Warren A. Gage, J.D., Ph.D.,
Professor Emeritus of Old Testament, Knox Theological Seminary
Assistant Minister, Coral Ridge Presbyterian Church, Ft. Lauderdale,
  FL, USA
Director, Florida Institute of Humanities and Culture

With the fifth book published in English in his History of Redemption series of twelve volumes, Dr. Abraham Park completes his consideration of the threefold series of fourteen generations in Christ's genealogy set forth in Matthew's Gospel. This new book is simply wonderful.

The Bible was written in an era long before there were standardized conventions about regnal years, co-regencies, consistent calendars (there are Tishri and Nisan, civil and ceremonial New Years, along with enthronement accessions or 'New Years'). It is a world where there are no clear markers and deep records or attestations of significant historical dates. Other imperial court registries (Egyptian, Assyrian, Babylonian) are marked with similar historical challenges. There are also differing methods of genealogical record keeping, with some records being ascendant, some descendant, some inclusive, and some stylized with numerous omissions. It is more than enough to cause the scholar to stagger, and has proven to be a fertile field for the biblical critic to mock the truth claims of Holy Scripture.

Dr. Park has a remarkable gift of sorting out, explaining clearly, and thus reconciling these often apparently contradictory data. He comes with a scholar's mind but also with a pastor's heart. He wants to secure the historicity of Scripture in order for his people to persevere in a deep confidence in the reliability and truth of God's Word. Dr. Park is uniquely gifted for both tasks.

The fifth book offers fascinating background into the last cycle of the genealogies prior to Christ being born of Mary, wife to Joseph who was descended from Abraham and David. It is a worthy addition to the previous books which looked at the first two cycles of fourteen generations.

Most of the names treated in this new volume arise out of the "four hundred years of silence" when the Spirit of prophecy was silent in Israel. But fortunately there are historical records still extant which providentially give us the context for these lives. Dr. Park is a master of this history as well as extra-biblical literary records. It is wonderful to see how God's providence was advancing the history of redemption through bringing to completion the ancient promise of the Seed of the Woman through the birth of Jesus Christ.

Dr. Park has wisely discerned that the *protoevangelium* of Genesis 3:15 is the dynamic that drives the history of God's redemption of His people. These genealogies are necessary to confirm the faith of the people of God in the authenticity of God's Word, which Dr. Park has already so ably helped us to see throughout the many centuries of the biblical drama.

Moses' valedictory to Israel challenged the people about to inherit the Promised Land to remember the generations that had persevered before them, all those who had only the promise of this inheritance to encourage them in their suffering. "Remember the days of old," Moses wrote. "Consider the years of all generations. Ask your father, and he will inform you, your elders, and they will tell you" (Deut 32:7). I can think of no better "father" and "elder" in the church today than Dr. Abraham Park. Ask him, and he will tell you that God is worthy of faith, for He has faithfully kept His promise in bringing the world a Redeemer, even Jesus Christ the righteous. Inquire of him, and Dr. Park will encourage you to join with all of us who have confessed our sins and known them to be covered by the blood of Jesus. Ask him, and Pastor Park will point you toward Jesus, Son of David, Son of Abraham, and Son of God! Jesus is all our hope. And He alone is worthy!

# Notes

1. Seock-Tae Sohn, *A Course on Genesis* (Seoul: Bible Reading, 1993), 33.
2. David Martyn Lloyd-Jones, *God the Father, God the Son* (Wheaton, IL: Crossway Books, 1996), 128. Also, Youngyup Cho, *Doctrine of God and Man's Sin* (Seoul: Lifebook, 2007), 207-8.
3. Shakespeare, *Hamlet*, Act 2, Scene 2.
4. The word translated as "or" (NASB, NIV) or "lest" (ESV, KJV) in the English Bible is the Hebrew word פֶּן (*pen*). According to *The Hebrew and Aramaic Lexicon of the Old Testament* (HALOT), when followed by an imperfect verb, as is the case in Genesis 3:3, the word can mean "so that not" or "lest." Furthermore, HALOT suggests a second possible meaning of the word when followed by the imperfect verb as "or else," "in case," or "perhaps" (Ludwig Koehler, Walter Baumgartner, M. E. J. Richardson and Johann Jakob Stamm, *The Hebrew and Aramaic Lexicon of the Old Testament*, electronic ed. (Leiden; New York: E.J. Brill, 1999), 937.). The Korean Revised Version has clearly opted for this second possibility in Genesis 3:3.
5. Warren Austin Gage, *The Gospel of Genesis: Studies in Protology and Eschatology*, Second Edition, (Warren A. Gage, 2010), 40-41. Also, Yong-Hwa Ra, *A Clear Christian Theology and Life* (Seoul: Christian Literature Crusade, 2010), 128.
6. Center for Ethnic Root Search Movement, *My Genealogy* (Seoul: Minyeseo, 2005), 21.
7. Sung-Hee Jung, *Sex Customs of Joseon*, (Seoul: Garam, 1998), 81.
8. Joachim Jeremias, *Jerusalem in the Time of Jesus* (London: SCM Press Ltd., 1969), 276-77.
9. Jong-Jin Choi, Significance of the Chronicler's Genealogy and Its Recording Format (Annals of Faculty), 18 (Seoul: Seoul Theological University, 2006), 350. Also, Walter A. Elwell and Barry J. Beitzel, *Baker Encyclopedia of the Bible*, (Grand Rapids, MI: Baker Book House, 1988), 845.
10. James T. Sparks, *The Chronicler's Genealogies* (Atlanta: Society of Biblical Literature, 2008), 29.
11. Jeremias, *Jerusalem*, 288-89.
12. Soo-Gun Lee, *Korean Family Names and Genealogies* (Seoul: Seoul National University, 2008), 59.
13. Mi-Young Kim, *Folklore on Family and Relatives* (Seoul: Minsokwon, 2008), 62, 66.
14. Mi-Young Kim, *Folklore*, 65.
15. Abraham Park, *The Unquenchable Lamp of the Covenant: The First Fourteen Generations in the Genealogy of Jesus Christ* (Singapore: Periplus, 2010), 78-80.
16. Jong-Jin Choi, *Significance of the Chronicler's Genealogy*, 369.
17. Jong-Jin Choi, *A Genealogical Study of the Old Testament* (Seoul: Seoul Theological University, 2010) 97-98.
18. Jong-Jin Choi, *Esther*, The Christian Literature Society of Korea's 100th Year Commemorative Biblical Commentaries, 15 (Seoul: The Christian Literature Society of Korea, 2005), 130-31.
19. One hundred ninety names – repeated names were counted once, and the names of families, chiefs, and women were also included. However, the chiefs of Edom (1 Chr 1:51, 54) were treated as names of places in accordance with the context of the sentence.
20. *Mattathias* means "gift of God." He was a priest from the famous Maccabean family. With his five sons, he resisted Antiochus IV (Epiphanes, 175-163 BC). In 142 BC, the Jewish people finally constituted an independent state and remained independent for 79 years until 63 BC. Bo Reicke, *The New Testament Era: the World of the Bible from 500*

*B.C. to A.D. 100* (Philadelphia: Fortress Press, 1974), 62.

21. William Hendriksen and Simon J. Kistemaker, *Exposition of the Gospel According to Luke*, New Testament Commentary, vol. 11 (Grand Rapids: Baker Book House, 1953-2001), 225.

22. Norval Geldenhuys, *Commentary on the Gospel of Luke* (Grand Rapids: WM. B. Eerdmans, 1979), 151-52.

23. Abraham Park, *The Unquenchable Lamp of the Covenant*, 71.

24. In Ruth 4:20 (in the original Hebrew text) and 1 Chronicles 2:11, the name *Salma* appears in the place of the name *Salmon* who married Rahab the harlot.

    (1 Chr 2:11) וְנַחְשׁוֹן הוֹלִיד אֶת־שַׂלְמָא וְשַׂלְמָא הוֹלִיד אֶת־בֹּעַז

    *Salmon* (שַׂלְמוֹן) means "garment" or "mantle" while *Salma* (שַׂלְמָא) means "strong" and "strength."

25. Abraham Park, *The Unquenchable Lamp of the Covenant*, 310.

26. Abraham Park, *The Unquenchable Lamp of the Covenant*, 74.

27. Abraham Park, *God's Profound and Mysterious Providence: As Revealed in the Genealogy of Jesus Christ from the Time of David to the Exile in Babylon*, (Singapore: Periplus, 2011), 215.

28. Jeremias, *Jerusalem*, 280.

29. Although it is unclear exactly why five children among Zerubbabel's seven sons and one daughter are differentiated from the rest (1 Chr 3:20), considering the traditional practice of differentiating the children in the genealogies if the mothers are different (1 Chr 2:19, 21-24; 3:1-9; 4:5-7), it is presumed that the five grouped together have different mothers from Meshullam, Hananiah, and Shelomith (daughter) mentioned before them. Carl Friedrich Keil and Franz Delitzsch, *Commentary on the Old Testament*, vol. 3 (Peabody, MA: Hendrickson, 1996), 424.

30. Samuel Fallows, ed., *The Popular and Critical Bible Encyclopedia and Scriptural Dictionary*, vol. 2 (Chicago: The Howard-Severance Company, 1907), 820.

31. Roddy Braun, *1 Chronicles*, Word Biblical Commentary (Dallas: Word, Incorporated, 1998), 52.

32. Walter A. Elwell and Barry J. Beitzel, *Baker Encyclopedia of the Bible* (Grand Rapids, MI: Baker Book House, 1988), 441.

33. Zerubbabel was a leader during the first return from Babylon in 537 BC (Ezra 2:2; 5:2). The Old Testament specifies that the minimum age requirement for those who serve in the temple is at least thirty years of age (Num 4:3, 23, 30, 35, 39), which shows that thirty is a mature age in which a person can carry out important duties. Thus, Zerubbabel was probably at least thirty years of age when he led the first return from Babylon, and it can be presumed that he was born around 570 BC.

34. Lord A. C. Hervey, *The Genealogies of Our LORD and Savior Jesus Christ* (Cambridge: Macmillan and Co., 1853), 123.

35. J. A. Bengel, *Gnomon of the New Testament*, vol. 1 (Philadelphia: Smith, English, and Co., 1860), 87.

36. Geldenhuys, *Gospel of Luke*, 154.

37. Jeremias, *Jerusalem*, 295-96.

38. Braun, *1 Chronicles*, 52.

39. Dual form indicates that two things are referenced.

40. Although some English translations of the Bible have "Jehoiakim" instead of "Zedekiah" in Jeremiah 27:1, it is clear that this was during the reign of Zedekiah. Most modern English Bibles like the NASB, NIV, ESV, and NRSV have "Zedekiah." Moreover, Jeremiah 28:1 tells us that the time Prophet Jeremiah delivered this prophecy was the "fourth year" of Zedekiah's reign, which would be 593 BC. There are some scholars

who assert that Zedekiah had gone to Babylon in 593 BC in order to make it seem as if he were not involved in the anti-Babylonian conspiracy (D. W. Baker, "Zedekiah," in *New Bible Dictionary*, ed. D. R. W. Wood, I. H. Marshall, A. R. Millard et al., 3rd ed. (Leicester, England; Downers Grove, IL: InterVarsity Press, 1996), 1267.).

41. Carl Friedrich Keil and Franz Delitzsch, *Commentary on the Old Testament*, vol. 8 (Peabody, MA: Hendrickson, 1996), 211.

42. Donald J. Wiseman, *1 and 2 Kings: An Introduction and Commentary*, Tyndale Old Testament Commentaries, vol. 9 (Downers Grove, IL: InterVarsity Press, 1993), 329–30.

43. E. R. Thiele, *The Mysterious Numbers of the Hebrew Kings* (Grand Rapids: Kregel, 1983), 186-87.

44. Jehoiachin was taken captive on the tenth day of the month of Nisan (first month) (Ref 2 Chr 36:10; Ezek 40:1). This was 596 BC according to the Nisan-to-Nisan calendar, but 597 BC according to the Tishri-to-Tishri calendar. Thus, when we calculate the date for the "fifth day of the tenth month in the twelfth year" since his captivity, it would be the fifth day of the tenth month in 586 BC according to the Tishri-to-Tishri calendar, or the fifth day of the tenth month in 585 BC according to the Nisan-to-Nisan calendar. However, Ezekiel 33:21-22 clearly states that the fifth day of the tenth month in the twelfth year since he was taken captive was after the destruction of Jerusalem (the ninth day of the fourth month in the eleventh year of King Zedekiah; 2 Kgs 25:3; Jer 39:2; 52:6). If Ezekiel were using the Tishri-to-Tishri calendar, then the fifth day of the tenth month in the twelfth year since captivity, in which the news of the fall of Jerusalem was heard, would have been before the actual fall. Thus, this proves that Ezekiel used the Nisan-to-Nisan calendar in his chronological calculations.

45. H. J. Lee, *How to Read Ezekiel* (Scripture Union Korea, 2008), 31.

46. Gleason Archer, Jr., *A Survey of Old Testament Introduction*, 3rd ed. (Chicago: Moody Press, 1994), 472.

47. Thiele, *Hebrew Kings*, 53.

48. S. H. Horn and L. H. Wood, "The Fifth-Century Jewish Calendar at Elephantine," *Journal of Eastern Studies* 13 (1954), 1-20.

49. Nahum compared the fall of Nineveh (BC 612) to No-amon (Nah 3:8). This city refers to Thebes, the capital city during the Eighteenth Dynasty of Egypt, which was destroyed around 663 BC by Ashurbanipal of the Assyrian Empire. Hence, Nahum's period of prophecy can be deduced to be sometime between the years of the destruction of No-amon and Nineveh, 663 and 612 BC, respectively.

50. D. A. Carson, R. T. France, J. A. Motyer, and G. J. Wenham, ed., *New Bible Commentary: 21st Century Edition*, 4th ed., (Leicester, England; Downers Grove, IL: InterVarsity Press, 1994), 815.

51. T. R. Hobbs, *2 Kings*, Word Biblical Commentary, vol. 13 (Dallas: Word, Incorporated, 1998), 289.

52. Thiele, *Hebrew Kings*, 176.

53. Stephen R. Miller, *Daniel*, vol. 18, The New American Commentary, (Nashville: Broadman & Holman Publishers, 1994), 222.

54. A.B. Bosworth, "Alexander the Great pt. 1: The Events of the Reign," in *Cambridge Ancient History*, vol. 6 (Cambridge: Cambridge University Press, 1994), 844-45.

55. St. Jerome, *Jerome's Commentary on Daniel*, trans. Gleason L. Archer, Jr. (Grand Rapids, Michigan: Baker Book House, 1958), 123.

56. Allen C. Myers, *The Eerdmans Bible Dictionary*, (Grand Rapids, MI: Eerdmans, 1987), 465.

57. Bengel, *Gnomon*, vol. 1, 88-90.

58. Geldenhuys, *Gospel of Luke*, 153.

59. John Nolland, *Luke* 1:1-9:20, Word Biblical Commentary, vol. 35A (Dallas: Word, Incorporated, 2002), 169-70.